CHRIST IN HISTORY;

OR,

THE CENTRAL POWER AMONG MEN.

BY

ROBERT TURNBULL, D. D.

"History, as a whole, is a successive revelation of God." — SCHELLING.

"All the intractable and contradictory problems of philosophy find their solution in Christ." — VINET.

"The gospel is the fulfilment of all hopes, the perfection of all philosophy, the interpreter of all revolutions, the key to all the seeming contradictions of the physical and moral worlds; it is life, it is immortality." — JOHN VON MULLER.

BOSTON:
PHILLIPS, SAMPSON, AND COMPANY.
LONDON: SAMPSON LOW, SON, AND COMPANY.
1854.

STEREOTYPED AT THE
BOSTON STEREOTYPE FOUNDRY.

Owing to the author's distance from the press, a few typographical errors have slipped into the work. The reader will please correct the following

ERRATA.

p. 22, line 8; for *are*, read *and*.
p. 30, line 5; for Pure, read *Practical*.
p. 36, Note, line 11; strike out *Histoire*.
p 40, line 4; for Plato, read *Pluto*.
p. 101, line 5; after *this*, supply *in*.
p. 201, line 13; for *Yet nature*, *Yes, nature*.

PREFACE.

To unreflective minds history appears only as an intricate or confused mass of details. Change follows change, revolution presses upon revolution. Now all is a dead level of monotonous usage, then all is unaccountable and startling transition. New forms of religion and politics, of customs and manners, play their brief hour or age, then, in their turn, grow old and vanish away. Empires rise, decline, and fall. Love and hate, piety and atheism, justice and injustice, peace and war contend for the mastery. At one time the world is luminous with hope, at another dark with despair. Individuals, families, and nations, like multitudinous waves, chase each other over the bosom of the deep, and are finally ingulfed in a stormy sea.

Under the steady gaze of philosophic, and especially, of Christian thought, much of this chaotic aspect of society disappears. Order begins to emerge; principles and laws are recognized; a progress and a purpose are discerned. To attain this, however, requires a lofty stand-point and a far-reaching vision. The whole domain of human affairs, like a landscape from the summit of a mountain, must lie in comprehensive unity beneath the gaze. Inspiration, indeed, long ago discerned, and in brief, pregnant utterances, indicated the true condition of humanity; but ages had to elapse before it could be comprehended, and above all exhibited, in any thing like a philosophical or coherent form. Indeed, the idea of universal history, or of history as a unit and a system, is the product of the seventeenth century. Even now there are cultivated minds, and among them a few distinguished historians, who can recognize in it no central or all-comprehending force. It is only occasionally, and as a compliment to religion, that they acknowledge the presence of the Deity in the affairs of man. Some of them would even eliminate all such conceptions from history as mystical and irrelevant. It is a happy circumstance, however, that the more profound and philosophical historians are the most inclined to recognize the divine element. Even those metaphysicians who have sometimes been suspected of pantheistic infidelity, Vico, Fichte, Schelling, and Cousin, have given this idea the most distinct expression. Cousin, especially, has recognized it in the fullest and most eloquent terms. It may now be regarded as the settled conviction of the leading thinkers of the world.

Bossuet, in his Universal History, was the first to elucidate and apply this great thought. Still his work is neither thorough nor philosophical. It possesses the character of a grand historical sketch, intended for popular impression. In several respects its range is narrow and ecclesiastical, being confined too much to the mere theocracy of the Jews, and the hierarchy of the Papal church. The state is absorbed in the church, and the march of history is described only from the Roman Catholic view. The historical details are meagre, and sometimes inaccurate. Still it possesses the great merit of recognizing the presence of God in the affairs of men, and describing the succession of events with a grave eloquence.

Much more profound and philosophical is the sublime idea which runs through the New Science (*Scienza Nuova*) of John Baptist Vico, that singular Italian thinker, who united the brevity and obscurity of Heraclitus to the depth and force of Plato. He maintains that the divine element underlies humanity in all its phases, and may be recognized even in the superstitions of the heathen *cultus*. Still he gives undue prominence to the mere natural element, and falls into some singular crudities and absurdities. Had Jonathan Edwards been more familiar with general history, and in his History of Redemption applied the leading thought which pervades that work to the general course of human affairs, he would have created an era in historical, as he has done in theological research. Herder, with less depth of intellect or force of character, but with a wider and more liberal range of study, starts from the same fundamental position as Bossuet and Vico, and shows how art, science, language, poetry, and religion mingle in the march of humanity towards ideal perfection. His system, however, is too narrow and empirical for a complete explanation of the phenomena of history. F. W. Schlegel follows in the same track, with considerable reach of thought, and a distinct recognition of fundamental principles. He does greater justice than his predecessors to the influence of the remoter Oriental nations; still his work strikes us as superficial and fragmentary. Like Bossuet, he is too much under the influence of Papal views, and fails to give a complete or philosophical exposition of the subject.

Bunsen, in the first volume of his Hippolytus, presents, in aphoristic form, a comprehensive sketch of the philosophy of history, in a manner much more complete and satisfactory than Schlegel. Marred by rationalistic fancies, and obscure or incomplete ontological statements, his view, upon the whole, is the most satisfactory we have seen. It distinctly recognizes the great truth of God in manifested form, and especially in Christ, as lying at the foundation of all religious and historical development. From his vast learning, Bunsen clearly sees that humanity cannot permanently rise, except through the influence of the new and supernatural force imparted by Christianity.

Of late years two or three works, chiefly of a practical character, have appeared among ourselves, under the title of the Hand of God in History, or, more briefly, God in History, — one an eloquent discourse by the Rev. Dr. Cheever, with special reference to the history of the United States; another, of greater extent and detail, by the Rev. Hollis Read. The object of these is not, by a philosophical analysis, to prove the presence of God in universal history, but rather, by a citation of facts, in connection with the teachings of Scripture, to indicate his providential sway, or what they fitly designate the "Hand of God in History." In fact, the title "God in History," in the case of Mr. Read's work, is an after thought, less appropriate, perhaps, than the original title; for his sole object, as stated in the preface, is to point out "the providence of God in the events of history." This he discovers, especially in striking junctures or turns of affairs, sometimes called "interpositions," rather than in the general movement of universal history. He makes no attempt to analyze the fundamental forces of society, and entirely omits the consideration of ancient history. His work, though interesting and profitable, breathing an excellent spirit, and "vindicating the ways of God to man," cannot be said to be an adequate exposition of "God in history."

We have made these remarks upon the literature of the subject to which the following work in part belongs, in order to assist us in pointing out its object and aim. And here, at the outset, we beg distinctly to say, that it does not pretend to be a *philosophy* of history, or to be strictly a philosophical or scientific work. Its form, in fact, is rather popular than philosophical, though based upon fundamental principles, and aiming to elucidate and apply essential elements. The title "Christ in History" limits its character to an exposition of the relations of Christ (here taken as the highest expression or manifestation of God) to universal history.

Hence it takes the Incarnation as the central or "turning point" in the history of mankind, and attempts to show how all the forces of society converge around it, how all preceding history prepares for it, how all succeeding history dates from it. In order to develop this fact, the reader is taken back to central facts and principles, in other words to the fountains of history in the nature of God, and the nature of man; and the attempt is made to show that the history of the world, ancient and modern, can be understood only with reference to Christ. This is not assumed dogmatically, but evolved by an exposition of historical facts.

Many things which would naturally be discussed in a complete philosophy of history are omitted. Some also are taken for granted, as known or conceded by the reader. Indeed, the attention is necessarily limited to the specific view which it is the design of the author to vindicate.

In the course of the investigation, Christianity is shown to be not only an historical reality, but a divine and supernatural power, by which all other realities and powers are explained and controlled. The theories of the sceptical rationalists, to account for Christianity on natural, local, or superficial grounds, are shown to be untenable. The natural or human factor, of course, is not denied; another, however, is added, namely, the supernatural or divine. In a word, Christianity, in its interior relations and vital energies, is shown to be nothing less than the presence of God, through Jesus Christ, among men, renovating the hearts of individuals, and preparing the transformation of society.

The author has endeavored to conduct the investigation in the freest and most liberal manner, holding himself aloof as much as possible from unproved preconceptions, and less anxious, therefore, to favor or deny orthodoxy, heterodoxy, or what Luther calls cacodoxy, than to establish the simple truth.

On a theme so vast and comprehensive, his work cannot be otherwise than imperfect. No one can be more sensible of its defects than himself. Though the labor of years, it is not offered as any thing approaching a complete or scientific view of the subject, but rather as a slight contribution, or preparation for such a view. Perhaps he might venture to call it an introduction to universal history, or at least an introduction to the history of Christianity.

CONTENTS.

APPENDIX.

CHRIST IN HISTORY.

CHAPTER I.

THE CENTRAL POWER.

THE farther science advances, the more clearly is the great fact discovered that all things have their centres of life and motion, and that they belong to a single system. Acting and interacting, moving, now this way, now that, all at last tend one way. The stars revolve around their suns, and suns themselves, with attendant planets, revolve around a central orb. Unity and variety, as in a circle, with its starlike radii, the unity ever passing into variety, and the variety into unity, pervade the visible creation. Nothing is insulated, nothing irregular. One mysterious law comprehends and governs the whole. All proceed from, and gravitate to, one centre.

Not only the larger masses, suns, and constellations, gravitate thus, but the inferior parts, the minutest atoms, fibres, and crystals. All plants and animals are organized around their centres. By accretion, growth, and assimilation, they form themselves, according to a fixed law, from interior forces. The rose unfolds itself with petals and leaves, from a vital root. The dew is globed by the force of gravitation. The bubble which floats in the sunbeam, the joy of childhood, obeys the same invisible power. It is sphered like a star, and carries upon its bosom all the splendors of the rainbow. A particle of sand, the sport of every breeze, is formed on the strictest mathematical principles. Scrutinized, it will be found piled up in fair proportions, like a huge crystal, with its lines, sides, and angles. The down upon an insect's wing, scarce visible to the naked eye, grows like a forest of palms. All nature is vital and moving, even when it seems to be still as the grave. Plants and animals have a sort of double life, a life in common with the rest, and a life in themselves, and all therefore tend in one direction. Their movement is ever from, and to, centres of action and development. The human body grows like a germ, is fed and developed from an interior force. It has its own centre, to which it gravitates, while gravitating with all other things, earth, sun, and stars, around a common centre.

Society also, in order to live and prosper, must

have an appropriate centre. It gravitates around some vital force, being, or principle, which constitutes its life. Men may seem to be insulated as individuals, but they grow together; and not only so, but they intergrow. They are many, yet they are one, like the myriad globules of water that form the rushing stream. No two are alike, yet all are alike. They move apparently in diverse orbits, and yet they move together in a common orbit. One spiritual, all-pervading force, or aggregate of forces, impels them in the same direction.

Hence they rise or fall together, move in peaceful order within the great sphere of duty, or dash tumultuously into the abyss. Strange varieties of costume, color, form, language, notions, prevail among the nations, yet "their hearts are fashioned alike." Their blood is the same; their reason and their affection, their hope and their fear, their origin and their end, are the same. Free indeed, and thence capable, within certain limits, of virtue or of vice, of holiness or of sin, of religion or of atheism, they diverge in their choice and destiny as individuals; yet they are formed on the same model, obey the same impulses, may share the same destiny.

Those who have read history with any attention know that society is always organized, if organized with any degree of permanence, around some divine idea or force. No society can be kept together without religion; and for the simple reason that man, imperfect, — nay, more, fallen, — has his origin and his end in God. The Deity, in other words, the true, the good, the holy, — what we fitly term "the divine," — is our centre and life. We gravitate harmoniously only around this eternal force, at once centripetal and centrifugal, attracting us to a centre, and at the same time propelling us in beautiful order around the orbit of duty.

This characteristic of man, like the cerulean color of the ocean or atmosphere, may not indeed be visible in detached fragments, but is always obvious enough in the whole. Morally, as well as naturally, the finite lies in the infinite. God and man are bound together by mysterious ties.

For the same reason, each individual soul has its proper centre. As a divine product, a child of the infinite Spirit, it belongs to God, and finds its felicity in him. No matter if morally severed, by disturbing causes, from its absolute Source, the principle or fact remains the same. The sun and its star, the centre and its radius, wherever they may be, are made for each other. Drawn off into "the abysmal dark" by the destructive influence of sin, the soul wretchedly wanders in the void, seeking rest and finding none. If not restored to its source, it must finally perish. To be pure, peaceful, happy, each of us must find God, and in God attain the true and the holy; and thus drinking the beams of the eternal Sun, revolve around him in glory and in joy forever.

Thus, in all ages, we find lofty souls, even in darkness and sorrow, "feeling after God." Thales, Pythagoras, Socrates, Plato, Cicero, Plutarch catch a glimpse of his glory, and proclaim, with exultation, the stupendous thought. Somewhat bewildered, and with only partial views, they yet reach towards the Divine as their centre and their end. Nay, the poor African, in a deeper night, feels the mighty fascination, without knowing what it is. Said Sekesa, a native of Southern Africa, of the Bechuana tribe, to a missionary from whom he had been hearing of God and immortality, "Your views, O white man, are just what I wanted and sought for before I knew you. Twelve years ago, I went, in a cloudy season, to feed my flock along the Tlotse, among the Malutis. Seated upon a rock in sight of my sheep, I asked myself sad questions; yes, sad, because I could not answer them. The stars, said I, who touched them with his hand? On what pillars do they rest? The waters are not weary; they run without ceasing at night and morning alike;

but where do they stop, or who makes them run thus? The clouds also go, return, and fall in water to the earth. Whence do they arise? Who sends them? It surely is not the Barokas (rain makers) who give us the rain, for how could they make it? The wind — what is it? Who brings it or takes it away? makes it blow, and roar, and frighten us? Do I know how the corn grows? Yesterday there was not a blade to be seen in my field. To-day I return and find something. It is very small; I can scarcely see it; but it will grow up like a young man. Who can have given the ground wisdom and power to produce it? Then I buried my head in my hands.

"Again I thought within myself, and I said, We all depart, but this country remains; it alone remains, for we all go away. But whither do we go? My heart answered, Perhaps other men live besides us, and we shall go to them. But another thought arose against it, and said, Those men under the earth, whence come they? Then my heart did not know what more to think. It wondered. Then my heart rose and spoke to me, saying, All men do much evil, and thou, thou also hast done much evil. Woe to thee! I recalled many wrongs which I had done, and because of this my conscience gnawed me in secret, as I sat alone on the rock. I say

I was afraid. I got up and ran after my sheep, trying to enliven myself, but I trembled much."

Moffat informs us that some of the tribes of Africa are so degraded as, apparently, to have no idea of a supreme power; but this is the exception, not the rule.* As intelligence and civilization advance, the idea of "the Divine" becomes, in all countries, more distinct and luminous. It rises with science and virtue, appropriates to itself all beautiful forms, and "sits enthroned on the riches of the universe."

It is owing to the depth and permanence of this original instinct or intuition, blind as it occasionally seems, and much perverted by ig-

* Further investigations show decisively that the exception scarcely exists, even among the most superstitious tribes of Africa; the word *Morimo*, which means the Supreme Spirit, is found as a relic of some better knowledge now lost. Mr. Livingston says that the recently-discovered tribes in the interior of Africa have an idea of a supreme God. This is corroborated by Mr. Bowen, who says the people in Yarouba believe in one God, though the national worship is directed to inferior deities, both benign and malignant. They speak of him as "over all," and call him "the Owner of heaven." Their language contains those terms which enable the missionary to speak to them intelligently of the Deity, of sin, guilt, moral obligation, &c. Some of their traditions would indicate an Oriental origin. Every where the ark is an object of reverence. Mr. Tanner, a half-breed Indian missionary, well acquainted with the Indians, says that those tribes who have been secluded from intercourse with the whites have a distinct idea of a supreme Spirit. They worship other spirits, but especially venerate the Great Spirit, and recognize the eternal distinction of right and wrong, with the doctrine of reward and punishment. This is corroborated by Mr. Catlin and Mr. Schoolcraft.

norance and lust, that the race, as such, especially in its more active centres, has always occupied itself with the problem of God, or the gods, those supreme and eternal powers supposed to preside over the universe, and has always organized itself, as we have said, around some fundamental belief in reference to duty and destiny. Thus Plato over and over again affirms that a belief in God, or the gods, is a natural and universal instinct.* "Examine," says Plutarch, in his tract against Coletes, the Epicurean, "the face of the earth, and you may find cities unfortified, unlettered, without a regular magistrate or distinct habitations, without possessions, property, or the use of money, and unskilled in all the magnificent and polished arts of life; but a city without the knowledge of God or religion, without the use of vows, oaths, oracles, and sacrifices to procure good, or of deprecatory rites to avert evil, no man can or ever will find." So also in his *Consolatio ad Apollonium*, he declares, "it was so ancient an opinion that good men should be recompensed

* See especially *De Legibus*, (lib. x.,) *Contra Atheos*. Plato, indeed, sees clearly enough that the instinct referred to is often feeble, as well as subject to great perversion. In himself, it was not entirely free from superstition; yet who, with the slightest knowledge of his works, will deny the strength and grandeur with which it developed itself in his sublime speculations on the *true*, the *beautiful*, and the *good*, as eternal *entities* in the bosom of God?

at death, that he could not reach either the author or the origin of it." In his Tusculan Questions, Cicero bears the same testimony. "As our innate ideas," he says, "discover to us that there are gods, [or *a God;* for Cicero often uses the term *gods*, when he means simply God,] whose attributes we deduce from reason, so, from the consent of all nations and people, we conclude that the soul is immortal." In another place, he affirms that this, as well as the sense of justice, must be "a law of nature." *

Errors and superstitions of course mingled with ancient myths and traditions; but they were based upon an original intuition, if not an original revelation. In corroboration of this view we find Aristotle averring that "it was an ancient saying, received by all from their ancestors, that all things exist by and through the power of God, . . . who, being one, (εἱς,) was known by many names, according to his modes of manifestation" — a testimony as striking as it is profound.†

* Tus. Disp. i. 30. "Omnis autem in re consensio omnium gentium *lex naturæ* putanda est." Compare *De Natura Deorum*, i. 43, as also lib. ii. 12. Cicero, being an Academic, often presents his opinions in the form of doubts; but his real sentiments were unquestionably favorable to the doctrine of God and the immortality of the soul. How striking, for example, is the following: "Esse præstantem aliquam æternamque naturam, et eam suspiciendam admirandamque hominum generi, pulchritudo mundi ordoque rerum cœlestium cogit confiteri." — *De Divin.* lib. ii.

† See *De Mundo*, c. 6, 7. A similar passage is referred to by Ne-

It need not surprise us, then, that the great thinkers of the race, those who have gone beneath appearances to grasp the reality of things, have always tended to a common centre of speculative thought. The absolute and eternal has always swept them within its mystic circle. God, the soul, and immortality; the eternal past, the eternal future, are the all-embracing essence in which they become one, are the majestic themes which have occupied their lives. The old Chaldean, Hindoo, and Egyptian sages, the Pythagoreans, the Sophists, the Socratists, Plato and Aristotle, the Academics, the Stoics, the Neo-Platonists, in fact every class of Grecian thinkers, as also the Roman philosophers, though much inferior to the Grecian in vigor and comprehensiveness of mind, took a more or less distinguished part in the discussion of these subjects. Among the questions which the ancients considered as lying at the foundation of all science and philosophical reasoning were the following: 1. Whether there was a creative power in the universe; 2. Whether this power was invested with the attributes of wisdom, goodness, and truth; 3. Whether the mind of man formed a

ander, as quoted by Plutarch, (*De Defectu Oraculorum,*) from the Antigone of Sophocles; but we have been unable to verify it in the Antigone as now extant. Compare Plutarch, *Adver. Stoicos*, c. 22. Cicero, *De Legibus*, lib. ii. 107.

part, or was made analogous to the divine mind, or principle; 4. Whether this intellectual part of man was of an absolutely spiritual nature, and was endowed with immortality; 5. Whether there is any thing absolutely true or absolutely good in the nature of things; 6. Whether the true and the good relative to man be the same in the essence as the true and the good relative to the divine nature; 7. Whether man was an object of care or interest in the divine economy, and whether he had any means of ascertaining the fact. 8. Whether we have any definite meaning in the mind when we make use of such words as *justice*, *power*, *existence*, *intelligence*, *benevolence*, *virtue*, *vice*, &c.*

Their methods of reasoning, somewhat variable, may be deemed fallacious; but the fact remains that, even in their logical and philosophical investigations, these were the great questions from which they started, and to which they constantly returned. A few philosophers, subtle and penetrating, but cold and sterile, like Epicurus and Comte, have lingered in mere mechanism, never transcending the outward and perishable. Others, like Aristotle and Hegel, have lost themselves in abstractions, even while recognizing absolute and eternal being; and

* Blakey's History of Logic, pp. 66, 70. See Ritter's Hist. of Ancient Ph., passim. Compare Aristotle's Metaphysica.

others, like Pyrrho and Lucretius, driven by doubt, arising from their limited natures, or the disturbing influence of a chaotic era, have plunged into the horrible abyss of atheism. But the majority of profound thinkers, and still more of great actors, in all ages, have recognized, with more or less fulness, the supremacy of spirit, the government of God, and the immortality of the soul.

Nay, sometimes in the deepest labyrinth of error, whole communities have longed after God. Groping in the dark amid the monuments of ancient superstition, or the deeper gloom of a false philosophy, they have stretched themselves towards the divine, like confined flowers, instinctively seeking the sun. In Athens, with its thirty thousand gods, we find an altar, if not several altars, to "the unknown God." The symbol worship of ancient Assyria, with its vast and shadowy forms, the mystic faith of Egypt, based upon some vague but sublime idea of the unity of God and the resurrection of the dead, although cold and massive as its stony images, and especially the gorgeous pantheism of India, at once monstrous and impressive, were shadows of the sublime reality. Zerdusht and Menu, as well as Pythagoras and Plato, penetrated beyond external forms, and saw quivering beneath them those eternal energies which they referred to being and thought.

This accounts for the supposition of a golden age, that era of religion simple and sincere. Then the Divinity walked among men, and all nature was glorified with his presence. Miracle was law, and law was miracle; for all was wonder and worship. Harmony and joy pervaded the earth, bathed, so to speak, in celestial sunlight. Refracted, indeed, through mythic and legendary mists, after all "'twas light from heaven." Its origin was supernatural and divine. The first Eden, or the reign of God upon earth, alone can account for it.

Of some such age or state all the ancient nations have traditions more or less perfect.* It gleams as a dim remembrance in all their poetry, philosophy, and history. In some cases it may be accounted for by the natural desire of all nations to glorify their origin and ancestry; but this will not account for it in all, and especially for the peculiar traditional form in which it often

* The Egyptian, Babylonian, and Persian mythologies recognize it with great distinctness, and describe the change which ensued as "a fall from glory." In the Vishnu Purana of the Hindoo tradition, we have the following: "The beings who were created by Brahma were at first endowed with righteousness and perfect faith; they dwelt wherever they pleased, unchecked by any impediment. Their hearts were free from guile. They were pure, and made free from soil by the observance of sacred institutes. In their holy minds Hari dwelt, and they were filled with perfect wisdom, wherewith they contemplated the glory of Vishnu." See a quotation from Pausanias in Neander's Church Hist. vol. i. p. 12; as also various references in Knapp's Theology, p. 198.

appears. It obviously supposes the existence of some higher civilization, lost in the dim shadows of the past, and not only so, but of a purer form of religion, or at least a deeper sense of its divine beauty and power.

The earlier and stronger communities, those even which lapsed into symbol worship, Egypt, Assyria, Persia, India, Greece, Etruria, and Rome itself, in the palmy days of the republic, as Strabo and Polybius distinctly testify, had a strong and all-pervading faith.* The Hebrew commonwealth was made prosperous and permanent only as a theocracy, or divine republic. When it ceased to be religious, it fell into imbecility, and became a reproach among the nations. The great and good men of all times, around whom society has clustered, the kingly spirits of history, martyrs and patriots of by-gone days, all have been distinguished for their piety. The founders of states, the reformers of laws and manners, Moses, Menu, Zoroaster, Solon, Constantine, Mohammed, Charlemagne, Alfred, Washington, derived their greatest force from the religious element. "God and the right" has been the battle cry of civilization throughout the world.

* Some may call it, and perhaps justly, *a superstition*; but this itself must have originated in the religious instinct. The universality of superstition is a natural mystery, which cannot be accounted for, except by reference to the spiritual and immortal nature of man.

Tyranny, indeed, knowing the immense power of this element, has often abused it; but what noble and generous thing has not tyranny abused? The diamond is a diamond still, though gleaming on the brow of pride. No abuse can deprive religion of its original beauty, its inherent and eternal power.

Hence, not only in ancient, but in modern times, we find ample recognition of the indestructible religious tendency of the race. "Whether true or false, sublime or ridiculous," says M. Thiers, "man must have a religion." The historian of the Consulate and Empire, quick, versatile, and well informed, but not profound or philosophical, is far from seeing the reason of this great fact; but his testimony is none the less valuable. It gives us a glimpse of the deepest secret of human nature.

Most instructive, as bearing upon this matter, is the history of Benjamin Constant,* who, seduced by the superficial materialism of Voltaire and the Encyclopædists, at first denied the reality and validity of the religious sentiment, and consequently the existence and moral government of

* Born at Lausanne, in 1767. He was educated in Germany, and became one of the greatest authors and most able orators of the liberals, or constitutionalists, in the French Chamber of Deputies. His great work on religion (*De la Religion, consideree dans sa Source, ses Formes, et ses Developpements*) was published in Paris in 1824.

God. Of noble and generous impulses, and longing for the emancipation of his own mind and that of his countrymen from the bondage of error, he embraced, with eagerness, those views of nature and society which promised this result. The dominant faith of continental Europe, associated with tyranny and superstition, seemed the greatest obstacle to its realization, and he sympathized with the powerful attacks made upon religion by some of the most brilliant writers of his time. His mind was too noble and aspiring to bear the burden of doubt. He longed for certainty and freedom. He was compelled, therefore, to undertake a patient and thorough examination of the whole subject. His great work on religion, however, was commenced with a far different aim from that which he actually reached. He intended it, at first, as a contribution to the cause of infidelity. He supposed that he could show, by an appeal to history, that the religious sentiment in man was always the product of a delusive superstition, and that in all its forms it was destructive to the best interests, and especially to the progress, of society. But one after another his prepossessions vanished. As his investigations advanced, he found that religion was a universal and indestructible principle in the nature of man. Thence his inquiries took an entirely different direction, and the issue was, the production of a work which may be regarded as one of the most striking testimonies to the validity and worth of religion. "My work," says he, in a letter to a friend, "is a singular proof of the remark of Bacon, that a little philosophy leads a man to atheism, but a great deal to religion. It is positively in the profound investigation of facts, in my researches in every quarter, and in struggling with the difficulties without number which they bring against incredulity, that I have found myself forced to return to religious ideas. I have done this most certainly in perfectly good faith; for I have not taken a single retrograde step without cost. Even to this moment all my habits, all my remembrances, are on the side of the sceptical philosophy; and I defend, post after post, every spot of ground which religion gains from me." *

Constant shows, by an analysis of the nature and susceptibilities of man, compared with the facts of history, that he is a spiritual being, and has affinities and relations with infinite perfection and immortal existence; that, although many things check and oppose this tendency in the race, it lives and grows, ever longing for its object, ever attempting its realization. He finds the highest development of this principle in the

* Specimens of Foreign Literature, by George Ripley, vol. ii, p. 273.

theism of the Jewish faith, so far transcending the people and age in which it is found, and especially in Christianity, which "brings life and immortality to light." Kant's Kritik of the Pure Reason, (*Der Praktischen Vernunft,*) after the strictest analysis of the moral wants and tendencies of the human soul, comes to precisely the same result. Comte himself has recently avowed the necessity of religion, and has given an exposition of his views upon this subject, in his "positive theory of human unity." *

Indeed, it must be obvious to every candid thinker that the welfare of the individual as well as the welfare of society depends upon the depth and purity of their religious convictions. "The first principle," says Lord Bacon, touching, in his brief, expressive way, the very core of the matter, "of right reason is religion." † On this rests, as its lowest foundation, the entire super-

* Developed in the second volume of his "*Systeme de Politique Positive.*"

† The whole passage in which this occurs is well worth attention. "I had rather believe all the fables in the Talmud and the Alcoran than that this universal frame is without a mind. God never wrought a miracle to convert an atheist, because his ordinary works confute atheism. A little philosophy may incline men to infidelity; but a further proceeding therein brings them back to religion. For when the mind looks on second causes scattered, it sometimes rests in them; but when it beholds them confederated and linked together, it must needs fly to Providence and to Deity. After all my studies and inquiries, I dare not die with any other thoughts than those of the Christian religion."

structure of the social state. Without it, man is nothing — society nothing. Destroy religion, and our very nature

> "Sinks under us, bestorms, and then devours."

The fact is, a community of atheists cannot exist. Infidelity is essentially disorganizing. It uniformly breaks up society, and rushes to ruin. France, indeed, once proclaimed herself atheistic, but it was in the midst of a revolution the most appalling and bloody. The delusion lasted only the briefest space. Reaction was instant and decisive. Atheism, we grant, yet lingers in that beautiful country, but only as an individual opinion. Besides, that it is an element of disorganization, even in this form, must be obvious to the most superficial observer. If France ever falls, as fell the old dynasties of the world, it will fall through scepticism and lust.

Of course, religion, like all other things, — science, morals, literature, social life, government, &c., — will represent the nature of those who profess it. As men are imperfect beings, in most cases ignorant, — nay, more, positively sinful, — having suffered some fatal lapse, their religion will rarely, if ever, rise to any thing like perfection. Their creeds will often be crude, visionary, superstitious; nay, sometimes positively degrading. For the well-known adage of Horace is universally true, that the best things abused always become the worst. Liable to error and passion, our religion, perverted, sometimes proves the direst curse. Hence, in the matter of piety and morals, we find, among men, strange action and reaction. For now, by the force of what may be called their better nature, they are attracted to God, and anon, by the force of their evil nature, repelled from him. They vibrate, like a pendulum, between holiness and sin, vice and virtue. After all, God is their portion, perfection their true and eternal destiny.

Hence superstition is the symptom of a deeper want. It is the hunger of the soul feeding upon husks, the thirst of the spirit drinking poison. In its wildest vagaries, even idolatry is the shadow of diviner worship. That young Hindoo mother, who has thrown her first born into the Ganges, has all the affection of a mother, and her heart, torn with anguish, goes after her little one sinking in the waves; but she has made the sacrifice (in her view, sublime) of that dearest treasure, for the salvation of her soul. Nations set up a Moloch or a Juggernaut, not because they love cruelty for its own sake, but because a blind, but irresistible instinct impels them to seek some relief to the terrible famine of the spirit.

The fact is obvious, that in all ages religion,

in some form, has been the central force of society, the keystone of states and empires; and for this simple reason, that, being divine, it is the only thing which controls the inner life. It is the law which a community carries, not in its government archives, but in its heart. It requires no magistrate to pronounce sentence, no police to seize, no executioner to punish. Its domain is invisible and all comprehending, like the magnetic forces which pervade universal nature.

A true history of the world, then, especially of its civilization, its progress or decay, would be a history of religion in its relations to society. This every where is the pervading and abiding power. This marks the degree of elevation or depression in all. As this rises so rises society in prosperity and strength. As this falls, so falls society into barbarism and decay. Corrupted, abused, debased, like government, law, organization, freedom, every thing, in a word, which has power, it is a reality the most sublime, a good the highest and deepest of all.

It is on this ground we maintain that God, in some manifested form, or an organized belief, and especially in Jesus Christ and Christianity, to which Judaism is an introduction, is the centre of all history, past, present, and to come. So that those who would know Christ must know history, and those who would know history must know Christ.*

But we must go back to primeval fountains, and trace the central element or principle referred to, namely, God as a personality, more especially "God in Christ," either as a hope or a possession, in the great powers which ruled over ancient society, in religion, philosophy, and what men call the common, but in reality divine, succession of events.

* "By him," says St. Paul, "all things consist," (συνεστηκεν,) literally, *stand together*; that is, *in him, and around him, all facts converge.*

CHAPTER II.

THE CENTRAL PRINCIPLE, OR CHRIST IN ANCIENT RELIGION.

We cannot here trace, with any detail, the history of religion from the earliest times, but a brief and comprehensive sketch, indicating its general character, and especially its relations to Christ, will be in place.

Leaving out of the account, for the present, the teachings of the Scriptures as to the primitive form of belief in the early ages of the world, we begin with religion as it existed in the form of nature-worship, symbol-worship, and idolatry. The most eminent archæologists and historians give it as their opinion that these, in the elder and more civilized nations, were the corruptions of a purer faith; or at least that the traditional influence of a purer faith mingled with these in all their successive transformations. "The more I investigate the ancient history of the world," says A. W. Schlegel, "the more I am convinced that the civilized nations set out from a purer worship of the Supreme Being; that the magic power of nature over the imagination of the successive human races, first at a later period, produced polytheism, and finally altogether obscured the more spiritual religious notions, while the wise alone preserved within the sanctuary the primeval secret.*

Among all these nations, especially in the writings of the poets, and in the primitive religious or mythological traditions, scattered memorials are found of a belief in the existence and moral government of God and the immortality of the soul. Plutarch, in his treatise on the *Isis* and *Osiris* of Egyptian worship, informs us, that "it was a most ancient opinion handed down from

* Those who wish to investigate this subject are referred to Cudworth's Intellectual System, civ., passim; the first part of Warburton's Divine Legation of Moses, compared with Mosheim, *De Rebus ante Const.* p. 17, et seq., (in Dr. Murdock's edition of Vidal's Translation, pp. 20–48;) Neander's Church Hist. vol. i. pp. 5–34; F. W. Schlegel's Language and Wisdom of the Indians; and Mueller's Intro. to a Complete System of Mythology. With reference to the Mysteries, see Creuzer's *Symbolik und Mythologie*, iv. 3, et seq.; Limburg Brouwer's *Histoire de la Civilisation des Grecs*, tom. 2, cxiv.; Bryant's Analysis of Ancient Mythology, vol. iii. p. 400, et seq. Lobeck, in his celebrated *Aglaophemus Histoire* has ingeniously defended a different view; but the verdict of recent mythologists is against him. The arguments upon this subject are summed up in an ingenious and eloquent article in Blackwood's Mag. for February, 1853. On the opinions of the Ancient Egyptians, see Prichard's Analysis of Egyptian Mythology; as, also, Kenrick's Ancient Egypt, particularly vol. i. pp. 302, 306. Meiners, in his too highly-estimated work entitled *Hist. Doctrinæ de Deo Vero*, has maintained that the heathen received their first idea of the true God from Athanagoras; but his reasoning is one-sided and unsatisfactory. The views of Neander, Schleiermacher and the later German theologians are much nearer the truth.

legislators and divines to poets and philosophers, the author of it entirely unknown, but the belief of it indelibly established not only in tradition and the talk of the common people, but in the mysteries and sacred offices of religion, both amongst Greeks and barbarians spread all over the face of the earth, that the universe was not upheld fortuitously, without mind, reason, or a governor to preside over its affairs."

This is especially true of the Egyptians, Chaldeans, Assyrians, and probably the Hindoos, as also, to some extent, of the elder Greeks and Romans. *Zeus* himself, (from the verb signifying *to live*,*) the head of the Olympian conclave, is but a corruption, as the name imports, of the one "living" and eternal Jehovah, the basis of which undoubtedly is, the "I am that I am," or *The Existing One* of Moses, "King of kings and Lord of lords." Occasionally, in the Greek dramatists and elsewhere, he is described as the One Fountain of life, "the Father of gods and men."

* This derivation is given by Plato in the Cratylus, (28.) "For in reality," he says, "the name of Zeus is, so to speak, a sentence, and persons dividing it into two parts, some of us make use of one part, and some another; for some call him Ζῆν, and some Δις; but these parts, combined in one, exhibit the nature of the God, which, as we have said, a name ought to do. For there is no one who, in a higher sense, is the *cause of life*, both to us and every thing else, than he who is the Ruler and King of all. It follows, therefore, that this God is rightly named, through whom life is imparted to all living beings."

Thus, in the Troades of Euripides, we have the following: —

> "O thou who guid'st the rolling of the earth,
> And o'er it hast thy throne, whoe'er thou art,
> Most difficult to know, the far-famed Zeus,
> Or nature's law, or reason such as man's,
> I thee adore, that, in a noiseless path,
> Thy steady hand with justice all things rules."

In the Œdipus Coloneus we read, —

> "Thou power supreme, all power above,
> All-seeing, all-performing Jove."

But in the Philoctetes of the same poet, the earth is apostrophized as the mother of all things: —

> "O Earth, thou mother of great Jove,
> Embracing all with universal love."

In the Prometheus of Æschylus, the most original and powerful of the Greek tragedies, Jove is described as a usurper. Prometheus, the half-divine, half-human Sufferer and Savior, (as it were a dumb prophecy of Christ,) is the true friend of man. It is only by glimpses and flashes that the Greek poets give any just conceptions of a supreme, all-righteous Deity. Eusebius, for example, in his *Preparatio Evangelica*, quotes from a lost tragedy of Euripides these striking words:—

> "Thou self-sprung being, that doth all infold,
> And in thine arms heaven's whirling fabric hold,"

reminding us of Bryant's beautiful lines, —

> "Whose love doth keep
> In his complacent arms the earth, the air, the deep."

It is well known, however, that in all these dramatists, and in the popular Greek theogonies, Jupiter, the apotheosis of a Phrygian tyrant, is most frequently represented as the son of Chronos, (Time,) as also of Gaea, (Earth,) as controlled by the Fates, as actuated by base passions, as the usurper of a throne held by a race of elder gods, as subject to violent changes, nay, as in danger, some time or other, of losing his dominions. But, alas! what can be expected from minds left to the sole guidance of nature and fancy? Still we discern in them all the struggles of a better faith, the faint traditional gleams of a purer era.*

To the same effect some of the Christian fathers, especially Clement of Alexandria, and Justin Martyr, quote several traditionary passages from Orpheus, Musæus, the Sibylline Oracles, and other Greek poems, some of which may be supposed to be genuine. Of these we translate one or two specimens:—

> "I adjure thee by heaven, the work of the wise and great God;
> I adjure thee by the voice of the Father."

* Plato, it is well known, excludes the poets from his ideal republic; not that he was averse to poetry, — far from it, — but because some of them, by their prurient fancies had corrupted the spiritual truths of religion, and, by consequence, injured good morals. Hesiod is sometimes charged with *inventing* the gods. The Orphic hymns are based upon a sort of pantheism, recognizing one supreme God, from whom issue both gods and men.

Some doubt, however, may be thrown upon the genuineness, or at least the absolute antiquity, of this. More reliable is the following:—

> "One God, one Plato, one Bacchus,
> One God in all——." *

That from the pseudo author of the Sibylline Oracles, indorsed as Justin Martyr affirms, by Plato and Aristophanes as a *vates*, could we rely upon its genuineness, is peculiarly striking.

> "One God there is, (Εις δε Θεὸς μόνος,) alone, great, uncreated,
> Omnipotent, invisible, seeing all,
> Himself unseen by mortal flesh." †

We will not, indeed, urge these as absolute authorities upon the point in question; still they are fair specimens of many similar expressions which were afloat in the current traditionary literature of Greece. Of the authors of these the profound Heraclitus, five hundred years before Christ, had said, "Their unadorned, earnest words, spoken with inspired mouth, reached through a thousand years." The passages from the elder Greek poets quoted in the *De Monarchia* of Justin's works are equally striking, and certainly more reliable, as most of them can be

* In striking correspondence with this was the ancient Greek inscription on the Egyptian obelisk in the Circus Major at Rome: Μεγας Θέος θέογεννήτος παμφὲγγης—*the great God, the Begotten of God, and the all-radiant One.*

† *Opera Justini Martyris*, (Otto's ed.) pp. 53–55. Compare what he says in the *De Monarchia*, p. 125, et seq.

verified by reference to the originals.* Cudworth, who justly rejects a large proportion of the collection called the Sibylline Oracles, as "a useless farrago," quotes the following as genuine, from the works of Pausanias: —

> "Zeus was, Zeus is, Zeus shall be, O great Zeus." †

In a word, it can be proved beyond a doubt, that the Greeks, as well as some of the neighboring nations, did occasionally recognize the existence of some supreme Numen, Governor or Spirit of the universe, and that the idea was taken up, and in some cases vindicated, by their philosophers.

Xenophanes, one of the early philosophical rhapsodists, and founder of what is called the Eleatic school, exclaims, with wonderful clearness and force, —

* Most of the Orphic and Sibylline hymns are regarded by scholars as spurious. Many of them were undoubtedly invented by the Neo-Platonists of Alexandria. It is certain, however, that some of them, in a more or less perfect form, were afloat, as traditionary fragments, in the common literature of Greece, and that several of these were quoted or referred to by Greek classic writers as early as the days of Plato. Orpheus is spoken of by them as a sort of "inspired theologer." The best edition of the Orphic poems is that of Hermann. The question of their antiquity has been thoroughly discussed by Bode, in his prize essay on this subject. On the Sibylline Oracles, an admirable article may be found in the Christian Review for March, 1848. Compare Neander's Ch. History, i. 177.

† Works, vol. i. p. 382. The quotation from Pausanias reminds us of the inspiration on the temple of Neitha in Egypt, as reported by Plutarch, (*De Isid. et Osi.*,) Ἔγω εἴμι παν τὸ γεγονος καὶ ον κα εσομοένον, etc.

"There's but one God alone, the greatest of gods and of mortals,
Neither in body to mankind resembling, neither in ideas.*

Pythagoras and the Pythagoreans, though bewildered by the duality of the universe, and the apparent duality in the nature of the infinite mind, yet taught that God, as essence, is one; that he is present in all things, governing the world; and that from him our souls derive their origin. They taught also, though in the form of metempsychosis, the immortality of the human soul, as well as the reality and eternity of virtue.†

It is a generally received opinion that the great philosophical writers of Greece derived some of their loftiest notions from Egypt and the East. The philosophy of Plato, whatever its origin, is but a combination of the Grecian and Oriental minds. The acknowledgment of one Supreme and eternal Deity, by him and others, is not so much a speculation as an intuition, if not a tradition from India or Egypt; perhaps from Judea itself. Be this, however, as it may, the German critics are right when they designate the philosophy of Plato as at once "speculative" and

* Ritter Hist. of An. Ph. vol. i. p. 432. The quotation is from Clemens Alexandrinus, and is as follows: —

Εἷς Θεὸς ἔν τε θεοῖσι και ἀνθρωποισι μεγιστος,
Οὔτι δέμας θνητοῖσι οὐδε νοημα.

† Cicero, *De Natura Deorum*, i. 11.

"traditional." He himself demands assent to it, mainly on the ground of its being σοφία θεοπάραδοτος — *God-given wisdom.*

Socrates, indeed, gives proofs from adaptation and design, after the manner of Cicero and Paley, for the existence and moral government of God; after all, it is evident that the idea existed in his mind, and in the mind of Plato before the proofs referred to were cited in argument.* These reverent and lofty souls caught the grand idea as it floated upon the stream of time, amid the fragments of a primeval revelation. They found it, indeed, connatural to their own reason; but they did not claim it as an original or independent thought, which had sprung up spontaneously in their mind, or had been excogitated by speculation and argument.†

* In the Platonic dialogues the existence of God is generally assumed, or based upon, an original intuition. Plato, if called upon for a proof, would refer to the very nature of being and thought, as essential, immutable realities.

Socrates, in Xenophon, refers to adaptation and design. See Xenophon's *Mem.* lib. i. c. iv.

† The ancient fathers, Justin Martyr, Cyril, Tertullian, and others, constantly affirm that Plato derived many of his ideas of God from the writings of Moses. After having quoted the celebrated passage from the *Timæus*, "that to know the Father and Maker of all is very difficult, nor, having found him, is it safe to tell to all persons," Justin Martyr (*Cohortatio ad Græcos*, c. 22) adds, "When Plato had learned these things in Egypt, and had been greatly delighted with what was said concerning the one God, he did not think it safe to mention the name of Moses, a teacher of the one and only God, being in fear of the Areopagus." (Opera, vol. i. p. 61.) This may be taken for what it is worth; we cite it as curious.

The Deity, as recognized by the Stoics, though frequently approaching the nature-divinity of pantheism, had sublime attributes, as the well-known hymn of Cleanthes strikingly testifies. It sounds like the echo, or the refrain, of a purer faith.* Yet, generally speaking, the God of the Stoics is represented by them as "devouring his own offspring," (a truly pantheistic conception,) and thus assuming the character of a blind, inexorable power, to whom, willing or unwilling, they must submit. They doubted, sometimes denied, the immortality of the soul, the consequence of which often was a mournful despair, under the influence of which Cleanthes himself committed suicide. Others regarded themselves as equal to God, and, like Prometheus, defied his power. A few only submitted gracefully to their destiny, giving back what they had received from *the All*. But amid all their speculations gleamed the central idea of the unity and eternity of God; and it is this which gives such grandeur to some of their expressions, and its fine moral charm to the hymn of Cleanthes.

A similar and perhaps more striking instance of this primitive, perhaps foreign, element in the religion of Greece is from the poet Aratus, as

* How grand and striking the commencement:

> Κύδιστ' ἀθανατων, πολυώνυμε παγκρατὲς αἰεὶ,
> Ζεὺς φύσεως ἀρχηγε, νομου μετα παντα κυβερνων,
> Χαῖρε.

quoted by St. Paul, in his address before the Athenian Areopagus, on which occasion the great apostle recognizes the religious spirit incrusted by superstition, even in their heathen *cultus*. He declares unto them "the unknown God, whom," says he, "ye ignorantly worship." It appears that Eudoxus of Cnidus, a contemporary of Plato, about 370 years before Christ, sent forth a description of the face of the heavens, containing the names and characters of the constellations recognized in his day. Though this production has perished, a poetical paraphrase of it was made by Aratus, a Cilician, and probably a native of Tarsus; and this is the poem from which St. Paul quotes. It opens with a statement of the dependence of all things upon Zeus, whose children all men are, and who has given the stars as the guides of agriculture:—

"With Jove (Zeus) we must begin, nor from him rove,
Him always praise; for all is full of Jove!
He fills all places where mankind resort,
The wide-spread sea, with every sheltering port.
Jove's presence fills all space, upholds this ball;
All need his aid, his power sustains us all;
For *we his offspring are*,* and he in love
Points out to man his labor from above,
Where signs unerring show where best the soil
By well-timed culture shall repay our toil."

* The original expression is τοῦ γαρ καὶ γένος ἐσμέν. Similar expressions may be found in Plato. See the passage respecting the creation of man, as translated by Cicero, quoted in Knapp's Theo. p. 197.

It is questionable, indeed, whether Aratus felt the full force of his own words. They probably convey to us a far sublimer conception than ever dawned upon his mind. For the fact is, while gleams of diviner light occasionally flashed upon some of the Grecian intellects, most of them were far from realizing the spiritual unity and supremacy of the all-comprehending Spirit. Their religion was only a poetical, often a very licentious nature-worship, in the form of polytheism. Their gods were seldom better, often vastly worse, than themselves.*

By a natural process of deterioration, the primitive and purer worship, in all nations, was gradually merged in superstition. Those undefined feelings which mankind naturally cherish towards some superior power were transferred either to symbolic representations, or to material objects. The principles and forms of idolatry, at first few and simple, were gradually multiplied. The system was invested with greater pomp, and modified by more numerous and elaborate ceremonies. The knowledge of the true God grew dim, and was all but effaced from the minds of men. Only its image or echo remained. A vague but still sublime impression of "something far more deeply interfused," a "motion" and a

* See Grote's History of Greece, vol. i. pp. 3–19.

"presence," vast and mysterious, dwelling in the light of setting suns, whispering in hoary woods and mountain solitudes, or residing, in supreme but hidden grandeur, above the blue concave, amid radiant suns and constellations, led them to seek emblems of the Deity in the more brilliant and magnificent forms of nature. Nature, indeed, was substituted for God. The fragment was taken for the whole; the world for the world's Creator and Lord; the life, the beauty, the motion for the great and eternal Spirit from whom they spring. The motions and uses, especially of the heavenly bodies, were observed. They were supposed to exert a baleful or benignant influence not only upon the earth, but upon the soul and destiny of man. They seemed the very eyes of God, or of the Gods; nay, more, the very power and presence of uncreated glory, burning, with unconsuming fires, in the depths of "the eternal night."

Besides, it is natural to give outward form and expression to inward feelings and conceptions, to symbolize, in permanent shape and image, abstract principles and modes of being. Hence the language of signs, of hieroglyphs, and emblems, common to all the ruder nations. Hence the symbols even of the Holy Scriptures, the signs and ceremonies of the old temple worship among the spiritual Hebrews.* Mr. Layard thinks that the magnificent, winged, lion-headed, and human-headed animals, excavated from the ruins of Nineveh, were emblems of the attributes and perfections of the old Assyrian deities.

"What more noble forms," says he, "could have ushered the people into the temple of their gods? What more sublime images could have been borrowed from nature by men who sought, unaided by the light of revealed religion, to embody their conception of the wisdom, power, and ubiquity of a Supreme Being? They could find no better type of intellect and knowledge than the head of a man — of strength, than the body of a lion — of rapidity of motion, than the wings of a bird. These winged, human-headed lions were not idle creations, the offspring of mere fancy. They had awed and instructed races which flourished three thousand years ago. Through the portals which they guarded, kings, priests, and warriors had borne sacrifices to their altars long before the wisdom of the East had penetrated to Greece, and had furnished its

* The Jews were not forbidden the use of symbols as such, but only of idolatrous images; that is, of idols or figures representing the divinity. Their whole history, temple service, and even domestic rites, were symbolic. The cherubim above the mercy seat symbolized the divine attributes. It is not symbols, but symbol-worship, or idolatry proper; that is to say, the substitution for the eternal God of outward forms, or created beings, which is so abhorrent to the pure Theism of the Bible.

mythology with symbols long recognized by the Assyrian votaries." *

But man unregenerate has earthly and carnal tendencies. He speedily loses the knowledge of the spiritual and eternal. Thence, in process of time, among all the ancient nations, the sign assumed the place of the thing signified.† God was forgotten, while his image remained. Principles were lost, but emblems and usages continued. The outer aspects and forces of nature were deified and adored. These, again, by an easy descent into error, came to be considered as separate powers ruling over the various departments of the universe. In this way the primitive form of idolatrous worship was the adoration of the earth and the blue concave with its innumerable fires, and especially the sun, moon, and brighter planets, perhaps as the symbols of the Divinity, then as the real aspects and attributes of his nature, and finally as separate gods. Artificial emblems of these, in their turn, were formed, either by means of painted or of sculptured images; and thus, in succeeding ages, the Brahma, Vishnu, and Shiva of Hindoo

* Nineveh, vol. i., p. 69.

† Doubtless there were, in all, individual exceptions. The influence of tradition, of natural reason and conscience, and the secret working of the divine Spirit, not entirely withheld from the heathen, preserved in devout hearts the worship of the one true God.

mythology — the ancient Belus or Baal of Chaldean and Phœnician worship — the Moloch or fire-god, Ashtaroth or Astarte, the moon-god, and Remphan, the star-god of Canaan and the neighboring countries — the Osiris or sun-god of Egypt — with the Jupiter and Apollo (Phœbus or the sun-god) of Greek and Roman superstition, took the place of the more simple and beautiful objects of early adoration.*

If Layard has given us the true import of the ancient Assyrian images, they had lost it as early as the days of the Hebrew prophets, who justly represent the Assyrians as abject idolaters. Various monuments on the Assyrian sculpture even now prove that they adored the powers of nature and "the host of heaven." If they had any conception of a supreme Divinity, he was probably regarded only as the first among many. The sun was the principal object of Chaldean worship, originally, we doubt not, as the symbol of Jehovah, but subsequently "in and for itself," as Baal or Belus, whence the Greek Apollo (*Ηλιος*) or the sun-god, corresponding, in a remarkable degree, to the sun-god of ancient Peru.† The magnificent bull-god

* Ritter, Hist. An. Ph. i. p. 81, and F. W. Schlegel's Ph. of Hist. pp. 214–227.

† See Prescott's Conquest of Peru. Introductory account of Peruvian civilization.

with human head and spreading wings, less appropriate and beautiful than the sun-god with streaming rays, or in the form of a majestic, irradiated man, the Apollo of later times, was probably the symbol of divine power; but the symbol itself, in the worship of the people, as the calf in the Hebrew idolatry, doubtless, took the place of the true and eternal Jehovah. "These be thy gods" — *thy Elohim, or God, symbols of thy God,* "*O Israel!*" In all the tombs and temples of Assyria and Chaldea, and even of Nubia and Egypt, are sculptured representations and inscriptions of these divinities — "the chambers of imagery" seen by Ezekiel in his prophetic visions.

The process of change and deterioration to which we have referred is strikingly developed in Egyptian history. We find among them, in the first place, some vague idea of a Supreme Being, with attributes of omnipotence and eternity, to whom all things are referred, and who was too holy to be named by any one except the priests, finally figured on all the sculptures as the Sun-god, whence the term *Phre* or *Phra*, and thence *Pharaoh*, the emperor or Cæsar of Egypt, who derived his power from the Divinity, and who, in his absolute dominion, mirrored the might and supremacy of the eternal Sun.*

* Sir Gardner Wilkinson says that the Hebrew *Phra* is taken from the Egyptian word *pire*, or *phre*, signifying the sun, and rep-

This supreme and "hidden" God was *Amun*, afterwards called *Zeus*, or *Jupiter Ammon*, symbolically represented under the figure of a ram, with the disk of the sun upon his head, to indicate that he is the God of the sun, as that luminary enters the sign of the Ram.* In Egyptian theogony, Amun is represented as manifesting himself through Phtha, the god of light or fire, in the creation of the world, and thus forming gods and men. The government of the universe, under him, is committed to twelve principal gods, each of whom has for his symbol one of the twelve signs of the zodiac, with three attendants or satellites, and these again with their attendants, and so on in succession, until the last class of subordinates amount to three hundred and sixty. These, with various orders of demons, good and bad, preside over the earth and heavens, and so divide the year. Hence the study of astrology, to which the Egyptians and other ancient nations were so much addicted.†

According to this system men are the em-

resented in hieroglyphics by the hawk and globe, or sun, over the royal banner. — Egypt, &c., by Dr. Hawks, p. 101.

* Whence *Heliopolis*, the sacred city of the sun.

† We ought to state here that the latest authorities deny the general prevalence of any one system of religion in Egypt. It would appear that various gods were worshipped in different parts of the country. Polytheism must have been prevalent at a very early period. See upon this subject Kenrick's Ancient Egypt, vol. i. p. 305.

bodied spirits of a higher order of beings, who, prompted by curiosity, formerly passed the boundaries of the celestial spheres, and received corporeal frames from the god Hermes. Falling into discontent and misery, they lost their primitive purity, and became a burden to the earth and elements, who complained of them to their creator. Pitying them, he sent Osiris and Isis upon the earth to redeem them.

Hence followed the sensual worship of Osiris as the sun, and Isis as the moon, generative powers of nature, with Typhon, the serpent or destroyer. Osiris was regarded as the tutelar deity of the Egyptians, and his spirit or soul was supposed always to inhabit the body of the bull Apis, a black animal with a white spot like a triangle on his forehead, another resembling a crescent on his right side, and under his tongue a lump or protuberance, somewhat resembling a beetle.

Thus beast-worship became universal in Egypt; for the symbolic meaning of the bull-god was known only to the priests.

Such a system, of course, readily mingled with the lowest forms of fetichism, springing spontaneously from the soil, or introduced into Egypt from the neighboring countries. So that we finally find throughout the land a monstrous and degrading worship of all sorts of gods in the heavens above, and in the earth beneath, and in the waters under the earth — cats, serpents and other reptiles, plants and flowers, rivers and fountains of waters, and especially the old prolific Nile with its ibises and crocodiles.

"Among the Egyptians," says Clement of Alexandria, "you find temples and porticoes, and vestibules and sacred groves; their halls are surrounded with numberless columns; the walls are resplendent with foreign stones and beautiful paintings; the temples are brilliant with gold and silver, and amber and many-colored gems from India and Ethiopia, while the adyta are curtained with gold embroidered hangings; but if you go into the deep interior of the place, and eagerly seek to see what you suppose will be most worth your attention, — the statue which occupies the temple, — a priest of dignified aspect, from among those who offer sacrifice in the most holy place, singing a pæan in the Egyptian tongue, lifts the veil a little aside, as if to show the god; then you find occasion for hearty laughter; for instead of the god you are seeking, you will find but a cat, a crocodile, a serpent of the country, or some other beast worthy only of some cavern, den, or marsh, rolling upon purple coverlets!" *

The vast and monstrous superstitions of the

* Pædagog. lib. iii. c. 2. For further information on the subject of Egyptian superstition, see Pritchard's Analysis of Egyptian Mythology, Iconographic Cyclopedia, vol. iv., art. Mythology;

Hindoo mythology are founded upon material pantheism, or nature-worship. Brahm, the supreme deity, written in the neuter gender to indicate his negative character, being simple existence without consciousness or will, all at once becomes prolific, and distributes himself "lying on eternity and the stars." The gods Brahma, Vishnu, and Shiva are the result, being the creating, preserving, and destroying powers of Brahm or the Universe, adored, however, as separate and even contending divinities. Indeed, all things are deified in the Brahminic faith, men and devils, sun, moon, and stars, all mountains and valleys, all seas and streams, all hills and groves, all plants and animals, all insects and reptiles. These, in fact, are but the natural development of the supreme divinity. All the powers of nature, male and female, are adored with appropriate rites. Vice itself is deified and adored in endless forms, and the result is universal superstition, universal beast-worship; we might add vice-worship, for Kalee, the goddess of murder, has myriad votaries. The Thugs or Stranglers are her sedulous devotees. They murder as an act of devotion.

In Brahminism the most hideous ceremonies,

Jablonsky's Pantheon Ægyptiorum; Wilkinson's Manners of the Ancient Egyptians; De Pauw, *Recherches Philosophiques sur les Egyptiens et les Chinois*; Kenrick's Egypt under the Pharaohs.

and even the most revolting crimes, are strangely mingled with sublime imaginings and thrilling fancies. God, as the absolute, is the beginning and end of all, an echo and exaggeration of the truth, but in this system a monstrous error. "His oneness," say the *Shastres*, "is so absolute, that it not only excludes the possibility of any other god, coördinate and subordinate, but excludes the possibility of aught else, human or angelic, material or immaterial." Thence he is conceived not only as *in all* and *through all*, but as positively and exclusively *All*, whether sun or star, weed or flower, reptile or man, vice or virtue. "Possessed of innumerable heads," says one of the *Vedas*, written, according to Sir William Jones, 1500 years before Christ, and according to Mr. Colebrooke even earlier than that, "innumerable eyes, innumerable feet, Brahm fills the heavens and earth; he is whatever was, whatever will be; he is the source of universal motion; he is the light of the moon, the sun, the fire, the lightning. The Veda is the breath of his nostrils, the primary elements are his sight, the agitation of human affairs is his laughter, his sleep is the destruction of the universe. In different forms he cherishes his creatures; in the form of air he preserves them, in the form of water he satisfies them, in the form of the sun he guides them in the affairs of life, and in that of the moon he refreshes them in sleep; the progression of time forms his footsteps; all the gods to him are as sparks of fire. To him I bow, I bow."

Hence a return to Brahm, — the silent, the unconscious, the eternal, — becomes the dream and desire of all. Utter absorption is the longing of the Brahmin and the Soudra, the philosopher and the peasant, the saint and the sinner. Through countless migrations from body to body, he hopes at last to reach the abyss.*

In Budhism the idea of the divine seems all but lost; but this, we doubt not, was its original foundation; though now the majority of its votaries deny the existence of an eternal, that is, of a conscious, ever-living God, and long for absolute *nigban*, annihilation or absorption. Gaudama, or Budh, was once on earth, but passing away has himself reached annihilation, or the *Burchan* state. Budh, indeed, is properly a generic term, meaning the divinity, while Gaudama (among the Burmans, particularly) is the name of their last Budh, regarded by some of the Hindoos as the ninth incarnation of *Vishnu*, the same, there-

* For a brief popular account of the Hindoo religion, see F. D. W. Ward's India and the Hindoos, pp. 267–277. Those who desire more extended information must consult Colebrooke's Essay, Miscellanies, &c., Sir William Jones's Works, Ward's View of the Hindoos, and The Journal of the Asiatic Society. Compare Van Bohlen's *Das Alte Indien*, and A. W. Schlegel on the *Bhagavad Gita*.

fore, as *Krishna*, who is supposed to have lived about the sixth century before Christ. Among the Burmans and others, he is simply a deified man, who has attained nigban. They expect another Budh many thousand years hence; in the mean while, they worship only images, and literally have no god.* Here, then, amid forms and beliefs, which at first sight appear atheistic, we have the indestructible longing after absolute and eternal Being, which, in its reality, is God. The return to *the All* is but the dim shadow, perhaps the fatal corruption of the sublime idea of the soul's return to the "Father of spirits." It would seem, indeed, as if the entire Oriental mind revolved around this idea, and longed, blindly and instinctively, for this ineffable result. After all, their Burchan state is not absolute extinction, but impersonal repose in the bosom of God.

Another great element of the faith of the Orientals, which we find in many diversified forms, is the possible coming of God to man, as well as the

* Malcom's Travels, vol. i. pp. 241–248. Mr. Malcom endeavors to show that Budhism is older than Brahminism. But his arguments are not satisfactory. The probabilities are all in favor of its being the last result of material pantheism. It exists in different forms among the nations of Farther India. The best authorities represent it as a branch or a shoot of Brahminism. Its essential principle, namely, *absorption*, after endless changes, in *Brahm*, or the All, is the same. See Ritter, Hist. of An. Ph. i. p. 93; see also the second part of F. W. Schegel's Language and Wisdom of the Indians; Icon. Cyclo. vol. iv. p. 233.

possible return of man to God. The idea of God's becoming man, and man's becoming God, is the mystic circle in which all their thoughts revolve. Nothing is more familiar to their minds than the possibility of divine incarnations, and the consequent possibility of human transformations. Somehow, God and man, the infinite and the finite spirit, must become one.

Is not this, too, in reality, the basis of all our western religions? Nay, is it not the very essence of all religion, as a spiritual power intended to restore man to the lost image of God, and thus make him one with God? The western mind indeed clings to the great fact of personality, maintaining not only the personality of man, but the personality of God; but it recognizes the possibility of interior and eternal unity, and consequently easily adopts the doctrine of a divine incarnation, and on the basis of this, the idea of a human transformation. Hence "the incarnation" and "the new birth" are the fundamental and most profoundly cherished truths of Christianity.

In a word, from his very nature man longs for some special manifestation of God, in such form as he can appreciate, and on the ground of this, for some sacred and eternal union with the Source of being and happiness. He must have a Redeemer and a heaven; in default of which he invents his Brahmas, his Krishnas and Osirises, his "lords many and gods many," his *Nigbans* and *Burchans*, his *Mount Merus* and *Elysian Fields.*

This, however, by the way, for our sketch is not yet completed. What remains we reserve for another chapter.

CHAPTER III.

THE CENTRAL PRINCIPLE, OR CHRIST IN ANCIENT RELIGION.

One of the most interesting and well-developed religions of the ancient world, the remains of which yet linger in many parts of Asia, especially in Persia, is that of the Zend-Avesta, (Fire-kindler, or Living Word,) the sacred book of the Parsees, or ancient fire-worshippers. Considerable dispute exists as to the primitive form of this religion, and some apparently well-grounded doubts have been cast upon the genuineness of the Zend-Avesta. Many learned men, however, allow it, in the main, to be the work or compilation of their great religious teacher, Zerdusht, or Zoroaster, who is supposed to have flourished before the time of Cyrus. Still the work is fragmentary, consisting mainly of occasional institutes, prayers, and other liturgical forms. Those most competent to form an opinion say that it has the appearance of a work consisting of some original materials, with successive additions and emendations. It was brought originally from India by Anquetil Du Perron, by whom it was translated and published in 1771, and has ever since been the subject of frequent discussion among Oriental scholars. Upon the whole, we are compelled, from the present state of the evidence, to conclude that its genuineness, or at least its extreme antiquity, is a matter of great doubt.* Zerdusht himself begins to appear almost as a mythic character.† Still the probability is, that there was such a personage, and that he gave form and pressure to the old Magian faith. Dean Prideaux and some other learned men think that the compiler of the Zend-Avesta derived much of his knowledge from the Hebrew Scriptures, perhaps from Daniel, and the Jewish exiles long resident among the Magi at the court of the Chaldean monarch. The supposition may not appear incredible, though not decisively confirmed by historical facts. Be this, however, as it may, it is well known that, while the Jews of Babylon preserved intact their own religious views, holding them, in the later days of their exile, with an exclusive and tenacious grasp, they

* At a recent meeting of the Bombay Asiatic Society, Dr. Wilson read the opinion of Professor Westergaard, of Copenhagen, "the first of Zend scholars," that the sacred books of the Parsees have no such antiquity as has been claimed for them, but are written in a dialect of modern Persian, disguised by a corrupted alphabet.

† "Zoroaster," says Niebuhr, Ancient Hist. i. p. 53, "whatever has been said as to his historical existence, is for us no more than a mythical name."

communicated them extensively to others. It is also certain that at some period or other, perhaps at successive periods, Magianism was greatly modified from some extraneous source. If, then, we find in it sentiments akin to those of Judaism, it need occasion us no surprise. Still it has a character of its own, sufficiently indicating its mythical nature and human origin.

The primitive religious system of the ancient Persians, upon which it was ingrafted, was simply a worship of the elements of nature, fire, air, earth, and water, the winds and starry heavens, especially the sun, moon, and brighter planets. Having no temples, they sacrificed, upon the mountains, living animals, but without burning their bodies. From Media came new views and forms, which were probably incorporated with this service of nature, whence originated what is called the Medo-Persian or Magian religion. *Hom*, greatly venerated by his successors, was the founder of the Magi, and of the first form of the Magian faith. It was from Zerdusht, however, according to Persian translation, that the system received its highest development. To him the composition of the Zend-Avesta is generally ascribed.

It teaches the doctrine of one supreme and eternal Being, (*Zeruane Akherene*, translated by some *Time without Bounds;* rather, as we suspect,

Existence without Bounds,*) who, like the *Brahm* of Indian pantheism, seems to be impersonal and incomprehensible, and yet has some features akin to the One Eternal Jehovah of the Hebrew Scriptures. He is represented as the great primal Cause or Creator, but appears, as Gibbon and others have observed, rather as a metaphysical abstraction (like the celebrated *Das Nichts* of Hegel) than as an active and presiding deity. Hence the series of emanations, spiritual and material, divine and demoniac, to which the supposition gives rise.

It differs, however, from *pantheism*, in being a system of *dualism;* though, we confess, the dualism is lost in what metaphysicians would call the principle of a higher identity; so that, as all things flow from unity and perfection, all return thither again. From the original source of existence, according to the Zend-Avesta, sprang *Ormuzd* and *Ahriman*, the one representing the principle of good, the other representing the principle of evil. These, though sometimes spoken of as created by the Supreme Deity, after all are but the development, as we understand it, of absolute and eternal being. Both, indeed, at first

* Du Perron and Kleuker translated it "Time without Bounds." Van Bohlen says that it is analogous to the Sanscrit, *Sarvam Akaranam*, the *Uncreated Whole*. Fred. W. Schlegel translates the equivalent expression as *Unum Indivisibile*, Indivisible One.

were good; but Ahriman, through envy or some other cause, fell into sin, and became the representative and agent of evil. Sometimes he is spoken of as bad from the beginning, and only suffered to come into existence; but in a legendary system like this we must expect some incongruities. The idea of the One God being gradually lost, or retained as a mere metaphysical entity, Ormuzd and Ahriman were worshipped as the supreme divinities, from whom are all beings and all things, good and bad. Hence the dualism and contest of the universe; but Ormuzd, being regarded as superior to Ahriman weakened by sin, Ormuzd will finally obtain the victory, and introduce an eternal reign of righteousness and peace.

Ormuzd is pure, eternal light, the fount of all beauty and perfection. He created, through Honover, from an ethereal substance, (like the Hylé of Plato,) the source of air and water, the whole universe, and completed his work in six periods. At first he created his own dwelling, the heaven of light, and the pure spirits who occupy it. From him are the Amschaspands, good angels and spirits, of whom there are different orders, a sort of angelic or divine hierarchy, of which Ormuzd is chief. One of these is lord of the empire of light, king of the universe, and dispenser of all happiness; another is the genius of fire; another the lord of splendor and metals; another the source of all fruitfulness; another the genius of water and of time; and another protector of the vegetable world, and the cause of growth in all living things.

In the second class of spirits which he created are the Izeds, of whom there are twenty-eight of both sexes, presiding over the elements and all pure things. Among these *Mithras*, the Sun, is the chief, being the source of all vivifying and fructifying power.

All these, including Ormuzd, and all other beings, as in the Platonic theogony, have their *Feruers*, or types, being ideas or emanations of the eternal mind embodied. These occupy the world of light where Ormuzd dwells, where they sparkle with ineffable light, and constitute the fundamental idea of a perfect world. Every emanation or creation of the great central being is but the manifestation, in some palpable form, of a new Feruer. Each, too, constitutes a sort of divine messenger, with spreading wings, flying to the protection of the good whenever invoked by them.

The bad spirits, of which there are various orders, superior and inferior, Devs and Archdevs, the impersonations of vices, impurities, and all noxious things, are from Ahriman, who created a rival world, and opposed the reign of Ormuzd.

In the mean while, Ahriman being confined in the kingdom of darkness, Ormuzd continued to create the outer world, with its suns and stars, winds, clouds, and fire, mountains and seas, vegetable and animal life. He created the bull *Abudad*, from whose blood all living things have sprung.

The good and happy spirits at first dwelt with Ormuzd in light. All were created pure, and for a long time (three thousand years) lived in happiness under Ormuzd. At last Ahriman, let loose, attempted to storm the heavens, and being repulsed, attacked the earth, and killed *Abudad;* but the body of the bull became the germ of all kinds of animals and of the first man, whom also the Devs put to death. Ormuzd then made a plant, *Reivas,* — "man and woman combined," — to grow out of the body, from which sprang, at the end of fifteen years, fifteen pairs of human beings, the progenitors of the present race.

Disappointed in his previous failures, Ahriman sought now to destroy the new-made creation. He blackened the fire with smoke, formed various kinds of noxious animals, and finally seduced from their allegiance the human race. In course of time, he gained such influence over them that he led them wholly to forsake the worship of

Ormuzd, and join the Devs, or Devils, in all their practices.*

Ormuzd, who pitied the human race, sent to them his law, first by Hom, and then by Zerdusht; but the people paid no regard to it, and so Ahriman remained victorious for three thousand years.

Ahriman will thus continue to reign until the expiration of time, when *Sosiosh*, the promised Savior or Redeemer, will come and extinguish the powers of the Devs, raise the dead, and pronounce judgment upon angels and men. A

* The following is a different form of the tradition, and strikingly akin to the scriptural account of the origin and fall of man. "The world itself was created during five succcessive periods, and during a sixth man himself received his being. After his production, man enjoyed a period of innocence and happiness in an elevated region, which Ormuzd had assigned him. But it was necessary to his existence in this state that he should be humble of heart, and humbly obey the divine ordinances; pure he must be of thought, pure of word, pure of deed. And for a time the first pair were thus holy and happy. But at last Ahriman, the Evil One, appeared and beat down their good dispositions, and under the influence of his glossing lies, they began to ascribe their blessings to him. Thus Ahriman deceived them, and to the end will seek to deceive. Emboldened by this success, Ahriman, the liar, presented himself again, and *brought with him fruit, of which they ate;* and in that instant, of a hundred excellences, which they possessed, all but one departed from them, and they became subject to misery and death." Another statement compresses the legend into this brief myth: "Ahriman, after having dared to visit heaven, descended to the earth, and approaching man in the form of a serpent, poisoned him with venom, so that he died. From that time, the world fell into confusion. The destroyer mingled himself with every thing."

general conflagration, through the casting down of the comet Gurzsher, will ensue, and the remains of the world sink downwards into Duzakh, forming a place of punishment for the wicked. After a long lapse of time, Ormuzd will have compassion upon them, and admit to heaven those who seek it by penitence and prayer. Even Ahriman and the Devs, after a longer period of punishment, and a proper submission to Ormuzd, will be admitted to the regions of eternal day.

"The kingdoms of Ormuzd and Ahriman," says the Zend-Avesta, "are in continual contest with one another; but Ahriman will hereafter be conquered; the reign of darkness will be altogether at an end; the rule of Ormuzd will be universally extended; and an all-embracing kingdom of light will alone remain." *

The night, with its innumerable stars, the "old eternal night," as the Magians deemed it, was the proper symbol of the great primal Cause, and in early times, as we have seen, was an object of religious homage. It was ever deemed sacred by the Oriental philosophers, and was the principal season of Magian worship. But as Ormuzd was the fountain of light, the sun was his fittest symbol, and in the absence of the sun,

* The whole period over which the system passes is that of twelve thousand years, subdivided into periods each of three thousand years.

the sacred fire, which they kindled and kept constantly burning under the open heavens. Other symbols were used, as the chariot and horses of the sun, which the ancestors of King Josiah, after the example of the Mehestani, or followers of Zoroaster, introduced into Jerusalem. The sun was considered by the Mehestani the eye of Ormuzd, and next to the Amschaspands, the greatest of all divinities; nay, they supposed him to be the body or residence of one of them. They described the chariot of the sun as being of a white color, and wreathed garlands of flowers. The sacred horses were white also, of the Nisean breed, and four in number.*

In this way the worship of the sun, the sacred fire, and other symbols, with a host of angels and spirits, usurped the worship of the true God, and must be recognized as a form of superstition, in the end nearly as degrading as that of Jupiter or Apollo.†

But how striking an image or shadow of the truth this whole Magian system! Blended with errors, it yet reminds us of the great and eternal principles recognized in the pure theism of the Scriptures. But losing the proper conception

* Jahn's Bib. Archæology, p. 521.

† See Hyde, *Historia Relig. Vet. Persarum;* Du Perron and Kleuker on the Zend-Avesta; Rhode, *Heilige Sage der Zendvolks;* Ritter's An. Ph. 1. p. 51, et seq.

of the one supreme Jehovah, lapsing first into nature-worship, and then into symbol-worship, it serves to prove not only the indestructible religious tendency of man, but his proneness to idolatry, and through idolatry to sin.* Mingling with astrology and magic, the religion of Zoroaster became as monstrous and bewildering as the other Oriental superstitions.

Thus idolatry, with its equivalent, nature-worship or demon-worship, was introduced and perpetuated among some of the most enlightened nations of antiquity; and it seems to be an acknowledged fact, that, once established in a community, it becomes fixed there forever. Man appears to possess no power to deliver himself from its terrible domination. Hungering after the divine, he knows it not. By a necessary descent into error "he changes the glory of the incorruptible God into an image made like to corruptible man, and to birds, and four-footed beasts, and creeping things."

* By idolatry here, we do not mean the formal worship of idols, from which the Parsees are free, but idolatry in its essence, which is the substitution in the place of God, of any beings or things, as objects of adoration.

† The case of the Arabians under Mohammed is no exception. Accepting the Old Testament revelation as to the unity of God, and acknowledging the divine mission of Moses and of Christ, Mohammed availed himself of extraneous aid to banish idolatry from his system.

With the elements of superstition thus engendered, were mingled from time to time, both among the nations of the east and of the west, the ideals and fictions of poetry, the forebodings of fear, and the delusions of oracular divination. Every where man felt and acknowledged his guilt, and longed for expiation and deliverance. Victims bled upon ten thousand heathen altars. Life was given for life, as an avowal of its forfeiture by sin. Designing men, of course, took advantage of the popular belief, and dreams, portents, prodigies, oracles, were rapidly accumulated. To gratify human pride, never extinguished even by a sense of guilt, and yet meet the natural longing for a godlike form of man, as the most beautiful symbol, perhaps dwelling of the divine, and especially to extend the influence of the priesthood, heroes and sages were elevated to the celestial regions and adored as divinities. Nor was this so unnatural as many suppose; for who more likely to be transformed into divinities than those who had done nobly for their race? Every hill, valley, and stream, every house and craft, must have its tutelary god. The woods were filled, as in Greece, where the popular superstition was somewhat elegant and cheerful, though profoundly sensual, with nymphs, fauns, and satyrs; the air was replenished with genii, the ocean with nereids and tritons. All nature throbbed with spiritual forms, some beautiful and good, but many dark and malignant. Poetry and passion, selfishness and even lust, venerable usage and the traditions of "eld," all combined to consolidate and extend the bewildering error. The dim notions of a supreme Numen, or Deity, to which we have referred, were overborne by universal superstition. So that neither in Assyria, Persia, India, Egypt, nor Greece, during any historical period with which the moderns are familiar, was any *general* or *intelligent* worship paid to the eternal God. If recognized at all, it was only as *primus inter pares*, or as the changeless essence, the absolute and incomprehensible fountain of gods and men. With the single exception of "the chosen people," themselves at first idolaters, the whole ancient world fell under the curse of idolatry, or nature-worship, and instead of casting off the baleful incubus, only sank, during the lapse of ages, deeper and deeper into the abyss.*

Where a moral and prudential code was the principal aim, as in the case of Confucius, (Confutse, or rather Chung-Tse,) the great religious teacher of China, who seems to have cherished but a comparatively feeble idea of an invisible and eternal state, superstition elevated the master to the place of God, and adopted him as "the

* See Appendix, Note A, at the close of the volume.

way, the truth, and the life." But Budhism, and in many instances the lowest Fetichism, became the prevalent superstition of the Celestial Empire.* So that every where men "worshipped and served the creature more than the Creator, who is God over all, blessed forever."

Among the Oriental nations, grand, massive and immovable, like the vast plains or lofty mountain ranges of that part of the world, the

* The original religion of China was a sort of nature-worship, based, as F. W. Schlegel thinks, upon the unity of God. *Tian*, who represented the heavens, was their principal deity. Other spirits, presiding over the earth, the stars, the winds, &c., with the souls of deceased ancestors, were adored. Lao-Tse first reformed, or perhaps corrupted, this religion, by a modification of Lamaism, which he found in Thibet. He inculcated a sort of stoical indifference and serenity; but his system is Epicurean as a whole. It is idolatrous, and yet it is sceptical. The higher classes in China are its votaries. But Chung-Tse, or Confucius, as we call him, is the great teacher of the Chinese. He endeavored to bring back the people to the religion of their fathers, but his chief object was to inculcate moral principles, among which are sobriety, prudence, reverence for superiors, justice, and obedience to the laws. He recognized a great first Cause, but only as an impersonal principle, or power, from which emanated *Yang* and *Yen*, the one the perfect principle, and of the masculine gender, and the other the imperfect, and of the feminine gender, from whom are all things. Confucius forbade his followers to make images of the supreme Cause, and conjoined with his worship the adoration of the elements, which he comprised under the name of *Tien*, heaven. But Confucius himself, or his *tablet*, and deceased ancestors, are the chief objects of reverence among his followers. The great body of the people, however, including the emperor and court, are Budhists. Foism, another name for Budhism, Lamaism, also a modification of Budhism, and Fetichism, the lowest form of idolatry, are spread over the whole of India beyond the Ganges.

forms of idolatry were more fixed and permanent. In Greece and Rome, and even in Egypt, and some parts of Western Asia, they were quite variable. The spirit of doubt and inquiry always actuated the Grecian mind. Some of the acutest intellects doubted the popular myths even as early as the times of Plato and Aristotle. Socrates, it is evident, though not entirely free from the common influence, perhaps saw through them, while recognizing their great underlying truths.* He was averse, however, to the destructive spirit of some of the sophists, who made them a subject of ridicule. Feeling the necessity of faith in a supreme Power, it was his aim, by means of some of the more legitimate and beautiful myths, to rise into a higher sphere. Plato frequently uses the vulgar superstitions as illustrations of his grand and thrilling conceptions. Aristotle says expressly, "It has been handed down to us in a mythical form, from the remotest times, that there are gods, and that the divine (το θεῖον, the divinity) compasses entire nature.† All beside this has been added after the mythical

* We say *perhaps* here, for much put into the mouth of Socrates in the Platonic dialogues is to be ascribed rather to the scholar than to the master. Socrates himself, as reported in Plato's *Apologia*, averred his belief in the popular religion. In practice, he sedulously worshipped the national gods. He taught nothing inconsistent with polytheism.

† The word θεῖον here translated the divine, is elsewhere used by Aristotle as equivalent to θεος, the supreme divinity.

style, for the sake of persuading the multitudes, and for the interest of the laws and the advantage of the state. Thus men have given to the gods human forms, and have even represented them under the figure of other beings, in the train of which fictions followed more of the same sort. But if we separate from all this the original principle, and consider it alone, namely, that the first essences are gods, [divine,] we shall find that this has been divinely said ; and since it is probable that philosophy and the arts have been several times, so far as that is possible, lost, such doctrines may have been preserved to our times, as the remains of ancient wisdom." *

At last, both in Greece and in Rome, the popular mythology lost its hold at once of the more cultivated and the common intellect. The doubts of the philosophers diffused themselves among the vulgar. Although religion, as such, could not altogether be abandoned, it is evident that the people generally had outgrown the crude mythological faith of their fathers. The conduct of the gods, as well it might, became a standing joke to the comic writers, and multitudes of all classes fell into blank atheism.

Hence the great problem of serious and candid minds was to find, either in connection with

* Quoted by Neander from Aristotle's Metaphysics.

the myths, or back of them, some fundamental ground of belief. The populace indeed fell into vice, or hankered after new superstitions, but thinkers and moralists longed for principles. Some endeavored to rest upon the idea of a supreme Cause and the immortality of the soul, though both of these truths were only imperfectly conceived, and not always fully realized even by the best minds. Cicero himself, in his *De Natura Deorum*, though believing in a supreme Power, and affirming the necessity of religion, often seems at a loss what to believe respecting the gods, and refers to the perplexity of others upon the same subject. His writings, while theistic as a whole, abound in academic doubts. Quite a number fell into a sort of natural pantheism, and resigned themselves to *The All*, whence they had come and whither they must return. Stoicism, with its stern indifference, often assumed this attitude. Many strong minds lapsed into despair. Denying the value of all religion as superstition or fancy, they saw nothing in the universe but an eternal cycle (κύκλος) or circular succession of changes, in which by and by they must forever be ingulfed. Man appeared like a vexed bubble upon the heaving tide, now in sunshine, then in shadow, and anon broken and forever lost. "All religion," says the elder Pliny, with Epicurean scorn, "is the offspring of necessity, weakness, and fear. What God is, if in truth he be any thing distinct from the world, it is beyond the compass of man's understanding to know. But it is a foolish delusion, which has sprung from human weakness and pride, to imagine that such an infinite Spirit would concern himself with the petty affairs of men. . . . The vanity of man, and his insatiable longing after existence, have led him also to dream of a life after death. A being full of contradictions, he is the most wretched of creatures; since the other creatures have no wants transcending the bounds of their nature. Man is full of desires and wants that reach to infinity, and can never be satisfied. His nature is a lie, — uniting the greatest poverty with the greatest pride. Among these so great evils, the best thing God has bestowed upon man is the power of taking his own life." * It was in this temper, that Pliny was willing to perish under the ashes of Vesuvius.

Others, however, could not be satisfied with doubt; and so they tried to solve, as best they could, the strange enigma and contradiction of human nature. They could not altogether believe, neither could they altogether renounce religion. Some, as Euemerus, resolved all mythology

* Pliny, Nat. Hist. ii. 4, apud Neander, Ch. Hist. i. 10.

into a poetical history of nature or of society; while others, like Plutarch, saw in it the corruption of a purer faith, though without the power of realizing fully their own grand and beautiful idea. Many sought refuge in foreign opinions and usages, though not with much satisfaction ; and a few insisted, that, while superstitions ought to be abandoned, religion, of whose divine beauty they had some conception, was good and true. Seneca recommended his disciples to worship the gods, as a thing due to good manners, but to rely upon something else as a ground of conviction and hope in reference to duty and destiny.

It thus came to pass that ingenuous inquirers after truth hardly knew what to believe, or what to disbelieve, in perusing the writings or attending the teachings of the so called philosophers. Some plunged irremediably into the prevalent Epicureanism, and so lived for the hour. Others committed suicide, or willingly lost their lives in battle ; while others, like Clemens Romanus and Justin Martyr, alternated constantly between belief and unbelief, hope and despair. They went from the Peripatetics to the Stoics, and from the Stoics to the Platonics, but all seemed to them confusion, contradiction, and doubt.*

* Is this wonderful when even Xenophanes, whose sublime acknowledgment of the one God we have already quoted, found in the little he knew only doubt and difficulty ? His state of mind is strik-

This, in fact, was the period of transition, when paganism, incapable of emancipating itself, proclaimed its vanity and weakness, and yet gave incontestable token of "man's old eternal want."

For in all ages, amid error and superstition, certain elder truths, certain instinctive convictions, maintained their place with more or less persistence. The idea of worship, of dependence upon spiritual powers, of obligation to the divine, the hope or dread of a future state, figured under the dream of Tartarus and the Elysian Fields, the necessity of mediation and atonement, of reunion and eternal life in the bosom of God, were never altogether lost. Often the night was dark and portentous; but anon the everlasting stars were visible in the heavens. Nay, the hope of some spiritual deliverer, especially among the more thoughtful nations, the longing for a divine Teacher, to which reference may be found in

ingly described by Timon, the Sillograph, who puts into the mouth of Xenophanes these words: —

"O that mine were the deep mind, prudent, and looking to both sides!
Long, alas! have I strayed on the road of error, beguiled,
And am now hoary of years, yet exposed to doubt and destruction
Of all kinds; for, wherever I turn to consider,
I am lost in the *One* and All."

The difficulty with Xenophanes lay in his pantheism, or rather his inability to distinguish between the ONE and the ALL. See Ritter, Hist. of Ph. i. 443.

Plato,* some mighty Redeemer, Son of God, or Savior of man, developed itself, with more or less significance, through the long lapse of ages. The sun had not yet risen, but lights were gleaming at distant intervals, relieving the terrible gloom of the long polar night, or heralding the dawn of the approaching day.†

It might be desirable in this connection to trace the origin and transmission of the great primeval faith, scattered in "sporadic revelations," as Neander aptly calls them, or in traditional fragments, among all the nations, from the first Eden down through the antediluvian believers, the Seths and Enochs of that early time, and subsequently through the patriarchs and prophets, with other saintly and priestly men of the postdiluvian age; the Noahs, the Abrahams, the Melchisedecs, the Jobs, and the Moseses of ancient inspiration; but this we defer for the present, which we do the more readily from the fact that the subject is somewhat familiar to all. Our knowledge of the Adamic and patriarchal ages is derived exclusively from the Scriptures, whose

* In the Second Alcibiades and elsewhere. See Dr. Lewis's Platonic Theology, pp. 367, 368.

† Those who wish to see this idea carried out, and more amply discussed, are referred to Trench's Hulsean Lectures, where the "unconscious prophecies of heathenism" are cited and discussed with much candor and ability.

simple annals bring down the history of true religion from its first revelation in Paradise to its final establishment in the kingdom of Christ.

In the mean while we will devote a chapter to the consideration of ancient philosophy, as cultivated among the more enlightened heathen nations, as an element of progress, and a preparation for Christ.

CHAPTER IV.*

THE CENTRAL IDEA, OR CHRIST IN ANCIENT PHILOSOPHY.

The human mind is under the necessity of bringing all things into unity: it is itself a unit; nature therefore must appear to it as a unit, or universe. Again, each man, as well as each society, and of course the entire race, stands, so to speak, between two infinites, or two eternities; though these are only one, in which we are embosomed, like islands in a boundless sea. And as nothing can happen without the supposition of an adequate cause, mankind must ascribe their origin to the One Supreme Power, whether named Mind, Reason, Spirit, Creator, or God.

Thus man, the moment he begins to reflect profoundly, finds himself pressed on all sides by the idea of the Infinite and Eternal. Thought presupposes and necessitates this idea. It begins with this, ends with this; for it ever starts from a limit, as it comes to a limit, beyond which it must acknowledge the presence of

* This chapter, with some modifications, was published as an article in the January number of the Christian Review for 1853.

absolute and eternal being; precisely as a part begins with a whole, ends with a whole. The segment of a circle, nay, its slightest line or radius, presupposes the existence of that circle; time presupposes eternity; the mind of man presupposes the mind of God. For if there be a finite, there must also be an infinite mind. The temporary thought of man necessitates the eternal thought of God. This is the mysterious circle, within which, whether he sees it or not, all the reasonings of man revolve.

There are those, indeed, who, in their investigations, keep assiduously within the fragmentary and mechanical; notwithstanding their inquiries are always coming to a limit, beyond which may be descried that infinite ocean into which they so much fear to plunge. As finite minds they lean upon God and eternity, as all their science, else limited and perishable, leans upon God and eternity, even at the moment that they hesitate to acknowledge the stupendous fact. Their philosophy, however, is shallow and transient; and though useful perhaps to material interests, leaves them without any real beauty or grandeur of thought.

But the great majority of thinkers will constantly transcend such narrow bounds, and press the inquiry, *Whence are we, and whither do we go?*

This is the real origin of speculative philosophy, especially in its higher range — a philosophy ever soliciting attention, ever attracting thinkers. The ocean of thought, indeed, is boundless, and many swift ships go down into its mysterious depths; nevertheless all human souls, freighted with any great ideas, must sail thereupon. Shore or no shore, they must adventure their all upon its heaving billows. Hence one of the most interesting elements of ancient civilization, especially in the more enlightened communities, is speculative philosophy. Its relation to Christ, though hinted at already, deserves our candid consideration.

The early fathers of the church, Justin Martyr, Clement of Alexandria, the author of the Epistle to Diognetus, (sometimes ascribed to Justin Martyr, but assigned, by Semisch and Neander, to another,) Tertullian, Origen, and others, while acknowledging its obvious defects, allow that it embodied portions of the truth, and formed a preparation for Christ. The apostle Paul himself refers to the manifestation of God in the mind of the heathen, as rendering them "without excuse" in departing from the truth. "Because that which may be known of God is manifest in them; for God hath showed it unto them; for the invisible things of him from the creation of the world are clearly seen, being understood by the things that are made, even his eternal power and godhead; so that they are without excuse."* He affirms, indeed, in another place, that "the world by wisdom knew not God," that is, adequately and satisfactorily; for, after all, philosophy, especially in its later developments, was a failure. It gave no rest to the weary conscience of man, and left the way of life in the greatest obscurity. Still it nourished a few great characters, and produced a dim and often passionate longing for a higher light. Some pious and learned men have even gone so far as to regard Socrates, Plato, Plutarch, and some others, as a sort of Christians by anticipation. So charmed was Erasmus with the character of Socrates, that we find him on one occasion exclaiming, *Sancte Socrates, ora pro nobis!*

This, doubtless, is carrying the matter too far; nevertheless, it must be allowed that many of the Grecian sages, considering their circumstances, made some remarkable approximations to the central truths of the divine unity and supremacy, and the possibility, on the part of man, of union and fellowship with God. In his *Stromata*, Clement of Alexandria uses the following remarkable language: "Indeed, before the coming of the Lord, philosophy was needful to the Greeks, for the reformation of their lives; and

* Rom. chap. i. v. 19, 20.

even now it is an aid to piety, supplying, as it does, some rudimentary teaching for those who subsequently may receive the faith upon conviction. For God is, indeed, the cause of all good things, of some preëminently and directly, as of the Old and New Testaments; of others indirectly, by means of reason and argument; as philosophy, which he probably gave to the Greeks before the Lord himself came, in order to call them also to his service. For philosophy acted the part of a schoolmaster to the Greeks, as the law of Moses did to the Jews, for the purpose of bringing men to Christ, and thus preparing the way for such as were to be advanced by him to perfection." *

It is well known that the philosophical systems of the ancient world, often meagre, as well as variant and contradictory, generally revolved around the idea of *the Infinite*, and in their higher forms recognized the existence of a supreme Intelligence, and the immortality of the soul.† It must not, however, be supposed that speculative inquiry, in any age, grasped fully these great truths, or held them for any length of time with persistent consistency.

* *Stromata*, lib. i. c. v.

† The doctrine of the immortality of the soul, however, in their view, was always associated with that of the *metempsychosis*. See Ritter's History of Ancient Philosophy, i. p. 156.

It is possible, however, that, in all ages, fragments of primitive revelation have been floating about in the common mind. God has never, in this respect, left himself without a witness; and who shall say that some special divine influence may not have been exerted upon the minds of certain thoughtful and virtuous men among the heathen? Still, ancient philosophy never assumed any thing like a perfect or permanent form, and certainly never discovered the great truths of what is called "natural religion," except by occasional glimpses and irradiations.

It will be allowed that the views of none ever rose higher than those of Socrates and Plato. In them, ancient philosophy gained its culminating point. And yet Plato himself must have regarded his inquiries as only the beginnings of a speculative system. Every one, familiar with his writings, must be struck with their variant and fragmentary character. His modes of reasoning are far from uniform; his opinions by no means coherent. A thousand questions are started without an attempt at solution. Many are left purposely obscure, as if for the sake of confounding inquiry.* Portions of his works are clearly myth-

* This is strikingly exemplified in the *Theætetos*, where his attempts to define science seem to fail. It is true that with Plato science is the *real*, the *essential*, the *permanent*; but the question recurs, What is the *real*, the *essential*, the *permanent*?

ical, yet how far believed by himself is an unsettled question. At times he despairs of any but a few philosophical spirits arriving at the truth. He feels that none can reach the knowledge of the absolute and ineffable Essence, from whom are all things. Hence his mournful confession, "To discover then the Creator and Father of this universe, as well as his work, is indeed difficult, and when discovered, it is impossible to reveal him to mankind at large." *

Still, Plato did teach, in forms more or less perfect, the existence of an infinite God, and the immortality of the soul, insisting strongly and often beautifully on its high capacity for virtue and everlasting life. Socrates, as an interlocutor in the Platonic dialogues, declares his belief of this consolatory doctrine. In his last hours he referred to it, and died, apparently, in the hope of a better world. We say *apparently*, for he certainly does not express the profound assurance and joyful expectation which a Christian is permitted to cherish. On other occasions he defends the immortality of the soul, as a speculative tenet; but here he admits the possibility of a doubt. He seems like one "treading the common path into the great darkness," hoping to find a home, yet not knowing whether even "a

* *Timæus*, c. viii. Compare *Repub.* vi. p. 506.

thread" of consciousness will remain "to tell how still it is."

"We may hence conclude," he says, "that there is great hope that death is a blessing. For to die is one of two things; for either the dead may be annihilated, and have no sensation of any thing whatever, or, as it is said, there is a certain change and passage of the soul from one place to another. And if it is a privation of all sensation, as it were a sleep, in which *the sleeper has no dream*, death would be a wonderful gain.* For I think that if any one, having selected a night in which he slept so soundly as not to have had a dream, and having compared this night with all the other nights and days of his life, should be required on reflection to say how many he had passed better or more pleasantly than this, I think that not only a private person, but the great king himself, would find them easy to number, in comparison with other days and nights. If, therefore, death is such a thing, I say it is a gain; for thus all futurity appears only as a single night. But if, on the other hand, death is a removal hence to some other place, and what is said be true, that all the dead are there, what greater blessing can there be than this, my judges? For if, on arriving at Hades,

* The Italics are ours.

released from those who pretend to be judges, one shall find those that are true judges, and who are said to judge there, Minos and Rhadamanthus, Æacus and Triptolemus, and such others of the demigods as were just during their own lives, would this be a sad removal? At what price would you not estimate a conference with Orpheus and Musæus, Hesiod and Homer? I indeed should be willing to die often, were this true. Most admirable would it be for me to sojourn there, where I should meet those ancient heroes who died by an unjust sentence. The comparing my sufferings with theirs would, I think, be no unpleasant occupation. But the greatest pleasure would be to spend my time in questioning the people there as I have done those here, and discovering who among them is wise, and who not, except in fancy. . . . For surely the judges there do not condemn to death; for in other respects those who live there are happier than those that are here, and are thenceforth immortal, at least if what is said be true."

After remarking that all which happens to a good man is wisely ordered, and forgiving his judges for their injustice, thus giving evidence of a noble and serene temper, he closes with these memorable words: "But it is now time to depart, for me to die, for you to live. But which of us is going to a better state is known only to the gods." *

But it may be said that ancient philosophy never went further than this; nay, could never afterwards be sustained at an equal elevation. It rather deteriorated, now lapsing into scepticism on the one hand, or materialism on the other, or, in despite of these, into an unreasoning mysticism.

Among the Orientals, especially of India, it never much transcended a sort of vague nature-worship, or the acknowledgment of the Infinite, as *The All*, from which the mystic thinkers of those dreamy regions believed they had come, and whither they expected to go. In one of their schools, it assumed the form of atheistic materialism.† In another, it terminated in absolute idealism. It readily blended with polytheism, as an emanation from the fountain of life, and cherished the hope, not of an individual conscious immortality, but of complete absorption in the Deity or Universe.‡

Among the Greeks, speculative inquiry, with inconsiderable exceptions, as in the case of Pythagoras, Socrates, and Plato, a few of the Academics and Stoics, was rarely practical in

* Plato's Works, *Apologia*, 32, 33.

† See Cousin's *Hist. de la Philos.*, 2d series, tome ix. 5th Leçon, *La Sensualisme dans L'Inde*, p. 110.

‡ Ritter's Hist. of An. Ph. i. pp. 90, 93.

its results. The common people never received it. Plato himself regarded them as incapable of philosophy.* Nor did it ever thoroughly free itself from polytheism. Occasionally it mingled with popular superstitions, and modified the character of the "Mysteries," especially among the higher classes of society, giving to religious rites a deeper significance, yet oftener divesting them of all their power. Its most common and popular effect among the patrician families was scepticism and indifference, frequently downright Epicureanism.

Its fundamental problems, too, were never thoroughly solved. Even in modern times, few, indeed, among the profoundest metaphysical thinkers, consider them solved. A coherent system of spiritual philosophy, or of absolute science, does not exist. By many, indeed, all ontology, as a positive science, is regarded as impossible.† Perhaps all such inquiries, at least in their higher relations, transcend the unaided powers of the human mind. The relation of

* This was the sentiment of all the ancient philosophers. Their feeling is well expressed by Horace, who says, "Odi profanum vulgus, et arceo." The idea of teaching the common people, as such, rarely, if ever, occurred to their minds.

† Among them Sir William Hamilton, the first philosophical critic of the age. See Morell's History of the Philosophy of the Nineteenth Century, p. 656. Compare Discussions, &c., by Sir W. Hamilton, p. 31, et seq. (Eng. ed.)

matter to thought, or of thought to matter, the origin and duration of matter, the origin and duration of mind, the relation of the finite to the infinite, the possible production of the finite from the infinite, or of matter from thought, the creation of the world, and the creation of man — these and kindred topics were debated constantly by the Grecian thinkers, without any one reaching a solution which satisfied the whole, or even any considerable number. With occasional flashes of light, and glimpses of beauty, radiant and eternal, the whole seems to most readers an endless logomachy. One feels, while endeavoring to follow them, as if he were revolving on Ixion's wheel.

"In reviewing the history of Greek speculation," says Lewes, who has too much reason for the remark, "from the Water of Thales to the Absolute Negation of Plotinus, what a reflection is forced upon us of the vanity of metaphysics! So many years of laborious inquiry, so many splendid minds engaged, and after the lapse of ages, the inquiry remains the same, the answer more ingeniously absurd! Ah, truly was it said that metaphysics was *l'art de s'egarer avec methode.*"

Socrates was generally, though not always, practical. He was really more of a moralist than a metaphysician. Plato was speculative and transcendent; so much so that few have ever pretended to understand him in all respects, and it is highly questionable whether he thoroughly understood himself. How God should reveal himself, or create the universe, is a problem he constantly suggests, but never solves. He speaks of the Supreme Being, the original absolute Essence or Idea, as inaccessible and incomprehensible. He consequently supposes the existence of another God in the outward universe, the Alter Ego, so to speak, of the Deity, the God manifested and embodied in finite forms. Occasionally he seems to present this second or manifested Deity, as a mere abstraction or ideal, though generally as the soul of the universe, embodied in the material whole.* His followers, the Neo-Platonists of a latter era, retained the distinction, and attempted to give it a more definite scientific expression. They departed, however, essentially from the views of Plato.†

Indeed, the idea seems to be founded, in some sense, in the nature of things, though inadequately and even erroneously expressed by Plato, and involving his speculations in inextricable difficulty. For now, he speaks of this cosmical Deity as if

* See the *Timæus*, passim. Compare *De Legibus*, x. p. 897. *Philebus*, p. 30. Idem, pp. 170, 171.

† For an extended account of the views of the Neo-Platonists, on the subject of the Trinity, see Cudworth's 'Intellectual System, ii. 735–40. Compare Ritter's Ancient Philosophy, vol. iv. pp. 521, 692.

he were uncreated and eternal, and thence equal to the supreme Intelligence, nay, constituting the supreme Intelligence, and then again as a sort of created and subaltern God. Still we must conceive of the absolute and eternal Essence, as manifested in the external universe, and thence limited, perhaps humanized. It is thus He discovers himself to us as a distinct personality. For we might well ask, How can the finite ever reach and comprehend the Infinite? And how, moreover, can the Infinite, who for this reason is the *one absolute, uuconditioned, and indivisible All*, create or produce the finite, the conditioned, the many? We believe the doctrine of course, nay, we know from revelation, perhaps from intuition, that the fact so exists; but in philosophy, the question is *How* does it exist? nay, *How can* it exist? How, in a word, (for thus the problem must present itself to the reason of a pagan philosopher,) how can the absolute and unchangeable Essence, who can never be more than he is, never less than he is, pass into or produce the external or multiform universe?

Plato's solution, if it may be called such, for it is only an hypothesis, involved him and his followers, both ancient and modern, in a sort of ideal pantheism, which has taken the form sometimes of a profound spiritualism, though more frequently, perhaps, of an arid rationalism.

We have said "a sort of ideal pantheism," for it is only such by implication. His system may be described as emanative; for he has first the Supreme Reason, the Everlasting God, then the Kosmos or Universe, which also is a God, with soul and body, produced according to an eternal archetype, and in this sense eternal also, though in its present form a production of time; then inferior gods, who in their turn are also creators, and finally the souls and bodies of men.* He believes that all things have their opposites; so if there be good there must be evil also, and so on, in which sense his system perhaps may be styled *dualistic* rather than *pantheistic*, though springing from an absolute unity, in which mind and matter, good and evil, are involved, and thus verging, as the merest tyro can see, towards an ideal or spiritual pantheism. Plato, however, vacillates, both as to the origin of the material universe and the origin of evil; for sometimes he seems to derive evil from matter, while matter itself is represented only as the grosser or more exterior form of that ethereal substance or essence which forms, so to speak, the body of God, or a kind of universal and eternal plenum, from which he produces all external things.

Souls or finite spirits also, according to Plato,

* Plato's Cosmogony is developed chiefly in the *Timæus*. See especially the 8th to the 17th chapters, inclusive.

are not created, but rather projected into formal or outward bodily existence, from which finally ascending, they will return to the immortal state.*

Thus the genius of Plato, held in the fetters of matter, yet tended to the spiritual and divine; and though his system, logically carried out, may be termed ideal, perhaps pantheistic, it certainly possessed this redeeming feature. His own lofty spirit longed for the perfect, the beautiful, and good, in their absolute and eternal archetypes. God and immortality were the starting point, and the goal of his reasoning and his life. Yet the unsettled question ever recurs, How does God come to us? How do we come to God? He is ours, and we are his — but *how?*

To relieve his theory of its main difficulty, Plato, as we have stated, in addition to the one inaccessible and universal Reason, who forms the root of all existence, supposed a God of this world, a sort of divine Logos, as he is named, a term given by St. John to Jesus Christ himself, as the Word, or manifestation of the invisible Father. But Plato's god of the world, or external universe, is a derived and limited deity, and cannot therefore be made to cohere with any just ideas of the divine Unity.

This deity, however, in the Platonic philosophy,

* *Phædo*, 128. Compare *Phædrus*, 51, 56, 61.

is simply the embodied soul of the universe, represented as a living creature. Plato's reasoning upon this subject is curious. The world has warmth, is composed of various elements, has motion like a human body, &c., therefore it must have a soul. "As soon as the soul, that image of the eternal gods, or ideas, the vast animal, began to move, *God looked upon his work, and was glad.*" Had Plato seen the Bible? See the *Timæus*, cxiv. In the *Phædrus*, (55,) he uses this remarkable language: "But the immortal derives its name from no deduction of reasoning; but as we neither see nor sufficiently understand God, we represent him as an *immortal animal*, possessed of soul as well as body, and these united together through all time." Here the idea is different from that in the *Timæus*, which closes thus: "We are now at length to say, that our discourse concerning the universe has reached its conclusion; for, not only containing, but full of mortal and immortal animals, it has thus been formed, a visible animal embracing things visible — a sensible (manifested?) god of the intelligible, (spiritual?) the greatest, the best, and most perfect — this one *only begotten universe.*" Plato's universe is thus a *created god*, a god whom he worshipped, for he begins the Critias with imploring, "*that God,* (the universe,) *long, long ago created in fact*, to confirm" the truth of his recent discussion, &c.

On the same ground, and springing from the same speculative difficulty, he cannot solve the question of the soul's immortality. He thoroughly believes it, and in the *Phædo*, devoted to this particular discussion, he presents many ingenious arguments in its favor, though none of them can be regarded as demonstrative; and in the last analysis he is compelled to base it on the doctrine of the *metempsychosis*, including the preexistence and transmigration of souls.* Indeed, Plato would seem to hold the past eternal existence of the soul in God, whence he deduces its future immortality. Its preëxistence he endeavors to prove by the doctrine or fact of reminiscence, an idea hinted at in Wordsworth's beautiful ode entitled Intimations of Immortality from Recollections of Early Childhood.

"Our birth is but a sleep and a forgetting;
The soul that rises with us, our life's star,
Hath had elsewhere its setting,
And cometh from afar;
Not in entire forgetfulness,
And not in utter nakedness,
But trailing clouds of glory, do we come
From God, who is our home."

Taken in some large poetic sense, all this is doubtless true; for we do come from God as the

* *Phædo*, 47–49; *Phædrus*, 61, 62. See also *Timæus*, clxxii.

fountain of our being; but evidently we are creatures of time, so far at least as the past is concerned. Our souls, grand and capacious as they may become, have yet their specific, individual beginning or creation; and all back of this,

> "That immortal sea
> Which brought us hither,"

is unknown and ineffable.

Plato, however, is not satisfied to deduce the immortality of the soul from its capacities and possibilities, and especially from those deep and beautiful harmonies and aspirations, of which he so touchingly speaks; he must go further; he must solve the problem philosophically; and hence back of all *a posteriori* considerations, back of all the facts of its present human existence, he boldly assumes the fact of its eternity; in other words, its absolute existence in God, from which its future immortality flows, as a natural and eternal necessity. And yet he seems to intimate the possibility of the destruction of bad souls; one of those singular inconsistencies into which the profoundest intellects not unfrequently fall.*

Logically carried out, as every thoughtful person must acknowledge, the doctrine of the

* *Phædo*, 130.

eternity of the soul involves its divinity; in other words, its identity with God. And as God, the infinite and immutable, cannot consist of parts, and thence can neither be divided nor multiplied, the identity of the soul with God would prove it God, and so pantheism would be the necessary logical result.*

The subject of the origin and duration of matter, to which Plato frequently refers, is left, as one might naturally suppose, in inextricable confusion. As a substantial, external thing, with its attributes of extension, divisibility, form, color, and so forth, he seems to regard it as simply phenomenal; and yet its basis, which he denominates *Hylé*, a sort of ethereal essence, contemporaneous with God, is regarded not simply as eternal, but occasionally as the seat of sin; so that on this ground he cannot successfully solve the problem of human redemption, to us the most immediate and thrilling of all problems. He sees and laments the strange "necessity" (ἀνάγκη) which gives rise to sin and misery, that apparent duality and contradiction in the nature of things, and especially in the nature of man, which the Bible refers to the fall of the race from its primitive integrity; but his chief remedy is

* It was on this ground that Lessing, a Spinozist, held the doctrine of the preëxistence of souls.

the renunciation of the outward and bodily, the contemplation of archetypal ideas, and a return, if possible, to the original and eternal essence.* These things, we know, are echoes of the truth, as it were imperfect glimpses of the reality; but much was wanting which ancient philosophy never supplied. Indeed, neither Plato nor any of the old speculative thinkers apprehended fully the nature of sin, as the voluntary lapse and transgression of the soul. They seemed to regard it as a natural and inevitable evil, for which there was no adequate cure, except in a return to absolute spiritual existence.† The idea of *redemption*, by a divine transformation, or regeneration of the soul, in its present limited and imperfect state, never dawned upon their minds. Plato evidently struggles with the dread necessity, and longs for emancipation in the bosom of the Infinite, but gives no distinct information as to the method of its attainment. True, he dwells upon the necessity of *goodness*, as the soul's eternal life. He speaks eloquently of virtue, as *μεγίστην και καλλίστην τῶν συμφωνιῶν*, "the deepest and most beautiful of all harmonies," and vaguely hints at the means of reunion with

* *Repub.* l. vii. 1, 2.

† In the *Timæus*, (lxix.,) he says expressly that the soul is "rendered morbid and unwise by the body," and that "no one is voluntarily bad."

God; but perplexed with the fatal proclivity to evil, in the very constitution of the external world, and the physical nature of man, he fails to answer those two great questions which are ever pressing the race, *How shall man be just with God? How shall man become sinless and happy?*

Plato sees clearly enough that nature is a manifestation of God; but he perverts, or altogether loses sight of the divine personality. His only personal deity is the actual universe, as a living creature, with its inner spirit and its external form, or, as he terms it, its body and soul. Thus he degrades the idea of the divine personality, making it commensurate, both in scope and duration, with the created universe. Leaving this, however, he naturally passes into the idea of the infinite and absolute nature of God, and here actually loses, as he must, all conception of personality. His notions become abstract and misty; so that his eternal Essence, or God, is found to be little more than an abstract idea or power, absolute and inaccessible, whom no man can know or love.*

The fact is, the great truth of the personality of God, and the possibility of union and fellowship with him, as a distinct intelligence, and

* See upon this point Ritter's Hist. An. Ph. vol. ii. p. 287. Compare pp. 272, 273.

especially as a Father and Friend, wanted, for its full expression and confirmation, an actual incarnation in some perfect, tangible form. This while preserving the fundamental truth of the divine unity and supremacy, would bring home to the intellect and the heart the idea of a personal God, distinct from the universe, with whom we might enter into relations of fellowship and love.

Yet Plato, as we see, clung to the fact of a divine manifestation, while incapable of realizing it in scientific form. It constituted, indeed, a pervading element of his system, and entered into all subsequent speculations conceived in his spirit. Nay, whenever, in the history of the past, any approximation was made, either in philosophy or religion, to the great truth of a First Cause, the necessities of human nature uniformly removed this primal deity beyond the sphere, not only of the senses, but of the mere finite intellect. The truth was held, as by a superior sense or faculty, as a great and unutterable reality; and intercourse with such a being, either on his side or on man's, was supposed possible only through some kind of intermediate power. For the same reason, the outward creation and government of the universe were always ascribed, as among the Oriental theosophers, to some emanating Essence or Deity, or, as among the Platonists, to the divine Logos, the Wisdom or Reason of the great Supreme, in the form, not only of an abstraction, but of a *personality*. That is to say, a personal God, the only conceivable God, to them ever was but an image, reproduction, or manifestation of the one absolute and eternal Being.

This was the doctrine, in some form or other, of all the old religions, of all the Indian and Egyptian philosophies and mythologies, of Magianism and of Platonism, though often appearing in a most imperfect, and even degrading form. This too was the doctrine of the Hebrew sages.* Numerous passages might be cited from Philo Judæus, born at Alexandria, in Egypt, only a few months before our Savior, and par excellence the philosopher of the Hebrews, on the impossibility that the self-existent Deity should become cognizable to the intellect or senses of man, and consequently that there must intervene between him and us some divine mediation, some eternal Logos, Reason, or Word. Sometimes he speaks of this intermediate divinity as the image, or still more adequately as the shadow of God.† Nay, he goes further, and maintains that as God is the

* For example, the Targumists, the earliest Jewish commentators on the Scriptures. Lightfoot, Schoetgen, and others have collected numerous passages in which the Messiah is represented under this idea. See some admirable remarks upon this point in the introduction to Tholuck's Commentary on John.

† *Leg. Alleg.* ii. The term here used is παράδειγμα της εἰκονος.

prototype of the Word, so again the Word is the archetype of other things, and of man among the rest. It is on this ground that he describes the Deity as a light, which not only illuminates himself, but also emits ten thousand rays, which form the supra-sensible world of his energies, the pleroma or "fulness of him that filleth all in all." * So that the *Messiah*, or Word, would be, as the Athanasian creed expresses it, *God of God* and *Light of Light*, or, as St. Paul, more beautifully, "the effulgence of the Father's glory, and the express image of his nature."

Philo does not carry out the idea quite consistently, neither does he conform, in all respects, either to the Platonic or the Hebrew conception.† He mingles with it some conceits and refinements which it is difficult to understand, and proposes to reunite man to the Deity by means of mental abstraction and theosophic mysticism.‡ It is impossible also to say whether he derived his ideas chiefly from Plato and the Oriental theosophers, or from the ancient Scriptures. His method of interpreting the divine Oracles is allegorical. The literal and even natural sense he often rejects, or modifies at pleasure; and endeavors, like Origen and Swedenborg, to find the real import

* *De Cherub.* xxviii. 156.

† He rarely, if ever, gives the idea of a personal Messiah.

‡ *Leg. Alleg.* iii. 9, p. 93.

beneath external words, facts, or appearances. His style is Grecian and Platonic; his ideas are Oriental and mystical, though frequently beautiful and affecting. He pours contempt upon outward things, the sciences, and even political affairs, and dwells with infinite complacency on the excellence and happiness of a contemplative life.* He praises especially the Therapeutæ, or the Jewish anchorites of Egypt, who despised society, mortified the body, and endeavored, by strange ceremonies and mystic contemplation, to reunite themselves to the Deity.†

These notions exerted a great influence upon the Jews of Egypt, who had multiplied there exceedingly during the reign of the Ptolemies, so as to amount to something more than a million of souls. In subsequent times they mingled, to some extent, with Christian ideas, and originated, probably, the monastic life of the early Christian devotees, so numerous in that country.

But the belief of Plato and Philo in regard to the Logos was cherished in a somewhat different form, perhaps, by the Jewish people, especially by their more thoughtful, religious teachers. He was

* See *De Vita Contemplativa.*

† *De Migra. Abrahah.* 2, 3, 10, 11, compared with *De Vita Contemplativa.* In other places, however, Philo rebukes the extreme asceticism and extravagant usages of the Theraputæ. See *Profugis*, 7.

called, as in the Old Testament Scriptures, the *Messiah*, or Anointed One, the *Shiloh*, or Peace-maker, the *Divine Presence*, or the *Angel of His Presence*, who led them through the wilderness, the *Metatron* or *Mediator*, though most frequently the *Memra* or *Word*, for as a word is an outgoing or utterance of mind, an embodiment or manifestation of spirit, so they regarded the Messiah, for whose incarnation in the fulness of the times they constantly longed, as the embodiment or manifestation of Jehovah—as it were God personified, that is, revealed, in such limited but appropriate form as mortals might understand.

And it is a curious fact, which we may state in this connection, that this very appellation, Word or Reason, is found not only in the Hebrew, but in the Indian, the Persian, the Chinese, and Egyptian philosophies and religions. In the Indian mythology, *Vach*, signifying speech, is the active power of *Brahma*. In the Egyptian hieroglyphics, *Amun* is "the hidden God," while *Phtha*, the god of light, or fire, by whom he produces the world, (as in the Rosetta stone,) is "the *Apparent*" or *Manifested God*. Hence the sovereigns of Egypt are styled "the beloved of *Phtha*." In the Persian religion, *Ormuzd, the good*, creates the universe by Honover, the *Word*.* *Lao-tsue*,

* Ormuzd is himself a manifestation of Zeruanc Akherene, or absolute Being.

one of the Chinese sages, teaches the creation of the world by "*the Primordial Reason.*" *

The same term may also be traced in some of the most ancient poets — a tradition doubtless of some primeval revelation, if not an intuitive conviction of the human mind. Passages of this kind are cited by Justin Martyr, Clement of Alexandria, and others, and though liable to some suspicion on the score of genuineness, are not to be utterly rejected. We do not indeed urge them here as conclusive proof, for they require to be sifted by a thorough and candid criticism. It is enough to say, that Philo-Judæus, as also the early Christian fathers, uniformly, and with considerable plausibility, maintain, that amid many errors of view, the ancient writers, poets, and philosophers derived the knowledge of one eternal God, and one eternal Word or Reason, by whom the worlds were created, from the sacred Scriptures, or from some original revelation, and thence, though bewildered by superstition, bore testimony to the fundamental principles of religion.† The light shone upon them as through broken clouds, often lost out of

* "La raison a produit un, un a produit deux, deux a produit trois, trois a produit toutes choses." — *Memoire sur la Vie et les Ouvrages de Lao-tsue, par M. Abel Remusat.*

† See Justin's *Cohortatio ad Græcos*, 15. (Otto's ed.) vol. i. p. 53.

sight, but anon reappearing amid the drifting shadows.

"Hence," says Clement, "if the truth be but one, however numerous the modes of error, we may suppose the different schools of philosophy, barbarian as well as Greek, seizing on it as the Bacchantes seized on Pentheus, and having torn it to pieces, each bearing off a part, and then boasting itself of possessing the whole. Yet I think the dawn of that light in the east illuminated them all; for it may be proved that all who sincerely sought after the truth, whether Greeks or barbarians, did in fact carry off, in some cases, not a little of the truth which they sought, the fragments of which being collected and reunited, the perfect Logos (Reason) or truth is then fully seen and known; for he who can with propriety be called a Christian philosopher must be imbued with all knowledge." *

Plutarch, one of the best of the ancient thinkers and moralists, at a later day than Orpheus and Plato, in his treatise on the *Osiris*, or Sun-god of Egypt, the symbol, as he deems it, of an eternal Sun, has a similar conception. While recognizing the superior and universal Reason or Mind as the fountain of all existence, he speaks of him as inaccessible and incomprehen-

* *Stromata*, lib. i. c. 13.

sible, except through some external manifestation, like that of the embodied Logos.*

Doubtless all the symbols and deities of the ancient pagan sages and religionists were false, or at least inadequate; nay, many of them bestial and bewildering, the fruit of superstition and fancy. Perhaps none of them ever rose to the true conception of the Divine Logos, or Reason, and all were liable to lose sight of the spiritual and divine in the carnal and terrene. Yet they felt the need, as many now feel the need, of some special manifestation of the Deity, over and above that of nature, which might meet the wants of man, and which, while bringing down the Infinite to the level of the soul, might at the same time lift the soul to the level of the Infinite.

And what can all this be but the general acquiescence of the human mind in the necessity of some Divine Mediator, some celestial Messiah, or Son of God, who should reunite the extremes of heaven and earth, of man and God, and so bring the Deity, the great Father of us all, within the sphere and compass of human thought and affection? †

But philosophy, both ancient and modern, has only hovered around the problem, never solved

* Ritter's Ancient Ph. vol. iv. p. 497.

† A striking passage as to the necessity of a mediator, even on natural grounds, may be seen in Bacon's Works, ii. p. 407.

it, and nothing can equal the bewilderment of the heathen mind in regard to this and kindred questions.* The difficulty, so far from being diminished, was only deepened by time. Where it did not find its issue in a sort of philosophic stoicism, or in absolute scepticism, as it often did, it became an agony of desire, which could be satisfied only with the divine reality.

The supposed case of Clemens, a noble Roman, will illustrate what we mean, and show how philosophy, with its high imaginings and strange perplexities, was a means of preparing the soul for Christ. In the commencement of his book, entitled *Recognitiones*, he gives a most interesting account of his mental struggles, and subsequent conversion to Christianity, beginning, "Ego Clemens in urbe Roma nata," etc. A considerable portion of his narrative may be found in Neander's Church History, vol. i. pp. 32, 33, admirably translated by Professor Tor-

* The same bewilderment is visible among the philosophers of modern Europe. The whole problem of the German and French Ontology, developed in the writings of Leibnitz, Kant, Fichte, Hegel, Schelling, and Cousin, is the relation of *subject* and *object*, and, at a higher point, of the *finite* and the *infinite*. With them the absolute Essence ever images or reproduces himself in the *finite*; so that they are compelled to believe in a certain Trinity. The idea is brought out very strikingly by Schelling and Cousin. See Schelling's *Philosophie und Religion*, pp. 23–30. Cousin's *Histoire de la Philos. Intro.*, p. 95.

rey.* All we can give here is a condensed abstract. From his youth he was haunted with the questions, which had entered his soul, he hardly knew how, "Will my existence terminate with death? What will be my fate then? Will it be as if I had never been born? When and how was the world created? What existed before it? Will it end, and if so, what will then take place?" Incessantly agitated by such questionings and doubts, he grew pale and emaciated, little aware, as he tells us, that he had a celestial friend guiding him to truth and peace. He tried to rid himself of his anxiety, but found it impossible. He attended the schools of philosophy, but without satisfaction. He saw nothing but endless and ever-varying notions, "building up and tearing down of theories." He was driven to and fro, now hoping and then despairing, now believing, and anon doubting the immortality of the soul. His case grew worse. He then resolved to visit Egypt, the land of mysteries and apparitions, and hunt up a magician who might summon for him a spirit from the other world. The appearance of such a spirit would give him demonstrative evidence of the soul's immortality;

* The genuineness of the *Recognitiones* is called in question by scholars; but the case will serve for an illustration of what might take place, and of what, indeed, has actually taken place in other cases.

and he should never again be permitted to doubt. But a philosophic friend advised him against this course, as unlawful and undesirable. In this state of mind, full of doubts, undecided, inquiring, agitated and distressed, he came in contact with the gospel of Christ, preached in demonstration of the Spirit. His doubts were dispelled, his mind was enlightened, his heart was renewed. He found God and immortality in Christ, and rejoiced with joy unspeakable and full of glory.

Very similar to this was the conversion of Justin Martyr, who though born in Flavia Neapolis, was educated in the religious belief of the Greeks, to which his parents belonged. He was fond of study, and especially attached to the Greek poets and philosophers. In the beginning of his dialogue with Trypho, the Jew, he describes his hopes and disappointments in the study of the Greek philosophy, and shows how he obtained certainty and truth only in the Christian religion. He first joined himself to a disciple of the Stoa, but soon left him with bitter disappointment, because his teacher could say little or nothing of that Deity, whose nature he so much longed to know. With a Peripatetic he had still less success, for he found under the cloak of the philosopher a sordid love of gain. This, however, did not abate his confidence in philosophy, and so he betook himself to a Pythagorean, who rang changes upon the glories of music, geometry, and astronomy, as essential to all elevated spiritual attainments, and finally excluded Justin from his teachings, because he professed ignorance upon these subjects. Justin almost despaired of attaining the truth in this way, when he learned that a noted Platonist had opened a school in the place where he was sojourning, with whom he resolved to make one more attempt to attain the object of his wishes. Here he was not altogether disappointed, for the conversations of the philosopher furnished his mind with the richest materials of thought. He was much impressed with the symmetry and grandeur of the Platonic system, and especially with its ideal and spiritual tone. His philosophic knowledge increased daily, and he thought himself on the verge of consummating his Platonic attainments, by the direct intuition of the Deity.

In this state of mind, he was wandering, one day, in a lonely spot by the sea shore, where he was unexpectedly joined by a venerable man, of gentle and imposing aspect, supposed by some to have been a philosophically educated Jewish Christian, by others the Bishop Polycarp. This good man informed him, that he had come down to the beach to wait for some absent relatives, whose return he was anxiously expecting. Justin could not resist the temptation of communicating his thoughts to the venerable man, informing him that he had repaired to that spot for philosophical speculation. " You are a lover, then, of discourse, (Φιλόγος,) but no lover of deeds, (Φιλεργος,) nor by any means a lover of truth ; for you do not try to be a practical man, but rather an ingenious disputant." To this Justin demurred, affirming that nothing could be more worthy of a man than to make it manifest that all things were governed by intelligence, and to detect the undivine and the erroneous in all other pursuits; that philosophy was the true source of wisdom, and ought to receive the homage of all.

The aged man inquired how philosophy led to happiness, and what was its proper definition. Being told that it was " the science of being, and the knowledge of the truth, happiness being the reward of this knowledge and wisdom," he showed that philosophy, when it depended upon its unaided resources, could never solve the problem. Because the knowledge of God, the highest object of all, and especially of Platonic speculation, could never be acquired by an empirical or formal method, or by discursive contemplation, like music, arithmetic, or astronomy. He proved that God himself must teach us, through some divine medium, to which philosophy could make no pretensions. Reason, indeed, might ascertain the truth of the divine existence, and of moral principles; but could not behold the essence of God. Besides, according to a postulate of the Platonic philosophy itself, only the pure and righteous can attain to the actual vision of God; so that the reason or intellect plays but a subordinate part. "The pure in heart shall see God."

He then dwelt upon the errors of the Platonic philosophy, especially with reference to the doctrine of the metempsychosis and the immortality of the soul; since the former was absolutely useless, teaching that while wicked men passed into the bodies of brutes, they had no consciousness of their former aberrations, nor any sense of their present degradation. As to the immortality of the soul, he showed that it was founded by the Platonics, on the *assumption* of its absolute and eternal nature, and involved not simply its future but its past eternal existence. The soul, indeed, created in the image of God, is capable of immortality, and is thus susceptible of future reward or punishment. Hence it endures, in order to realize the idea of retribution, not only from its own nature, but through the will and power of him who gave it existence.

Justin was profoundly impressed by the wisdom and eloquence of the venerable man. He began to lose confidence in his philosophical speculations. "What, then, shall we do?" was his exclamation; "on what teacher can we rely, and from what quarter derive infallible truth?" He was directed to the prophets, "organs of the Divine Spirit," and especially to "Christ, the way, the truth, and the life." The old man then left him, and he saw him no more. Eagerly he sought the Scriptures, and the instructions of those known as the friends of Christ. And there he found what he sought — truth and rest, God and immortality.*

It may be concluded, then, that ancient philosophy was a longing and a preparation for Christ. "For it appears to me," said Simmias, in Phædo, addressing himself to Socrates, who concedes the correctness of the statement, "that to know them (the truths pertaining to the soul and its destiny) clearly in the present life, is either impossible or very difficult: on the other hand, not to test what has been said of them in every possible way, to investigate the whole matter, and exhaust upon it every effort, is the part of a very weak man. For we ought, in respect to these things, either to learn from others how they stand, or to discover them for ourselves; or if both these are impossible, then taking the best of human reasonings, that which

* For a more extended account of Justin's conversion, see Semisch's Life, Writings, and Opinions of Justin Martyr, vol. i. pp. 8–18.

appears the best supported, and embarking on that, as one who risks himself upon a raft, so to sail through life; unless one could be carried more safely, or with less risk, on *a surer conveyance*, or some DIVINE (Logos) REASON." *

Hence, also, in the Second Alcibiades, we have the still more remarkable declaration, "That we must wait patiently until some one, either *a god*, or some *inspired* man, teach us our moral and religious duties, and, as Pallas in Homer did to Diomed, remove the darkness from our eyes." †

* Plato's *Phædo*, 78.

† Alcib. ii. 150.

CHAPTER V.

THE CENTRAL RACE, OR CHRIST AMONG THE HEBREWS.

As in society at large we find a central power, in religion a central principle, and in philosophy a central idea, it may be presumed, that in the succession of human affairs, we shall find, among the nations, in a more or less perfect form, a central or a chosen people, whether named church, theocracy, or kingdom of God. We may expect not only a succession of divine facts, maintaining religion in the world, but a succession of individuals, families, and communities, perhaps some one community differing from all the rest in gifts, attainments, and usages, fitted to retain and transmit to all generations, and finally to the whole world, the principles and hopes of a perfect religion. Other nations may not, on this account, be proscribed, except for their vices. Much of their ignorance and superstition may be "winked at," or *overlooked*, at least for a season. In none of them will God leave himself without a witness for the truth; but the state of the world may be such as to demand a chosen people, a religious or prophetic race, who shall stand at the centre of history, and form a vehicle or medium for the transmission of the truth to all ages, and its diffusion among the nations.

This would be analogous to the divine procedure in other cases; for in all times we find central communities, in the matters of science, literature, refinement, arts, legislation, arms. So also we find central families, and central individuals, great lights in the world, whose mission and ministry have been a blessing to all. Insignificant, sometimes, in position, personal attractions, and other gifts of an external kind, often, too, great sufferers, and not always realizing for themselves the good of which they are the chosen depositaries, they have conveyed to others, sometimes during their lives, but oftener afterwards, vast and permanent benefits. Thus good of all sorts is ever found radiating from specific centres. In former times Greece was the central nation of philosophy and art; Rome of political power and civil law. From Plato sprang the speculative spirit; from Homer that of poetry and song.

If, then, we find in the Hebrew people the centre of a pure religion for ages, it will not be a matter of surprise; for if we study them thoroughly, we shall find that, in early times at least, they had the qualifications necessary for this purpose.

Or if this be denied them, as an original gift of nature, it will be allowed that they were disciplined for this end, and so successfully, that they actually succeeded in maintaining a pure and lofty Theism, and transmitting it to modern times.

But let us go back a little, and see how this thing was provided for in the very dawn of society.

Those who have studied human nature, and the history of the race, with the greatest attention, will not need to be told that it must have suffered some terrible lapse. Under the supposition the most natural that can be formed, that man was created innocent and happy, with a pure faith and a gentle discipline, it is clear that he has since departed from God. "The gold has become dim, the most fine gold is changed." The first Eden, the peaceful reign of purity and love, did not long continue. The knowledge of the true God, as we have seen, was speedily tarnished, and finally all but lost in universal idolatry. The ancient historical nations, with one, perhaps two exceptions, were idolaters.* Evil clung to the race.

* We have said perhaps *two*, the reference being to the Jews and the Persians. The latter, however, were nature or symbol-worshippers, adorers of the sun and fire; in this respect, therefore, to be classed with the Peruvians.

All the ancient philosophers, as well as prophets, felt this. Plato, who may be regarded as representing the whole Oriental and Occidental worlds, speaks of it in various forms, now as an ignorance, then as a discord, then as a constitutional necessity, and sometimes as a fatal, eternal duality, which he cannot understand. Some ascribed it to matter. This was the notion of most of the Oriental mystics, who thence mortified the body, and longed for absorption in the divine. The same view is taken by Proclus and most of the Platonic philosophers.

It is evident, however, that they often felt it to be a moral perversion, which had come upon man, and which ought to be remedied. Nearly all the mythologies recognize it as a fall; and some of the philosophers describe it much as the Bible describes it, as a fatal departure from God. One of the most striking things in all the works of Plato is that wherein he represents the soul under the image of Glaucus, who, having bathed in some fountain of life, had become immortal; but losing the secret, could not point out the fountain to others, and so threw himself into the sea, to be swept around all shores, by the violence of the waves. "We are now telling the truth," says Plato, "concerning it, [the soul,] such as it appears at present. Indeed, we see it in the same condition in which they see the marine Glaucus, in whom they cannot discern his ancient nature; because the original members of his body are partly broken off, while others are worn away, and altogether he is damaged by the waves. Besides this, other things are grown to him, such as shell fish, seaweed, and stones; so that in every respect he resembles a beast, rather than what he naturally was. In such a condition do we behold the soul under a thousand evils." * He adds that it ought to be restored to its original condition; but alas! Plato himself seems to despair of this, with reference to the mass of mankind wholly sunk in ignorance, superstition, and vice. How striking an evidence of the fact, too well known, and too well authenticated by all history, sacred and profane, that, at a very early period of the world's career, "all flesh had corrupted its ways!" †

God, then, must provide for his own. Hence he selected individuals and families to be recipients of his truth, and its teachers to mankind. There were those, in the antediluvian ages, who were styled "his sons," and who preserved, from

* *Republica*, c. xi.

† Even Theodore Parker says, "In the higher stages of polytheism man is regarded as fallen. He felt his alienation from his Father. Religion looks back longingly to the golden age, when God dwelt familiar with men. It seeks to restore the links broken out of the golden chain." —*Discourse of Religion*, p. 79. See Appendix B.

generation to generation, the great principles of religion. A Redeemer was promised; a sacrifice of reconciliation was provided. Penitence and prayer were found available, through the mercy of God, for the redemption of the soul. Devout men called upon the name of the Lord, and worshipped at his altars. Enoch, the seventh from Adam, is peculiarly distinguished as a prophet and teacher. Subsequent to this we find Noah a worshipper of the true God, and a preacher of righteousness. Saved from the flood, he became the father of a new race, the type of a new redemption. For, the rescue from water, in ancient times, might have been regarded as a symbol of a higher deliverance from sin. The bow which spanned the heavens was a pledge of hope to the world. Whatever view may be taken of this event, such is its moral import and design, and hence its profound impression, not only upon single families, but upon all the ancient nations. Preserved, in its most perfect form, among patriarchal and Hebrew traditions, we meet with it in nearly all the mythologies of the more ancient nations. One of the most striking of these is the Chaldean legend, as given by Berosus, among the fragments of his history, preserved by Josephus, Eusebius, and others.* He gives first the mytho-

* Berosus, we are aware, is poor authority with many, in matters strictly historical. Even in this department, however, he has been

logical period of Babylonian history, consisting of ten kings who reigned before the flood; the first of whom, Alorus, corresponds with Adam, the last, Xesuthrus, corresponds with Noah. With Xesuthrus commences the second or real historical period. Of this Xesuthrus Berosus gives the following legend: Chronus appeared to him in a dream, and warning him that mankind should be destroyed by a flood, commanded him to build a ship, into which, having previously stocked it with provisions, and introduced into it a certain number of fowls and four-footed beasts, he, with his friends and nearest relatives, as also a band of pious men, should enter. Xesuthrus did as he was ordered. He built a huge ship, the dimensions of which are given, stocked in the manner described, in which he himself embarked with his family and pious associates. By and by the flood came; and when it began to abate, he let fly some birds, which soon returned to the ship. After a few days he sent them out again, and they came back with their feet darkened with mud; but when for a third time he dismissed them, none of them ever returned. The ark floated towards the mountains of Armenia, and when the waters had

too much undervalued. Niebuhr's estimate may be seen, Lectures on Ancient Hist. vol. i. p. 48. In matters purely traditional, of course, all will admit his validity.

subsided, the just men there disembarked and returned to Babylonia.*

A similar tradition is found in the religious annals of India. It is related in the Padina Puran that Satyarota, whose miraculous preservation from a general deluge is told at length in the Mataja, had three sons, the eldest of whom was called Jyapeti, to whom he gave all the regions to the north of the Himalaya, in the Snowy Mountains, which extend from sea to sea, and of which Caucasus is a part; to Sharma, (corruption for Cham or Ham,) the countries to the south of these mountains, &c. † We do not present these legends as proofs of the scriptural account of the deluge, but simply as illustrations of the wide-spread influence which might have been exerted by Noah, as a preacher of the truth, upon the more ancient nations. ‡

Later we meet with Abraham, styled the

* For an account of the Babylonian cosmogony and flood, see Niebuhr's Lectures on Ancient History, vol. i. pp. 48–51.

† Asiatic Researches, iii. pp. 312, 313.

‡ The tradition of the flood must have spread far beyond the central nations of Asia. We find it even among the legends both of the South and of the North American Indians. The Mexicans and Peruvians have accounts of its occurrence in singular coincidence with the main features of the Mosaic narrative. See Humboldt's Researches, ii. 65; Clanigero, Hist. Mexico, i. 204; Thacher's Indian Traits, ii. 148, 149; Kitto's Bible Illustrations, i. 152, 154, where the reader will find some interesting citations on the subject. See also Prof. Hitchcock, in the Biblical Repository for 1836; Iconographic Cyclopædia, art. Mexican Mythology.

"father of the faithful," recognized as such both by Jews and Arabians, and by some of the neighboring nations. He was called from "Ur of the Chaldees," into the land of Canaan, that as a prince, patriarch, and priest in his family and among his dependants, he might found a nation of worshippers, who should be numerous as the stars of heaven, and a blessing to the world. At this period, nature-worship, and perhaps idolatry, was prevalent in Chaldea. The word *Ur*, Abraham's native place, signifies *fire*, and is supposed to have been one of the seats of Sabæan worship, a sort of Heliopolis, where the "host of heaven" were adored with superstitious rites. Be this as it may, it is quite evident that the family of Terah, Abraham's father, was involved in the prevalent superstition, as we learn from Joshua xxiv. 2: "Your fathers dwelt on the other side of the flood [the River Euphrates] in old time, even Terah, the father of Abraham, and the father of Nachor, and they served other gods." It is even asserted by Epiphanius and others, that Abraham's father and grandfather were makers of idolatrous images; but we have no means of verifying such a statement. Around the fact of Abraham's supposed conversion from idolatry, and his assertion of a pure theism, have gathered many striking Oriental traditionary fictions, one of the most beautiful of which is the following. "As Abraham was walking by night from the grotto where he was born, to the city of Babylon, he gazed on the stars of heaven, and among them on the beautiful planet Venus. 'Behold,' said he within himself, 'the God and Lord of the universe!' But the star set and disappeared, and Abraham felt that the Lord of the universe could not thus be liable to change. Shortly after he beheld the moon at the full. 'Lo,' he cried, 'the divine Creator, the manifest Deity!' But the moon sank below the horizon, and Abraham made the same reflection as at the setting of the evening star. All the rest of the night he passed in profound rumination; at sunrise he stood before the gates of Babylon, and saw the whole people prostrate in adoration. 'Wondrous orb,' he exclaimed, 'thou surely art the Creator and Ruler of all nature! but thou too hastest like the rest to thy setting! neither then art thou my Creator, my Lord, or my God!'"*

The fact, however, is obvious enough, that Abraham and his family were isolated from their idolatrous kindred and people, and made the vehicle for the transmission of a pure religion to their descendants. From him came the hope of a Messiah, or divine Deliverer, which formed the polar star of the Jewish mind.

* Milman's Hist. of the Jews, i. p. 9.

Thus Abraham commenced a new era in the history of mankind, among whom, at the time of his birth, idolatry, or nature-worship, so far as tradition can teach us, was prevalent, not only in Chaldea, his native land, but throughout the world. Nations were in process of formation; civilization advanced slowly; the relations of the sexes, the foundation of all permanent national prosperity, were uncertain; slavery was a common evil; multitudes of nomadic tribes, without fixed habitations, roamed from place to place; religion, such as it was, gradually assumed a more narrow and sensual character, while war was conducted with extreme cruelty, prisoners being tortured or enslaved, at the caprice of their masters. In Egypt, the seat of ancient civilization, idolatry was becoming constantly more and more gross, while caste and slavery were stereotyping some of the deepest evils of its social and political state.* Hence it was important that, in some great centre, a counteracting power should be established and perpetuated, from which it might gradually diffuse itself among the nations. Abraham and his family are chosen as its depositary. Thus God enters into covenant relations with man. The unity of God, the hope of a Messiah, the spirituality of the human soul, and the beauty of virtue, are involved in this arrange-

* See the bas-reliefs in Wilkinson and Rosellini

ment. Idolatry is checked. The dawn of a brighter day rises upon the world.

To the same era is referred Melchizedek, (Melchi-Zedech, *King of justice*,) King of Salem, which is interpreted "King of peace," who lived, according to some, at Jerusalem, but according to others, at a place of the same name near Scythopolis, where a ruin, called Melchizedek's palace, was shown in the time of Jerome. He united in his own person the offices of prince and priest, was a worshipper, and, of course, a teacher of the one eternal God, in whose name he blessed Abraham, when returning from the conquest of his country's invaders. His priestly descent, as well as succession, according to St. Paul, are unknown. He stands alone in history, "without father or mother, without beginning of [priestly] days, or end of life, that is, of official succession, a beautiful type of the one great" High Priest of our profession, for whose advent all the ancient believers longed.

Whether Job, or the author of the book which bears his name, belongs to this era, or to one subsequent, is an unsettled question. The book itself bears unequivocal marks of a remote antiquity, and teaches a Theism of the purest character.* In this sublime composition, God, as

* Its reference to the prevalent Sabæism, or nature-worship, the simplicity of its diction, the peculiar social usages which it de-

Creator, Judge, and Redeemer, is clothed with all the attributes of boundless majesty and perfection. His omnipotence, above all, his infinite holiness and mercy, are celebrated in strains of the loftiest poetry.* It was much, in that early

scribes, the name of Job's friends, the absence of all reference to the events narrated in the Pentateuch, with other circumstances, have compelled the most judicious critics to assign it to an epoch anterior to the exodus, somewhere about two thousand years before Christ. Its authorship has been ascribed to Moses, but this is a mere conjecture, to which there are serious objections. Job himself is more likely to have been its author. Even admitting that in form and embellishment it is imaginary, its principal events must be real occurrences. Job is universally recognized in the Scriptures as a real character. See the testimonies in Ezekiel xiv. 14, and James v. 2.

* The late Daniel Webster, whose vast intellect and exquisite taste fitted him to appreciate the sublimities of the old prophetic writings, regarded the Book of Job as the first of all epic poems. Referring to an interview with him at Marshfield, the editor of the Boston Atlas says, "He talked of the books of the Old Testament especially, and dwelt with unaffected pleasure upon Isaiah, the Psalms, and especially the Book of Job. The Book of Job, he said, taken as a mere work of literary genius, was one of the most wonderful productions of any age or of any language. As an epic poem, he deemed it far superior to either the Iliad or the Odyssey.

"The two last, he said, received much of their attraction from the mere narration of warlike deeds, and from the perilous escapes of the chief personages from death and slaughter; but the Book of Job was a purely intellectual narrative. Its power was shown in the dialogues of the characters introduced. The story was simple in its construction, and there was little in it to excite the imagination or arouse the sympathy. It was purely an intellectual production, and depended upon the power of the dialogue, and not upon the interest of the story, to produce its effects. This was considering it merely as an intellectual work. He read it through very often, and always with renewed delight. In his judgment it was the greatest epic ever written. We well remember his quotation of some of the verses in day, to be able to say, "I know that my Redeemer liveth."

Allowing this book, in the main, to be a real history, and not simply a dramatic or epic fiction, belonging to a remote epoch, we have, soon after the age of Abraham, or a little later, a magnificent testimony to the fundamental truths of religion, and a decisive evidence that groups of individuals, here and there, worshipped "the living and true God." In a word, Job, with Melchizedek and Abraham, belong to that sacred succession, through which flowed the stream of pure and undefiled religion, till the advent of the Messiah and the preaching of the everlasting gospel.

Abraham, however, is the principal figure among the patriarchs and teachers of the patriarchal age, and has left the impress of his character upon much of the Oriental world. To him it was announced, by a divine inspiration, that from his loins should proceed a wondrous race, through whom the one eternal Jehovah

the 38th chapter: 'Then the Lord answered Job out of the whirlwind, and said, Who is this that darkeneth counsel by words without knowledge? Gird up now thy loins like a man; for I will demand of thee, and answer thou me. Where wast thou when I laid the foundations of the earth? Declare, if thou hast understanding,' &c. Mr. Webster was a fine reader, and his recitation of particular passages, to which he felt warm, was never surpassed, and was capable of giving the most exquisite delight to those who could appreciate them."

should manifest himself to mankind, and bring them into a new and peculiar relation with himself. The promise was renewed to Isaac, as also to Jacob, who, in his dying hour, predicted the coming "Shiloh," or Peacemaker, to whom "the gathering of the people should be."*

Thence, as all our readers know, sprang the Hebrew nation — first nurtured and disciplined in Canaan, as a patriarchal family; then in Egypt, as a peculiar people; then in the wilderness, for many years, as a wandering tribe; then again in the land of Canaan, as a settled nation; and, finally, in all lands, as a sacred race; and all for the purpose of maintaining and transmitting to mankind the knowledge of one true God, one almighty Redeemer, and one eternal life.

This great fact in the history of the Jews, as a peculiar or chosen people, is beautifully indicated in the language of Moses, just before his death — "Remember the days of old, consider the years of many generations; ask thy father and he will show thee, thy elders and they will tell thee. When the Most High divided to the nations their inheritance, when he separated the sons of Adam, he set the bounds of the people according to the number of the children of Israel. For the Lord's portion is his people, Jacob is the lot of his inheritance; he found him in a desert

* Genesis xlix. 10.

land, and in the waste howling wilderness; he led him about, he instructed him, he kept him as the apple of his eye. As an eagle stirreth up her nest, fluttereth over her young, spreadeth abroad her wings, taketh them, beareth them on her wings, so the Lord alone did lead him, and there was no strange god with him." (Deut. xxxii. 8–12.)

The sacred writers do not disguise the imperfections of their nation; they dwell, with honest indignation, on their frequent apostasies and perversities, and describe them as "a stiff-necked and rebellious race." The most terrible judgments are denounced against them by the prophets, on this very ground—judgments literally inflicted in subsequent times, as all the world knows; yet the fact of their high and special destiny, as the chosen people, through whom divine truth was to be communicated to the world, is never, for a moment, lost sight of. For this purpose they were formed into a theocracy, or priestly nation, governed by inspired laws and sanctions; nay, more, by the immediate presence and guidance of Jehovah, symbolized in the Shekinah, or luminous appearance called the "glory of the Lord," which shone above the mercy seat, between the cherubim, first in the tabernacle, and then in the temple.

Well, indeed, they knew, as Solomon in his

prayer of dedication acknowledges, that the "heaven of heavens" could not contain the infinite Spirit, whom they worshipped as "the living God;" but they believed in the possibility of a divine manifestation, such as they could understand, the visible outward symbol of which was recognized in the supernatural splendor, which illumined the "holy of holies." In that shrine, too, were offered continually the sacrifice and incense prescribed by Jehovah, adumbrating, in no ambiguous form, the one great sacrifice of atonement, by which the world was finally to be reconciled to God. It thus became a centre of hope, and "a house of prayer," for all pious souls, whether in Palestine or other lands, until the true Temple and the true Shekinah were realized in the person of Jesus Christ. Around it gathered the hopes of the entire Hebrew race; to this, even in far distant countries, they directed their devotions; fulfilling, in this way, the remarkable words used at its dedication — "But will God, indeed, dwell on the earth? Behold, the heaven and the heaven of heavens cannot contain thee; how much less this house that I have builded! Yet have thou respect unto the prayer of thy servant, and to his supplication, O Lord my God, to hearken unto the cry and the prayer which thy servant prayeth unto thee to-day, that thine eyes may be opened towards this house, night and day, even towards the place of which thou hast said, *My name shall be there*, that thou mayest hearken to the prayer which thy servant shall make towards this place. And hearken thou to the supplication of thy servant, and of thy people Israel, when they shall pray towards this place; and hear thou in heaven, thy dwelling-place, and, when thou hearest, forgive." (1 Kings viii. 27–30.)

The Temple then taught to the Israelites, and, through them, to the neighboring nations, this great and thrilling truth, that Jehovah, though the infinite and ineffable Spirit, "whom no man hath seen, or can see," does manifest himself in mercy to man, that he hears the prayer of the penitent, and restores his erring child to his favor and image.

With the same view, God raised up among them a long succession of prophets, men of high inspiration and saintly virtue, who, controlled by the Spirit of truth, uttered oracles of divine wisdom, denounced the judgments of the Almighty against sin, and proclaimed, in grand and passionate numbers, the advent of the Holy One, the Redeemer of Israel and the hope of the world. Moses announced him as "the Prophet, like unto himself," whom all were bound "to hear;" Jacob, as "the Shiloh," unto whom should "the gathering of the people be;" Isaiah, as "the Wonderful," "the Mighty God," "the Prince of Peace," who, while "making his soul an offering for sin," should yet "prolong his days," and reign over his people forever; Daniel, as "the Ancient of Days," the "Messiah," or the "Anointed and Princely One;" and Malachi, the last of the ancient prophetic line, as "the Sun of Righteousness," who should "arise with healing in his wings."

They speak of him as gentle and lowly, "despised and rejected of men, a man of sorrows, and acquainted with grief," and yet of kingly might, "glorious in his apparel," "travelling in the greatness of his strength," and "mighty to save," as David's Son and David's Lord, the Sovereign of the Temple, and the Messenger of the Covenant; as "giving his back to the smiters, and his cheek to them that plucked off the hair," dragged as "a lamb to the slaughter," "stricken, smitten of God, and afflicted," "numbered with transgressors," and finally "cut off out of the land of the living," by a premature and ignominious death; and yet as living, reigning, triumphant, a God confessed, loved, and adored by myriads, his power resistless, his reign universal and everlasting — contrasts the most singular, and yet the most singularly fulfilled in the person of him, who, ages after, was described by the last of the apostles as "the Root and Offspring of David, the Bright and the Morning Star." *

The physical or geographical position of the holy people corresponds to their character and destiny. They were planted in a goodly land, in a singularly protected but fertile heritage among the mountains, with Asia on the one side, and Europe on the other, quite near to Egypt and Ethiopia, and not far from Greece and Rome; with rivers, roads, and seas around them, sufficient, when the time came, to link them with the commercial, political, and religious destiny of the world.

For the same end, they were made to pass through a severe and peculiar discipline, until their idolatrous tendency was completely burned out, and the whole nation became as much distinguished for their hatred of idolatry, as, in former times, for their strange proclivity to this very sin.

This was the true secret of the exode from Egypt, and the peculiar circumstances in which that took place; and this too was the principal reason of their long captivity in "the far East."

Nothing could be better fitted than the exode, and the splendid series of miracles by which it

* See Hengstenberg's Christology, passim, for admirable criticisms and explanations of the Messianic predictions.

was preceded and accompanied, to cure their idolatry, contracted from long residence and bondage in Egypt, and train them for their peculiar destiny as a sacred race. The Sun-gods of Egypt, the sacred Nile, the holy priesthood and animals of pagan adoration, were stultified and conquered before the God of Israel. How singularly, too, was Moses prepared for his high destiny, nurtured first in Egypt, and then in the far wilderness, alone with nature and with God, a man of a simple, energetic mind, with no pretensions to those oratorical gifts which gain the public attention, but a devout Theist, with an utter abhorrence of idolatry, and a profound sense of the all-pervading presence and spirituality of God. He appears with his brother Aaron, more highly gifted as a speaker than himself, in the presence of his people, and calls upon them in the name of God, from whom he had received his commission, to cast off the bondage of Egypt, and return to the land of their fathers. Reluctant and doubtful, they finally yield to what seems to be the evident command of God. Application is then made to the Emperor of Egypt, who, like other Oriental monarchs, probably held open court to hear the petitions and try the causes of his people, for permission, at the command of God, to pass into the wilderness, to offer a solemn sacrifice. This is peremptorily denied;

new burdens are imposed upon the people, who murmur against Moses and Aaron, as the cause of these calamities. Then the contest between Theism and idolatry, freedom and despotism begins. Moses had come from converse, in the wilderness, with the ineffable "I am that I am," and presented his claims to attention, in the name of the God of Abraham, of Isaac, and of Jacob, who appeared to him in the bush. He must therefore vindicate his commission, and prove, before all, the supremacy of Jehovah, in whose name he acted. How this was accomplished, the following extract from Milman's History of the Jews will strikingly show. "Again they [Moses and Aaron] appear in the royal presence, having announced, it should seem, their pretensions to miraculous powers; and now commenced a contest, unequal, it would at first appear, between two individuals of an enslaved people, and the whole skill, knowledge, or artifice of the Egyptian priesthood, whose sacred authority was universally acknowledged; their intimate acquaintance with all the secrets of nature extensive; their reputation for magical powers firmly established with the vulgar. The names of the principal opponents of Moses, Jannes and Jambres, are reported by St. Paul from Jewish traditions; and it is curious that in Pliny and Apuleius the names of Moses and Jannes are recorded as celebrated proficients in magical arts.

"The contest began in the presence of the king. Aaron cast down his rod, which was instantaneously transformed into a serpent. The magicians performed the same feat. The dexterous tricks which the Eastern and African jugglers play with serpents will easily account for this without any supernatural assistance. It might be done either by adroitly substituting the serpent for the rod, or by causing the serpent to assume a stiff appearance like a rod or staff, which, being cast down on the ground, might become again pliant and animated. But Aaron's serpent swallowed up the rest — a circumstance, however extraordinary, yet not likely to work conviction upon a people familiar with such feats, which they ascribed to magic. Still the slaves had now assumed courage, their demands were more peremptory, their wonders more general and public. The plagues of Egypt, which successively afflicted the priesthood, the king, and almost every deity honored in their comprehensive pantheon, which infected every element, and rose, in terrible gradation, one above the other, now began. Pharaoh was standing on the brink of the sacred river, the great object of Egyptian adoration, not improbably in the performance of some ceremonial ablution, or making an offering to the native deity of the land. The leaders of the Israelites approached, and renewed their demand for freedom. It was rejected; and at once the holy river, with all the waters of the land, were turned to blood. The fish, many of which were objects of divine worship, perished. Still the priesthood were not yet baffled. The Egyptians having dug for fresh and pure water in some of these artificial tanks or reservoirs, the magicians contrived to effect a similar change. As their holy abhorrence of blood would probably prevent them from discharging so impure a fluid into the new reservoirs, they might, without great difficulty, produce the appearance by some secret and chemical means. The waters of the Nile, it is well known, about their period of increase, usually assume a red tinge, either from the color of the Ethiopian soil, which is washed down, or from a number of insects of that color. Writers who endeavor to account for these miracles by natural means, suppose that Moses took the opportunity of this periodical change to terrify the superstitious Egyptians. Yet that Moses should place any reliance on, or the Egyptians feel the least apprehension at, an ordinary occurrence, which took place every year, seems little less incredible than the miracle itself. For seven days the god of the river was thus rebuked before the God of the stranger; instead of the soft and delicious water, spoken of by travellers as peculiarly grateful to the taste, the fœtid stream ran with that of which the Egyptians had the greatest abhorrence. To shed, or even to behold blood, was repugnant to all their feelings and prejudices. Still the king was inflexible, and from the sacred stream was derived the second plague. The whole land was suddenly covered with frogs. The houses, the chambers, even the places where they prepared their food, swarmed with these loathsome reptiles. It is undoubtedly possible that the corrupted waters might quicken the birth of these creatures, the spawn of which abounded in all the marshy and irrigated districts. Hence the priests would have no difficulty in bringing them forth in considerable numbers. The sudden cessation of this mischief, at the prayer of Moses, is by far the most extraordinary part of this transaction, — in one day all the frogs, except those in the river, were destroyed. So far the contest had been maintained without manifest advantage on either side. But the next plague reduced the antagonists of Moses to a more difficult predicament. With the priesthood the most scrupulous cleanliness was inseparable from their sanctity. These Bramins of Egypt, so fastidiously abhorrent of every kind of personal impurity, that they shaved every part which might possibly harbor vermin, practised ablutions four times a day, wore no garments but of the finest linen, because woollen might conceal either filth or insects, heard with the greatest horror, that the dirt had been changed into lice, and that this same vermin, thus called into existence, was spreading over the whole country. After a vain attempt, notwithstanding their prejudices, to imitate their opponent, they withdrew for the present from the contest. But the pride of the king was not yet broken, and the plagues followed in rapid and dreadful succession. Swarms of flies, ... in unusual numbers, covered the whole land; by the intercession of Moses they were dispersed. Next, all the cattle, of every description, were smitten with a destructive murrain, all but those of the Israelites, who were exempt from this as from the former calamity. This last blow might seem to strike not merely at the wealth, but at an important part of the religion of Egypt, their animal worship. The goat worshipped at Mendes, the ram at Thebes, the more general deity, the bull Apis, were perhaps involved in the universal destruction. Still this is by no means certain, as the plague seems to have fallen only on the animals which were in the open pastures; it is clear that the war horses escaped. If this plague reached the deities, the next was aimed at the sacred persons of the priesthood, no less than at the meaner people. Moses took the ashes of the furnace, perhaps the brick kiln in which the wretched slaves were laboring, cast them into the air, and where they fell the skin broke out in boils. The magicians, in terror and bodily anguish, fled away. It is impossible to read the following passage from Plutarch, without observing so remarkable a coincidence between the significant action of Moses and the Egyptian rite, as to leave little doubt that some allusion was intended. 'In the city of Eilithuia,' as Manetho relates, calling them Typhonian, (as sacrificed to Typhon,) 'they burned men alive, and winnowing their ashes, scattered them in the air and dispersed them.' The usual objects of these sacrifices were people with red hair, doubtless their old enemies the shepherds. Had any of the Israelites suffered in these horrid furnaces, it would add singular force and justice to the punishment inflicted on the priests and people. It would thus have been from the ashes of their own victims, that their skins were burning with insufferable agony, and breaking out into loathsome disease. The next plague, though in most tropical climates it would have been an ordinary occurrence, in Egypt was an event as unusual as alarming. All ancient and modern writers agree that rain, though by no means unknown, falls but seldom in that country. It appears to be rather less uncommon now than formerly. According to Herodotus, it rained once at Thebes, and the circumstance excited general apprehension. 'There, at present,' says Belzoni, 'two or three days of moderate rain generally occur during the winter.' But lower down, in the part of the valley where these events took place, it is still an uncommon, though not an unprecedented phenomenon. Hasselquist saw it rain at Alexandria, and other parts of the Delta; Pocock saw even hail at Faiume. Ordinarily, however, the Nile, with its periodical overflow and constant exhalations, supplies the want of the cool and refreshing shower. Now, according to the prediction of Moses, a tremendous tempest burst over the country. Thunder and hail, and fire mingled with the hail, 'that ran upon the ground,' rent the branches from the trees, and laid prostrate the whole harvest. From the cultivation of flax, Egypt possessed the great linen manufacture of the ancient world; on the barley the common people depended for their usual drink, the rich soil of Egypt in general being unfit for the vine. Both these crops were totally destroyed. The rye and the wheat, being later, escaped. This tempest must, therefore, have taken place at the beginning of March. By this time the inflexible obstinacy of the king began to fail; on the deliverance of the country from this dreadful visitation, he engaged to release the bondmen. At the word of Moses the storm ceased. Still, to deprive the whole land of so valuable a body of slaves, seemed too great a sacrifice to the policy, and too humiliating a concession to the pride of the monarch. To complete the desolation of the country, the corn lands were next laid waste by other means of destruction. The situation of Egypt usually secures the country from that worst enemy to the fertility of the Asiatic provinces, the locusts. As these insects fly in general from east to west, and cannot remain on the wing for any length of time, the width of the Red Sea presents a secure barrier to their invasions. Their dreadful ravage is scarcely exaggerated by the strong images of the prophets, particularly the sublime description in Joel. Where they alight, all vegetation at once disappears; not a blade of grass, not a leaf, escapes them; the soil seems as if it were burnt up by fire; they obscure the sun as with a cloud; they cover sometimes a space of nine miles, and thus they march on in their regular files, till '*the land which was as the garden of Eden before them, behind them is a desolate wilderness.*' Such was the next visitation which came to glean the few remaining signs of the accustomed abundance of Egypt, spared by the tempest. A strong and regular east wind brought the fatal cloud from the Arabian shore, or, according to the Septuagint translation, a south wind from the regions of Abyssinia. The court now began to murmur at the unbending spirit of the king; on the intimation of this new calamity, he had determined to come to terms. He offered to permit all the adults to depart, but insisted on retaining the children, either as hostages for the return of the parents, or in order to perpetuate a race of slaves for the future. Now he was for an instant inclined to yield this point; but when the west wind had driven these destroying ravagers into the sea, he recalled all his concessions, and continued steadfast in his former resolutions of resistance to the utmost. At length, therefore, their great divinity, the Sun, was to be put to shame before the God of the slave and the stranger. For three whole days, as Moses stretched his hand toward heaven, a darkness, described with unexampled force as a DARKNESS THAT MIGHT BE FELT, overspread the land; not merely was the sun unable to penetrate the gloom, and enlighten his favored land, but they could distinguish nothing, and were constrained to sit in awe-struck inactivity. The king would now gladly consent to the departure of the whole race, children as well as grown-up men; yet, as all the latter plagues, the flies, the murrain, the hail, the locusts, the darkness had spared the land of Goshen, the cattle of that district, in the exhausted state of the country, was invaluable; he demands that these should be surrendered as the price of freedom. 'Our cattle also shall go with us, not a hoof shall be left behind,' replies his inexorable antagonist. Thus, then, the whole kingdom of Egypt had been laid waste by successive calamities; the cruelty of the oppressors had been dreadfully avenged; all classes had suffered in the undiscriminating desolation. Their pride had been humbled; their most sacred prejudices wounded; the Nile had been contaminated; their dwellings polluted by loathsome reptiles; their cleanly persons defiled by vermin; their pure air had swarmed with troublesome insects; their cattle had perished by a dreadful malady; their bodies broken out with a filthy disease; their early harvest had been destroyed by the hail, the latter by the locusts; an awful darkness had enveloped them for three days, but still the deliverance was to be extorted by a calamity more dreadful than all these. The Israelites will not depart poor and empty handed; they will receive some compensation for their years of hard and cruel servitude; they levy on their awe-struck masters contributions in gold, silver, and jewels. Some, especially later writers, have supposed that they exacted these gifts by main force, and with arms in their hands. Undoubtedly, though the Israelites appear to have offered no resistance to the Egyptian horsemen and chariots which pursued them in the desert, they fight with the Amalekites, and afterward arrive, an armed people, on the borders of Canaan. Josephus accounts for this, but not quite satisfactorily, by supposing that they got possession of the arms of the Egyptians, washed ashore after their destruction in the Red Sea. But the general awe and confusion are sufficient to explain the facility with which the Israelites collected these treasures. The slaves had become objects of superstitious terror; to propitiate them with gifts was natural, and their leader authorized their reception of all presents which might thus be offered. The night drew on, the last night of servitude to the people of Israel, a night of unprecedented horror to the ancient kingdom of Egypt. The Hebrews were employed in celebrating that remarkable rite, which they have observed for ages down to the present day. The Passover, the memorial that God passed over them when he destroyed the first born of all Egypt, has been kept under this significant name, and still is kept as the memorial of their deliverance from Egypt, by every faithful descendant of Abraham. Each family was to sacrifice a lamb without blemish, to anoint their door posts and the lintels of their houses with its blood, and to feast upon the remainder. The sacrifice was over, the feast concluded, when that dreadful event took place, which it would be presumptuous profanation to relate, except in the words of the Hebrew annalist. 'And it came to pass, that at midnight the Lord smote all the first born in the land of Egypt, from the first born of Pharaoh, that sat on the throne, unto the first born of the captive that was in the dungeon, and all the first born of the cattle. And Pharaoh rose up in the night, he and all his servants, and all the Egyptians; and there was a great cry in Egypt, for there was not a house where there was not one dead.' The horrors of this night may be better conceived, when we call to mind that the Egyptians were noted for the wild and frantic wailings with which they lamented their dead. Screaming women rush about with dishevelled hair, troops of people assemble in tumultuous commiseration around the house, where a single corpse is laid out — and now every house and every family had its victim. Hebrew tradition has increased the horror of the calamity, asserting that the temples were shaken, the idols overthrown, the sacred animals, chosen as the first born, involved in the universal destruction. While every household of Egypt was occupied in its share of the general calamity, the people of Israel, probably drawn together during the suspension of all labor, caused by the former calamities, or assembled in Goshen to celebrate the new national festival already organized by a sort of discipline among the separate tribes; with all their flocks and herds, with sufficient provisions for an immediate supply, and with the booty they had extorted from their masters, stood prepared as one man for the signal of departure. During the night the permission, or rather entreaty, that they would instantly evacuate the country, arrived, yet no one stirred before the morning, perhaps apprehensive lest the slaughter should be attributed to them, or in religious fear of encountering the angel of destruction. The Egyptians became only anxious to accelerate their departure, and thus the Hebrew people set forth to seek a land of freedom, bearing with them the bones of their great ancestor Joseph."

Thus were the Jews organized, and fairly committed before the world as the chosen people, and submitted to that long train of change and discipline, by which they were fitted to be the vehicle for communicating the truth of God, to the nations of the modern civilized world.

Hence their long sojourn in the wilderness, their reception of the law from Sinai, their final planting in Canaan, and the peculiar institutions, rites, and usages by which they were distinguished from all the world besides. The whole was intended to extinguish idolatry, and introduce both among Jews and Gentiles the reign of God.

It is on this ground we may justify the command to exterminate the Canaanites, inveterate and even bestial idolaters, indulging as they did in the grossest sensuality, and making their children pass through the fire to Moloch. It was absolutely necessary to the preservation among the Jews of any thing like purity of character, or spirituality of worship. Nothing, indeed, but a special divine injunction could legalize the procedure; but this given, it was found the strongest protest against idolatry, and the most effectual means of preserving the national virtue. Had it been fully carried out, the Jews would have remained in their own land, a beacon light to the surrounding nations. That many of the Canaanites were left in the country, and permitted to form alliances with Hebrew families, and finally, through the influence of Jeroboam and others, "who made Israel to sin," to introduce their pagan rites among the Jews, is a fact well known. It is also the only one which accounts for their final apostasy, from the fatal consequences of which they were saved only by foreign exile. Their long captivity under the kings of

Chaldea and Persia, brought out more distinctly the national character, and finally saved them from idolatry.

Being separated at first, as was meet, from all the nations of the earth, by a severe, and what some have deemed a barbarous discipline, they were subsequently, by a series of the most singular dispersions, such as no other nation has ever experienced without extinction — war, migration and commerce, intestine divisions and external calamities — scattered over the world in Assyria, Persia, Greece, and Rome, in Egypt and the parts about Libya and Cyrene. They were very numerous in Babylon, where they long remained, first through captivity, and then through choice, and in that and many of the adjacent countries, became the teachers of their conquerors. They had synagogues in all the principal cities of Asia Minor, in Persia, and even in India. Temple worship was performed in Alexandria, and thousands, both of Jews and Gentiles, in Egypt, read in their own vernacular, the translation of the Old Testament, called the Septuagint. Many Jews lived in Arabia, and so spread their Messianic hopes among the tribes of the wilderness, as well as among the more cultivated communities of the ancient world. Other nations passed away; but they remained, partly among the heathen, partly in their own land; their views the same, their hopes the same. They had gained numerous proselytes in heathen lands about the time which preceded the advent of Christ. Hence the universal expectation of this event, cherished through the Oriental world. Hence, especially, the existence of this hope among the sages of Babylon, or Arabia, according to some, and its final realization by the Magi, who came to Jerusalem to worship the new-born King.*

* See Appendix, Note C.

CHAPTER VI.

THE CENTRAL RACE.—PRELUDES AND PREPARATIONS.

THAT the Hebrews, as "a peculiar people," possessed the character and performed the functions ascribed to them in the preceding chapter, can admit of no reasonable doubt; for the fact stands before us, account for it as we may, that ancient history, in its higher relations, revolved around them, and finally converged at Jerusalem in the cross of Christ.

The most inveterate sceptic, at all familiar with the annals of the past, must allow that one of the great purposes, served by this old Hebrew stock, was the preparation of the world for the Messiah, and his actual advent, in the fulness of the times, from the very bosom of the race that rejected him as their king. Strange that they should reject him, and yet give him to the world. Yet such is the actual fact. So that they and all other nations have been "as clay in the hands of the potter," for the production of this sublime result. Let the rationale of the thing be as it may in the view of speculative minds, the hand of God is visible in the whole history of the Jews, and of the neighboring nations, who actually do homage to this politically insignificant race; the consequence of which is not only a Messiah, but a pure and perfect religion, a new era in history, a new power in the heart of society, a new life in the soul of man. Great is Rome, on account of her colossal power, complete organization, martial energy, and legal force. Great also is Greece, greater even than Rome, from the breadth and grandeur of her philosophic thought, and, above all, from the exquisite beauty of her poetry and art. The power of law, and the grace of form, are represented by these, the most highly cultivated of all the ancient nations; but all this, as even the merest tyro knows, has been drawn into the Christian civilization. Blending with the idea of the divine, and the hope of a glorious immortality, and especially the spirit of universal charity, the purest product of faith, all that is really valuable in ancient civilization has been perpetuated through Christ, and not only so, but sublimed to higher use. Law now is recognized as having its seat in the bosom of God, and beauty shines upon us, radiant and immortal, from the face of Jesus. Both are discovered to us as eternal powers.

The character and position, then, of the Hebrew race, are to be estimated with especial reference to Christ, and the amazing influence thence exerted in the history of mankind. It is obvious, even to the most superficial view, that the elementary forces of modern society are derived from this peculiar nation. Scattered and peeled as they have generally been, and as they still, to some extent, are; often dispersed and trampled upon by the nations, and, indeed, with many obvious defects of character, which their own writers freely acknowledge, they have done a work for the world, the stupendous consequences of which can be estimated only at the close of time. The old forms of religion in the East are dead or dying. All their civilizations are undermined, and tottering to their fall. Not one of the pagan nations is making the slightest progress. To such progress idolatry and polygamy, the power of caste and the power of superstition, oppose effectual barriers. All are stationary, or absolutely dying out. The religion of the crescent, with some elements of power, but more of weakness, has long since reached its culmination. Its rapid decline is obvious to the world. All Mohammedan communities are suffering from sterility and weakness. A vigorous blow from without would dash them to pieces. Judaism, shorn of its early strength, and standing simply as the *nominis umbra*, the shadow of a reality, which has passed into Christianity, is ready to vanish away. Christianity and the Christian form of civilization, yet imperfectly evolved, alone are strong and progressive. Every where they penetrate with their new views, new aspirations, and activities. Under their influence, industry and the arts, science and social life prosper. Especially is this the case in those nations and communities which have formed the clearest and loftiest conceptions of Christianity, as a living, practical power. God is in them, because Christ is in them. And where God is, there charity, freedom, and activity abound.

Now to whom, under God, do we owe all this, but to that old Hebrew stock, or, at least, *that portion of it* who are "the true Israelites, to whom pertaineth the adoption, the glory, and the covenants, and the giving of the law, and the services of God, and the promises; whose are the fathers, and of whom, as concerning the flesh, Christ came, who is over all, God blessed forever?" (Rom. ix. 45.) And even if, by their rejection of Christ, the modern Jews, as a nation, are "cast away," have they not become, on this very account, as St. Paul shows, "the riches of the world?" *

If, then, among the nations at large, we find a general preparation for Christ; if in this respect Jesus, as "God manifest in the flesh," is proved to be the centre of a new spiritual sphere,

* In the eleventh chapter of his Epistle to the Romans.

and "the Desire of all nations," we shall find among the Hebrews a special preparation, nay, more actual "preludings," as one of the English divines has called them, of his advent and incarnation.* In the sphere of matter, shadows follow realities; in that of religion, they go before them.

Hence the various theophanies, or divine manifestations in human form, granted to the patriarchs, the prophets, and the Jewish people generally, recognized in the New Testament as appearances of the divine Word, or the Messiah. The Jews had the same idea of God, which has approved itself to the profoundest speculative intellects, — Plato, Philo, Anselm, Bacon, Leibnitz, Newton, Kant, Schelling, and Cousin, — namely, that the absolute, invisible Jehovah, who is above all things, and yet comprehends all things, can never adequately reveal himself to the finite intellect. All passing into the finite, on his part, must be by limitation. At least, it must so appear to our faculties. To us, then, God cannot be known in himself, that is, in his infinite or absolute perfection. He must appear in another self, the same, and yet not the same, that is, in some divine Logos, Son, or Messiah, who, as a definite personality, may reveal himself to us in an august, but limited and shaded form.

* Bishop Bull.

Hence the more eminent Hebrew writers, and among these the apostles John and Paul, ascribe the creation of the world to Christ, "by whom are all things," and "for whom are all things," and "in whom all things consist." When God creates, he goes forth, so to speak, into space and time; but this being impossible for an infinite Essence, he must go forth as a *Word* or *Image* of himself, in which sense only, can God be regarded as a conceivable personality. So that the Hebrew notion upon the subject is founded in the very nature of things, and commends itself to every thoughtful mind. It is only thus that God can discover himself to us, only thus that he can enter into personal relations with his creatures. "In the beginning," then, "was the Word, and the Word was with God, and the Word was God." That is, the Word is the manifested Deity, whether embodied in the outward universe, or incarnated in the person of Jesus Christ. This is that Voice, or Word of God, that appeared to our first parents in the garden of Eden; that discovered himself to Enoch, walking with him as a friend; that revealed himself to Abraham, Isaac, and Jacob, as their portion, being familiarly known as "the God of Abraham, of Isaac, and of Jacob," appearing to them as a divine or angelic man, often conversing with them, or performing on their behalf acts of benignity and help. This was the Angel-God adored by Moses in the bush, who discovered himself to the prophet as the "I am that I am," that is, the manifested form of the absolute and eternal ONE, in whom all being is centred, and from whom all life forever flows. God in Essence is invisible, and even inconceivable, as Moses well knew; for he never lost sight of his absolute spirituality; Him, therefore, he could never behold "face to face;" but his Image, or Voice, could be made manifest and conceivable to his finite reason. This imaged or embodied Essence, then, is the God who spoke to Moses, "face to face," as one man speaks to another, by visible or audible signs, and who, when the prophet stood in the cleft of the rock, made his glory pass before him, declaring himself to be "the Lord, the Lord God, merciful and gracious," whose "face," that is, whose direct and essential glory could not be seen, but whose "back parts," more properly, whose *train*, that is, the subdued and shadowed reflection of his ineffable brightness, like the train of burnished clouds which follow the sun, sinking beneath the horizon, could alone be made visible to mortal eyes. This was "the Angel of his Presence," or simply the *Divine Presence*, the Angel of the Covenant, in whom was "the name," or *nature* of God, and who went before the Israelites in their journeyings through the wilderness; a fact distinctly recognized in the dying address of St. Stephen, as well as in the language of the Pentateuch.* This, too, was "the Captain of the Lord's host," worshipped by Joshua, and "the angel," or rather "the Lord," who appeared to Manoah and his wife, and "did wondrously" with the sacrifice on the rock. This, in fact, is that "Lord of hosts," who appeared to the prophets, sometimes in the temple, sometimes in the wilderness, and sometimes in their own humble dwellings, from whom they received their commissions, and whose high behests they were ever willing to perform. "In the year that king Uzziah died," writes Isaiah, with solemn and thrilling words, "I saw also the Lord sitting on a throne, high and lifted up, and his *train* filled the temple. Above it stood the seraphims: each one had six wings; with twain he covered his feet, and with twain he did fly. And one cried unto another, and said, Holy, holy, holy is the Lord of hosts, the whole earth is full of his glory. And the posts of the door moved at the voice of him that cried, and the house was filled with smoke. Then said I, Woe is me! for I am undone; because I am a man of unclean lips, and I dwell among a peo-

* Compare Exodus xxiii. 20–22; xxxiii. 14, 15, with Acts of the Apostles vii. 38, 39, and 1 Cor. x. 41; as also v. 9.

ple of unclean lips; for mine eyes have seen the King, the Lord of hosts." * In a word, this was the manifested Divinity, who, in shadowy form, discovered himself to the chosen people, and who finally, in actual human shape, became incarnate as the Son of God, the Savior of the world. Hence the peculiar phraseology of the Psalms, in which this great truth is frequently recognized: "The Lord said unto my Lord;" in the Hebrew, "Jehovah said to my Jehovah, Sit thou on my right hand, till I make thine enemies thy footstool;" a passage applied to himself by Jesus Christ, who, when the Pharisees had admitted that the Messiah was the Son of David, put to them this pertinent question: "How, then, doth David call him Lord, [Jehovah, as in the Hebrew,] saying, The Lord said unto my Lord," &c.? †

Indeed, the great truth was well understood by the ancient Hebrew believers, and recognized in their whole Talmudic literature, that the Messiah, who should spring from the family of David, and from the tribe of Judah, was to be at once *David's Son and David's Lord.* "Rabbi," was the devout confession of a true Israelite, when he discovered

* Isaiah vi. 1-5. Compare St. John xii. 31. "These things said Esaias when he saw his glory."

† Matt. xxii. 42-46.

the Messiah, "thou art the Son of God; thou art the King of Israel!" *

The fact, then, is established, that it was among this strange people that the true idea of God, manifested as a distinct personality, through the divine Word, was cherished and perpetuated, and that religion, in its severe grandeur, received its highest development in ancient times. When Pompey entered the Holy of Holies, in the temple of Jerusalem, he was astonished to find no image there, such as all other nations worshipped. But the Hebrews were a Heaven-instructed race, who recognized the eternal Jehovah as an infinite and ineffable Essence, revealed to them only "in part," and thence longed for that more perfect manifestation of his glory, in the coming Messiah.

Thus it is seen, that the dispensation of Moses, in comparison with the higher form of religion under Christ, is but the raw spring, to the refulgent summer, or the crude and somewhat unsightly root, to the resplendent flower. Nor is this unnatural. For it is ever God's method, both in nature and in society, to discover himself, and accomplish his designs, by gradual steps and processes. The first, indeed, is as vital as the rest, but, in comparison, it seems narrow and defective. For, in the dark root lies the stem, in

* The various theophanies of the Old Testament are given, in their order, in the first volume of Hengstenberg's Christology.

the stem the leaf and bud, and in the bud the blushing rose. Cold winter, sterile as it may seem, carries in its bosom the palpitating spring, the spring the radiant summer and abundant autumn. The child, too, with its crude simplicity, is "father to the man;" while the weak and ill-formed society, governed, perhaps, as a patriarchate or a nomadic tribe, is parent to the free and prosperous commonwealth. We are not, then, to judge of Judaism by its unsightly root, or its rough and prickly rind; not by the accidental circumstances with which it was environed, or the stormy changes through which it passed, and by which it was developed; not by the faults of its early members, or the crimes of those who succeeded them; above all, we are not to judge of it by the obvious imperfections in legislation and social life, for a season permitted, or rather overlooked, by Jehovah, in order to be finally corrected or entirely extinguished; but by its interior spirit, its elemental powers, its grand spiritual truths — God and the soul, the union of the human and divine, and the final marriage of heaven and earth by the mediation of a divine Messiah — in a word, by the glorious flower evolved through spiritual forces from its bosom, expanding in the fair sunlight, and filling the whole earth with its heavenly aroma.

Some persons, poorly informed upon the subject, or occupied with sceptical prepossessions, have represented the God of the Jews as narrow and local, like the god of the hills, or the god of the vales, of whom the Canaanites dreamed.* It is true, the Jewish conception of God, at times, may have caught some such taint; but, in the Scriptures, the God of Israel is represented ever as supreme over all worlds and all nations; the All-mighty, the All-holy, the All-merciful, the one, living, and true God, who created and who sustains the heavens and the earth; the *I am that I am;* as if all being, boundless and everlasting, belonged to him; the King of kings and Lord of lords, "gracious and long-suffering, slow to wrath, forgiving iniquity, transgression, and sin." Thus was he revealed to Moses, and thus to all the prophets. Thus is he represented in the Psalms, those sublime lyrics, from which poets, in all ages, have borrowed their loftiest images of Him, who is "above all, through all, and in all." †

So, also, it has been concluded that, in the Old Testament, the immortality of the soul is not

* Goethe, for example, in the first volume of his *Dichtung und Wahrheit.* It first appears, however, in Spinoza's *Tractatus Theo. Politicus.* Of course it figures largely in the works of Strauss, Parker, and Newman.

† See Gen. i. 1; Exod. xx. 8–12; xxxi. 17; Deut. iv. 23. Compare Gen. xiv. 18–20, xvii. 1–9, xviii. 16–25, xxxix. 9, l. 20; Exod. vi. 3; Deut. iv. 32–36; Deut. x. 14–18; Psalms ciii. and civ.; Isai. xl. 12–18, 25–31.

recognized; whereas that great truth is necessarily *involved* in the spirituality of God, and especially in the doctrine of his union and fellowship with man. Long after the patriarchs were dead, Jehovah speaks of himself to Moses as the God of Abraham, of Isaac, and of Jacob, whence our Savior deduced the doctrine of the spirituality and consequent immortality of man, or what he termed the doctrine of the *anastasis*, or resurrection state, that is, the spiritual existence of man subsequent to death, on which the fact of a literal resurrection must ultimately be based, saying, "God is not the God of the dead, but of the living." And not only our Savior, but all the ancient prophets, deduced from it the same great truth; so that the hope, not only of the dying, but of the living Jew, ever passed the precincts of mortality; while all the prophets sang triumphantly of a spiritual and everlasting kingdom beyond this world and time.* Long before our Savior appeared, the doctrine of the spirituality of the soul, and even of the resurrection of the dead, was strongly held by the great

* We admit that the immortality of the soul is not specifically taught by Moses. So far as this is concerned, Warburton is right in his main position. It does not follow from this, however, that it is not implied in the doctrine of the spirituality of God, and of the consequent spirituality of man, formed, according to Moses, in the image of God. It is taught plainly enough in other parts of the Old Testament. For the proof texts, see Jahn's Bib. Arch. p. 397.

body of the Jewish nation. Dimly and imperfectly realized, it is true, yet still known and believed; a circumstance which explains two facts: first, that the Jews, in our Savior's time, in their conversations with him, speak often of the resurrection, or resurrection state, (e. g., "in the resurrection whose shall she be?") and, secondly, that, in the flood of glory with which Christ invested the doctrine, and in the vivid realization which he gave it, by his own resurrection, and final ascension, or return to the spiritual sphere, he is justly said to have "brought life and immortality to light."

As a people, whatever their faults and aberrations, the old Hebrews lived under the government of the one eternal God, "the God of the whole earth," a practical theocracy, or rather divine commonwealth, and longed for the coming of the Messiah. Amid all their corruptions and dispersions, this was the polar star of their history, their cloud by day and pillar of fire by night. Among the hills of Canaan; on the banks of the sacred Nile; in the beautiful Damascus; by the ancient Euphrates, where they hung their harps on the willows; in Antioch and Jerusalem; in Babylon and Alexandria; in Corinth, and in Rome; wherever, indeed, they were scattered in later years, this was the "consolation of Israel." Never did this heaven-inspired hope forsake them. In the strange vicissitudes of their history, and even in their deepest debasement, cured forever of their idolatrous tendencies, severed completely by fire and sword, by famine and privation, by spiritual discipline and providential dealing, from the corrupted mass of heathenism then enveloping the globe, and thus preserved, as the ark of truth and hope amid the sullen waves, they never lost the idea of one supreme Jehovah, or the hope of the coming Messiah, who should set up an everlasting empire of righteousness and peace.

That which in other nations was dimly and imperfectly apprehended, associated with error and idolatry, or taught only to the select few as an esoteric doctrine, or a mere philosophical speculation, was the common heritage of this singular people, obviously under the inspiration and guidance of the Almighty.

It is clear, moreover, that neither the doctrine of God, nor of the immortality of the soul, nor of the union of the human and the divine, and thence of the reunion and restoration of mankind to their common Father, sprang spontaneously from the genius of the Hebrew people. These truths were communicated to them from a higher source, nay, drilled into them by long and peculiar discipline. The Jews were not philosophers. They knew nothing of metaphysical speculation. The idea had never dawned upon their minds, till the time of Philo, and scarcely then. Neither were they given to historical research, or curious learning. What they knew, they knew only as a tradition, or an inspiration. They could give no account of it, except that it came from heaven. This is strikingly exemplified in their views of the perfect spirituality of God, notwithstanding their acknowledged anthropomorphism, and constant proclivity to idolatry, as also in reference to the immortality of the soul, in which, all admit, the later Jews thoroughly believed. Indeed, these great truths are in absolute contrast with their singular narrowness, bigotry, and fickleness, as a nation. But God was their King, and disciplined them into these high and immortal beliefs. At first trained as rude children, under a theocratic government, saying little of the far distant and invisible future, yet clearly holding it in reserve, they were subjected to immediate reward and punishment. Quick, decisive, palpable, it came upon them in waving harvests and joyful prosperity, or in blighted crops and sweeping death. Obedience was the uniform rule, the clear and infallible test. The doctrine of immortality was safe enough under such a regimen.

The grand defect of all other extant religious systems lay in their idolatrous and licentious spirit. God, or, if *he* was forgotten, the gods were materialized and degraded. Faith became fear, worship superstition, happiness pleasure, if not absolute lust.* Philosophy, too, even when it reached the idea of the great First Cause, reached it as a speculation which could not be taught to the people. If God was supposed to discover himself in the flesh, it was an incarnation, not of purity and love, but of simple power, or human wisdom; nay, more, of brutal passion. Polytheism clung to the systems of the best thinkers, Athanagoras, Socrates, Plato, Plutarch. Even while admitting the existence of a Supreme Being, it was only as the source or creator of gods, demons, and men.† Sin was not understood, and the immortality of the soul, sometimes taught, but as often doubted, as Cicero, in *De Natura Deorum*, over and over again informs us, was regarded simply as the onward process in its eternal transmigration. Redemption was longed for, but never thoroughly understood, never truly realized. Sin was felt as a horrible discord, and a desire was cherished, by a few, for that divine life, that pure

* Of all the gods of Greece and Rome, none were adored more sedulously than Venus. Lust was sanctioned by deification. The temples, in later times, were scenes of great impurity.

† Plato declares that "no change" ought to be made in "any established religion," and he "who thinks of it must have lost his senses." — *De Legibus*, v. Socrates gave it as a maxim, that every one ought to follow the religion of his country.—Xenophon's *Memorabilia*, lib. i. When charged with denying the gods adored by the public, he defended himself from it as from a crime. — *Apologia*, in Plato.

and peaceful condition of the soul, which Plato describes as the deepest and most beautiful melody;* but if some attained it, as charity may hope, alas! the great mass of the heathen did not even know what it was.

Blood flowed from innumerable pagan altars, but it was a blind homage to the gods, or a sort of dumb, instinctive confession of guilt, not a reasonable and acceptable service, which exerted upon the heart any high moral influence.

But among the pious Hebrews, with no philosophy, no literature, no arts, there existed a profound idea of the spirituality, eternity, justice, and compassion of God; a longing for a true revelation of him in the coming Messiah, who should "restore all things;" a definite conception of sin, as a wrong against God and man; and a clear idea of redemption, through penitence and faith. By their sacrifices and ablutions, they confessed their guilt, acknowledged the great fact that life was forfeited by sin, and if restored, must be restored by another and higher life. Their symbolic ritual prefigured the one great sacrifice, Jesus Christ, "whose blood," in other words, whose life, given for the redemption of the world, "cleanseth from all sin." So they believed in God, in the soul, in immortality; believed these things as

* *De Legibus*, i. 3.

divine and authoritative truths, believed them as practical and eternal realities; and through Christ have given them to the world. Or rather, we ought to say, God, through them and the Messiah, who came from them, has given these truths to the world, for the enlightenment and salvation of all.

For it came to pass in process of time, that while retaining the great outlines of truth, permanently embodied in the Old Testament Scriptures, the Jews gradually lost the true spirit of their ancient faith. Their expected Messiah, described in the prophets as a spiritual Redeemer, came to be invested with temporal attributes, foreign to his nature and dispensation. He was still regarded as divine in his origin and resources, but this belief was carnalized, by the narrow conceptions and political longings of worldly hearts. Hence in the days of the Maccabees, and in the age just preceding the advent of Christ, they longed for the celestial and the divine, only that the terrene and sensual might be consummated and enthroned.

The sect of the Pharisees, derived from a word signifying purity or separation, which sprang into existence during the reign of the Asmonean kings, for the sake of maintaining the worship of God in its primitive integrity, grew proud and ambitious, and finally controlled the nation. It was only about sixty years before Christ that the brothers Hyrcanus and Aristobulus made war upon each other for the priesthood, to which was attached the royal dignity. This was the fatal moment when commenced the downfall of the Jewish nation. From that resulted the interference of Pompey in the affairs of Syria; and Judea fell under the control of the Romans. Through their influence the sovereignty of the land passed out of the hands of the native princes, and fell into those of Herod, a stranger and an Idumean. Under his powerful and cruel dominion every thing was changed. The temple indeed was rebuilt, with considerable splendor; but the principles and usages of Judaism were fatally marred. Restive and unhappy, hating the usurper, and longing for freedom, the nation was compelled to be the slave of Herod, while Herod himself was the slave of Rome.

It was then that the great body of the people, especially the Pharisees, longed, with deeper intensity than ever, for the coming of the Messiah; but it was a Messiah fierce and conquering, who might destroy their enemies, and crown them with earthly glory. Whence we conclude that it was only by a true incarnation, a divine and supernatural process, that Jehovah, through such a people, could bring salvation to the world. The morning must come from the bosom of night;

life itself must spring from the silence of the grave. In a word, God, as of old, must say, Let there be light! and the morning stars shall sing together, and all the sons of God shout for joy.*

* Those who desire further information on the topics embraced in the two preceding lectures are referred to Dean Prideaux, Connection of the Old and New Testament, though this work is liable to some slight critical abatements; Dr. W. Alexander's (Edinburgh, Scotland) Congregational Lectures on the same subject; Faber, G. S., Treatise on the Genius and Object of the Pat., the Levit., and the Christian Dispensations; J. P. Smith's Scripture Testimony to the Messiah; Hengstenberg's *Christologie;* Jahn's Hebrew Commonwealth; Jahn's Bib. Archæology; Knobel, Aug., *Prophetismus der Hebraer. Vollständig Dargestellt;* Bähr, K. Ch. W. F., *Symbolik des Mosaischen Cultus;* Barnes's Commentary on the Book of Job; Pareau on the Doctrine of the Immortality of the Soul, as taught in the Book of Job.

CHAPTER VII.

THE FULNESS OF TIME.

History is like a river, or like a number of confluent streams, proceeding from some high table land, or lofty mountain range, rushing through the plains beneath, now diverging, then again approaching, finally flowing together in some common channel, and by a single mouth or mouths falling into the sea. One great principle or law predominates over the whole. All tend one way, all find themselves together in the ocean. Thus, from some common origin in the depths of Asia, we find mankind diverging into various communities and peoples, long separated from each other, then mingled together, by means of war, commerce, literature, religion, and other causes, evermore tending in one direction, and passing on to some common destiny. The hand of God presides over the rushing millions, evolving grand and benignant purposes, preparing the world for new eras and revolutions, and above all for the peaceful and eternal reign of the Messiah. Thus history has two aspects, the one superficial and gloomy, like a sea vexed with storms, the other clear and calm, like the same sea in its profounder depths. It has two movements, the one temporary and tumultuous, setting in towards time, the other permanent and majestic, setting in towards eternity.

Hence we find the ancient nations brought together, revolutionized, thrown into new shapes and positions, or utterly extinguished in the process of human civilization. But amid all changes, there is an onward movement. Truth is preserved among men, and in the lapse of ages, discovered in greater beauty, comprehensiveness, and power. Religion, like a deeper life, having its sources in the infinite, advances to its goal, now apparently lost amid the heaving surges of human passion, then again reappearing with greater force, and evidently moving, with the progress of events, to some august consummation. So also the chosen people, with whom it is mainly deposited, are preserved and pushed forward, in connection with the truth, to the same final issue. Dynasties rise and fall with reference to this alone. It weaves itself, like a supernatural agency, which it really is, in all their affairs, and when these have served its purposes, it leaves them for a new, and perhaps wider career with others. Thus God used the old Assyrians to punish his people, and convey his truth into the remoter Oriental world; so that even in the courts of Nineveh and Babylon he had witnesses for the truth; he used the Persians to provide them a congenial home, to restore them to their native land, to rebuild the temple and reëstablish their ancient worship; he compelled Alexander of Macedon and his early successors, both in Syria and Egypt, to protect them; he permitted Antiochus Epiphanes, by bloody persecution, to try their faith and test their devotion; but he put "a hook in his nose," and said, "Thus far shalt thou come, and no farther;" finally, he brought the Romans to enslave them, yet, by this very means, to maintain, within certain limits, their national integrity, and above all to save them from the vengeance of the kings of Syria, who longed for their destruction. By these and similar means he not only preserved them in the land of Palestine, with their inspired books, sacred places, and Messianic hopes, but he scattered them also through the civilized world, in Rome, Greece, Egypt, Arabia, Syria, Babylon, and even India, into which places they carried their peculiar principles and expectations; so that great numbers of the heathen became their proselytes, and cherished, in form more or less perfect, their peculiar hopes.

How singularly, in its external aspects, not to speak of its interior forces, was the world prepared for the establishment and propagation of Christianity!

It was a time of transition and convergence, such as the nations had never before seen. The old dynasties were subdued, and Rome was every where dominant. The languages of the most intelligent and aggressive civilizations, the Grecian and the Roman, spread with the advance of their conquering armies. Greece herself had fallen into decay, but her language, from a great variety of causes, had become almost cosmopolitan. It was spoken not only in its old native haunts, but throughout Asia Minor, and in many parts of Syria, especially in all the great centres of commerce and power, Rome, Damascus, Babylon, Jerusalem, Cæsarea, Antioch, and Alexandria. Thus the nations were brought together. Thus the streams of history were converging to some central issue.

Indeed, that was a most peculiar and critical era, which closed, in some sense, the troubled drama of the ancient world, and prepared mankind for a new order of things.

The existing religions, and consequent civilizations, all of which, with a single exception, embodied the element of idolatry, and what is worse, of selfishness and lust, had fallen into a state of dotage. Their old fiery hearts ceased to beat. A strange torpor seized them all. Indeed, mankind, in consequence of their advancing intelligence, had outgrown their religions, while their morals were becoming more and more corrupt. The splendid visions of Grecian polytheism had long been tarnished. Olympus was deserted. Magnificent temples, beautiful poetry, exquisite statuary remained, but all earnest worship was lost. The whole was thoroughly penetrated by the spirit of doubt and lust. The stronger, but equally idolatrous faith of Rome gave signs of decay. Like the civil polity which it supported, it was tottering to its fall. Superstitions enough remained, but all profound and coherent faith, even in idolatry, was breaking to pieces, and vanishing away. The whole array of the priesthood began to be contemned, nay, what is more significant, began to contemn themselves. Philosophers, who despised the vulgar notions, often spoke with contempt of superstition; then again urged a more rational veneration of the popular divinities, but without the slightest success. The awe-struck imagination of the elder pagans, which prostrated itself in burning adoration before the starry host, the sacred fire, or the Olympian Jove, could nowhere be found. Sacrifices enough were offered, especially by the magistrates, but rather to appease the hunger of the populace than to attract the favor of the gods. Xenophon tells us that the common people regarded them only as a pleasant means of securing a good meal.* The festivals and ceremonies of religion were observed for amusement and pleasure. They did more to corrupt, than to preserve the morals of the people.

A new era, in fact, was opening upon the world; but what it was to be could scarcely be foretold, by reference to the existing state of things. For idolatry was replaced by scepticism, and scepticism resulted in anarchy and crime. Atheism, in its practical forms, was stealing into the halls of legislation, the cabinet of kings, and the closets of philosophers, and with it the most hideous crimes. "Darkness covered the earth, and gross darkness the people." Abominable vices, vices which we do not even name in this age of the world, polluted every pagan country, not as unfrequent and startling enormities, but as common every-day occurrences. Indeed, this taint always pervaded these countries, especially Greece and Egypt, and to some extent Rome; for even Plato and Cicero, in their pages, refer familiarly, and by way of illustration, to one of the most detestable of these vices. Free themselves from sensual indulgence, they speak of it, in such easy terms, as would indicate its extensive prevalence.† But now vices of this kind

* In his *Athen. Republica*, c. 2.

† See, in the *Phædrus*, the illustrations of love in its various forms. It is well known that both the Epicureans and Stoics allowed and

had increased to an amazing extent. Occasionally checked by civil penalties, as in the case of the Bacchanals at Rome, they broke out again with fresh energy. Every where, also, slavery, in a form vastly worse than any thing in modern times, pervaded the Roman empire, and entailed upon all concerned the most fatal vices. Life was cheap, chastity still cheaper; and a man, especially a patrician, might maim or murder his slaves with impunity. Amid much exterior refinement, the greatest brutality of manners prevailed. Justice was sacrificed, in the terrible struggle of contending politicians, and the republic, so long the boast and glory of Rome, ignominiously fell. The most astounding debaucheries were mingled with the most terrible cruelties.

Egypt, never distinguished for its morals, and Syria under wretched misgovernment, were sunk in venality and crime.* Greece was effeminate

defended *παιδεραστία*, as well as *incest*, reckoning these flagitious crimes among things (ἀδιάφορα,) *indifferent*. The classical reader will remember Virgil's *Corydon amabat Alexin*, as well as Horace's numerous allusions to the same thing. Plutarch tells us that even Solon practised this monstrous crime. Diogenes Laertius says the same of the Stoic Zeno.

* We learn from Rosellini, Wilkinson, Bunsen, and others, who have made Egyptian history a special study, that the Egyptians, while eminently skilled in many of the arts of life, were coarse and disgusting in their habits. Their very monuments furnish indisputable evidence of their sensuality and cruelty. Their feasts end in "bestial excesses," on the part of both sexes. Gentlemen are

and powerless, hungering, as of old, after pleasure, but without the redeeming force and elegance of former times. The great Roman heart, which swayed the world, grew gross and languid, under the dominion of cruelty and lust. The dream of heroic virtue and freedom had passed away. Despotism, unprincipled and capricious, ruled the nations. The morals even of those called sages, with few exceptions, were rank and bestial. The condition of the hungry masses, in the Roman empire, grew more and more intolerable. What may be termed the higher philosophy, not yet entirely abandoned by thoughtful men, here and there shone, like a vessel on fire, amid the fury and darkness of a tempestuous night. At the best, it never reached the masses; and hence the doctrine of God and of the immortality of the soul, which lingered in books, and in the belief of a few lofty souls, left like rocks amid the tide of corruption, exerted upon the community no conceivable influence. Nay, this higher philosophy, at the time of which we are speaking, was itself becoming sceptical and lewd. The reign of Epicureanism was all but complete. A few philosophical spirits, like Cicero in Rome, or Philo in Alexandria, admired Plato,

carried home in a state of insensibility, and even ladies give token of their preceding intemperance. All know how licentious was the worship of Isis.

and caught something of his generous spirit. Remains of the Chaldean Magi, descendants of those associated with Daniel, devoted themselves to devout contemplation. But the majority, even of thinkers, throughout the bounds of the civilized world, including Rome and Greece, portions of Asia Minor, Syria, and Egypt, were the followers of a sensual or sceptical materialism. The better portion were Academics, whose distinguishing feature, at this time, was a spirit of universal doubt. While rejecting the grosser materialism, and in some cases living a virtuous life, they held themselves aloof from all fixed opinions on the higher metaphysics.* The superior orders of society were distinguished only by an intenser corruption. Their motto was, "Let us eat and drink, for to-morrow we die." Even their females had often to be put to death secretly for their crimes. The old Lucretian chastity was lost. Once distinguished for their purity of manners, the gentler sex were corrupted by the coarse and sensual indulgences, which, with foreign religions, and abounding luxury, had

* We learn from Sallust, in *Catilina*, c. 57, p. 309, that Julius Cæsar made no scruple in denying before the people that man had any thing to hope or fear after death; and even Cato, the stoic philosopher, in this applauded his noble philosophical spirit. Cicero informs us (*De Inventione*, lib. i. c. 29,) that the majority of the philosophers of his day were considered the enemies of the gods and religion.

infected Rome. Divorce and consequent licentiousness of manners were excessively prevalent, especially among the higher classes. Cato the Censor made desperate, but vain efforts to restore the ancient simplicity of manners, and check the progress of national demoralization. The senate, once the pride of Rome, on account of its stern integrity, was tainted with crime. Rome, indeed, even in her palmiest days, was relentless and cruel. But the gladiatorial exhibitions, of which even delicate females were passionately fond, grew more and more bloody. Whole hecatombs of men were sacrificed, under the eyes of pleasure-loving crowds. The young patrician beauty, languishing on purple couches, "by a sign of her jewelled finger," condemned the poor gladiator to die, to amuse herself with the sight of his expiring agonies. The banquets of the wealthy were scenes of debauchery. As the luxurious Egyptians placed a real skeleton at their feasts, to whet the appetites of the guests, and deepen the pleasure of the passing hour, so the Greek and Roman epicures, on festive days, placed upon their tables, at their orgies, (fit emblem of intellectual and moral despair,) the skeleton of ivory or silver, as a memento of the rapidity of life, and the duty of "quick and unlimited enjoyment." So much was despair the fashion of the times, that even Stoicism, the only moral strength of this period, was much less an heroic struggle than a mournful resignation.*

The very poets, rising occasionally in the olden time to the character of prophets, laughed to scorn, not merely the mythologies of bygone times, but the doctrines of the existence of God, and the immortality of the soul. The sublimest of them all, Lucretius, born ninety-five years before Christ, was an atheist, and his spirit only represents the spirit of the age in which he lived,† Virgil has no moral character. Horace is gay and licentious. Lucian among the Greeks, and Persius and Juvenal among the Latins, somewhat later, joke and sneer, as, perhaps, was natural in their circumstances, at all things, sacred and profane. In some of these writers the reader will find the most detestable affections treated with much detail, as things of daily practice, both among the vulgar and the refined. The temples themselves were not free from pollution; from which circumstance Ovid takes occasion to advise those females who would preserve their honor not to visit such places. In the city of Rome, according to Valerius Maxi-

* For an account of the private manners of the Greeks and Romans see Bekker's *Charicles* and *Gallus*. See also *Pericles*, by one of the authors of Small Books on Great Subjects.

† The ancients intimate that Lucretius was somewhat insane, (they say from a love philter,) and that he wrote his work under this influence. He committed suicide in his forty-fourth year.

mus, there were seven thousand Bacchanals, among whose mysteries prostitution and murder found a prominent place. Opposed by the government, and partially suppressed, they were never wholly banished from the city. Crimes without a name continued to be enacted in their secret orgies. A very few moralists, chiefly Stoics, said fine things on the subject of virtue, but could offer no resistless motives to enforce it. The tide of popular corruption swept onward, in spite of their subtile theories and fine-spun imaginings. Their attempts at reform were spider webs to bind Leviathan, straws to stem the currents of the ocean. The later sophists and rhetoricians, a heartless and infidel race, controlled the popular will, and gave law to society. In a word, "the foundations were destroyed." Old things were passing away. Night and chaos were enveloping the moral world.

If any one should call this declamation, or incline to think our picture too deeply colored, let him read attentively the pages of Lucian and Juvenal, or let him visit, as we have done, the disintombed cities of Herculaneum and Pompeii, and especially the Bourbon Museum, at Naples, in which are preserved, for the private inspection of scientific gentlemen, some of the most secret ornaments, sculptures, and paintings, found both in private houses and in the temples of the gods, and he will be satisfied that our statements are literally correct. Indeed, persons not familiar with the subject have no idea of the extreme corruption of manners, which polluted the most polished of the ancient nations. The revolution effected by Christianity, in this respect, is immense. Imperfect as it still is, owing to partial development, the change is one of the most striking and benignant in the history of man.*

* The following, from a source not usually suspected of over-statement on such matters, will corroborate this: "While religious scepticism was thus in the ascendant, morality, public and private, had reached its lowest landmark. Those incitements to vice, of which our laws prohibit even the sale, were, as Juvenal assures us in a satire (Sat. ii., near the commencement) specially levelled against the sensualism of the period, publicly paraded in every street, and filled the infant mind with impressions that stifled the development of its moral nature. The only part of their mythology for which the people seemed to have any relish, was that which administered to the passions, so easily excited; and the only temples that could command a crowd were those of Flora and the Bona Dea. At the festivals of those deities, before the Roman day had sunk to its shortlived twilight, crowds, not only of courtesans, but of orderly matrons, might be seen wending their way to the shrines of these goddesses in the *Via Sacra*, not simply with unveiled breasts, or with bodies negligently exposed, but in an absolute state of nudity. In the spacious and magnificent baths which the prodigality of successive emperors had reared in the imperial city, both sexes were indulged, at the vile price of a farthing, in promiscuous bathing. In the crowded theatres, when the first scenes of the play had been acted, and the minds of the auditors were inflamed with obscene verses, a sea of voices usually called out, *Nudentur mimæ*, and the order was no sooner issued than obeyed. — *Valerius Maximus*, lib. ii. c. 5. Obscenities far more polluting than any to be seen in the worst penny theatre that attracts the dregs of our London population, were enacted in the Flavian amphitheatre for the amuse-

Externally, however, the condition of the nations, at the time of which we are speaking, was favorable to the establishment of a new system both of religion and civilization. The larger portion of the known world was occupied by a single empire, in whose bosom elements of change and dissolution were at work. From beyond the Pillars of Hercules to the Caspian Sea, sweeping through the forests of Germany on the one side, and the sands of the Libyan desert on the other, about a hundred and fifty millions of persons, of diversified climate and character, were consolidated into one vast commonwealth. Diverging from the city of Rome, which might be called the metropolis of the world, magnificent roads stretched in every direction, connecting, by social and commercial ties, distant and flourishing cities. The old separate kingdoms, most of them immobile and stationary, governed by caste, and opposed to progress, which once occupied this vast area, were broken up, and a political brotherhood was

ment of the emperor and the highest ranks of Rome; *and crimes at which we now shudder, as unnatural, cleave to the greatest names of that epoch.* Vice had attacked the *foyers* of society, and *families were expiring so fast that a premium was offered to the man who should transmit a legitimate offspring to posterity.* Human kind was gradually dying out, and if the process of dissolution had continued unchecked by the infusion of a purer blood and a chaster creed, the race must have become extinct." —*Martial and his Times. Westminster Review.*

established throughout the bounds of the civilized world. It was a colossal power, appearing to grasp and control the whole destiny of man. But it had long passed its meridian. The prevalent civilization, based upon idolatry, polygamy, and slavery, was about to find its issue. Internal, ever-augmenting corruption was gradually working its overthrow. In a word, the hand of God, through natural agencies, seemed to be preparing the way for some vast and glorious change, or for some deep and universal catastrophe.

The condition of the Jewish people, at this time, differed little from that of the neighboring nations, except in their hatred of idolatry, their contempt of all other people, and their hope of a conquering Messiah. The vital energy of their ancient faith had given place to formalism and superstition. For a hundred and fifty years before the birth of Christ, their Mishna, in which were embodied "the traditions of the elders," had been growing in their esteem.* By this they made void the law of God, now all but obsolete. Hence their division into sects, the Pharisees and the Sadducees, the one clinging to traditions, the other rejecting them. The Pharisees, however, were by far the most power-

* The *Mishna* was the title given to the collection of traditions made by Rabbi Judah Hakkadosh, about B. C. 150.

ful party in the state, both in religion and politics. Ambitious and intriguing, they controlled the popular will, and inflamed it with their bigotries. Hence they yielded reluctant obedience to the ruling monarch, Herod the Idumean, whose ambitious and selfish character is well known. The Sadducees, as much distinguished for their national pride and intolerance of foreigners, were equally disaffected to the government of Herod, and longed to be delivered from what they deemed a degrading servitude. The nation, therefore, was ripe for rebellion and political change.

In these circumstances, the religion of their fathers, yet revered as a form, had become cold and sterile, a mere engine of political strife. Long had the Shekinah departed from the temple. The voice of its oracles was dumb. More free from the tendency to idolatry than in ancient times, and preserved untarnished in the ancient books, Judaism had lost all regenerative force. The spirit of prophecy was extinct. No holy seers predicted the glories of the Messiah's reign, or denounced the judgments of God against the workers of iniquity. No Deborah sang under the palm tree, between Ramah and Bethel. No Ezekiel thundered between the porch and the altar. The word indeed remained; but it was a dead letter to the great body of the people.

The formalism of the Pharisee on the one hand, and the scepticism of the Sadducee on the other, paralyzed all pure and earnest feeling. The people, subjected to the galling oppression of a foreign yoke, were discontented and furious. Unheard-of atrocities, which easily account for the subsequent "murder of the innocents," no more strange or monstrous than some of his other crimes, had been perpetrated in the family of the elder Herod, whose days of mingled splendor and crime were about to close, in horror and blood.

In addition to this, infidel and pagan notions, introduced through the influence of the court, began to prevail in some portions of Judea, particularly in Cæsarea, the Roman capital of the country; while the mass of the people, especially in the larger cities, were intoxicated with a savage fanaticism. Hence the origin of the sect or clique, as it may be called, of the Herodians, who saw no harm in mingling the rites of heathenism with the pure ceremonial of their own worship, and whose cringing sycophancy and easy submission to a foreign yoke excited the disgust of their countrymen. Some holy hearts, here and there, in the temple and among the mountains, consecrated by the memories of the past, brooded over the prophecies, and longed for the reign of God upon the earth. The Essenes, the anchorites and mystics of the Jewish faith, were distinguished for their simplicity of manners; but they lived in seclusion, and took no part in public affairs. Separating themselves from their fellow-men as unclean, and making no attempt at the reformation of others, they shut themselves up, in the profound solitudes adjoining the shores of the Dead Sea. The same may be said of their brethren, the Therapeutæ, in Egypt, yet more distinguished for their mystic and ascetic habits.

But the great body of the people were ignorant and superstitious; and though free from idolatry, narrow and sensual in their feelings. They cherished, indeed, the hope of a Messiah, but so mingled with selfish and fanatical views, that it rather exasperated than soothed their passions.

There prevailed, also, at this period, even in the Roman world, a wide-spread expectation of some august revolution, to be achieved by the sudden appearance of a mighty and mysterious personage. This dim idea was floating about not only in Syria, but in Rome, in Egypt, and Babylon. So familiar had it become, that it attracted the attention of the Roman poets and philosophers. Virgil is supposed to refer to it. "Among many," writes Tacitus, "there was a persuasion that in the ancient books of the priesthood, it was written, that at that precise time the East should become mighty, and that the sovereigns of the world should issue from Judea." * "In the East," says Suetonius, "an ancient and consistent opinion prevailed, that it was fated there should issue at this time those who should obtain universal dominion." † This general expectation is to be traced, doubtless, to the predictions of the Hebrew prophets. Daniel's "weeks of years" were supposed to be on the point of expiring. The sceptre, in some sense, had "departed from Judah," and therefore the Shiloh, or the Peacemaker, was about to come. What he was to be, few indeed understood. The views of his character and mission were modified by the dispositions of those who cherished them. Josephus, a shrewd, selfish man, false to the hopes of his nation, false even to the principles of honor, subsequently pretended to recognize him in the person of the Emperor Vespasian! Some expected a mighty King, a half divine, half human conqueror; others, but a comparatively small number, a great Moral Reformer or Spiritual Redeemer; and fewer still, the Son of God, the Savior of the world. But the majority of the na-

* In the language of Tacitus, the *East* means *Syria*. — *History*, v. 13.

† Suetonius, Ves. p. 4.

tion looked only for a temporal deliverer, his footsteps tracked with blood, and his long reign of earthly power and splendor encircling the globe.

Hence the general state of the Jews, though favorable enough to political change, was quite unfavorable to the reception and acknowledgment of a spiritual Messiah, whose peaceful reign should be that only of righteousness and love. Carnal and besotted, they were more likely to crush than to honor the Son of God.

What mankind every where needed, was a divine transformation, a complete spiritual and interior revolution in the domain of religion and morals; a regeneration, in fact, of the heart and the life of individuals and families; and that consequent political transformation, on the basis of which, might spring up a new and more perfect form of civilization. But the idea had not even dawned upon the Grecian or the Roman mind, and though clearly predicted in the Old Testament Scriptures, was utterly lost sight of by the Jewish people.

Indeed, taking the world as a whole, it was a dark and godless era. The race, as if abandoned by Heaven, staggered like a crazy vessel amid the gathering storm, and seemed on the point of being forever ingulfed.

Yet there were watchers on the hills of Palestine, and far off, even in the depths of the Orient, wise and good men were longing for the coming of the Deliverer. Long years had they brooded over the prophecies, and like Simeon and Anna, hoped to see the Messiah before closing their eyes in death. But all was still in the heavens above. A deep and portentous gloom, unrelieved by a single star, brooded over the world.

CHAPTER VIII.

THE ADVENT.

We can easily imagine the sceptic, at the era referred to in the preceding chapter, pouring infinite scorn on the predictions of the Messiah's reign, saying, Where is the promise of his coming? for since the fathers fell asleep, all things continue as they were from the foundation of the world. The course of nature moves on as usual; the sun rises and sets, the stars circle in the heavens, spring, summer, and autumn come and go, by an unvarying law. Divine advents are no more. Miracles are a legend of the darker ages. The season of faith in the supernatural is passed. A religion other than instinct, or nature, is but the dream of sick-brained enthusiasm. Prayer is folly and presumption. The creation of the world as a work of time, the first Eden, the fall of man, the flood, the call of Abraham, the exode from Egypt, the pillar of cloud by day and of fire by night, the passage of the Red Sea, the giving of the law from Sinai, divine revelations through Moses and Isaiah, inspiration, miracles, and wonders, are simple myths, or traditionary legends, in which a few grains of truth are mingled and preserved in a huge mass of error. But the time for believing such things is gone by. This is the eighth century from the foundation of Rome. The age is too enlightened to be caught by fictions. And as for a new and special revelation, of a grander and purer character than has ever been dreamed of by saint or sage, and above all, the advent from the spirit world of a divine messenger, whose kingdom is to be coeval with time, and spread over the globe, reason must pronounce it the most absurd chimera.

Yet nature moved on as usual; and no sign or promise of the new order of things so long expected, and so much needed, was visible in the earth or sky. Mankind were eating and drinking, sinning and suffering, as usual. Millions were rushing after vanity, and the weary nations were sinking into deeper and still deeper night.

But as nature is often silent, intensely silent, before the bursting forth of some grand or fearful change, which is to affect, for weal or for woe, the destiny of thousands, and as such change is often like the sudden protrusion of a hand from the dark, or a flash of lightning at midnight, so now, the fulness of the times being come, Jesus was born into the world — in a humble town, in the hush of night — among strangers who cared nothing for the event — in a condition of lowliness and poverty peculiarly striking — and without any general and imposing demonstrations. And why? Simply because he was to be a spiritual Teacher, a divine Redeemer, whose "still small voice" of love and mercy was gently but irresistibly to penetrate the human heart, and transform it into the divine image.

Natural, for it was only a birth; supernatural, for it was the birth of the Divine among men. Natural, for he seemed to glide into the race, as a new star glides into the heavens; supernatural, for a higher form of gravitation in the spiritual sphere began to act upon society, fitted to change and modify it forever. Natural, for no laws were counteracted or suspended; supernatural, for a deeper and more comprehensive law controlled them all. Indeed, it may be said, that in the unity of a higher and more comprehensive law, the natural and supernatural are one — a fact of which the incarnation is a proof and illustration.

Little is recorded of this unostentatious but august event. It was proclaimed, as has been often said, not in the streets of Jerusalem, or the purlieus of the temple, but in the quiet scenes of the country; not to the Sanhedrim of the Jewish nation, nor to the priesthood in solemn conclave, but to a few pious shepherds, as they watched their flocks by night on the plains of Bethlehem.

In all this we discern much of divine wisdom.

God, in creating and blessing, is not so much in the "whirlwind and the storm," as in "the still small voice." His mightiest changes are achieved by invisible, and apparently trivial means. He works not at the surface, but at the centre; not by mechanism, but by spirit. He comes rather in the solitude and silence of night, like the dew beneath the stars, than in the glare and tumult of day. In this respect he reverses all the expectations of man. "Without observation," like his own reign of purity and love, he accomplishes the designs of his grace. Not with the might of kings, or the tread of armies, but with the quiet majesty, the still, but resistless force of supreme and all-pervading will. He taketh "the weak things of the world to confound the mighty, and things that are not to bring to nought things that are, that no flesh may glory in his presence." Evermore he magnifies purity and love over might and display.

Moreover, the incarnation of Jesus Christ was a veiling rather than a revealing of absolute power. Indeed, every embodiment or manifestation of God must possess this character. Properly speaking, the heaven of heavens cannot contain him; the entire visible creation, in magnitude, bears no conceivable relation to his infinity. "In all," he is yet "above all," transcendent and ineffable. Further, it was love, rather than absolute or physical might, which assumed the human form.* By a new and peculiar manifestation, "grace and truth" were to be discovered as the greatest powers in the universe. Enthroned by the death of the Son of God, they were to be proved resistless and eternal. It was meet, therefore, that in lowliness and poverty the birth of Christ should correspond with his death, the beginning with the end of his earthly career.

Indeed, we cannot judge correctly of the dignity or magnitude of any event, and especially of the glory of any divine manifestation, by its external aspects, or its immediate effects and accompaniments. Its spiritual relations and future results are the measure of its importance. If it link itself with the affections and destinies of unborn generations, turn the whole tide of human affairs, and pass on in ever-deepening and widening currents of influence, it proves itself worthy of the infinite mind. Men, it is true, from the narrowness and meagreness of their views, are more powerfully affected by brilliant and imposing demonstrations; it would seem natural to them, when the Divinity comes visibly to earth, that the heavens should bow, and the earth tremble to its centre. But how different

* We use the term *absolute* or *physical* here as equivalent to what is sometimes called *natural*, in distinction from moral, though both terms are imperfect and inadequate.

the reality, and, when duly considered, how much more affecting and beautiful!

"Thou wast born of woman; thou didst come,
O Holiest, to this world of sin and gloom,
Not in thy dread, omnipotent array;
And not by thunder strewed
Was thy tempestuous road,
Nor indignation burned before thee on thy way.
But thee a soft and naked child,
Thy mother undefiled,
In the rude manger laid to rest,
From off her virgin breast.

"The heavens were not commanded to prepare
A gorgeous canopy of golden air;
Nor stooped their lamps the enthronéd fires on high.
A single, silent star
Came wandering from afar,
Gliding unchecked and calm along the liquid sky;
The eastern sages leading on
As at a kingly throne,
To lay their odors sweet
Before thy infant feet." *

* Milman's Fall of Jerusalem. The intelligent reader will here call to mind the words of Milton, in the grandest of lyric strains: —

"But peaceful was the night,
Wherein the Prince of Light
His reign of peace upon the earth began;
The winds, with wonder whist,
Smoothly the waters kissed,
Whispering new joys to the mild ocean;
Who now hath quite forgot to rave,
While birds of calm sit brooding on the charméd wave.
The stars with deep amaze," &c.

Milman has given, in beautiful form, the general aspect of the case; but we are not to forget what, perhaps, he has overlooked, that

There was a profound spiritual significance in the fact that Jesus should be "born of a virgin," for then would it be seen that he was "the Holy One of God." The unstained innocence of the mother, her serene beauty and gentleness of character, and the entire separation of Christ, by means of his supernatural birth, from the corrupted mass of humanity, would form a peculiar attraction for all pure minds. Then, also, would it be understood by the world that he "came forth from God," the immaculate incarnation of righteousness and love. It was meet, also, that the advent of the Redeemer should be a sacred mystery, around which the affections of his followers should linger with delight and awe. This feeling, indeed, has been exaggerated and vitiated both by the Greek and Roman churches; but it is a natural feeling, and not only so, but productive of the best results.

For how could Christ come into the world as one of the race, except by a birth? and how could he be recognized as the Divine, except by an immaculate birth? "That holy thing that shall be born of thee shall be called the Son of God." On this account, there is something inexpressibly touching in the thought expressed

"suddenly there was with the angel *a multitude*," perhaps more than "a single choir" of *the heavenly host*, praising God and saying, "Glory to God in the highest, on earth peace and good will to men."

by Wordsworth, that in the virgin mother were "blended and reconciled" those singular but beautiful contrasts —

> "Of mother's love and maiden purity,
> Of high and low, celestial with terrene." *

Rude minds have wondered that "the Highest" was born of woman, especially that the Godhead was enshrined in the person of a child. But more thoughtful and spiritual minds have discerned, in this very thing, a meaning and design which awaken their profoundest awe. They cannot allow that mechanical greatness, or material expansiŏn, though of suns and systems innumerable, have aught in them akin to the nature of God, or that adventitious circumstances, however grand and imposing, can add any thing to his infinite excellence! Indeed, they look beyond all the depths of the starry heavens, and all the immensities of the visible creation, to find his indivisible essence, and his boundless majesty. Not physical grandeur, or mechanic force, but spirituality, purity, love, infinite and unutterable,

* The nations could never imagine how the Divine should come into the world, and live itself into our historic existence, except by an incarnation, and that too from a pure virgin. Budh, Hercules, Zoroaster, Confucius, and others, considered divine men, were supposed to have virgin mothers, — a fiction obvious enough, but a natural one, so natural that the fact, or reality, when it does come, corresponds to it.

constitute their idea of his glory. Hence they can adore the indwelling and manifestation of that glory, as well in the person of "the holy Child," as in all the magnificence of the universe! God is a Spirit! God is love! And since man, in his unstained innocence, was made in the image of God, no fitter temple of the Deity can be found than that of a sinless Messiah.

The true tabernacle of God is not so much nature as man; not indeed man fallen, but man redeemed, or rather *man the Redeemer*. "Man," says the celebrated Jean Paul Richter, in one of his transcendent flights, where he touches on the very borders of the infinite, "man is the Isis-veil of the Divinity." "Ye are the temple of the living God," is the clearer, more appropriate language of St. Paul. So that we may well affirm that God is closer to man than most of us imagine.

It will be admitted, we think, by all, that man is greater than the whole material or visible universe; and yet God is in the latter, by a special presence and manifestation. Here we behold his glory. How much more intimately present must God be in man, who is matter and spirit at once, and thus the fittest vehicle for the divine manifestation. "All religion," according to an erratic but vigorous thinker, "stands upon this; not paganism only, but far higher and truer religions, all religions hitherto known." Hence he says, "Hero-worship, heartfelt, burning, boundless, for a noblest, godlike form of Man, is it not the germ of Christianity itself?" To which he adds, "The greatest of all heroes is one whom I do not name here." *

This testimony is important; it is an echo of the deepest truth. The apparent pantheism upon which it is founded, of course, we regret; but pantheism, in its better sense, that is, the idea of God *in all things*, as their Creator and Lord, and especially in man, as his highest and holiest temple, we maintain, on the plainest scriptural authority. God is "all and in all;" not, however, as a simple, all-comprehending force, or law, but as a personal agent, "in whom are all things, and by whom are all things." So that the great fact of Christianity, the incarnation of God in the man Jesus Christ, is a truth the most rational and conceivable. Even those who doubt historical Christianity — Hegel, Strauss, Carlyle, Parker — confess the fitness of Christ, simply as a form, for the indwelling and manifestation of the Deity. Indeed, an ideal or perfect man, from Plato downwards, has been the fascination of the world, the desire of all nations; especially a godlike man, a son of God, a deliverer, in whom should be found blended all per-

* Hero-Worship, p. 13.

fection with all gentleness and love; nay, more, a divine man, a true Prometheus or Apollo, in whose hands nature and his fellows should be pliant as clay in the hands of the potter, has been the longing of poetry and religion, even among the heathen. This, in a still higher form, was the polar star of the Jewish mind. Moses and Isaiah, as well as the Talmudists, alike magnify this mightier Prophet—this super-angelic Logos, or Revealer—this divine Metraton, or Reconciler of God and man. It seems to us, indeed, that every heart, beating true to nature and its higher instincts, must long for it. Dissatisfied with all common men; dissatisfied with all heroes, even with the kingly spirits of history,—for in beauty, worth, and power we can always conceive something beyond them;—nay, more, dissatisfied with angels, whether the angels of the Bible, of Dante, or of Milton, august and lovely as they seem, we are still yearning for the perfection of man; that is, man sinless, infinite, immortal. It seems an anomaly, an impossibility, a contradiction in terms; but we are made for it, as we are made for God and glory.

Some of those who reject the supernatural element in the Bible, and look upon the gospel as a figment or myth of a darker age, sometimes betray the instinct to which we refer; and, while rejecting a divine Redeemer, describe just such a being as "the want" of the world. Emerson, for example, who, in his transcendental gyrations, has long ago left Christianity behind him, thus describes what he calls "the old want:" "There is no man; there hath never been. The intellect still asks that *a man* may be born. The flame of life flickers feebly in human breasts. We demand of men a richness and universality we do not find. Great men do not content us. It is their solitude, not their force, that makes them conspicuous. There is somewhat indigent and tedious about them. They are poorly tied to one thought. If they are prophets, they are egotists; if polite and various, they are shallow. How tardily men arrive at any result? . . . Thus a man lasts but a very little while, for his monomania" [that he has the secret of the universe] "lasts but a very little while. It is so with every book and person; and yet — and yet — we do not take up a new book, or meet a new man, without a pulse-beat of expectation. And this invincible hope of a more adequate interpreter, is the sure prediction of his advent. . . . .

"We no longer hold it [nature] by the hand; we have lost our *miraculous* power; our arm is no more strong as the frost, nor our *will equivalent to* gravity and the elective attractions." *

* The Method of Nature. Addresses and Lectures, pp. 187–189.

What does this imaginative, half pagan poet or philosopher want? Turning away from Him whom he acknowledges, in one place, as "the true prophet of nature," who, with "open vision," looked upon "its secret," and called himself "divine," he yet longs for a perfect godlike man, under whose hands nature should be plastic as wax; whose movements should be miracles; whose powers should equal the elective and attractive forces; whose great heart, of such "richness and universality," should comprehend and control all other hearts.

Such a man we find in Jesus Christ, whose advent into the world, as a sinless child, we have briefly described. Beyond him nothing can be conceived, nothing can be desired.

Sensual and mechanical minds may doubt here; but pure and lofty spirits, who have caught only Platonic fire, well know what we mean.

The truth is, man is *from* God, as to his origin, and *to* God as to his end. We are apt to date him from his fall, and think of him only as severed from God and lost to perfection; but he dates from an era anterior to the fall. God is the fount of our being; so that in a close and peculiar sense, we are the divine offspring. Æschylus, the sublimest of the heathen poets, had slight glimpses of this truth. So had Euripides and others. Plato grasped it thoroughly, though exaggerating its import, and thence inferring, though by no means unnaturally, the preëxistence of souls. He shows, in language of surpassing beauty, that they came from God, and, though fallen into earthliness and sin, yet becoming "winged," that is, as we understand him, renouncing all sensual delight, and longing for the pure and perfect, they rise again into the bosom of God. He puts this refined speculation into the mouth of Socrates, conversing with a youthful friend, under the shadow of an agnus castus, beyond the city walls; whence we infer that it is not impossible that the idea was cherished by Socrates himself.*

Indeed, the idea of a divine paternity has been recognized, with more or less distinctness, by all lofty minds; nay, has been descried as from afar by the common heart of humanity. It runs through the whole Bible, and finds one of its most striking expositions in the address of St. Paul before the Athenian Areopagus. "God, that made the world, and all things therein, seeing that he is Lord of heaven and earth, dwelleth not in temples made with hands, neither is worshipped with men's hands, as though he needed any thing; seeing he giveth to all life, and breath, and all things, and hath made of one blood [nature?] all nations of men, for to dwell on all

* *Phædrus*, 25.

the face of the earth, and hath determined the times before appointed, and the bounds of their habitation, that they should seek the Lord, if haply they might feel after him, and find him, though he be not far from every one of us; for in him we live, and move, and have our being; as certain also of your own poets have said, *For we are also his offspring*."

Thus, then, from his origin, man bears the impress of Divinity. The image, indeed, like some beautiful statue, fallen into barbarous hands, may be defaced, but it is extant in all. For as God is a Spirit, so man, in his higher nature, is a spirit also; as God thinks and wills, so man thinks and wills; as God is the conscious, the holy, and ever blessed, so man is conscious, responsible, joyful, and, if "born from above," holy and blessed forevermore. In fine, as God lives, and loves, and acts, so man lives, and loves, and acts, as his image or echo on earth. Man dwells in God as the root of his being and well being. All the streams come from one fountain, all are filled with the same life. Take away God, and all the channels of human existence are dry and desolate. Hence, every where man "feels after God," longs, sometimes indeed blindly and madly, but still longs for the perfect, the boundless, and eternal. When pure and peaceful, filled with love and joy, he stands the fairest image of the Uncreated Beauty, like the great ocean mirroring, in some clear and placid hour, the everlasting heavens.

If God, then, should ever come to man, in other words, reveal himself to us in closer contact, and with a deeper and more tender significance than in all suns and stars, he would come in some godlike form of man, in some immaculate, yet earth-born Messiah, through whose eyes of love he might look upon us in pity, through whose voice of strange power and pathos he might speak to us, through whose unfathomable heart he might love us, and through whose inscrutable sufferings for sin he might expiate our guilt, and reconcile us to himself.

Moreover, man had run down to the lowest point, as we have seen, previous to the Christian Epiphany. The fall had produced its bitter fruits. Superstition and atheism had ripened, and all base passions, all personal and national lust and imbecility, were the result. A new beginning, a new and stronger life, was needed. Some divine power must be given: but how given, except in a living form, such as men could understand and feel, and to which, in spiritual bonds, they might be personally linked?

The help must come from above, that is clear; and yet seem to spring from the bosom of humanity: in other words, it must be human and divine, in order to inspire sympathy, confidence, and love, and thus impart a new and everlasting life to the race.

That is to say, stating the matter in such language as we possess, the divine Redeemer must be born into the world, born of a pure virgin, a holy, sainted spirit, born as the Son of God, grow up by natural steps, develop himself by a process akin to the workings of nature, or the manifestation of God, in the advancing spring, or the growing corn, till, matured and perfected, he should once more pass, by a common path, that is, death or dissolution, which is only final change and transition, into the invisible and immortal state.

Such an incarnation is by no means an unnatural or unfamiliar idea among men. Nay, it is one of the most natural and spontaneous. The Oriental world, with its grand, though bewildering conceptions, teems with incarnations, — exaggerations indeed, nay, caricatures,— but still hints, and, so to speak, shadows of the possible reality. The Grecian mind, in lower forms, conceived the divine, as born amid the hills and vales. Mythical, we grant, but not unnatural, not even irrational, except in the meagreness of the form, and, above all, in the crude superstition and debasing sensuality with which it was invested. The immeasurable superiority of the Christian incarnation is seen at a glance; for the former, at best, were mythical incarnations of beauty and power, sometimes of passion, carnal and evanescent; the latter is a real incarnation, a divine embodiment of purity and love. In Prometheus we see strength of will, in Apollo beauty and wisdom; but in Christ we see "all the fulness of the Godhead." The former were symbols and myths, the latter is "God manifest in the flesh."

But what do we mean by an incarnation? Not the limitation, or humanization, (forgive the word,) of an infinite Essence, for that is impossible; but the special presence, energy, or manifestation of that Essence, itself boundless and unutterable, in an exterior human form. It is thus that God reveals himself in all outward things, though here in Christ, by a special impersonation. Each spring, however, is but a "renewing," by means of a spiritual presence beneath the surface, "of the face of the earth." The poor Indian sees the Great Spirit in the thunder cloud; we ourselves devoutly acknowledge him as the light and life of all we see. The heavens and earth are his garment, according to the lyric poetry of the Hebrews, the outer costume in which he robes himself.* The doctrine of a presence in nature, belongs not merely to the-

* Psalm civ.

ology, but to science. And what is that idea of presence but the prelude, or intimation of a more specific advent, or presence among men? Why should not the Deity become visible before our eyes? Why should not the infinite Spirit, as well as the finite spirit, be capable of an embodiment? Certainly, with all our science and mechanism, our outward notions and carnal views, we cannot be averse to this; for as a matter of fact, the spiritual comes into this world only as a birth — the soul *is born* into the joys and sufferings of this material sphere, of this carnal and mortal life. Spirit is ever superior to matter — comes *to it*, not *from it*. It is a *cause*, not an effect; a power independent and immortal; an essential and vital force, created, indeed, but still essential and vital, which wills and acts, in and through the material organization. The sensual philosophers teach that it is not primary, but secondary, a mere product of mechanism, or organization, evolved, as some of them say, from the action of the body, like the electric or magnetic forces from a common battery, and so passes away with the organism which gave it birth. But this is to confound cause and effect and not only so, but it is to confound cause and occasion; for even the electrical or magnetic machine may simply supply the occasion or medium through which acts that all but spiritual force which we call electricity or magnetism. But the soul *is* a productive cause — a dweller in the body, controlling that body, and using it for its purposes, by the force of its original will. Besides, we are plainly taught in the word of God, that the spirit was *imparted* to the bodily organization, when formed and fitted for its dwelling-place, and that the spirit through that body communicates with the external world of forms. Spirit, then, is superior, not inferior or posterior to the body; and thence is a proper *incarnation.** Every man coming into the world, by birth, comes into it just as Jesus did; and the only difference between them is, that the one comes as a spirit finite and feeble, because created and dependent, the other as a spirit infinite and immortal, because uncreated and divine. Besides, that spirit of ours, made visible in human form, though dependent and limited, is vastly more than the body; it is, so to speak, of grander dimensions, of more stupendous powers. And yet, there it gleams through its narrow dwelling, there it loves and acts, grows and expands in its

* If any one prefers to say that the body is first created, or produced, and that then the soul is given to it by a divine act, be it so; the force of the argument remains the same. But the vital force and interior spirit one would think necessary to the very possibility of organization and growth. Our own opinion is, that though created by God, spirit is first, and that it is necessary to human existence.

fleshly tabernacle, from which, by and by, sublimated and glorified by the change which men call death, it will pass, once more, into the spiritual and immortal state.

Why, then, should it be thought a thing incredible that the Divinity should become incarnate, that the eternal Spirit should take up his dwelling, and perform his high work for humanity, in the limited, but fitting form of the man Jesus Christ? Nay, is not this the most natural, the most credible thing in the universe? What were a body without a soul? and what were Christ without the indwelling God? What, on the other hand, were the soul to us without the body; and what to us even the invisible God, without the manifestation of himself in the man Jesus Christ? We might have known him dimly and distantly, as the heathen know him, but never as we now know him, the Father, the Friend, the Redeemer of us all.

In the estimation of the sceptic and the worldling, the advent of Christ may seem a small event; nay, more, a thing impossible and incredible. "Yet it was the turning-point of the world's history," as Schelling, the greatest of the modern German philosophers, cheerfully avows. Then the "Day-star" from on high visited us. Then the "Sun of righteousness arose with healing in his wings." Then sprang to life a form of civilization, which was to penetrate the nations with an invisible but resistless force, and which, at the present time, as Jouffroy, one of the clearest and profoundest thinkers of the French eclectic school, has demonstrated, is the only thing active and diffusive in society, constituting, in fact, what Vinet terms the gravitation of the moral world.*

Thus the birth of Christ, insignificant in its seeming, was inexpressibly great in its reality. Apparently the advent of a simple child, it was the incarnation of the Godhead. A mere incident, in an obscure corner of the earth, which disturbed neither the course of nature nor the course of society, it was the origin of untold revolutions, the beginning of a new civilization and a new religion, of a new world and a new heaven. No wonder, then, that it was hymned by angels, as was the creation of the world at first, when the morning stars sung together, and all the sons of God shouted for joy. Not only on the plains of Bethlehem resounded the glad acclaim, but in the realms of glory. For as soon as the news was announced to the shepherds, "suddenly there was with the angel a multitude of the heavenly host, praising God, and saying, Glory

* See Jouffroy's *Melanges Philosophiques;* Vinet's *Essais de Philosophie Morale*, p. 189.

to God in the highest, on earth peace and good will to men."

Much of this has been styled a myth or legendary fiction by the sceptics of continental Europe, and their imitators in this country; after all, the thing, the reality remains. No hypothesis can explain it away. It is an effect of which some adequate, and therefore divine cause must be supposed. If any fact in history is well established, it is that of the extraordinary birth of Christ, and the wonderful change thereby wrought in the history of the world. But if the birth of Christ must be conceded, as the first step, in the series of stupendous facts connected with his mission, then the mystery of the incarnation, the song of the angels, the visit of the Magi, and the star in the east, or the luminous appearance which guided their steps to the place of his nativity, all, in a word, connected with this event, natural, or supernatural, may be allowed. The same testimony which proves the one, proves also the other. If the one is natural in the circumstances supposed, so is the other. The miracle of Christ himself, his very presence in the world, with its vast influence among men, so clearly divine, easily accounts for all the rest. The sun in the heavens is not alone there, cannot be alone there. Stars follow in his train. Planets and satellites are his natural attendants. Light and beauty supernal flash along his pathway. If Christ, then, be the Son of God, how natural and becoming the angelic announcement! how beautiful "that soft hosanna's tone" from celestial choirs! how glorious that refulgent star, leading on the believers of the Orient — first fruits and representatives of the Gentiles — to Christ, and standing like a thing of life over the place where the young child lay! how dignified and touching the homage of the shepherds, and the adoration of the Magi, with their gifts of gold, frankincense, and myrrh!

Let us draw nigh, then, and behold this great sight, this transcendent wonder, this true Shekinah of the Godhead. Away with curious imaginings and impotent speculations. The Word is made flesh and dwells among us, and by faith we behold his glory, the glory as of the only-begotten of the Father, full of grace and truth. Not by the vulgar senses, not even by the mere formal intellect, but by that higher exercise of the soul which discerns the true, the beautiful, the good, absolute and eternal, palpitating beneath the thin vesture of external forms and finite existences, can we recognize and appreciate the glory of God in the face of Jesus. Life only can apprehend life. Souls echo to souls. Love is their interpreter. It is only thus that God himself can be known to man. Spirit answers to spirit, finite to infinite, the love of the believer to the love of God.

Hence the incarnation is a sacred mystery, to be known and cherished in the secret depths of regenerate hearts.

CHAPTER IX.

THE DISCIPLINE.

NATURE is progressive. Principles and forces remain, but organic forms and living creatures are gradually developed.* The powers beneath the surface are often concealed from human observation, and apparently restrained and limited by an invisible hand; but they are essentially, and at all times, the same, as God is the same. Working on, however, they give rise to the most diversified appearances, and actually seem to gather strength and volume as they proceed. The change is generally from the less to the greater, as the dawn advances to the perfect day. Thus the stars are born, taking their place in the galaxy of night. Thus the rivers rise, and the forests grow. Thus the earth itself is projected into the realms of space, with its accumulating freight of living beings. Hence in the Scriptures we find "the beginning" of all things recognized,

* Of course we do not here indorse "the Development Theory" of the author of "The Vestiges of Creation," now pretty thoroughly exploded. We maintain an original and perfect creation of distinct and independent species. But when created, these, as well as other organic forms, are gradually developed. Growth succeeds creation.

and as in the discoveries of geological science, so here we behold the first creation of the great masses, "chaos and elder night" succeeded by the beautiful and all-penetrating day, then the deep strata of the earth's foundations, the alternations of sea and land, the green herbage with plants and trees, the old monsters of the deep and of the wilderness, fishes and birds, in their order, then the higher animals, and finally man, to crown the whole; the six days of successive change and improvement, with the seventh of completion and perfection, or, as some have it, the six great periods and revolutions of time, figured under the symbol of the common week, with its six periods of social activity, and its seventh of sacred rest.

Man himself appears as a feeble beginning, first as an individual, and then as a single pair, after which follow families, communities, states, empires, that mighty and multiform thing which we call mankind, or the race. In the individual man, also, as now developed, we see the same wonderful process; for he first appears as an embryo, and then as a child, feeble and dependent, with the majestic soul within, wrapped up, so to speak, in the tissues of the flesh, or in the secret chambers of the brain, but of vital and productive energy, capable of all growth and enlargement of thought, purpose, and will, expanding with the body, and finally arriving at the stature of a complete and well-proportioned man, with his stalwart limbs, clear eye, energetic hand, and all-comprehending mind. Strange that a Newton, with all the grandeurs and complications of scientific thought, should lie in that little child. It would seem impossible; but there he is, as vital, as energetic, as great, absolutely, as when gazing through starry worlds into the very centre and essence of things.

This, then, is God's method to work outwardly and onwardly, as from a centre, — gradually evolving his beautiful creations, and although unchanged in all the energies and resources of his nature, discovering himself in external things, by a limited, but constantly expanding process. He would seem thus to confine himself, to bring down and compress his energies in finite forms and forces, that an external universe, men and angels, might come into existence, — who, in due time, should recognize him as "all and in all." We have called this the progress of nature; but nature is nothing separate from God. It exists by him and for him, with a view to the outward and eternal development of his glory. Hence Cowper is entirely justified in representing what we call nature, as but "a name for an effect, whose cause is God." It would seem, then, that God, in outwardly revealing his nature, voluntarily subjects himself to an apparent process of limitation and development.

Now, in the incarnation, the second and more perfect outgoing or embodiment of the Divine, we should naturally expect something analogous; as first of all, the promise and the preparation, then the birth of the Divine among men, in the form of a wondrous child, pure as the opening day, or the first effluence of light from its primal fountain, penetrating the darkness of chaos, and turning it into radiant gold; a nature infinite and transcendent, but hiding itself in this limited and lowly shape, which grows and expands till the Godhead shines refulgent through the whole. So we find "the holy Child" passing into the boy — the thoughtful and spiritual boy, who, true to his original nature, "must be about his Father's business;" then into the man, the man active, and the man suffering, through all the duties and exigencies of this mortal life, through the family, the church, and the state, through the garden, the cross, and the sepulchre, through all, indeed, of joy and sorrow, of obligation and attainment, which comes between the cradle and the tomb, until, *perfected*, he ascends, by inward force, "far above all principality and power, and might and dominion." Strange, men may say, that in that humble stable, in that lowly manger, in that feeble child, though beautiful as a star in the gloom of night, should lie concealed the divine Redeemer, with all the depths of his unutterable love, and all the resources of his infinite power. But no more strange than true; no more strange than the dwelling of a finite spirit, yet to become a seraph, with vast power and eternal joys, in a similar form; no more strange than the dwelling of the infinite Jehovah in the universe he has framed; for, *above all*, he is yet *in all*. And so also the gradual development of Christ as a child, a boy, a man, the lowly life he led, and the sharp discipline through which he passed, to the full perfection of his nature and work, are no more strange or anomalous than the course of creation, through its various throes and changes, to the full revelation of the creating God, in this fair, harmonious world. Clearly did the high soul of Milton discern the *glory* of the new-born child, even in the manger of Bethlehem, as he sang, in lofty numbers, that wonderful event, in which all heaven and its angelic choirs sympathized as a new creation, and in which hell, with all its brood of demons, felt that its empire was gone; for he saw, as the angels saw, the mighty change thence to be wrought not only in the person of Christ, but in the entire history of man.

"The oracles are dumb,
No voice or hideous hum
Runs through the archéd roof, in words deceiving.
Apollo from his shrine
Can no more divine,

> With hollow shriek the steep of Delphos leaving;
> No nightly trance, or breathèd spell
> Inspires the pale-eyed priest from the prophetic cell.
>
> . . . .
>
> Peor and Baalim
> Forsake their temples dim;
>
> . . . .
>
> And sullen Moloch, fled,
> Hath left in shadows dread
> His burning idol all of blackest hue;
>
> . . . .
>
> Nor is Osiris seen
> In Memphian grove or green,
> Trampling the unshowered grass with lowings loud —
>
> . . .
>
> "He feels from Judah's land
> The *dreaded Infant's* hand;
> The rays of Bethlehem blind his dusky eyne;
> Nor all the gods beside
> Longer dare abide,
> Not Typhon huge, ending in snaky twine.
> *Our Babe*, to show his Godhead true,
> Can in his swaddling bands control the damnèd crew."

Thus, in the principle of change and progress, the "Holy Child" is recognized as embodying "all the fulness of the Godhead," as much at his birth as when enthroned in the heavens. But the progress and development of the higher manifestation or incarnation of the Divine must be common and natural. It must take place in such a land as Judea, under such a reign as that of Herod, of Archelaus, and Herod Antipas, in such a house as that of Joseph, in some humble occupation or trade, and by such ordinary ministrations as fall to the lot of mortals. Jesus must be prepared for his great work, and in every phase and form of existence, of trial and suffering, discover to man the divine love and pity. Thus he must be persecuted even when a child, go down into Egypt to escape the wrath of the king, wander about in lowliness and poverty, hold fellowship with nature and man, be tempted even of the devil, pass through all stages of change and fiery trial, and finally of agony and death, for the redemption of the lost.

It is only thus he can make himself *known*, only thus he can fully discover to us his indwelling glory, and bring down to man, not simply the absolute nature, but the very heart of the great God, yearning for the return of his offspring; only thus that he can sanctify for our benefit, life, death, and the grave; and so become our Forerunner to glory.

It is on this ground that one of the Christian fathers (Irenæus) has remarked that Jesus "came to save all by himself, all who through him are regenerated unto God — infants, little children, boys, young men and old." Hence "he passed through every age, and for the infants he became an infant, sanctifying the infants; among the little children he became a little child, sanctifying those who belonged to that age, and, at the same time, presenting to them an example of piety, of well-doing, and of obedience; among the young men he became a young man, that he might set them an example, and sanctify them to the Lord." * The thought is not only beautiful, but just and scriptural; for our Savior did, by means of his childhood, youth, and maturer life, confer dignity upon all, and prove that all may be made pure and happy. He thus fitted himself to become, in our human affections, the true brother and friend of man, in all possible relations. How profoundly this single circumstance has affected the sympathies of mankind, all must be aware. Childhood and old age have felt it alike. The mother, gazing upon her infant, has felt it through all the depths of her being. The child itself has felt it when hearing that mother sing of the Holy One, "cradled in a manger," and "fed with the beasts of the stall." All ranks and conditions have acknowledged it. The poor man in his cottage, and the prince in his palace, the wild Indian, converted to Christ, and the polished European, consecrating himself and his family to God.

"O, who, that feels the spell which Heaven
Casts round us in our infancy,
But, more or less, hath homage given
To childhood, half-unconscious why?

* Neander's Church History, vol. i. p. 311.

A yet more touching mystery
Is in that feeling comprehended
When thus is brought before his eye
Godhead with childhood strangely blended."

The same fact has tended to impart a peculiar dignity and worth to human nature itself, and to the whole life of man, married thus to the celestial and divine. The majesty of the Son of God seems thereby to be veiled, and doubtless, in some partial and relative sense, it really is so. But how immeasurably exalted is our poor humanity, and what treasures are thence in store for us, when we, too, are made "partakers of the divine nature!" Certainly it was an infinite condescension on his part to "take upon him the seed of Abraham," and appear among men, as one of the least and lowliest of all, going down to the deepest deeps of human sorrow, that he might lift us up to God. But the Divinity was not thereby degraded, as some have rashly concluded, any more than a Howard or a Fry in prison, and among thieves, is degraded. Indeed, the Divine is equally glorified in descending as in ascending; so that we conclude that the mysterious union between the highest Essence in the universe and the lowliest form of men was at once natural and becoming. We know of no shrine of the Deity so beautiful as the spotless body of "a holy child." The infinite lies nearer to the souls of children than we are aware. Indeed, it is "all about us in our infancy." And when one is found absolutely stainless, that child forms a temple of the Deity more refulgent than all the starry spheres. Even on the cross, marred and dying, there is a grandeur in the person of the man Jesus Christ, for which the presence of the indwelling Divinity alone can account.

Let us not, then, be surprised if we find the Son of God, who is equally the Son of man, subjected to the will of his human parents, increasing in years and strength, and "in favor with God and man," performing the accustomed round of duties, secular and sacred, mingling with his neighbors and kinsfolk in the humble town of Nazareth — asking and hearing questions with the doctors in the temple, working at the occupation of a carpenter, or celebrating the rites of the Jewish faith. Let us not be surprised if we find him "a hungered," or "athirst," or "weary" at the close of day, tempted of Satan, "troubled in spirit," or rejoicing with deep and peculiar joy, "weeping with those that weep, and rejoicing with those that rejoice," mingling in life's festal or mournful scenes, partaking of common pleasure, and bearing, in all things, the sorrows and infirmities of man. Serene and self-possessed in his higher nature, he is yet linked to man, as the soul is linked to the body, and while the union lasts, must sympathize in all which is common to the race. "It behooved him in all things to be made like unto his brethren." Why? That we might be able to recognize him as "a merciful and faithful High Priest in things pertaining to God." We need not, then, be shocked, if we hear his townspeople speak of him contemptuously, as "the carpenter's son," whose kinsfolk they know, or if we find him "despised and rejected of men, a man of sorrow, and acquainted with grief." If the life of man, is "a great and inscrutable mystery," — if the life especially of a good man, in the lowest walks of poverty and sorrow, has in it something divine, — let us not wonder that the Son of God should pass through such a life, and thereby make it unutterably sublime.

Night must come to reveal the stars. The beacon shines brightest in the fiercest storms. Love is the most intensely beautiful amid long watchings and agonies. And so best is the glory of God revealed in the poverty, lowliness, and suffering of Christ. The love, too, of a long and checkered life is better than the love of a single act, or even of many detached acts; and thence Jesus must live and labor, and suffer through many years, the vivid incarnation of the infinite heart yearning for the restoration of the lost. It is only thus that the overwhelming conviction is brought home to our souls, that we must and can be "regenerated unto God," and though sinful, fitted for glory and immortality.

Little or nothing is recorded of the first thirty years of our Savior's life; and in this we see the profound continence and wisdom of the sacred writers. It was a season of preparation, of common every-day duties, common every-day trials. With a slight exception or two, it had nothing in it of the strange or marvellous, such as fictitious writers would have easily found. And hence the "Gospel of the Infancy," as it is called, an apocryphal Gospel of early times, differs, *toto cœlo*, from the inspired records, indulging, as it does, in all sorts of foolish stories and extravagant figments, unworthy of the simple grandeur and serene beauty of our Savior's character. It represents him as a capricious, revengeful child, working the most preposterous miracles, on the slightest and most insignificant occasions. How superior to all this the sober narratives of those who copied from the divine original, and narrated only what they knew to be fact and reality! In boyhood itself, Christ must "be about his Father's business," as he told his virgin mother. Even then, the consciousness of an ineffable union with "the Father," of a high spiritual destiny, and of an actual preparation for it, is indicated amid the common cares and sympathies of his life.

An interesting question here presents itself, to which we may profitably devote the remainder of this chapter. How and where was Christ educated? Or rather, perhaps, was Christ educated at all, in the ordinary sense of the term? Among what learned rabbis, or in what sacred school, if any, was he trained as a teacher of righteousness? The question has been debated chiefly by the enemies of Christianity, who maintain that Christ acquired his wonderful knowledge by ordinary means, and that there is nothing really original in his system, admirable, especially in its moral aspects, as they are compelled to acknowledge it.* The sublime truths taught by our Savior, the spirituality, purity, and comprehensiveness of his views as a Reformer of society, and especially the simplicity, sublimity, and perfection of his moral code, confessed alike by infidels and Christians, must be accounted for. There is no effect without an adequate cause; those, therefore, who deny the divine origin and authority of Christianity, must explain it on natural grounds.

Now, it may be allowed that Jesus had access to the Old Testament Scriptures, which he tells us he came "to fulfil," not to destroy; and thence doubtless might derive some of his grandest con-

* Strauss, Bruno Bauer, Newman, and others, represent him simply as an extraordinary man, taught, probably, by the Essenes.

ceptions of God, of duty, and immortality; but this will not account for the whole, sceptics themselves being judges; for he left behind him, in the old dispensation, all that was temporary, local, and ceremonial, all that was narrow, crude, and imperfect; and not only so, but he added certain peculiar principles and precepts, organized the church, and thence society on a new and wider basis, and gave the whole a grandeur, force, and comprehensiveness utterly unknown to Moses and the prophets.

Did he derive his information, then, from other books and documents? Alas! there were none from which he could derive them; unless he possessed that peculiar alchemy of heaven, of extracting all the good out of every book and system, leaving nothing behind but the poison and the dross. Were this really the case, it would prove him as much inspired as if the whole proceeded from his unaided mind. It would be collecting by a power which none but God, or a God-inspired being, could possess, the fragments of truth, scattered, as Milton finely imagines, over the face of the earth, like the mangled remains of the god Osiris.* Imagine the broken parts of a magnificent temple lying promiscuously over a wide and tangled wilderness. What genius, but of that of a

* Works, vol. i. p. 185.

Michael Angelo, were it possible even for such as he, could bring them together, and constitute them into the fair proportions of an original work? That Christ should be fancied by sceptics to have gathered all the good of Oriental theosophy, Grecian wisdom, as well as Jewish faith, into a fair and well-proportioned system, is a tacit acknowledgment of his amazing superiority.

But there is not the slightest evidence that he ever studied these systems, or had the least familiarity with philosophical speculations of any kind. Indeed, nothing is clearer than his decided rejection of all speculative theologies, as well as the mysteries and symbols of the ancient pagan faiths.

With the exception of a very short sojourn in Egypt, at a time of life when he could form no acquaintance with Egyptian literature and theology, he spent the most of his life at Nazareth. This was the place of his preparation for his public ministry. Remote from schools of learning, he gave himself, so far as we know, to the common duties of religion and of social life, and passed, among his acquaintances, as one of the common people. When the Jews listened to his remarkable style of teaching, they expressed their amazement, on the ground that he had never been taught, like other learned and godly men whom they revered. "Is not this the carpenter's son, whose kinsmen we know?" "How, then, hath this man this wisdom, and these mighty works?"

Some have maintained, that he might have been familiar with the works of Philo, the celebrated Alexandrian Jew, whose allegorical and philosophical explanation of the Mosaic faith presents some lofty and attractive features. But Jesus is free from the errors and fancies of Philo. His method of thought is entirely different. The one is allegorical and speculative, the other simple and spiritual. Philo speaks as a philosopher, Jesus as a prophet. The one is an ingenious but fanciful thinker, the other is a messenger from God. Philo, indeed, claims to be inspired, as, he believes, all wise and good men are, but writes with the air of one who relies much on his own philosophic genius. He allegorizes the simplest facts, adding or retrenching, glossing or explaining away, as he sees fit; and thus, while doing homage, apparently, to divine revelation, he goes far to diminish its strength and undermine its authority. Jesus never allegorizes the facts and doctrines of the Old Testament; but, extracting its spirit, proceeds, both in his teaching and life, to *fulfil it, or fill it out*, that is, complete and mature its teachings.*

* Philo seems to have no idea of a *personal* Messiah, especially of a suffering Messiah, and makes redemption, as in Plato, to consist in a return to the absolute and infinite, without any proper

Could Jesus have been educated among the *Pharisees*, or have derived from them the principles of his system? They were the most learned and rigid of the Jewish sects, and exerted a preponderating influence in the nation. They passed as the orthodox formalists of the times, and laid claims to the highest sanctity and worth. Venerating all the books of the Old Testament, they were rigid in attending fasts and festivals, and in observing all minute and ritual forms. Our Savior's spirit was just the reverse. He rejects all formalism and separatism, all assumed, external sanctity, all vain and superstitious ceremonies. Hence, in language of fire, he denounces the Pharisees as *a generation of vipers* — *whited sepulchres* — *hypocrites*. Thus, then, while agreeing with the Pharisees in their veneration for the fathers, the sacred books, and the law of God, as also with their views touching the spirituality of God, and the resurrection state, he renounces their spirit and aim as destructive to true religion and virtue!

Well, then, could the *Sadducees*, who rejected the great mass of Jewish traditions, and clung to the Pentateuch as the original and infallible reve-

conception of an atonement or a personal regeneration — principles which lie at the very foundation of Christianity. The Greek philosophy exerted upon him an immense influence. Hence it has been said that "either Plato philonized or Philo platonized."

lation of God, have been the teachers of Christ? Impossible; for their low and unspiritual views, their Epicureanism, as well as their scepticism touching the separate existence of spirits, and the immortality of the soul, were his abhorrence. The fact is, the Sadducees, a small but wealthy and influential class, were the materialists of Judaism. They denied the spiritual world, and, consequently, made as much of the present as possible; living a free and Epicurean life, and so caring little for man, or God, or immortality. They are associated, in the denunciations of our Savior, with the Scribes and Pharisees, as equally the children of perdition.

A single supposition only remains, and that will exhaust the subject, namely, that Christ derived his peculiar views of religion and morality from the Essenes, or Esseans, represented by Josephus and Philo as the third sect of Jewish religionists, or, as they choose to term them, *philosophers*, adapting their representations to Grecian and Roman modes of expression. The extreme anxiety of both these writers to recommend every thing Jewish to their pagan readers has thrown some doubt over their accounts. They vary somewhat, though both have a slight air of romance. Little or nothing is known, from other sources, of these Essenes, though Pliny speaks of them in favorable terms, and represents them as very ancient. His account, however, is, probably, borrowed from the Jewish writers, or from hearsay. It is questionable whether Josephus, or even Philo, knew much of them from personal observation. Their statements are rather vague and rhetorical. It is singular, too, that no mention should be made of them in the New Testament. So far as we can see, our Savior never came into contact with any of them. This, however, may be accounted for on the ground of the smallness of the sect, their monastic and retiring habits, and their residence at a distance from the principal scene of Christ's ministrations. They avoided cities and places of public resort; took no part in the questions or agitations of the times; shunned promiscuous intercourse, refusing even to eat with any but their own order. The name, according to Josephus, is derived from the Hebrew *asah*, because they practised the healing art; though Philo and others have suggested a different origin. It is well known that the Jewish high priest wore upon his breast a splendid ornament, in which twelve precious stones were inserted, representing the twelve tribes of Israel, the appellation of which was the *Essen*. It was worn especially when the high priest went into the holy of holies, and bore an intimate relation to the matter of divine communications. It was regarded as a means, or medium, of approach to the Deity; or at least signified, as the Urim and Thummim, a real fellowship, through the high priest, between Jehovah and the twelve tribes of Israel. Thus one mode of inquiring the mind of God was by Urim and Thummim. The society of the Essen, or the Essenes, then, according to this view, were a secret, mystical fraternity, who professed to have direct and peculiar access to the Deity, and thence claimed a sort of prophetic inspiration. As the Pharisees were the formalists, and the Sadducees the rationalists, so the Essenes were the mystics of the Jewish nation.

Their principal settlement was on the western shores of the Dead Sea — a region favorable, from its lone and desolate aspects, as well as its ancient and thrilling memories, to profound and melancholy thought. From this they slowly and secretly spread themselves through other parts of Palestine, and, it may be, southward as far as Egypt, where, according to some, they reappeared in the *Therapeutæ*, or Jewish ascetics of Egypt.

Both Philo and Josephus extol them for their rigid morality; their simplicity and purity of life; their quiet and gentle temper; their hospitality and piety. They generally practised celibacy, regarding all women as unchaste, though some of them did not altogether disapprove of marriage; paid great attention to the curative properties of plants, practising medicine; and, when not engaged in contemplation or devotion, spending their time chiefly in agriculture, or in other simple and rural employments.

They formed a fraternity, separate, secret, and exclusive—a sort of Freemason, or Eleusinian order—admitting members only after a novitiate of three years, and gradually passing them through four different stages, or classes, till they arrived at what they deemed the most perfect. Though oaths were strictly forbidden on ordinary occasions, no one was admitted to the society without solemnly binding himself, by the most awful oaths, to observe the rules of the order, and to keep its secrets, particularly those in reference "to the angels," about whom they cherished some superstitious notions. At the close of the first year, the candidate received a small hatchet, a white apron, or girdle, and a white robe, which had a mystical or symbolical meaning. They lived upon the simplest fare; held little converse with each other, except at meals; the four different classes really forming separate *castes*, who regarded contact with each other as *contamination*. They performed frequent ablutions, but held anointing with oil in abhorrence. Philo denies that they offered any sacrifices, but Josephus affirms that they only declined offering them at the temple. Among themselves they performed sacrificial rites, with fasting and prayer, at the dead of night, or at early dawn.

Justice and charity were regarded by the Essenes as cardinal virtues. Slavery among them was absolutely forbidden. They were also *communists,* having all things common in the matter of property and food.

They believed in one God, whom they worshipped chiefly in the night, regarding that season, in common with many of the Oriental religionists, as peculiarly sacred. It is said that they worshipped the sun, perhaps as the symbol or image of the divine glory — a circumstance which would indicate some connection with Oriental theosophy. At all events, they offered prayer and sang hymns at the dawn, with their faces towards the rising sun.

Their sacred books were kept secret, and used in divination, or prophesying; somewhat, we fancy, after the mode of the *Sortes Virgilianæ.*

Rejecting the great mass of Jewish traditions and ceremonial observances, the Essenes superstitiously observed some ritual usages of their own, and were distinguished by their rigid manner of keeping the Sabbath. Abstemious and ascetic, they despised and mortified the body, believing it to be the seat of evil. Josephus says that they wore their clothes till they fell to pieces. Their notion was, that the souls of men had fallen from the regions of purity and light into gross and sinful bodies, from which, in due time, through piety and penance, they would escape, and once more rise into the pure and spiritual state. Hence they rejected the resurrection of the body, and longed for reunion with God, through abstinence and death.

The Essenes have been divided into the theoretical and practical, the former being identified with the Therapeutæ of Egypt, who, as their name imports, devoted themselves, like the Essenes, to the healing art; unless we are to understand the term symbolically, as having reference to the health of the soul. *Matter*, the celebrated author of the history of Gnosticism, and *Neander*, the church historian, doubt the connection of these two orders of ascetics, supposing, perhaps justly, that the monastic tendency might develop itself spontaneously in both countries, as it did in various Oriental nations even among the heathen, and, in the middle ages, among Christians.* The Therapeutæ had their principal settlement on the tranquil shores of Lake Mœris, not far from

* Mosheim, in his Ecclesiastical Commentaries, also doubts the propriety of the distinction. His observations upon the Essenes are remarkably just and discriminating. Both he and Neander give it as their opinion that considerable varieties obtained among them.

the brilliant capital of Grecian Egypt, where they passed their lives in monastic seclusion, shut up in separate cells, devoted to prayer and contemplation. The sacred oracles formed the basis of their studies; but they interpreted them, after Philo and other theosophic writers, allegorically. Their usages were those of the anchoritic life. They exercised themselves in fasting and other ascetic practices, taking only one meal in the evening, consisting of bread and water. Indeed, they sometimes spent whole days without eating. They met together, in solemn assembly, each seventh day and more especially on the seventh week; partaking together of fraternal repasts seasoned with salt and hyssop, listening to theosophic lessons, singing in chorus ancient traditional hymns, and performing certain mystic dances.*

The fact is, the Alexandrian Judaism mingled too readily with the spirit of Oriental and thaumaturgic mysticism; and the usages of the Therapeutæ were but a mixture of Jewish and pagan notions, reduced to practice, in monastic seclusion and ascetic severity. Hence, while the Therapeutæ, as well as the Essenes, clearly possessed some noble and even beautiful traits of character, they fell into errors and extravagances,

* The view of the Essenes and Therapeutæ here given is based upon the explicit statements of Philo or Josephus. See Appendix D.

alien from the spirit, at once, of Judaism and of Christianity. Infinitely superior as the Essenes were, both to the Sadducees and the Pharisees, and embodying in their creed some elevated tendencies, their whole system was exclusive and ascetic, just the contrary of Christianity, as taught by our Savior, and exemplified in his life. Undoubtedly there are some slight coincidences in the two systems; but there are, also, the most obvious and striking differences. Christ was no Essene, — no monk, or ascetic, — for he mingled freely in society; approved of marriage, sanctioning it by his presence at the marriage in Cana of Galilee; partook of ordinary food and drink; so much so, that his enemies charged him, falsely enough to be sure, but with an apparent plausibility, with being "a gluttonous man, a wine bibber, a friend of publicans and sinners." His system is not allegorical, or mystical, in the technical sense of these terms; neither is it narrow, monkish, and exclusive; but all-comprehensive, practical, social, and free — a religion for man in all the relations of life and society. Like that of the Essenes, his kingdom is not of this world; but, unlike theirs, it has no tones provincial — no peculiar garb — no strange Shibboleth, or oath — no secret notions and usages — no worship of angels, or despising of the body — no superstitious reverence of the night — no worship of the sun or stars — no castes, or orders — no dread of society, or of common every-day duties. Like theirs, the church of the first ages often had a community of goods, and took special care of the poor, the sick, the sorrowful, the dying; but, unlike the Essenic fraternity, it was composed of all ranks and conditions of men, and went forth among the unregenerate and outcast, preaching a free gospel, and urging them to press, without hesitation, into the fold of the Redeemer. Like the Essenes, the primitive Christians, following Christ, abandoned the distinctions and vanities of the world, despised suffering and death, and were preëminently distinguished for their justice, veracity, hospitality, and fortitude; but, unlike them, were actuated by a burning zeal for the spread of the truth, and the salvation of the heathen. While the Essenes shut themselves up in their secluded settlements, the Christians went every where preaching the word, and diffusing among men the blessings of salvation.

But it is unnecessary to pursue the comparison further. It is clear, not only from the absence of the slightest historical testimony, but from intrinsic evidence, that Christ and Christianity could not have originated among the Essenes of Palestine, or the Therapeutæ in Egypt.*

* It is well known that Roman Catholic writers have claimed the Essenes and Therapeutæ as *Christian monks*, in order to justify the

Christ, even in the commencement of his career, was altogether peculiar and original. He does not even seem to belong to his age. Who thinks of him as a Jew at all? He is as much superior to his era, and his nation, as if he had descended, full grown, from a higher sphere; as if he had sprung immediately from the bosom of God. And indeed he did come forth from God, and, while on earth, dwelt, so to speak, in the bosom of the Father. "No man hath seen God at any time; the only-begotten Son, *which is in the bosom of the Father*, he hath declared him."

monastic system as ancient and apostolical. But the whole is an assumption, without historical basis. It is singular, however, that De Quincey, in two articles contributed years ago to Blackwood's Magazine, has defended this view, or at least a modification of this view, maintaining that the Essenes were primitive Christians, mistaken or misrepresented by Josephus (whom he bitterly denounces) as a Jewish sect. De Quincey, however, has presented no new facts upon the subject. His reasoning is altogether hypothetical, and we are compelled to say, fanciful. Indeed, De Quincey, with all his learning, is not particularly reliable in questions of this sort. He is not unfrequently carried away by his imagination, in opposition to plain historical facts. The testimonies of Philo he has not even considered. He makes no account of the deliberate, well-founded opinions of such historians as Mosheim, Neander, Hase, Matter, Gieseler, and others. Any one who will take the trouble of reading his articles will find his reasoning *conjectural* from beginning to end. We refer our readers once more to note D in the Appendix.

CHAPTER X.

INAUGURATION, OR JOHN THE BAPTIST.

Some time before the commencement of Christ's public career, Judea was reduced to the condition of a Roman province. Archelaus, after a weak and disastrous reign, as ethnarch, for nine years, was banished into Gaul. The country was subjected to the capricious despotism of Pontius Pilate, the Roman procurator, who took every opportunity of humbling the Jews, and breaking their national spirit. He was the fifth Roman governor of Judea, and received his appointment from Tiberius Cæsar. He occupied that position about ten years, and distinguished himself by his spasmodic energy and cruelty. He is known in history chiefly in connection with our Savior's death. He introduced, not only into Cæsarea, his ordinary residence, but into Jerusalem itself, the idolatrous standard of the Roman empire, and attempted to suspend certain bucklers, bearing the image of the emperor, in the palace of Herod. The Sanhedrim was still permitted to exercise some jurisdiction, but was sadly checked and degraded. This, as far as possible, they endeavored to conceal both from themselves and the people. Their claims seemed as lofty as ever; and they guarded with an intense jealousy the ancient institutions and usages of the nation. Throughout the country, publicans or tax gatherers, under the appointment of Rome, constantly reminded the people of her subjection to foreign domination. Galling burdens chafed them at every point. Their very religion was subjected to rude, pagan interference. The high priest was displaced at the pleasure of the Roman procurator, and sometimes with insulting levity and violence. No one could be initiated into that office without the sanction of Rome. Religious sects were inflamed against each other. The Herodians, as they were called, were universally hated. False to their ancient faith, they yielded their necks to the conqueror, and were active in modifying the spirit and institutions of their country. The most fierce and sanguinary fanaticism raged amongst the followers and imitators of Judas, the Gaulonite, the leader of those who attempted to throw off the yoke of Rome. There was something, indeed, noble in their spirit of self-sacrifice, for they contemned suffering and death, and fought only for their country and their religion. Judas and his followers, however, perished miserably. The nation every where was agitated by treasons and tumults, often repressed by the iron hand of Pilate, who more than once mingled the blood of the people with their sacrifices. Indeed, the whole country was in a ferment, resembling a volcano heaving and dashing beneath the thin surface, previous to a violent eruption.

John the Baptist, stern and majestic as a rock of the wilderness, where, in devout meditation, he loved to wander, was commissioned as the messenger or herald of the Messiah. Coming "in the spirit and power of Elias," according to ancient prediction, it was his office to introduce the Redeemer to the world, and so prepare the way for his public ministry. He made his appearance in the wilderness of Judea, by the banks of the sacred Jordan. As a reformer and preacher of repentance, John, though humble and devout, was severe, and even ascetic. He came to rouse the people from their spiritual slumbers, and announce the approach of the Deliverer. In awful and thrilling tones, like a voice from eternity, he proclaimed his coming and kingdom. In anticipation of this august event, he baptized, in the Jordan, multitudes who repented of their sins, and professed to receive his teaching in reference to the speedy establishment of the new spiritual kingdom of the Messiah. Many, indeed, both among the Sadducees and Pharisees, he rejected, discriminating thus between the sincere and the insincere, the false and the true hearted. His was not simply a baptism of external form, but of "faith and repentance," a symbol of a true inward change and preparation for the Redeemer, with his higher baptism of fire and of the Holy Spirit.

But few, even of those who listened to the teachings of John, understood the "spiritual nature of the kingdom of God," and all, with scarcely an exception, were expecting in the Christ a mighty conqueror, a glorious, earth-born king. That the great body of those who were baptized by John, in anticipation of the Messiah's coming, were sincere in their belief, so far as it went, cannot be doubted. A great and happy reformation of manners was the result. The attention of the whole community was excited. A strange thrill passed through them, as they listened to this new Elijah, recalling the long silent voices of the prophets. Then the way was prepared for the public appearance of the Messiah. The dawn of the new day was visible on the hills. The star, which heralded the approaching sun, shone bright and clear in the horizon.

As it is important to understand the character of John the Baptist, and his relations to Christ, we will enter a little into detail respecting his life and ministry. The son of Zachariah and

Elisabeth, of the tribe of Levi, and of the race of the priesthood, he was born a little before Christ, probably at Hebron, or Jutta, a sacerdotal city, situated among the mountains, or "hill country" of Judea. His birth had been foretold to his father, and his name given him, in anticipation, by an angel. He spent his early years, it is presumed, in his native town, far from the tumults of the world. It is said, in the sacred narrative, that he was "in the wilderness of Judea," [called such because it was a region of less fertility and population than the rest of Palestine,] until the commencement of his ministry, or, as it is expressed, "his showing, or manifestation to Israel." Here, in retirement and humility, he acquired, by grace divine, that purity and force of character necessary to the fulfilment of his mission. His manners were primitive and simple; his fare and his dress humble, and even ascetic. What was his precise education, we are not informed. Some have supposed that he must have received his peculiar views and habits from the Essenes. He has, we admit, somewhat the appearance and manners of those simple-hearted ascetics; he possesses their purity and love of solitude, their energy and dignity of character. And as God works by means in preparing the agents and instrumentalities of his will, it is not absolutely impossible that John may have associated somewhat with those primitive hermits, and acquired some of their views and feelings. But this is a mere conjecture at best, and, upon the whole, is not sustained by any facts in the case. For, in the first place, John might have possessed all his simplicity, self-denial, and energy, without ever having seen an Essene, or belonged to any of their fraternities. He could not have been educated among them without a regular novitiate, and, consequently, must have renounced the peculiar views of his father, and many of the usages of his immediate family and connections. But of this we have not the slightest hint. His food, "locusts and wild honey," upon which he chiefly subsisted in the wilderness, was the common fare of many poor people in that part of the land, and would not seem at all unnatural to them. Indeed, his life might have been simply that of a *Nazarene*, a thing by no means uncommon among all the Jewish sects. The quiet and solitary scenes in which he spent his youth, the simplicity, purity, and devotion of many of the "hill people," especially of some of the old sacerdotal families, would naturally foster his contemplative and even ascetic turn. His parents were pious and simple hearted, "walking in all the ordinances and commandments of God blameless." He was *the promised*, and, consequently, the *cherished child*, and thence their most precious *offering* to God. Like Samson, or like Samuel of old, he was brought up as a consecrated son, as a sacred Nazarene, who one day was to perform a great work for God and his church. We can easily understand how his mind would dwell upon the usages of the olden time, the simplicity and energy of the ancient Jewish faith, the noble examples of heroism and self-denial among the prophets, recorded in the sacred books, and how, consequently, he would be fired with a noble enthusiasm to emulate their example and fulfil his mission. His entire training, so far as his parents were concerned, would be directed to this single end. They knew that the herald of Christ was to come in the spirit of Elijah ; and as that illustrious prophet spent much of his time in solitude, and evinced a noble spirit of heroism and self-denial, being very "zealous for the Lord God," so would they encourage in their son similar habits and modes of life. Then, who can tell how early he felt the inspiration of God, moving him to undertake the high mission to which he was destined ; or how natural and easy he found it, even without instruction, to emulate the purity of the ancient seers ?

We have the highest proof of the correctness of this view, in the prediction of the angel, upon which, doubtless, his parents would act in his education. His course is described by the celestial messenger as that of a Nazarene: "For he shall be great in the sight of the Lord, and shall drink neither wine nor strong drink, and he shall be filled with the Holy Ghost, even from his mother's womb." Nay, further, his entire mode of life, as the "forerunner of the Messiah," is detailed — a circumstance, which, known to his parents, and in due time to himself, must have shaped his entire character and habits. "And many of the children of Israel shall he turn to the Lord their God. And he shall go before him, [the Messiah,] in *the spirit and power of Elias*, to turn the hearts of the fathers unto the children, and the disobedient to the wisdom of the just; to make ready a people prepared for the Lord." *

The same great truth is proclaimed by the father, in the peculiar style of Hebrew devotion and thanksgiving, at the birth of his son: "And thou, child, shalt be called the prophet of the Highest; for thou shalt go before the face of the Lord, to prepare his way; to give knowledge of salvation to his people, by the remission of their sins, through the tender mercy of our God; whereby the dayspring from on high hath visited us, to give light to them that sit in darkness

* Luke i. 15–17.

and in the shadow of death, to guide our feet unto the way of peace." *

Thus it will be seen that it was absolutely necessary for John to appear in the rude garb, and with the severe manners, of the ancient prophets, in order to be recognized by the people as the herald of the Messiah. So, also, it was necessary for him to dwell much in the wilderness, as Elijah did, for the sake of fortifying his spirit, and preparing for his ministry.

As he advanced in years, he grew "strong in spirit," acquiring clearer and profounder views of his mission, and animated by a constantly increasing zeal for its accomplishment.

The precise time of the commencement of his ministry is uncertain.† The word of God came to him in the desert, and instantly he traversed the mountains and valleys of Judea, announcing the baptism of repentance, and the remission of sins. He took up his position especially at Bethabara, one of the passages of the Jordan, where he baptized those who became his disciples, and the disciples, by this means, of the coming Redeemer. To the questions which the

* Luke i. 76–79.

† It was in "the fifteenth year of Tiberius, Pontius Pilate being governor of Judea," &c., as we are informed by Luke, but in what season of the year is a matter of conjecture. It is supposed, however, to have been in the spring of the year. John was then thirty years of age, six months older than Christ.

people addressed him respecting their future course, he replied in the most practical manner, advising each class to attend to their respective duties, to amend their lives, and in humble penitence, to anticipate the speedy advent of the Holy One.* His preaching and mode of procedure, are not those of a fanatic, but of a noble, self-denying reformer. He cheers the contrite, directs the wayward, humbles the proud, and exhorts all to reform their hearts and their lives. To the Pharisees and Sadducees, whose haughty spirit and whose sham religion he despised, he addresses the severest rebukes: "O generation of vipers, who hath warned you to flee from the wrath to come? Bring forth fruits meet for repentance; and think not to say within yourselves, We have Abraham for our father; for I say unto you, that God is able of these stones to raise up children to Abraham." Thus John announced the need of personal reform, and of a new spiritual kingdom among men. His views are elevated and comprehensive. Unlike the Pharisees and Sadducees, he does not rely upon outward forms and mere beliefs, and unlike the Essenes, he does not confine his teaching to a class, or attempt to form secret fraternities, but to reform the people, to benefit the race.

* Luke iii. 11-15.

Lustration by bathing in water was long practised before the time of John, by the Jews, and, indeed, by all the ancient nations. The performance, then, of the baptismal rite, as symbolic of a new spiritual change, or a new and divine faith, would naturally strike the Jews as an assumption of high ecclesiastical authority. This especially affected all ranks of the nation, and attracted the attention of the Jewish council, who sent a deputation to inquire into his claims. He distinctly acknowledged that he was not the Messiah, nor Elijah, (in the sense they understood it,) nor that old prophet, whoever he might be, who, according to Jewish tradition, was to precede the coming of the Messiah, and perform certain wonderful actions in the temple and elsewhere. "No," said he; "I am the voice of one crying in the wilderness, Prepare ye the way of the Lord, as saith the prophet Esaias;" thus disclaiming all personal supremacy or independent authority, especially disclaiming all design of founding a peculiar sect, or setting up a new system, yet clearly intimating that he was the herald of the Lord, whose "baptism of fire and of the Holy Ghost," that is, a complete and divine transformation both of the individual and of the church, was dimly typified by his inferior baptism in the waters of the Jordan.

What a beautiful and touching proof of the

profound humility and self-abnegation of this greatest of the prophets! No, he was not the Messiah; indeed, he was not worthy, as he tells us, to stoop down and unloose the sandals of that divine Messenger; he would claim nothing for himself; for, in his own esteem, he was nothing separate from Christ. "*I am only a voice*," said he, "*an echo in the wilderness*, proclaiming the coming of the kingdom." He would stand back, sink out of sight, *for the Son of God was at hand.*

While John was thus engaged preaching the kingdom, and attracting crowds of followers, Jesus himself appeared, and asked baptism at his hand. With respect and astonishment, John hesitated; for he probably knew him as one far his superior in sanctity and worth. Struck, too, with his appearance of dignity, and perhaps inwardly suspecting that he was the promised Messiah, though not yet "officially certified of the fact," as he himself informs us, John, who uniformly evinced the deepest humility, declined the service, saying, "I have need to be baptized of thee; and comest thou to me?" But, yielding to the authority of Jesus, who replied, "Suffer it to be so now; for thus it becometh us to fulfil all righteousness," — perform every duty, or, as George Campbell translates it, "ratify every institution," — he went down with him into the water, and administered the sacred rite. It had previously been announced to John, that the sign of the Messiah should be the descent upon him of the Spirit from heaven, in some special or symbolic form, at his baptism. As Jesus then ascended, a luminous appearance, in the form or with the undulating motion of a dove,* (in all ages the symbol of purity and gentleness, and, in this instance, of the Holy Spirit,) descended upon the head of Jesus, and a voice was heard from heaven, recognizing him as the Son of God, well pleasing to the Father, and his accredited Messenger to the world. It was at this point that John knew, for certainty, that Jesus was the promised Messiah; and from that hour he commended him to the people as "the Lamb of God, which taketh away the sin of the world." "For, although the Baptist had a glimpse of him," says Jeremy Taylor, "by the first irradiations of the Spirit, yet John professed that he therefore came baptizing with water, that 'Jesus might be manifested to Israel;' and it was also a sign given to the Baptist himself, that 'on whomsoever he saw the Spirit descending and remaining,' he is the person 'that baptizeth with the Holy Ghost.' And God chose to actuate the sign at the waters of Jordan, in great and religious assemblies, convened there at John's bap-

* Ωσεῖ περιστερὰν, Matt. iii. 16. Εν σωματικῷ εἴδει, Luke iii. 22.

tism; and, therefore, Jesus came to be baptized, and, by this baptism, became known to John, who, as before he gave to him an indiscriminate testimony, so now he pointed out the person in his sermons and discourses, and by calling him 'the Lamb of God,' prophesied of his passion, and preached him to be the world's Redeemer and the sacrifice for mankind." *

After his baptism, Jesus, it would seem, mingled with the crowd, or retired from the scene. John, doubtless, in private, announced to his own immediate disciples the appearance of the Messiah.

The next day, John seeth Jesus coming unto him, and saith, "Behold the Lamb of God, which taketh away the sin of the world. This is he of whom I said, After me cometh a man which is preferred before me," &c. "This is the Son of God." Again: on the day following, John stood and two of his disciples; and looking upon Jesus as he walked, he saith, "Behold the Lamb of God!" Thus John introduced the Messiah to his disciples, in consequence of which, several of them, immediately, or soon after, devoted themselves, doubtless in accordance with John's wishes, to the service of Christ. They were prepared to follow him, as the Son of God, the Redeemer of Israel. Among these were

* Works, vol. ii. p. 184, English edition.

Andrew, Simon, Philip and Nathanael, the latter of whom, receiving a convincing proof of the amazing knowledge of Jesus, exclaimed, "Rabbi, thou art the Son of God, thou art the King of Israel."

The testimonies cited from John the Baptist are important, as indicating his views of the character and mission of Christ. They prove that he regarded him as a spiritual and divine Redeemer, "the Son of God" by preëminence, "a name above every name," as St. Paul affirms; and not only so, but that he regarded his message as one not formal and local, or simply Jewish, but moral and universal. He designates him the *Lamb of God*, reminding us of the *paschal lamb*, the means of redemption to Israel in that terrible night when the angel of destruction *passed* over their houses, on which the blood of the *paschal lamb* had been sprinkled, and in all subsequent time offered in sacrifice, on the day of the great annual *passover*, thus indicating the character of Christ as a *spiritual Deliverer*, "*our paschal Lamb*," as he is styled by the apostle of the Gentiles, "the Lamb of God, *who taketh away* the *sin*" — not the political degradation and bondage, but *the sin* of Israel, and not of Israel only, but "of the *world*." How lofty, spiritual, and comprehensive are these views of John the Baptist! how much in harmony with those of the ancient prophets, of Christ himself, and of the whole Christian church!

John continued to preach these great doctrines to the people, and in various places, in Ænon, near to Salem, for example, by baptism, to prepare disciples for the Master. When a discussion arose between some of John's disciples and those of Jesus, about purifying, (perhaps the effect ascribed to baptism,) the Baptist declared his inferiority to the great Messiah, and his consequent unwillingness to form a school or sect separate from his. He avowed his mission to be subordinate and preparatory. "He must increase, but I must decrease."

Subsequently we find John cast into prison, for his stern fidelity to duty, in reproving Herod Antipas (who greatly respected him as a prophet) for having Herodias, his brother's wife, a fact referred to by Josephus. Here lingering in confinement, his disciples, come to him, and ask him about the Messiah, concerning whom they began, under the circumstances, to cherish some doubt. It is not, indeed, impossible, though it would seem highly improbable, that John, depressed in mind, might himself have yielded to doubt. But the circumstances seem to forbid such a supposition. And hence we conclude that the difficulty lay in the minds of his disciples, for whose satisfaction he sent them to Jesus, with the question, "Art thou he that should come, or do we look for another?" At the moment they arrived, Jesus was performing some of his wonderful works. Instead of answering them directly, he said, "Go and show John again those things which ye do hear and see: the blind receive their sight, and the lame walk, the lepers are cleansed, and the deaf hear, the dead are raised up, and the poor have the gospel preached unto them."* Then follows our Savior's beautiful testimony to John: "What went ye out into the wilderness for to see? A reed shaken with the wind? But what went ye out for to see? A man clothed in soft raiment? Behold, they that wear soft raiment are in kings' palaces? But what went ye out for to see? A prophet? Yea, I say unto you, and more than a prophet. For of those that are born of women, there hath not risen a greater than John the Baptist." "Nevertheless," he added, referring probably to the case of a disciple made perfect in the kingdom of God, glorified in body and in spirit, "he that is least in the kingdom of God is greater than he" — thus resolving all greatness into purity and love.† There could

* Matt. xi. 3-6.

† Perhaps, however, the reference here is to a disciple in the kingdom or church of God, fully established on earth, subsequent

be no diversity of opinion and purpose, then, between Christ and John ; both fully understood that the deeper radiance of the kingdom of heaven swallows up and absorbs all lesser lights. The one as the Sun of Righteousness, the other as the star which heralds his coming, advance, joyously, into the unobstructed effulgence of the eternal kingdom.

At length, John disappears from the scene. He was beheaded at the instance of Herodias, and thus entered glory, by a quick, though bloody passage. His work was done; Jesus alone must appear on the scene, and occupy the entire field of vison.*

to the descent of the Spirit on the day of Pentecost, and so possessing higher views and enjoying greater privileges than John. Though elevated, we are not to suppose the views of John to be as perfect, or as clearly defined, as those of the early Christians, who lived after the permanent establishment of the church. See Olshausen *in loco.*

* Some of John's disciples did not carry out the spirit of their master, but forming a peculiar sect, lapsed into narrow Jewish prejudices, and carnal usages. Hence the *Ebiontes.*

CHAPTER XI.

THE MYTHIC THEORY.

We have dwelt the longer, in the preceding chapters, on the preparation of Christ for his public ministry, as well as on the character and mission of John the Baptist, because they supply the materials for a refutation of one of the most plausible and ingeniously supported theories of modern scepticism — to account, on natural grounds, for the life and character of Jesus, as the acknowledged Messiah. We refer to the hypothesis of Strauss, developed in his Life of Jesus, and adopted in its fundamental features by the great body of sceptics in Europe and in this country, among whom we may name Theodore Parker, who has reproduced it for the benefit of American readers. We have already alluded to this theory, but we wish to take some further notice of it, as it is confessedly the boldest yet proposed, to account for a life, which Rousseau himself was compelled to consider a miracle.

It is based, we may premise, upon a fundamental denial of the possibility of miracles — a prodigious assumption, as most persons will regard it, yet a perfectly natural one to Strauss, who, philosophically, is a pupil of the pantheistic school, and, therefore, positively denies the existence of a personal God. Nature and God, in his theory, are confounded. He knows no God but "the Absolute Essence, which comes to consciousness in man." Nature, or the external universe, is but the necessary and eternal manifestation of the divine. All, indeed, is divine, as man is divine, and in its essence changeless and eternal. What we call change, or the relation of cause and effect, according to this theory, is but the ebb and flow of the uncreated being, who reveals himself in nature and in man. Under such a system, the idea of new beginnings or creations, whether in the natural or the spiritual worlds, of special interventions and revelations, as ordinarily understood, and, above all, of miracles and incarnations, is inadmissible. Such divine interpositions, beyond the sphere of natural or ordinary causes, Strauss pronounces impossible.*

Keeping this in mind, we present the following, as a fair statement of the substance of his theory: —

* It is on this ground that Neander designates the controversy commenced by Strauss as "a struggle between *Christian Theism* and a system of *world and self deification.* — Preface to his *Leben Jesu.*

"All that is miraculous in the life of Christ, as given in the gospel, and recognized by the church, is mythical; that is, it is the natural exaggeration of a credulous and superstitious age, anxious to exalt its heroes into divinities. There was such a man, such a teacher and reformer, as Jesus, the principal natural events of whose life are probably real historical facts; but all else, all especially that is supernatural, his birth from a pure virgin, the song of the angels, the star in the East, the miracles, the resurrection, the ascension, &c., are legendary or fictitious. He was a native of Nazareth, the son of Joseph and Mary. Some exhibition of uncommon intelligence may have given rise to the story of his sojourn in the temple, when twelve years old, though this is doubtful. He probably had some instructions from the Essenes or from the Jewish Rabbins, and intelligent persons whom he met at the feasts at Jerusalem. At about thirty years of age, he became a follower of John the Baptist, who appears to have belonged to the sect of the Essenes, and to have proclaimed the popular idea, very natural among an oppressed people, that the great national deliverer was at hand. Jesus probably remained a follower of John the Baptist much longer than the partiality of tradition would allow us to believe. At length he began to preach, at first the same doctrine with

John the Baptist, that the Messiah was about to appear. Gradually becoming conscious of his extraordinary power, the idea occurred to him that he was destined to fill that office. His conception of the Messiahship, at first probably similar to that entertained by the Jewish people, rose with his increasing experience, until, applying to himself the prophecies of the Old Testament, which speak of the Messiah as suffering, he was convinced that a violent death, which the malice of his enemies rendered probable, was a part of his mission. Having exercised the mission of a teacher and reformer of morals, he was at length put to death. He did not rise again, but the excited imagination of his followers presented his form in visions; a report spread of his resurrection, which was believed among his followers, and contributed chiefly to the success of his religion."

On this ground, Strauss and his followers ascribe no *fraudulent designs* either to Christ or his disciples. The whole conception of his Messianic character is attributed to the force of imagination. The myth, based upon a few fragmentary natural facts, grew, so to speak, by accretion, so that the church did not receive, but gave itself a divine Messiah. The followers of Christ, then, are in no sense impostors, but simply enthusiasts, who, finding certain things predicted of the Messiah in the ancient prophets, imagined that they must have happened, as matters of fact, in connection with the life of Jesus.

It hence follows, that the Christian records were the gradually accumulated result of traditions, hearsays, and imaginings; and thence, that they contain a few grains of truth amid a vast accumulation of legendary fiction.

This theory, apparently ingenious as an hypothesis, and supported by minute and laborious learning, is contradicted by the facts in the case. At the best, it is a mere hypothesis. Its basis is gratuitous. Its main positions are simple historical guesses. Nay, its truth would seem to be impossible in the nature of things. On such a supposition the gospel is a production without a producer, an effect without a cause.

It is inconceivable, for example, either that the apostles, or Christ himself, with his vast intellect and serene affections, could have thus imposed upon themselves. His relations to John the Baptist, with the teachings and aims of both, are inconsistent with the supposition.

How, moreover, could the apostles, with their peculiar views and prejudices, spontaneously form and develop the idea of Christ's peculiar character and life, so far transcending any thing which had ever dawned upon their minds — so far, indeed, transcending the whole spirit of the Jewish people? But, even supposing that they could have originated and sustained the idea, it is incredible that they should have persuaded themselves that it was actually realized in Jesus of Nazareth. Were such the case, we must conclude not only that their intellects, but that their senses, were deceived. The events to which they testify, in the most natural and deliberate way, are of the most striking and stupendous character. They happened, also, according to their own accounts, beyond their expectations, and often in opposition to their wishes. How is it credible, then, that they could have been deceived as to their occurrence? Would it be likely, for example, that sane men would imagine that they had witnessed the great events of the American revolution — the declaration of independence — the battles of Lexington and Bunker's Hill — the crossing of the Delaware — the surrender of Burgoyne — the inauguration of the first president — if they had never witnessed them, above all, if these events had never occurred? Even supposing them superstitious and credulous — nay, more, looking for an American Messiah — could they be made to believe that they had found such in the illustrious Washington? that they had seen him perform the most stupendous miracles? that, after his death, he had risen from the grave, and held many conversations with them? and, finally, at the end of forty days, had ascended, in their sight, to heaven? Above all, could any man with the calm intellect, sound heart, and generous nature of Washington, even if a religious enthusiast, be made to imagine himself the Son of God — a special divine messenger, who, possessing supernatural powers, and performing divine miracles, was first to die and then to rise again from the dead — and thus become the founder of a new religion? After having predicted his own death by violence, and his resurrection on the third day, is it likely that such a death, and, above all, such an imaginary resurrection, should become the basis of a great religious system, the most beautiful and comprehensive the world has ever seen?

After his death, "a report," says Strauss, "spread of his resurrection." Is Christianity founded upon a report? To say nothing of our Savior here, how could his apostles, who ever bore a decisive and uniform testimony to his miracles, especially the miracle of the resurrection, as the foundation of their faith, and that, too, immediately after the supposed occurrence of the events, have done so, if such events had never happened? By what strange device could they make themselves believe that these great and startling phenomena actually happened under their eyes? They testify not to opinions or notions, but to *facts*—facts never contradicted by their enemies—facts for which they were willing to lay down their lives.

Moreover, if the Gospels were a mere collection of traditions, hearsays, and notions, growing spontaneously from the spirit of the age, or the spirit of a self-constituted sect, based upon some natural facts, as Strauss supposes, they would embody all the prejudices of the times, and give us a Messiah corresponding to the crude and fanatical views prevalent in such an age, and among such a sect. The character of a Messiah, so conceived, could not be coherent or symmetrical, but one-sided and fragmentary. Rude peasants would not be likely, by spontaneous effort, to compose a Miltonic epic, or construct the dome of St. Peter's. One would say, such a thing is impossible. How then could an ignorant sect of Jewish enthusiasts, long after the times of the actual Jesus, for that is the real supposition of Strauss, construct, out of the simple traditionary relics of his career, the grand and beautiful edifice of his Messianic character and life?

The Gospels, we may say, are the basis of Christendom. They are the fruitful germs of all that is elevated and comprehensive in the morals and civilization of our modern world. They have accomplished the greatest, the most beneficial revolution in the history of man. They reveal the spiritual and paternal character of God, and the true and equal brotherhood of man. Simple they are, but of wondrous power and beauty. Their teachings not only transcend the age in which they appeared, but all ages — they yet transcend ours. They are far in advance of our meagre policies and imperfect virtue. Their light, even now, streams far into the future, revealing a brighter and holier age to come, in which love to God and love to man shall be the reigning impulse.

In these wonderful compositions, the life of a *perfect* being, at once human and divine, is carried successfully, and with singular dramatic power, through the most exciting and tragic scenes, to its sublime and triumphant close. The genius of Æschylus or of Shakspeare is brought out, especially in death scenes; but what death scene, real or fictitious, will compare with that of Christ? What great historian or tragic poet, in his loftiest flights, has reached an elevation making the slightest approach to this? Ah, well might Rousseau say, "If Socrates died like a philosopher, Jesus died like a God!"

It is incredible that the writers, some of them eye witnesses of the events which they narrate, with their natural and minute statements of facts, written each from his own peculiar stand-point, and without reference to the others, should have cheated themselves by the mere force of imagination. They state only what two of them at least heard, and saw, and felt, and the others knew to be true, from the testimony of competent witnesses, as they themselves, over and over again, affirm.

Take, for example, the Gospel according to John, which Strauss, Bauer, and others have made such fruitless efforts to set aside. Its genuineness has been triumphantly vindicated.* Indeed, we are justified in saying that it is as certainly the composition of John as the Life of Agricola is that of Tacitus. Well, then, could John, with his pure character and clear intellect, persuade himself, by the mere force of imagination, that he had witnessed miracles which he had never witnessed; especially could he persuade himself that he had seen the empty sepulchre of Christ, then Christ himself, subsequent to his resurrection; that he had conversed with him in open day, had walked with him towards Bethany, and seen him ascend into heaven, if these things had never happened? Would it be possible for him to invent, not fraudulently, but

* See Tholuck on John, Olshausen on the Genuineness of the Gospels, as also Norton on the Genuineness of the Gospels, particularly the first volume of that able and elaborate work; see also Bunsen's *Hippolytus*, in which the theory of the Tübingen school is refuted, vol. i. pp. 40, 41, 87, 88, and vol. iv. pp. 105, 106.

through the mere force of fancy, the entire Messianic character, and ascribe it to one with whom he had associated during the whole of his public ministry, and must have known to be a mere natural man like himself? *Credat Judæus.**

Again: a myth and mythic writings, such as are supposed by Strauss, take a long time for their formation. Religions do not originate in myths. These are the growth of a subsequent age. Even supposing it possible, a century or two, at least, would be needed for the natural growth of such a system as Christianity, and the production of such writings as the Gospels and Epistles. But Strauss himself does not take the ground that they originated beyond the latter part of the first century, or during the first forty or fifty years after the death of Christ. For which reason, we once more affirm that their production, within that time, as myths or legends, cannot be conceived; for the actors in the scenes referred to, as well as their contemporaries, many of them interested and bitter enemies, were alive to prevent it.

Further: the testimony in favor of Christianity, as a supernatural, yet historical manifestation, is all on one side; there is actually no counter

* The same reasoning will apply, of course, to Matthew, and indeed to all the primitive Christian witnesses.

testimony. If such had existed, it would have been produced. The next age at least would have produced it. Celsus, Julian, Porphyry, the Jewish and heathen adversaries of Christianity, would have urged it. But all are silent. Hence Strauss has drawn upon his imagination, rather than his learning, in denying the genuineness of the Gospels, and ascribing a mythic character to Christianity. The legend, if any, is in his own brain, the myth is woven from the tissues of his own fancy.

So much is this the case, that among the truly learned in his own country, Germany, the mythic theory is regarded as an exploded error.

The fact is, in the life of Christ, as the merest tyro must see, the supernatural or divine is so blended with the natural or human, that they cannot be separated, without destroying both. Nay, the supernatural or divine greatly predominates; it is not simply the coloring, but the substance of the whole. So that if you strike out that, you leave nothing. The sun has vanished from the heavens. Strauss, indeed, pretends to leave a wonderful teacher and reformer, perhaps a great philosopher, but only in his own imagination; for all the wonderful in his history has vanished, and the teacher, whoever or whatever he may be, is not the Messiah — is not, in fact, the historical character, acknowledged as the founder of Christianity. When the foundation fails, the superstructure must fall.

It is the supernatural which forms the origin and basis of the Christian church. Without this, its existence as an historical fact would be an effect without a cause. But the Messiah, so transcendant and wonderful, even as a conception, — a conception, for which, says an eminent German writer, one might consent to be branded and broken on the wheel, — is not the product of the church; the church is the product of the Messiah. To say that the church has given itself a Savior, as Strauss maintains, is to invert the pyramid, is to make the river run backwards. It would be a greater miracle than the one supposed; nay, rather, it would be an absolute monstrosity. We can easily understand how light illumines darkness, but how darkness generates light is beyond our comprehension. The primitive church of the New Testament, with its lofty conceptions of God and immortality, its simple institutions, its pure morals, and, above all, its divine life, so superior to all Jewish, to all Greek and Roman ideas, can be traced only to Christ, and through Christ to God. The fountain generates the stream, not the stream the fountain.

Every religion fully represents its founder. His image is mirrored there. It is thus with

Islamism. Mohammed is its inspiring genius. You see nothing more, nothing less than Mohammed. It rises no higher, falls no lower than the prophet. It is human as he is human. His knowledge, his genius, his enthusiasm, his morals, his aims, such as they were, all are mirrored here. Hence every one sees at a glance what *he was*, from what *it is;* and the result is an indelible conviction that it is good in some respects, but still human, and not divine. So also in Christianity we see Christ. His life, his death and resurrection, above all, his divine or supernatural character, majestic and beautiful as the Godhead, all are here as in a mirror. God is love — Christ is love, infinite and immortal. We behold "in this glass the glory of the Lord." And the result is, in all those capable of appreciating it, an indelible conviction that it is divine, as he is divine. In fine, Christianity does not project Christ as its image or reflection, but Christ projects Christianity. He is its cause and origin, its animating spirit and life. If, then, Christianity is a reality, Christ is a reality. It is the one day which flows from the one sun.

The apostles themselves, the writers of the Gospels, the first Christians, the early martyrs are the product of Christ. Their existence, their heroic lives, their triumphant deaths are impossible without him. The Christian records are but his echo, and whether absolutely or only relatively perfect, they are authentic and true. One might admit even their fragmentary character, and yet maintain their integrity. Christ is mirrored in them, as the serene heavens are mirrored in the sea. And what, we ask, is seen in Christ himself? All the fulness, all the love and pity of the Godhead.

One might as well tell us that the sun and stars do not shine in the heavens, as tell us that Christianity is a myth, and the Bible a legend. The owl-like spirit of infidelity may flap its boding wings under the sunlight, and cry, *Where is it?* But yonder in the far depths is the king of day, and here on earth we bask joyously in his beams.

The author of the mythic theory, not fully satisfied with it himself, has occupied the greater portion of his ponderous work in commenting upon the apparent discrepancies, inconsistencies, and contradictions supposed to be found in the four Gospels; but in this department of inquiry he has suggested nothing new. All may be referred, without straining, to such omissions and variations as might naturally be expected in the depositions of four honest, independent witnesses. Such variations, as Starkie (on Evidence) has remarked, though furnishing the adverse counsel with a copious subject of cavil, are perfectly consistent with substantial harmony. Nay, they become a collateral proof of integrity; for they are precisely such as must necessarily be found in the concurrent testimonies of frank and competent witnesses. Unity with variety is their most distinguishing feature. Even allowing, for the sake of argument, the occurrence here of occasional slight mistakes, in reference to matters of time, plan, succession of events, and other details, the fundamental integrity of these writings is not thereby impeached.* They still remain on the same platform of substantial authenticity with all other historical documents. Those, indeed, who claim their plenary inspiration, will not, of course, admit the possibility of such mistakes; but this is a point which we are not discussing now; nor does it really enter into the question either of genuineness or authenticity. All we need now to assert is the fundamental historical verity of the Gospel narratives, so consistent and harmonious, and yet so natural and free. They are such, at least, as to satisfy the keen, exhaustive criticism both of a Neander and a Niebuhr.† So that we feel ourselves fully

* For a specific refutation of Strauss's objections, sometimes on his own grounds, see Neander's Life of Christ.

† The critical and sceptical tendencies of Niebuhr, as well as his boundless historical learning, are well known. He stands at the head of all critical historical investigators, as Neander stands at the head of all ecclesiastical historians. After a thorough examination

justified in saying that, if the gospel history is not authentic, there is no authentic history in the world.

We conclude, then, that the theory of Strauss is the production of his own imagination, based upon false assumptions and erroneous statements, inconsistent with historical verity, inconsistent especially with the genius of Christianity, and only plausible on the hypothesis that there is no God, or that man is his own God. It denies the possibility of the supernatural, the possibility of an historical Christianity, nay, the very possibility of a personal God, that is, of an

of the Christian records, at a time when his rationalistic doubts were stronger than at a subsequent period, he says, notwithstanding his admission of the fragmentary and even imperfect character of the Gospels, "But here, as in every historical subject, when I contemplated the immeasurable gulf between the narrative and the facts narrated, this disturbed me no further. He whose earthly life and sorrows were depicted, had for me a perfectly real existence, and his whole history had the same reality, even if it were not related with literal exactness in any single point. Hence, also, the fundamental fact of miracles, which, according to my conviction, must be conceded, unless we adopt the not merely incomprehensible, but absurd hypothesis, that the Holiest was a deceiver, and his disciples either dupes or liars, and that deceivers had preached a holy religion, in which self-renunciation is every thing, and in which there is nothing tending towards the erection of a priestly rule, nothing that can be acceptable to vicious inclinations. As regards a miracle, in the strictest sense, it really only requires an unprejudiced and penetrating study of nature to see that those related are as far as possible from absurdity, and a comparison with *legends, or the pretended miracles of other religions*, to perceive by what a different actual divine Intelligence, who may interest himself in man, and who, in the plenitude of his love, may come to us as an incarnation, and reunite us to himself.

As we proceed with our inquiries, we shall find constantly accumulating evidence of the absurdity of the mythic theory. The more we investigate the life of Christ, and the history thence resulting, the more we shall be satisfied of his supernatural character and mission.

It will not be necessary, however, to enter into any formal details in reference to the public ministry of Christ, and especially the closing scenes

spirit they are animated." —*Life and Letters*, i. pp. 339, 340. At a later period of his life, when his views were more mature, he gives us the following, as reported by Neander, (Life of Jesus,) who hailed them as "*golden words* from one of the greatest men of modern times." "In my opinion," says he, "he is not a Protestant Christian who does not receive the historical facts of Christ's earthly life in their literal acceptation, with all its miracles, as *equally authentic with any event recorded in history*, and whose belief in them is not as *firm and tranquil as his belief in the latter* ; who has not the most *absolute faith* in the articles of the Apostles' creed, taken in their grammatical sense, who does not consider every doctrine and every precept of the New Testament as undoubted divine revelation, in the sense of the Christians of the first century, who knew nothing of a theopheustia. Moreover, a Christianity after the fashion of the modern philosophers and pantheists, without a personal God, without an immortality, without human individuality, without historical faith, is no Christianity at all to me, though it may be intellectual, very ingenious philosophy. I have often said that I don't know what to do with a metaphysical God, and that I will have none but the God of the Bible, who is heart to heart with us."

of his wonderful career, as these are presumed to be familiar to our readers. We shall group all we have to say, in reference to the whole, under two heads, namely his Teaching and Miracles.

CHAPTER XII.

TEACHING.

If it be atheism to exclude God from the realm of matter, it is equally atheism to exclude him from the realm of mind. As a supreme and universal Spirit, which the Scriptures teach him to be, he is "all and in all." The "Father of light," he is also the "Father of spirits," from whom "cometh every good and every perfect gift." Man, indeed, is endowed with reason and will, and thence has the power of choice, on which account he may morally depart from God; still he lives in God, and God lives in him as the essence of his being; so that, in order to be happy, man must return to God — in other words, recognize God as the very fountain of his spiritual life. In this sense, existence is not life; in the latter lies the element of love, and thence of happiness. Existence, indeed, may become the deepest curse, for it may be burdened with spiritual hate, which is death. In the world of mind, then, God reigns through the free choice and affection of each individual spirit. Harmony, interior and indestructible, is possible only through faith and love.

This is the essential teaching of Divine Revelation, as it is the essential teaching of nature, could we read it aright. It is the foundation principle of Christianity. In Jesus Christ this great truth is incarnated. It lives and glows in his wondrous career, as the Word of God, the Redeemer of men. "I in them, and Thou in me." In this central unity, which is God, all souls must converge. "This is the true God and eternal life."

Hence we find our Savior equally at home in the bosom of nature and in the bosom of God — in the inner and in the outer world. He is "the light of the world." He is "the life of man." In him dwelleth "all the fulness of the Godhead bodily." He possesses "all power in heaven and on earth."

So that Christ is ever found standing at the centre of things, whether in the sphere of matter or of mind, of history or of religion, "drawing all men," and not only "all men," but all angels, "unto him." By him "were all things created, visible and invisible" — he is "before all things, and by him all things consist," as Paul expressly teaches. That is, all things find their centre in him, come to order and harmony in him.*

* This, as stated in a former part of this work, is the import of the remarkable term *consist*, (Greek *συνέστηκεν*,) literally "in him all things stand together."

Men often acknowledge the supremacy of God in the world of external or material forms, but deny it in that of interior and spiritual forces. They discern the action of his creative and renovating spirit in the seasons. Joyfully they sing, —

> "O God, thou art the life and light
> Of all this wondrous world we see;
> Its glow by day, its smile by night,
> Are but reflections caught from thee;"

but they frequently close against him, both theoretically and practically, the domain of the soul, and deny the very possibility of a new creation, or renovation there. Hence their alienation and irreligion, even amid the forms and symbols of worship. Hence, also, their rejection of a profound spiritual religion, of real union with God, and that interior life fitly called divine.

But our Savior aims, both by precept and example, to bring men to the practical acknowledgment of God's supremacy, not only in nature, but in the soul; so that, spiritually, they may live in God, as God lives in them.

This is the true coming of the kingdom of heaven, not with outward movement, or mechanical force, but by inward life and spiritual control. "The kingdom of God cometh not with observation; neither do men say, Lo, here! or Lo, there! but the kingdom of God is within you."

Christ does not despise the outward, except

when it is forced into competition with the inward. On earth, he seems imbosomed peacefully in nature, which ever does him homage. Nay, more, he imbosoms himself in society. It seems his natural home. Rejected and despised by his apostate countrymen, he yet comes to them as a brother and a friend. His death itself does not remove him from the race. He abides there by his spirit. Through this means he organizes a church, or spiritual family, in which he may dwell, bound together by love, and observant of all holy precepts. Being himself the embodiment of the divine, he would ever give a beautiful body to a beautiful soul; so that the church is analogous to his body, and is even called by his name. Thus he has enshrined the kingdom, in its essential powers, in fair forms and usages, to be observed by his followers to the end of time. In this way, the reality within expresses itself by the image, or utterance without. But the interior power is first, as the soul is first, or as God, who is a spirit, is first. The spirit must generate the form, as God creates the universe, or renews the face of the earth, in the form of plants and flowers.

Clearly, then, the kingdom of heaven is inward, spiritual, immortal; and in that kingdom God, "the Father of us all," must be "Alpha and Omega, the beginning and the end."

This is only another mode of expressing the fact, that a religion, to be good for any thing, must be a religion of spiritual or vital force — a religion of inward light and love, all-comprehending and imperishable.

Such a religion, however, must be taught both by word and deed — that is, by the word within, and the word without — for all action is a kind of word. It must embody and exemplify itself in a divine and human life. God and man must be seen in company; the union, secret and indestructible, must be exhibited at once in speech and in action.

For this reason, Christ lives as the incarnation or embodiment of God. The Son reveals the Father. The one is the measure and manifestation of the other. Through the Son, the Father communicates his life to the world. Thus God comes, as Christ comes. His reign is acted into the historic life of man — into the life of each Christian soul. So that now "the tabernacle of God is with men." We dwell in him, he dwells in us. All are one, as God and Christ are one.

A religion, then, which stops short of God, and a true reign of heaven in the soul, has neither truth nor power. That only is real and divine which first brings God to man, and then brings man to God. Harmony, deep and eternal, is found only in the God-man, and the ineffable union thence secured between the soul of a believer and the Spirit of God — a result accomplished by a reconciling and regenerating power on the part of *Christ*, by a penitent and confiding faith on the part of the *Christian*. "God is in Christ, reconciling the world unto himself."

How plain, then, the proposition, already hinted, that Christ presents himself to us as an infinite central power, from which flows a spiritual influence to redeem the lost, and thus constitute a sacred organization, which may be the light and glory of the world!

All this is expressed by Christ in a few pregnant sentences, which he uttered in the form of supplication, just before his death. "That they all may be *one*, as *thou, Father, art in me, and I in thee*, that they also may be *one in us;* that the world may believe that thou hast sent me. And the *glory* which thou gavest me I have given them; that they may be *one, even as we are one; I in them, and thou in me*, that they may be made *perfect in one*."

The same great truth has been uttered in all ages by the church universal, in that prayer which Christ taught his disciples, the model and form of all true supplication: "Our Father who art in heaven — hallowed be thy name. *Thy kingdom come. Thy will be done on earth as it is done in heaven.*" This, then, is the key note of our Savior's teaching.

True to this grand conception, which, as a conception, is original and perfect, like the sun shining by its own light, Jesus Christ went forth "to teach and to preach" amid the hills and valleys, and in the cities and villages of Judea. He addressed himself chiefly to the common people, in language of marvellous simplicity and force. He spoke to them respecting God and the soul, sin and holiness, life and death, duty and immortality, as man had never before spoken. And not only so, but he looked all he said, acted all he said; so that he himself was a living Word, an embodied, eternal Discourse.

So striking and authoritative was his teaching, and yet so simple and clear, that all were compelled to acknowledge its force. Attracting to himself a few childlike souls, mostly fishermen, who longed for the coming of the kingdom, of which they cherished only dim conceptions, he made known to them gradually the design of his mission, and the principles of his kingdom. The terms used are so familiar and translucent, and yet so perfect and full, that while, from our familiarity with them, they seem the merest commonplaces, they yet contain the grandest and deepest verities. But they would never have become commonplaces, even to us, had they not possessed, at first, the most complete originality, as well as the most touching simplicity. Like the unchanging stars, familiar to us from childhood, they are more than they seem. Their beauty is of the infinite. Back of these luminous points lie undiscovered worlds.

Indeed, the language of Christ is not that of the schools, far less of the rhetoricians. It is scarcely language at all. So transparent is it, you see the things rather than the words. In fact, it is only when you see the things rather than the words, that you understand him. "Blessed are the pure in heart, for they see God." "There is joy in heaven, among the angels of God, over one sinner that repenteth." "Our Father." "Take no thought [care] for the morrow. Consider the lilies of the field, how they grow. They toil not, neither do they spin; and yet I say unto you, that Solomon, in all his glory, was not arrayed like one of these." "Peace I leave with you, my peace I give unto you." "In my Father's house are many mansions; if it were not so I would have told you. I go to prepare a place for you." "He that hath seen me hath seen the Father." "God is a spirit." "Labor not for the meat that perisheth, but for that which endureth to eternal life." "Two men went up unto the temple to pray, the one a Pharisee, the other a publican. The

Pharisee stood by himself and said, 'God, I thank thee that I am not as other men are, unjust, extortioners, or even as this publican.' But the publican, standing afar off, would not so much as lift up his eyes unto heaven, but smote upon his breast, and cried, 'God be merciful to me a sinner." How simple all this, but how full, how significant!

The teaching of Christ is that of inspiration, or, as we term it, of revelation, a revelation as rich and varied as nature itself; new and strange, like the well-known face of earth and sky, in which all forms are blended with a familiar, yet mystic beauty. In a word, it is the utterance of that eternal Wisdom (Logos) from which are all things, natural and divine. "Never man spake like this man." Sometimes in the synagogues, but oftener in the open air, by the wayside or by the well, on the mountain or by the margin of the lake, in the shadow of the temple or in the depth of the wilderness, he uttered his words of life. Nothing could be more natural, nothing more thrilling and impressive.

The originality, completeness, and imaginative beauty of his parables, in which the highest, most abstract, spiritual truths are embodied in familiar forms, which have all the vividness of life, must have greatly struck the minds of the people. Containing unknown depths of spiritual truth, they are yet simple and beautiful as the falling dew, or the blowing clover. God and the soul, in their mysterious relations, duty and happiness, sin and misery, the infinite and immortal state, regeneration and resurrection, the renovation of society, the restitution of all things, the everlasting life, the everlasting death, all are incarnated in these marvellous inspirations. The invisible world is made as patent as the visible; mysterious, indeed, as all things are mysterious, stretching away into the everlasting immensities, yet real, palpable, glowing. Every thing external and internal is set in motion; all around us, within us, and above us, trembles with life. The most delicate and affecting relations, the deepest feelings, the most amazing facts and changes in the realm of spirit, are bodied forth in shapes of grace and power.

Indeed, all outward things, in the parabolic and figurative language of Christ, are made to symbolize and describe invisible realities. The elder dispensations, the types and shadows of the Jewish worship, the temple with its mystic forms and magnificent ritual, all external changes and usages, earth and sky, mountains and streams, plants and animals, are made to range themselves, in figurative beauty, around his marvellous revelations.

But what is most peculiar in the teaching of

Christ is, that the whole is but an image or reproduction of himself. All that is human, all that is divine, meets in him, and thence utters itself in his words and deeds. Here is all the past, both of history and prophecy; here all the present, whether of earth or heaven, of natural or supernatural; here all the future, with its amazing changes, its restitutions and resurrections. In him dwelleth all the fulness of the universe, because "all the fulness of the Godhead;" power, purity, love, beauty, blessedness, — in a word, all the possibilities of the human and the divine.

Hence it is only as we come into fellowship with Christ that we come into fellowship with God and the universe, and feel that deeper love which is the harmony of all worlds. "I am the way, the truth, and the life." "No man cometh unto the Father but by me." "The Father loveth the Son, and hath given all things into his hand." "I in them, and thou in me." "I give my life for the world." "I give unto them eternal life." "Believe in God, believe also in me." "My Father will love you, and we will come and make our abode with you." "I and the Father are one."

Hence the force of his own most significant explanation: "This is life eternal, to know thee, the only true God, and Jesus Christ, whom thou hast sent." "This," says the apostle, as if repeating the Master's words, "this is the true God, and eternal life."

This leads us to remark, that the life of Christ is a unit, as his character is a unit, or as God is a unit. Hence his doctrine is a unit, also; for it has its great central principle, like the gravitation of nature, from which all other principles diverge, and to which they all return. This central, all-comprehending truth is, that God IS ALL AND IN ALL; and being such, that "HE IS RECONCILING THE WORLD UNTO HIMSELF."

It may be viewed, however, as it is taught in the words of our Savior and his disciples, who derived it *from him*, in its various details and applications.

What, in this view, then, are some of the leading principles taught by Christ?

1. *The "allness" of God*, including his *absolute spirituality*, *supremacy*, and *eternity*.

2. *The personality and paternity of God — "Our Father who art in heaven."*

3. *The spirituality of man, as formed in the divine image; the consequent possibility of his union and fellowship with God, and his immortality.*

4. *The atonement; that is, reconciliation or reunion between God and man, through Christ as a mediator; thence the doctrine of "justification by faith alone," faith being the link which unites the*

soul to Christ, and through Christ to God — "*I in them, and thou in me;*" *whence spring the freedom, strength, and joy of the Christian state.**

5. *Regeneration, or the new and eternal life in God* — "*born again*" — "*born from above*" — "*a new [spiritual] creation in Christ Jesus.*"

6. *The brotherhood of man, or the unity of the church* — "*one Lord, one faith, one baptism.*"

7. *Eternity, or the tendency of all things to fixed and permanent states; in other words, the final, absolute issue of all things according to their nature.*

8. *Responsibility, individual and common, involving the possible eternal divergence of character and doom, being the eternal life, or the eternal death.*

9. *The resurrection of the dead, or the completed perfection of the body and the soul; that is, of the whole nature of the renovated man — the earthly, carnal, and perishable being exchanged for the heavenly, the spiritual, and immortal.*

10. *Grace, or the Holy Spirit, a modification of the doctrine of the life in God, whence*

* The atonement, or reconciliation, is made by intervention and sacrifice. The sacrifice, of course, is voluntary and vicarious, that is, it is the suffering of the innocent for the guilty, the sinless for the sinful; not, indeed, as a *quid pro quo*, but as a *prerequisite* to union. On this ground the doctrine of mediation and sacrifice is fundamental. And, what is singular, it is recognized in all religions. See, upon this subject, Appendix, note E.

prayer, or the communion of the finite with the Infinite, the spirit of man with the Spirit of God.

11. *Charity, or the doctrine of overcoming evil with good, the method of Christ and of God.*

12. *The permanence of the church, or the organization of believers in Christ, as their central animating spirit, made visible in holy uses and worship.*

13. *The possible renovation of the race; on the ground of which we may cherish the hope of universal peace, and the brotherhood not only of individuals, but of nations. This would be the triumph of God in society. Then, not only in reference to himself, or his absolute nature and eternal purpose, but in reference to the race, and the actual condition of things, God would be all and in all.**

The sum of the whole is, *consecration of all things to God*, and *the restitution of all things in God*, a new law and a new life, a new body and a new soul, new heavens and a new earth; in its practical, every-day application, briefly and

* It is on the ground that society ought to be regarded as a divine institution, yet to be planted on its proper basis, and to subserve its proper end. Under God, therefore, all righteous governments are to be established, and all good and wholesome laws enacted. This would not be the union of church and state, as ordinarily understood; but the church and the state, in their separate spheres, guarded and governed by eternal principles, and thus aiding and strengthening each other.

popularly expressed by Christ himself in his exposition of the law, "Thou shalt love the Lord thy God with all thy heart, and thy neighbor as thyself. On these two commandments hang all the law and the prophets."

But the great truths taught by original minds are not at first received and appreciated by the mass of mankind. They are seldom thoroughly understood even by their immediate disciples. Thus, while the common people heard him gladly on account of his simplicity, purity, and force, such was the grossness of the age, such the carnality of its views, that few, perhaps none, adequately understood his doctrine, or his life. Its elementary principles, however, were lodged, as seed, in the hearts of a few thoughtful, Heaven-guided men. Checking their carnal views, correcting their prejudices, winning their affections, he gradually led them forth from the darkness of corrupted Judaism into the pure light of eternal truth. His public or more striking acts, his miracles, as we call them, (of which more in the next chapter,) at first few and unimposing, though most significant, were just enough to attract attention to his claims, and attest the divinity of his mission. They were all distinguished by their godlike and benevolent character. Like his parables, they were the expression of his nature, and had a profound spiritual import. The poor, the maimed, the halt, the sorrowful, the blind, the dumb, the paralytic, the lunatic, the lost, followed him, and "he healed them all." But while healing their bodily maladies, he never failed to administer to their spiritual wants, thus teaching his disciples, in all ages, that religion is intended for the redemption of humanity, in all its aspects and interests, being fitted to heal both the body and the soul, both the church and society.

Christ counteracted no laws of nature, which are laws of God, or the modes in which God acts in nature and among men; but he gave them infinite force, and threw them into new and marvellous combinations, the result of which was calm, not storm, health, not sickness, life, not death. Perhaps we may say that he introduced new laws, or new modes of communicating the central power, which is life. Thence we find him healing, quickening, controlling, and blessing both the bodies and the souls of men; in a word, bringing out, in new and glorious manifestations, the indwelling might of divinity. Thus he received the testimony of unprejudiced witnesses, who said, "He hath done all things well." But the outward, in his case, is only the symbol and expression of the inward; for it is the inward redemption, the inward health, the spiritual and everlasting life, mainly, which Christ communicates.

In this way he went about "doing good"— a mode of teaching the most impressive. The Platonic philosophers call the great primal and eternal Essence the First Good, while his Logos, or Word, is the Son, or expression of the First Good. We call it God, the old Saxon word for *good.* Christ, then, is the embodied Good, which is just the same as to say, the incarnate God. And what else can he teach, what else can he do on earth, but good, the highest proof of divinity? Thus every where he preaches, both by word and deed, righteousness, charity, and peace, directs the attention of his followers to the paternal character of God, the universal brotherhood of man, and inspires them with that holy love which unites them to God and to one another, in eternal bonds.

Finally, Christ crowns his teaching by dying upon the cross, dying, "the just for the unjust." This is the triumph of divine goodness, this the enthronement of disinterested love. In this mysterious act, to use the language of a great poet, "the divine depth of sorrow lies hid." * "Father, forgive them, for they know not what they do!" There speaks the heart of infinite grace.

This is teaching, this is acting like a God.

Surely the world can never forget the lesson of the cross.

* Goethe.

How the thought thrills us, thrills unnumbered millions, who softly but exultingly sing, —

> "In the cross of Christ I glory,
> Towering o'er the wrecks of time;
> All the light of sacred story
> Gathers round its head sublime."

CHAPTER XIII.

MIRACLES.*

The works of such a being as we suppose Christ to be, will possess a special divine character and import. They cannot, therefore, be considered apart from himself, or apart from each other. They belong to a supernatural system for the restoration of man to the lost image of God. Hence, in our humble judgment, a serious error has been committed in the discussion of this subject, by isolating the miracles from the essence of Christianity, as itself supernatural, just as if miracles did not form an integral part of the gospel dispensation, whose fair and massive proportions can be estimated only when contemplated as a divine whole. The majority who have written upon miracles have vindicated their title to our respect, as the external defence of Christianity, treating them simply as redoubts and outposts of the sacred citadel; on which account they have seemed to reason in a circle, proving

* This chapter, with some additions, appeared in the July number of the Christian Review for 1853.

Christianity by the miracles, and the miracles by Christianity. They have admitted, on Hume's own ground, that no amount of testimony will establish a lying wonder, or what may be termed an immoral miracle, that is, a miracle wrought in defence of error and imposture, all of them taking it for granted that such miracles may be performed through satanic or other equivalent agency.

Hence they have been compelled to defend Christianity by that which Christianity alone can authenticate as divine. Having courageously fought the battle of miracles, and, as they supposed, gained the victory, they have found themselves obliged to fight it all over again in defending Christianity itself. Thus it has come to pass, in the estimation of some of the ablest speculative thinkers, that, instead of being a defence to Christianity, miracles have proved its greatest hinderance. For, without the essence of Christianity, as a religion of purity and power, miracles, as supernatural manifestations, would be utterly indefensible. Some devout men have been able to retain the miracles only by means of the perfect and supernatural religion with which they are associated; a striking instance of which may be found in the case of the eloquent Schleiermacher.

For the same reason, sceptical writers, like

Hume, Spinoza, Comte, Emerson, Parker, and others, have readily disposed of technical and isolated miracles as simple prodigies, or, as they choose to call them, "violations of the laws of nature." Standing alone, outside of Christianity, they have easily swept them aside by the philosophy of "nature," or of immutable law, whether material or ideal. Even those of them who believe in a personal God, as Parker professes to do, have no hesitation in denying miracles, in themselves considered; for God, in their view, cannot be supposed to violate or even suspend the law of his own universe, that is, the common course and constitution of things. Miracles, even if admitted as possible, on the theory of these men, stand alone, and require for their establishment a peculiar kind and amount of proof. Hence they set themselves to weaken the force of that proof, often with apparent success, long before the gospel, as a system, is touched at all. Their assumption, too, about "the violation of nature," which, in some sense, may be considered impossible, is made plausible on the same ground; so that the Christian faith seems demolished before a single blow has fallen upon its proper fabric.

Let us pass, however, into the heart of the magnificent structure of our common Christianity, founded upon the Rock of Ages, and towering high towards the illuminated heavens; and even if we admit that the miracles, as such, are its outer buttresses, we shall see, at a glance, that they are a part of the whole, and only add to its symmetry and strength. The materials, too, are precisely the same, though the interior portions may present a more delicate architectural finish; for they are all the product of a celestial hand. The whole, as supernatural and divine, must stand or fall together.

Is there a personal God? Has he a distinct, productive, all-controlling will? In other words, is he, the all-creative One, a Spirit, immanent, it may be, in nature, and yet superior to nature? Is man, too, though finite, a distinct, productive will, a rational and responsible agent, formed in the image of God? Is the outer universe, then, or what we call nature, with all its forces, dynamic or mechanical, under God, a mere agent or instrument; and can God control it with the sovereignty of a master? If so, then creations and re-creations, vital changes and transformations, new species and new eras, renovations, redemptions, miracles, as supernatural divine manifestations, are possible, are probable. The spiritual, the supernatural, the religious, are all possible and real.

Here we have a foundation on which to base our reasonings in reference to Christianity, which we claim to be, under God, a supernatural system, a new beginning or spiritual creation, through the medium of the Divine Logos, or incarnate Word, in which miracles play a most important part, not in violation of nature, but as above and beyond nature, being the more direct and tangible demonstrations of the life-giving or creative power.

But "to the law and the testimony;" for in this matter we must correct and control all speculative reasonings by a reference to the facts in the case. How stands the matter in the Christian records? This is our first inquiry. It is proper, however, to remark, that our word *miracles* (which simply signifies wonders, though, in the use we now make of it, involving the idea of the supernatural or divine) is somewhat indefinite, and scarcely covers the whole series of supernatural acts or works, by which our Lord not only attested, but accomplished, his mission. In the New Testament, quite a variety of terms are used to designate them, not simply as wonders, but as special divine acts, such as might naturally constitute or accompany a divine mission. They are called "signs," as it were divine signatures or seals, "gifts," "gifts of the Holy Ghost," "powers," "works," "mighty works," that is, special divine operations, indicating the presence and sanction of the Deity.

In brief, they are such "wonders" as might be expected from the "Wonderful."

Though these may be represented as the signs or attestations of a divine mission, they are not exclusively such; and hence, in the department of Christian evidences, too much stress has been laid upon their merely physical or external aspects. They have been used as the main, and sometimes as the exclusive, proof of divine revelation. Whereas the character of Christ, who in reference to the miracles is the sun amid the stars, is the principal evidence. His very presence among men, like a new sun in the heavens, is sufficient proof of his divinity. The miracles can only be a collateral evidence, and in many cases, perhaps, chiefly useful to those who beheld them. They are parts of a great system, whose divine grandeur and perfection must be obvious to every well-constituted mind.

At any rate, they ought never to be regarded as insulated facts, but rather as the natural expression and accompaniment of a divine mission. That admitted as a possibility, the miracles follow as a matter of course.

For what is it we naturally expect in such a manifestation of God? The godlike, of course; and if the godlike, the wonderful — nay, far more than the wonderful, the omnipotent, the all-beautiful and good.

Such miracles, though transcending nature, would not be contrary to nature; for nature, as we use the term, is only God's method of acting in the sphere and time with which we happen to be familiar. In its philosophical sense, it is but the aggregate of those natural forces or laws by which the infinite Spirit acts in the visible universe. Nature then is only a part. God is the whole. While "in all," he is yet "above all." Certainly his powers are not exhausted in nature; over and above all its methods and all its forces, he may possess infinite methods, boundless resources.

Some inconsiderate theologians, and almost all sceptics, as we have intimated, have represented the Christian miracles as "a violation of the laws of nature," whereas they are only "over and above nature." It is only in the sense of being divine, that we deem them transcendent and wonderful.

If any thing is contrary to nature, it is sin. That violates the divine law, that opposes the course and constitution of nature, introducing among men disorder and death. So terrible is its influence, that it has become a power in the world, having the force of a law, to which we sometimes give the name of nature, because, from the force of habit, it has become a "second nature;" after all, it is most unnatural and accursed. It opposes God and goodness, darkens and desolates the soul of man.

Sin, then, is disturbance, or anarchy, and in this sense a violation of all laws, natural and divine. For its removal, a counteracting force is needed, a force above nature, and yet in accordance with nature, a force of renewal and regeneration. It is a great and fatal mistake, however, to confine the miraculous or divine to mere physical or external manifestations. Its highest sphere is the spiritual. Here its life-giving and transforming energies are chiefly seen. Christ himself, the truly divine, is the great miracle; all other miracles are streams from this fountain, rays from this sun.

The whole subject, generalized, presents itself to us in the light of the following question: What may be reasonably expected in an incarnation of the Deity, such as Christ claims to be? All, doubtless, which is peculiar to God, and the great object to be served by his advent among men.

God is the omnipotent Creator; hence works or manifestations of creative power.

God is the all-good; hence manifestations of boundless love and pity.

God is the life-giver; hence miracles of healing, of revival and resurrection.

In a word, the whole mission of such a being

would be a new moral or divine creation, and thence a life-giving or transforming power. Negatively, he would cast out the demon, the incarnated, indwelling spirit of evil; positively, he would bring all heaven, with its love and peace, into the soul.

In which case the inward and spiritual would be symbolized and expressed by the outward and physical. All nature would wait upon its God. So that works of atonement, reconciliation, and regeneration would naturally be associated with works of physical control, of healing and resurrection in the outer or material sphere.

Thus any kind of wonderful or supernatural works would not be a proof of a divine mission; and many signs of a striking but mechanical character would not be found in it. Such works the Messiah might decline, even as proofs of his divinity.* Besides, he would attach, as we ought, more importance to his higher spiritual works, which link themselves immediately to the great end of his mission, than to any thing external, however striking. He might even refuse to work appropriate external miracles, when he perceived that they would not subserve his great

* "An evil and adulterous generation seeketh after a sign, [such a sign as that referred to,] but there shall no [such] sign be given it."

spiritual design, or only minister to selfish appetites and carnal views.*

The main thing, then, in such a mission, would be the new spiritual force or life, embodied in the person of the Redeemer, and imparted to the race — the holy love, the eternal purity and joy given by his incarnation and atonement to mankind.

In fine, the mission of Christ, if divine, would be a new spiritual beginning, of which the first beginning, in the physical creation, supplies a beautiful type or symbol. The miracles clustering around it, illustrating or enforcing it, would be only its outer garniture, or rather its natural and graceful accompaniment, like the song of the morning stars, which hailed the new-made world.

An inquiry here suggests itself: Might false or imaginary miracles mingle themselves in the mere histories of such a life? The thing is not impossible, but the proof of the fact must be given. It is, indeed, quite conceivable how that, in subsequent time, and as the mere human result of such a mission, imaginary miracles might be supposed, and some natural events mistaken for

* Hence our Savior refused to gratify Herod in this respect. On one occasion it is said, "he did no mighty works there, because of their unbelief." It would have been "casting pearls before swine."

miracles. We do not here say that such is the case; we only say that such is not impossible, perhaps not improbable. But this would not affect the argument in favor of the great life-giving powers, the miracles of renovation and resurrection, which form the substratum of Christianity.

It is important here to remark, that all miracles, or all events claimed to be supernatural, are not credible. In ordinary circumstances, they might be regarded as positively incredible. For then they are effects without an adequate cause. On the other hand, it does not follow that all miracles are incredible. Indeed, some events of this sort, in themselves, may be highly credible; for they may bear the stamp of divinity on their very front. So far from being effects without a cause, they may be presumed to have the highest cause in the universe, that is, God. The spurious article, however abundant, by no means proves that the genuine is not to be found somewhere. Were all other religions mythical, and all other miracles false, the religion of Christ, and the miracles of Christ, might be real and divine. That they are real and divine is proved by the facts in the case. They are altogether peculiar; they are such as might naturally be expected; they are worthy of their divine origin; they are such as must ever be found in connection with a divine mission, nay, such as must ever constitute a divine mission. For we return here to our fundamental position, namely, that Christ is "God manifest in the flesh," and his whole life, from beginning to end, supernatural and divine. It can be regarded as consisting of different parts, and some of its elements, taken alone, may be called natural and human; after all, it is one in its more interior characteristics, in which view it far transcends any thing among men. As a whole, it is supernatural and divine, and thence the means of a new spiritual life in the world.

The whole question of miracles, in its fundamental relations, thus turns on the possibility of the supernatural. Such possibility the opponents of Christianity generally deny, those of them at least who make the slightest pretensions to philosophical thought.

But the supernatural, as connected with Christianity, is equivalent to a new creation, or the exertion of a divine creative power. For example, the birth of Christ is a new beginning or creation. He comes into the world as a divine or supernatural agent. So also the changing of water into wine, the restoration of sight to the blind and of life to the dead, the feeding of five thousand persons with a few loaves and fishes, and the resurrection of Christ himself, are all creative acts, or acts equivalent to creative.

Now, the possibility of the supernatural, in this view, can be denied consistently only by those who deny the possibility of all divine creations. If, for example, they deny the existence of God, or a supreme creative Intelligence, or if they maintain the existence of such a God as cannot freely and intelligently create, they can deny the possibility of miracles. This, in fact, is the position assumed by all the abler opponents of Christianity as a supernatural scheme — Spinoza, Hume, Hegel, and Strauss.

Hence miracles have been rejected, first of all, on the ground of atheism. Of course with the class of theorists who take this monstrous position, we can have no discussion here, except to remind them, that modern science has actually proved the fact of successive creations. Geology has set this matter forever at rest.* We might also remind them, that man, in some sense a productive will, and so far capable of acting above what we call nature, or the outward creation, is capable of certain acts at least analogous to the supernatural. And if a finite intelligence can act thus, can interfere at certain points, in the movement of nature, by means of new combinations of power, and thus perform wonders,

* All the great geological writers maintain this — Lyell, Agassiz, Brogniart, Buckland, Murchison, Mantell, Miller, Hitchcock, and others.

which appear to his fellows, as in the case of the steam engine and the electric telegraph, all but supernatural, why may not an infinite Intelligence interfere, by miracles so stupendous and thrilling as to be equivalent to the creation of worlds? But atheists usually deny the freedom and spirituality of man, as well as the existence of a supreme creative Power, making man the mere machine of the universal machine which they call nature.

For the same reason, miracles have been denied on the ground of materialism. Rejecting the existence of spirit, and even of thought and volition, except as the production of matter, such theorists maintain the absolute material identity of all things. If there be a God, matter is that God, universal matter, or aught else they may choose to call it, governed by necessary and eternal laws, consequently revolving in an endless cycle, without the possibility of new beginnings, supernatural changes, or creations. Perhaps such men do not positively say what matter is; they speak only of its laws, and thence, as in the case of Auguste Comte, refer all things to the uniform and eternal action of necessary forces, in which religion is a necessary, though temporary development, in the "hierarchie des sciences positives." Of course, in such a system, there can be no place for miracles. Both God and Christ, and even man, as responsible spiritual agents, are denied. Man is but a link in the eternal chain, a bubble on the surface of the ever-flowing stream.

Is it not clear, however, that such persons deceive themselves by words? Matter, they say, is the whole. Then the question arises, What is this matter of which they predicate so much? The question is not answered by calling it, as most persons do, a substance, formal, limited, tangible, divisible, &c.; for these philosophers say it is absolute and eternal, nay, that it is *all and in all.* It is not an effect, but a cause, or it is both. On this theory it is a power, an omnipotent power, for it produces all things, does all things. Is it not then intelligent, adapting means to ends, working according to method and law? Is it not, in fact, a conscious, self-controlling agent, and may it not be holy, just, and good? Substitute, then, the term *God* for *matter*, and what have we but the old, eternal doctrine of the Creator, supreme over all, as well as in all — whence the possibility of creations, revelations, and miracles.

But Comte and his followers would say, We do not refer the universe to matter, or call it matter; we simply affirm that the whole consists of necessary and eternal laws, from which come all the changes or phenomena of the universe. Laws! what are they? They must be either methods or forces. If methods or rules, they are the methods or rules of some subject or cause, that is, of God; for they display infinite power and intelligence. If forces, we ask again, forces of what? for forces are attributes of a subject, qualities of a being.

The fact is, we are so constituted as to be under a necessity of referring all qualities and changes to some Essence or Being in whom they inhere, or from whom they proceed. Evidently, the universe, as we know it, is a production, an organization, or congeries of organizations, which must have a beginning or cause. And, as we know of no new changes or products among men, which have not, back of them, an intelligent agent, which we call *mind*, we are compelled to conclude, that the universe, as an organism the most complicated and beautiful, has, back of it, an all-creative Mind. And if so, all sorts of creations, and miracles among the rest, are possible.

But, thirdly, miracles are denied on the ground of pantheism.

There are various forms of pantheism, but in its proper, absolute character, it denies the personality of God as well as the personality of man, and thus represents the universe as God, and God as the universe, without consciousness, freedom, or intelligence.* Hence it views all

* As involving limitation and succession, personality cannot be

things, and all beings, man among the rest, as only parts of a whole, or rather as only limited manifestations of a whole, which it calls Nature, God, or Spirit, as it pleases. Thus Spinoza made the universe to consist of *Natura Naturans* and *Natura Naturata.* The *Natura Naturata*, or the outward universe, according to him, is the necessary and eternal manifestation of the *Natura Naturans*, or the absolute Substance, which has two attributes, Thought and Extension. The laws of such a nature, of course, are absolute, necessary, and eternal. There can be no freedom or choice, no new laws, or new applications of old laws, no reserved forces, no new creations, and no miracles.*

Pantheism, however, may be divided into physical and spiritual. The physical, or grosser form of pantheism, as in the Brahminism of India, deifies and worships the visible universe, sun and stars, earth and man, rivers and fountains, beasts and insects. In such a system there can be no positive sin. Man is God, as an insect is God. He proceeds from, and will finally fall back into, the abyss. This kind of pantheism, among the western nations, takes the

ascribed to God. But as involving freedom, consciousness, and reason, in their absolute perfection, it undoubtedly can.

* Opera, vol. i. p. 208 et seq. Spinoza's views of miracles are developed in the sixth chapter of the *Tractatus Theo.*, Opera, vol. iii. p. 86, et seq.

form of materialism, already noticed. It recognizes only the outward and material, and, in our mechanical age, refuses to worship.

The spiritual pantheism is that adopted by some of the idealists in Germany and elsewhere. It regards the outward universe, or the universe of material forms, as simply phenomenal or apparent. God, or the interior, absolute cause of the universe, is spiritual, consisting simply of Being and Thought, or of Being and Thought together, without conscious personality. According to Hegel, all we can know is the relations of things. God, as absolute, is an infinite Abstraction, that is, the absolute and inconceivable Essence, which he has called *Das Nichts*, (or *Nothing*,) meaning by that, not an absolute Nothing, such as ordinary mortals would conceive the word to mean, but an absolute Abstraction, in other words, Being or Thought, from which all conceivable relations and conditions are abstracted. But in the process of thought, according to Hegel, this Absolute passes into reality, which is the universe. Both, indeed, are eternal, for the *All* is only an everlasting oscillation between the negative and the positive, the absolute and the relative, the spiritual and the concrete. God, as the eternal Thought, which lies back of all change, comes to consciousness only in man, on which ground man is divine.

His development is the necessary progress of all history, of all religion, and morals. On this basis Hegel builds the vast superstructure of his logical and philosophical system.

The apparent pantheism of Schelling, much modified of late years, differs from this in many particulars, and admits, whether logically or not we do not now say, of a divine incarnation and atonement, and, so far, does homage to Christianity as a supernatural system.

It is clear, however, that the theory of Hegel, adopted, in its fundamental principles, by Strauss, Bauer, and others in Germany, and in this country, to some extent, by Theodore Parker, R. W. Emerson, and his willing pupil, Mr. Henry James, strikes at the very possibility of a supernatural religion, and especially of miracles. It might admit, and indeed does admit, of the existence of Jesus Christ as a necessary development of the divine, in the sense understood by the Hegelians, but not more so than any other good man. Hence these speculatists do not deny the reality of Christ, as a remarkable character, and author of a beautiful system of religion and morals. They only deny him as a supernatural being, or as God incarnate.*

* This is eminently true of Emerson and James, who have interwoven the Hegelian pantheism in their somewhat elegant, but superficial lucubrations.

It would be out of place here to attempt a formal refutation of Hegelianism. Indeed, to most sane persons it refutes itself. Its grounds and conclusions are equally absurd, though, as a system, distinguished by vast logical power, and occasionally suggesting grand and comprehensive views.*

If we ourselves are free agents, and not mere machines, spiritual or animal, (and who at bottom can doubt this, that knows himself?) we are compelled, by the constitution of our nature, to regard God as a free agent, self-conscious and self-controlled; and if thus free, then creative, freely creative; and if freely creative, then capable of intervention and miracle. It is not, indeed, for us to say, what he may or may not do, in the way of supernatural manifestation; but, assuredly, the idea of creation, of incarnation, and miracle, ascribed to him, is neither impossible nor improbable. Indeed, nothing would seem to be more probable; a consideration which accounts for the universal expectation and impression on the

* Hegel professed to construct his system without assuming any thing, whether matter or mind, thought or volition. But this was impossible. Unconsciously to himself, he assumed his own powers of thought. His "Das Nichts," though *negative*, involve the *positive*, as a necessary idea. His abstractions, then, must involve realities, that is, man as an intelligent, voluntary thinker and actor; and if man, then God, as the free and intelligent Creator of the universe. In this way his system refutes itself.

subject. Admit the idea of a personal God, interested in man, and you can admit easily all the miracles of the New Testament.

In its more naked character, pantheism is a monstrous and fatal error, and yet it is only the exaggeration of a great truth, namely, that God, while superior to his works, is not to be considered as separate from them. While over all, he is yet "in all," by a universal presence. Here we behold him as the all-comprehending Power, the all-pervading Wisdom and Beauty, a thought which brings him close to the heart. But the God of Hegel and Strauss, who comes to consciousness only in man, is a monstrosity, rejected alike by reason and revelation.

But while we admit God as "in all," we instinctively feel, all instinctively feel, that we ourselves are distinct personalities, and though derived from God and even dependent upon him, that we have a will and a purpose, a character and a career of our own. So, also, we feel that the external world is not only distinct from us, but distinct from God, and consequently that God, being himself a free and omnipotent agent, can do as he pleases, in the matter of incarnation and miracle.

Yet as nature is from God and under God, all his actings, however strange and stupendous, will be in harmony with those great laws through which he is wont to act. These, however, have already admitted of creations, of new and wondrous beginnings, changes, and developments, in organic forms and animals, as Hugh Miller and others have shown; so that no new creations or beginnings, whether in the sphere of matter or of mind, need occasion us any surprise. All we want is proof of the fact.

We apprehend, however, that the philosophical objection to miracles, as new creations, lies in the attempt to conceive how something can come from nothing. Those who believe this, as a simple fact, of course will not feel the force of the objection; for however mysterious the thing may be, they are compelled to suppose that all created things are made from nothing. But this cannot be strictly or absolutely true, God himself being supposed as ultimate cause or ultimate something; for of course there can be no effect without a cause, in which sense the maxim is true, *Ex nihilo nihil fit.* God creates all things, say theologians, from "the word of his power;" he "speaketh and it is done, he commandeth and it standeth fast;" on which ground miracles are possible. The philosopher might prefer to say that God creates all things from or out of himself; but in saying this he throws no new light upon the matter. It is simply admitting the great principle of adequate cause. The mystery or the rationale of the fact remains concealed.

Now, it is on this ground we urge not only the moral but the philosophical possibility of the Christian miracles, including the birth and the resurrection of Christ. It can never be shown that they must necessarily be the product of nothing, even on the lower ground of appearances. While supernatural power came in at particular points, natural causes, and sometimes preëxistent materials and forces, were used. The miraculous wine, for example, was a product from water, just as the wine of the grape is a product from natural elements.

Christ, as a new creation, had two terms, the human and the divine; he was both natural and supernatural, but not an effect without a cause. So also the healing and restoring power, which gave health to the diseased and life to the dead, was in Christ as a cause. "Virtue went out of him." His own resurrection was the effect of his eternal divinity, or eternally divine and indestructible life. Thence, while he died as to his manhood, by the separation of the soul from the body, or the human from the divine, he did not die as to his spiritual and immortal nature. The union only was suspended. When restored on the third day, of course he rose again. So that the maxim, that "from nothing nothing comes," will not apply here.

We add, fourthly, that the miracles have been rejected on the *mythic theory.*

Not content with metaphysical or even philological objections, Strauss, Parker, and others have endeavored to show that all the miracles are only natural myths, clustering around the few elementary facts which form the basis of Christianity. Because the religions of most nations, as well as many historical facts and personages, in the earlier period of their history, are invested with myths or legendary fictions, it is inferred that such also must be the case both with Judaism and Christianity. We have already considered this theory; we will therefore now limit ourselves to the remark, that though the premises may be admitted, the conclusion may be peremptorily denied. Because there have been many false pretensions to freedom, are we to conclude that there is no such thing, or that there never can be such a thing, as freedom? Because many histories, especially in their earlier periods, are fictitious and extravagant, must we infer that all histories are of the same character? Because religion has frequently appeared in the garb of myth and poetic legend, must we accept the conclusion that God cannot give us the true religion without such appendages?

All the ancient nations, with the exception of the Hebrews, were idolaters. If, then, all the religions of such nations, in their mythical forms, were false, may not that of the Hebrews be true? If other forms of faith, growing up by a natural process, and thence invested with much human error, were associated with false or pretended miracles, may not Christianity, based, as Strauss and Parker are compelled to own, upon absolute and eternal truth, be associated with true miracles?

We might also inquire, How comes this universal belief in miracles? It is a fact to be accounted for. Why should all mankind, with inconsiderable exceptions, cherish the indelible conviction that they must be found somewhere? It seems to spring from an instinct, or an intuition, as deep and all-pervading as that which gives them the idea of God and immortality. Hence, instead of an argument against miracles, the mythic theory is a presumption in their favor. Only we must be careful to distinguish between the real and the spurious, the divine and the human. Both have their characteristics.

But the whole is a question of fact; and Strauss, unconsciously dissatisfied with his theory, has attacked the Christian miracles, chiefly on historical and philological grounds. He has gathered together all apparent discrepancies and contradictions, to falsify their claims. After all, the great historical verities, or fundamental facts, springing from the supernatural character of Christ, and forming the essence or basis of Christianity, are left untouched. No quibbling with particulars, or even the citation of real difficulties, can affect the history as a whole. It has woven itself, as an historical reality, into the very fabric of society; there it stands, in its divine and supernatural power, and there it will stand forever. The source of a river may be far inland, and much hidden among woods and hills, so that some dispute may be indulged respecting the localities of its origin, and particularly as to the individual streams which have swelled its current; but it has originated among those woods and hills, and yonder it comes, rolling its mighty tide of waters to the distant sea.

Finally, the miracles have been assaulted on the ground of experience.

Assuming that a miracle is "a violation of the laws of nature," which laws "are established by a firm and unalterable experience," "there arises," says Hume, "the contest of two opposite experiences, or proof against proof;" so that "the proof against a miracle from the nature of the facts is as complete as any argument from experience can possibly be imagined. On this ground he maintains that " no amount of testimony can prove a miracle ; " which is precisely the same thing as to maintain that a miracle is impossible in the nature of things. That this was his real theory, can admit of no question. Speaking of certain alleged miracles, he says, " What have we to oppose to such a cloud of witnesses, but the *absolute impossibility* or *miraculous nature* of the fact." The sum total, then, of Hume's argument is, *that a miracle* is to be rejected *because it is a miracle*, assuming it to be " a violation of the laws of nature," and thence *impossible*. But he forgets his own principles, and in the course of his argument, actually admits that there may be miracles of such a kind as to admit of proof from human testimony ; only he will not allow them in connection with religion ; and why ? Because " mankind have been so frequently imposed upon by pretensions of that sort ! " Thus he changes his ground and abandons his argument.

That miracles are possible, not as a violation of the laws of nature, but as a special manifestation of a Power beyond the resources of nature, or the laws which control its movements, must be conceded by every one who believes in a God. Even Theodore Parker, who more than once avails himself of Hume's sophism, admits their possibility. He says, " Discourse of Matters pertaining to Religion," p. 254, "There is no antecedent objection nor metaphysical impossibility in the case," namely, that a miracle may be what he calls "a transgression of all law known or knowable by man, but yet in conformity with some law out of our reach." "Finite man," he adds, "not only does not, but cannot, understand all the modes of God's action, all the laws of his being. There may be higher beings, to whom God reveals himself in modes that we can never know; for we cannot tell the secrets of God, nor determine *a priori* the modes of his manifestation. In this sense a miracle is possible. The world is a perpetual miracle of this sort. Nature is the art of God; can we fully comprehend it? Life, being, creation, duration, do we understand these actual things? How then can we say to the Infinite, 'Hitherto shalt thou come, but no farther; there are no more ways wherein thy being acts'? Man is not the measure of God."

We will not stop here to remark upon the latent argument against miracles, even in this concession, by the ambiguous use of the expression, *transgression of the laws of nature*, much the same as Hume's "violation of the laws of nature," upon which Mr. Parker seems to argue, in other parts of his book; we will take the passage as it stands, cordially thanking him for his important admission; for now the only question that remains touches the evidence of the fact.* Mr. Parker himself momentarily sees this, and immediately addresses himself to the evidence, which he demolishes (in his own view) by a few dexterous blows. But it is not so easily got rid of. Mere assertions will not disprove it. Declamation will not diminish its power. Pretended miracles, those, for example, of the dark ages, may seem to have as much and even more evidence; but this is a fancy easily disposed of. It is appearance only, and may deceive the unwary, but not thoughtful, well-informed men. No one in the slightest degree acquainted with legendary or monkish miracles will, for a moment, bring them, either as to their nature or their evidence, into comparison with the miracles of Christ. Fifty witnesses, in a court of justice, may testify on one side, and their evidence may seem to overpower and utterly extinguish the testimony of two or three simple and candid men, on the other side; but the instant their

* After all, we apprehend that Mr. Parker's concession is a mere logical or rhetorical ruse; for he must ultimately base his denial of miracles on their impossibility. Hence in his Two Sermons, 1852, he makes the following bold statement: "I do not believe there ever was a miracle, or ever will be; every where I find law — the constant mode of operation of the infinite God. I do not believe in the miraculous inspiration of the Old Testament, or the New Testament," &c.

true character and the circumstances of the case are fairly presented, the evidence of the fifty vanishes into thin air, while that of the two or three is established forever. Every thing, in such a question, depends upon *character* and *circumstances*. The thousand and one stories, then, of foolish monks or garrulous old women, — nay, more, the solemn depositions of learned and dignified bishops, besotted by superstition, — may well be dismissed from the account. In nothing but their name do they bear the slightest comparison with the divine mission or supernatural works of Jesus Christ.

But how is it with this matter of experience? There seems to be something in it, after all. What are its nature and bearings on the question at issue? If the word, as used by Hume, means any thing, it must mean our individual experience, or the experience of the race. If it means our individual experience, then it makes that which is necessarily limited and imperfect the standard of all possible events — an assumption utterly preposterous. If it means the experience of the race, including that of the first Christians, the apostles of Christ, and the writers of the gospel histories, then it takes for granted the very point to be proved. For we maintain that miracles were matters of experience in the days of Christ and his apostles. Hume, however, was too acute to mean any thing more than the general conviction of mankind, derived, as he thought, from experience, with reference to what may be termed the uniform action of the ordinary laws of nature, in the case of miracles, partly suspended or controlled, as we suppose, by some higher power or law beyond our knowledge. But nature can never be contrary to God, nor can God be contrary to nature; consequently an inferior law can never be contrary to the action of that higher law by which it is controlled. Even now the law of life controls, sometimes suspends, the action of chemical laws; but they are never contrary to each other. In Christianity, life is restored to the dead. Lazarus, for example, rises from the tomb at the command of Christ. That divine power, then, or power of life, by virtue of which this takes place, may be represented as the higher, or unknown law, which, in this instance, controls the ordinary laws governing organized beings. But there is no real opposition between them, no violation, transgression or perversion of any thing. A new and stupendous power has intervened, and a new and stupendous phenomenon is the result. This is ascribed directly to God himself, the great original Life-giver, who, when the darkness of primeval night brooded upon chaos, said, "Let there be light, and there was light."

Thus the uniformity and immutability of nature and its laws are not absolute, but relative; relative, we mean, to God, who presides over them with the supremacy of a master. Their uniformity for five thousand or ten thousand years is no proof that, previous or subsequent to that period, a change was or may not be possible. In a word, it does not follow, from the general uniformity of nature's laws, that God, "whose they are, and whom they serve," may not interpose at specific eras, by means of new creations, regenerations, and miracles. To deny this would make matter eternal, and God a mere natural and blind necessity, without freedom or choice.

Our experience, however, of the general uniformity of nature's laws, leads us, of course, to reject all pretensions to miracles, on ordinary or frivolous occasions, or on such occasions as a divine intervention cannot be supposed. "Lying wonders," in the garb of miracles, are essentially incredible; for they are derogatory, not only to the laws of nature, but to the character of God. Their external evidence or testimony may seem imposing, but it is never really adequate. Thoroughly sifted, it will ever be found partial, selfish, and contradictory. It may be allowed, then, *that no amount of such testimony can prove such a miracle.* A true miracle must have an adequate cause, and that cause God. And as it is fair to assume that God will always act consistently with himself, it follows that a true miracle will only be performed for a sufficient reason, or with reference to an adequate purpose. So that mere portents and prodigies, monkish marvels, and mesmeric wonders, whatever other character they have, may be rejected *as divine miracles*, without further examination. God, we repeat it, will always act like himself; and although we know little of his essence or mode of working, we know enough of his character to be certain that all his works will be holy, just, and good, with a certain air of simplicity and majesty, fitly styled "divine." Consequently, when he does interpose by miracles, as in the first act of creation, when "the morning stars sang together, and all the sons of God shouted for joy," or in the new spiritual creation ascribed to Jesus Christ, the occasion is worthy of his infinite majesty and grace, while the results are the most stupendous and beautiful that can be conceived. For once more the angels sing, "Glory to God in the highest, on earth peace, and good will to men."

Thus Hume's suggestion, misapplied and abused, as an argument against the supernatural character of Christianity, after all, has something good in it, as it supplies us with this practical rule, that our experience of the uniformity of nature's laws ought to make us suspicious of all miraculous pretensions on ordinary, inadequate, or frivolous occasions. We ought never to forget, however, that the spurious proves the possible existence of the genuine, the false of the true. Shadows cannot last forever. *Lux post nubila.* At last the morning of a heavenly day dawns upon the nations. The kingdom comes. The new creation, all aglow with the light of God, bursts upon the world.*

To enforce our meaning, and bring the matter to a practical issue, take the following illustrations: Were some one of ordinary credibility to inform us that a person apparently dead by drowning had been resuscitated by the means ordinarily used to restore suspended animation, we should believe it at once, without further inquiry, for the thing comes within the scope of ordinary experience, and is perfectly natural in the circumstances supposed. Were the same person to inform us that he had just seen, alive and well, a friend known to be dead and buried several days, we should probably be unwilling

* Parker and others lay great stress upon the assumption that more evidence is required to prove a strange or miraculous event than one of an ordinary kind. But that depends altogether upon *circumstances.* In our humble opinion, it is not so much a question of *quantity* as of *quality.* Something, too, depends upon the mind to be convinced. All the evidence in the world will not satisfy some men.

to credit the assertion. We should conclude that there must be some mistake in the case, for the dead cannot rise, under the action of the ordinary laws of nature. For the production of such a result, the exertion of a divine power, equal to creation, is needed, which cannot be expected, except at some grand or peculiar crisis. If, however, four, five, a dozen honest and competent witnesses were to testify to the occurrence of a similar fact, we should deem it quite extraordinary; still, we should suspend our judgment till the matter should receive a thorough investigation. There is, indeed, no *a priori* impossibility in the supposition that God should raise the dead, but certainly there is a high moral presumption against the exercise of such a power on ordinary occasions. Hence our hesitation and doubt, justified alike by religion, philosophy, and common sense; on which ground it may be assumed, that all pretensions to miracles, on common or frivolous occasions, are essentially incredible. Nay, we may go farther, and maintain that, in all probability, miracles, as special divine interventions, equal to creative acts, can be expected only once or twice in the history of the world, that is, at those peculiar and critical epochs when Jehovah must interfere by special divine manifestations for the establishment of a true religion, or the introduction of a new moral creation among men.

We have supposed an imaginary case. Let us now describe a real one. The world, by wisdom, knew not God. The leading nations had outgrown their pagan creeds, but could not replace them with a higher and purer faith. They were departing farther and farther from truth and duty. Darkness covered the earth, and gross darkness the people. New forms of scepticism, or of superstition, were eating into their hearts, yet they were longing madly and vainly for some heavenly light. An obvious crisis or turning-point had arrived in the history of the world. The nations were expectant. All nature was prepared for the advent of God. It had been predicted in certain ancient books, that at such a time a Redeemer should come, in lowliness and meekness, yet with transcendent wisdom and mighty power, to regenerate souls.

In these circumstances, a personage, claiming the character and function referred to, makes his appearance in the Holy Land. His aspect and manners correspond to the idea of a divine teacher. He speaks on the subject of religion and morals, of life and immortality, as man has never before spoken. His purity is unquestioned, his benevolence expansive and wonderful. He penetrates the secrets of nature, of man, and of

God, as by an intuition, and develops in language of amazing simplicity and force a system of absolute religion and morals. In every respect, he transcends his age, and indeed all ages. Simple and august, gentle, yet severe and commanding, he goes forth to do and to suffer the will of God, supplying not only in his creed, but in his person, a splendid illustration of the power of goodness, infinite and immortal. He performs many wonderful works, and suffers much from the persecution of the ungodly. He predicts his own death, looking forward to it as a great spiritual necessity, with a sublime and mysterious confidence. At last he dies by the hand of the public executioner, praying for his enemies, and exclaiming, "It is finished!" But previous to this, he had predicted not only his death, but also his resurrection, as the necessary completion of his career on earth and the crowning proof of his divinity. His disciples, indeed, are incredulous of the fact, and give up all for lost. Their hopes are buried in his tomb. His enemies, aware of his predictions, secure his sepulchre by the government seal and a guard of Roman soldiers. But on the third day the sepulchre is empty; the body of Jesus is gone. He appears, however, to some of his disciples, not once, but again and again, and in circumstances admitting of no delusion. At first, some of them doubt, but subsequently obtain ocular, nay, more tangible demonstration of the fact; so that all are entirely satisfied as to the fact of his resurrection. Such, at least, is their testimony — a testimony which they bear before the judicial tribunals and people of the Jews, and which they repeat in all conceivable circumstances to their dying day, in spite, too, of persecution, contumely, and wrong. At last they behold him ascend from the earth; in other words, pass into the spiritual and immortal sphere; in parting, they receive his blessing, filling them with unutterable peace. His spirit of might and love takes possession of their hearts, and they go forth in his name, to found among men a kingdom of righteousness and love.

Here every thing is natural and becoming. The testimony is ample and satisfactory. It is uniform and uncontradicted. The occasion is the most august and thrilling in the history of the world. The result is stupendous and beautiful. Life and immortality are brought to light, —

> "The gates of paradise
> Stand open wide on Calvary."

We have spoken of miracles. After all, Christ and his gospel may be represented as but one miracle, the miracle of eternal love, first embodied in Christ, and then embodied among men. He brought heaven to earth; and it is this which is now struggling for supremacy in the world. The miracle stands before us now, modifying the interior spirit and the historic life of man, transforming individual hearts, and penetrating, as a leaven of regeneration, into the great mass of fallen humanity. God has smitten the rock in the far wilderness, and the streams are flowing yet to refresh the weary millions.

CHAPTER XIV.

CHRIST IN THE PRIMITIVE CHURCH.

As a system, Christianity had not assumed a complete form till after the resurrection of Christ. Then all things were prepared for its full development and progress in the world. Rejected by the mass of the Jews, it was lodged as a hidden leaven in a few simple hearts, who, all at once, show themselves bold, resolute, resistless, as if inspired, as indeed they were, by a supernatural power. Fifty days after the crucifixion, the apostles began, with a commanding earnestness to which previously they were strangers, to execute the commission of their divine Teacher—"Go ye into all the world, and preach the gospel to every creature." This they did, first at Jerusalem, the very scene of our Savior's degradation, and the last on earth, one would suppose, in which such a commission could be executed with success. But they claimed to be filled with the Holy Spirit, and spoke the word with life-giving eloquence. Fearlessly they charged home upon their countrymen the guilt of crucifying the Son of God, "the Lord of glory," at the same time proclaiming to them the "glad tidings" of reconciliation and eternal life. This was the constant burden of their testimony, the great end of their labors. It was as a power of life, of renovation, reunion, and eternal joy that they announced Christianity to the world; the key note of which had been struck by angel voices on the plains of Bethlehem. Not as a philosophy, but as a fact; not as a policy, but as a power, superhuman and divine, did they proclaim it to all. Calmly they pointed, first to the crucifixion, and then to the resurrection of Christ, universally known and acknowledged as the ground of their testimony, while affectionately and tenderly, as if angel hearts had been given them, they besought men to be reconciled to God. As a consequence of this, no less than three thousand persons were converted and added to their number in a single day. Subdued by a power which they ascribed to God, they repented, believed; and hence they were baptized in the name of the crucified Redeemer. Soon their number was swelled to five thousand; and at the expiration of a year and a half, even while the labors of the apostles were confined to Jerusalem and its vicinity, multitudes, both of men and women, had received the truth, and "a great company of the priests were obedient to the faith."

At this time the converts were scattered abroad by violent persecution, and they went every where preaching the word. Though "the Master" was gone, so far as his bodily presence was concerned, his divine spirit of love and power was with them. As Christ died blessing his executioners, so died the proto-martyr Stephen. Both conquered agony and death by the might of a supernatural charity; and this was the Heaven-kindled flame which the first disciples carried over Judea and the neighboring countries. They travelled as far as Phœnicia, Cyprus, and Antioch; and in less than three years, churches were established in Judea, Samaria, and Galilee.

During this time, however, Christianity had been preached to none but Hebrews. Two years afterwards it was proclaimed to "the Gentiles," and before the thirtieth year from the death of Christ, the triumphs of the cross had extended to every part of Asia the Less, the isles of the Ægean Sea, to a large portion of Greece, and even to Rome. At these places the converts are described as "a great number," "great multitudes," "much people." They were especially numerous at Antioch and Ephesus. During the two years' residence of Paul at the latter city, "all Asiá," it is said, "heard the word of the Lord," meaning by the term "Asia," according to the ancient, and especially the Roman use of it, the beautiful and populous region, which lay eastward from the Mediterranean Sea, and occupied a considerable portion of what has been more recently designated Asia Minor. So numerous were the converts in Ephesus that a single class of them, who had dealt in magic, burned their books and implements to the value of fifty thousand pieces of silver, "so mightily grew the word of God and prevailed." *

In Jerusalem alone there were "many myriads," or many "tens of thousands" of believers. They multiplied there, and in the adjacent regions constantly, and no power of opposition or persecution could retard their progress. Their faith and joy struck the people. Their simplicity and devotion, their freedom and liberality, gave them power over the minds of serious and candid men. Miracles of life, especially in the spiritual sphere, every where indicated the presence of the Divinity, once incarnated in the body of Jesus, now enshrined as "Lord and King" in the bosom of the church. Baptized "in the spirit," they were one — one in their faith and life, one in their organization and action. When necessary, they had all things common; they loved one another, they pitied the poor, they sought the salvation of men, they conquered evil with good, and

* These statements, as will be obvious to all, are made on the authority of the Acts of the Apostles.

went forth, at the hazard of life, to the moral conquest of the world.

Thirty years from the day of Pentecost, or the inauguration of the church by the baptism of the Holy Ghost, Christians, during the persecution under Nero, were quite numerous even in Rome; for Tacitus says, that "a great multitude" of them were seized.* In the days of Trajan, not more than seventy years after, Christianity had spread so extensively throughout the Roman empire, that in many places the heathen temples were deserted. Pliny the younger, governor of Pontus in Bithynia, says, in his well-known letter to the Emperor Trajan, "that many, of all

* Tacitus obviously was ignorant of the character and claims of the first Christians. His testimony to their numbers, however, is clear and express. Narrating the facts of the burning of Rome by Nero, which the tyrant charged upon the Christians, Tacitus, after stating that they had derived their name from Christ, (or Chrestus, as he writes it,) who, in the reign of Tiberius, had suffered death, under the sentence of the procurator Pontius Pilate, adds, "For a while this dire superstition was checked; but it again burst forth, and not only spread itself over Judea, the first seat of the mischievous sect, but was even introduced into Rome, the common asylum, which receives and protects whatever is impure, whatever is atrocious. The confessions of those who were seized discovered *a vast multitude* (the expression is *ingens multitudo*) of their accomplices; and they were all convicted, not so much for the crime of setting fire to the city as for their hatred to mankind." It will thus be seen, not only from the expression "vast multitude," but also from the expressions "dire superstition," "checked," "burst forth," that the increase of Christians, even in Rome, must have been great and striking.

ages and of every rank, were accused to him of being Christians;" and adds, much in the style of Tacitus, whose precision in the use of language is the admiration of scholars, "that the contagion of this superstition" (as if it spread with the rapidity of a pestilence) "had seized not the cities only, but the smaller towns also, and the open country;" so that "few victims were offered for sacrifice, and the temples of the gods were almost deserted."

There can be no question as to the fact that about the close of the first century, say sixty or seventy years from the ascension of Christ, Christianity had penetrated, with more or less success, into every part of the Roman empire, the population of which could not be less than a hundred and twenty millions. It was planted in the cities of Rome and Carthage, in Athens and Alexandria, in Ephesus and Antioch, in Damascus, and even in Babylon; nay, more, it had reached, if we may credit the traditions of the fathers, as far as Spain on the one hand and India on the other. Christians were to be numbered by thousands in Palestine and Arabia, in Italy and Egypt, in Greece and Asia the Less. Justin Martyr, who flourished in the first half of the second century, describes the extent of Christianity in the following terms: "There is not a nation either of Greek, or barbarian, or any other name, even of those who wander in tribes, or live in tents, among whom prayers and thanksgivings are not offered to the Father and Creator of the universe in the name of the crucified Jesus." So also Clemens of Alexandria, a little later, says, "The philosophers were confined to Greece, and to their particular retainers; but the doctrine of Christianity did not remain in Judea, but is spread through the whole world, in every nation, and village, and city, converting both whole houses and separate individuals, having already brought over to the truth not a few of the philosophers themselves. If the Greek philosophy is interdicted by law, it immediately disappears; whereas, though, from the first appearance of Christianity, kings and tyrants, governors and presidents, with their whole train, and the populace on their side, have endeavored with their whole force to exterminate it, yet doth it flourish more and more." The following is the testimony of Tertullian, who lived in the second century of the Christian era. Addressing those who governed the Roman empire, he says, "We are but of yesterday, but we have filled every thing that is yours, cities, islands, castles, free towns, council halls, the very camps, all classes of men, the palace, the senate, the forum. We have left you nothing but your temples. We can number your armies; there are more Christians in a single province. Even if unequal in force, is there any war for which we, who so readily submit to death, should not be prepared and prompt, did not our religion teach us to be slain rather than to slay? Unarmed and without rebellion, should we only separate from you, we might *thus* fight against you, by inflicting the injury you might suffer from divorce. If we, such a multitude of men, were to break away from you, retiring into some remote corner of the world, your government would be covered with shame at the loss of so many citizens, whoever they might be. The very desertion would punish you. Without doubt you would be terrified at your solitude, at the silence and stupor of all things, as if the world were dead. You would have to look about for such subjects." It may be said that this, from the fiery Tertullian, is the language of rhetorical exaggeration. Be it so. After all, it must have rested upon some basis of fact, to give it even the semblance of force; for as it has been well remarked, "Tertullian was a writer of too much acuteness and eloquence to suffer the boldness and vehemence of his language to pass those limits, beyond which their only effect must have been to expose him to derision.*"

* Dr. Andrews Norton, who, in the first volume of his work on the Genuineness of the Gospels, has discussed this subject, especially

Nor is this the only occasion on which Tertullian asserts the great fact here referred to. The following, as it relates to specific facts, is, if possible, more striking than the quotation already made. He is addressing Scapula, the proconsul of Africa. "When Arrius Antoninus undertook to persecute the Christians, all of that persuasion immediately presented themselves before his tribunal. Then he, after ordering a few for execution, said to the rest, 'Wretched people, if you wish to die, there are precipices and ropes enough to be had.' — If thou wert inclined to do this here, [in Africa,] how wouldst thou dispose of so many thousands, as well men as women, persons of both sexes, of all ages, of all ranks, presenting themselves to thee? How many fires, how many swords wouldst thou need? What would Carthage herself, now about to be decimated by thee, have to endure, when every one should see among the sufferers his relations and friends; when he might see there, perhaps, and by thy order, dignified men and matrons, and all the principal persons of the city, the relations and friends even of thy own friends! Spare, therefore, thyself, if not us; spare Carthage, if not thyself. Finally, those whom thou considerest as thy masters, are men, and they too will

in opposition to the views of Gibbon, with great candor and ability.

die: but this sect will not diminish, which thou now knowest is but increased when it seems to be in the course of being extirpated. For whoever sees so much fortitude is tempted to inquire into the cause, and when he sees the truth he himself quickly embraces it." *

This language was used in Africa, within a a hundred and fifty years after the first promulgation of Christianity.

Unknown and despised, it was penetrating, like the electric forces, silently and irresistibly, into the hearts of mankind, in all quarters of the world. It had seized all the great marts of commerce and political power. Rome, long before it was aware of the fact, felt its secret energy. Judaism tried to crush it, but was itself crushed in the encounter. Polytheism struggled with it in deadly embrace, but finally yielded to its superior force, and, with pagan philosophy, first gave up the cities, then the smaller places, and at last the country itself. Every where Christianity was aggressive and triumphant.

How shall we account for this amazing power and progress? Gibbon has attempted the solution by a reference to natural causes. The following is his enumeration of these: —

"1. The inflexible, and, if we may use the

* *Ad Scapulam*, c. 5.

expression, the intolerant zeal of the Christians, derived, it is true, from the Jewish religion, but purified from the narrow and unsocial spirit, which, instead of inviting, had deterred the Gentiles from embracing the law of Moses. 2. The doctrine of a future life, improved by every additional circumstance which could give weight and efficacy to that important truth. 3. The miraculous powers ascribed to the primitive church. 4. The pure and austere morals of the Christians. 5. The union and discipline of the Christian republic, which gradually formed an independent and increasing state in the heart of the Roman empire." *

We accept the facts, for they lie on the surface, but the solution is not thereby found. The facts themselves have to be accounted for. The inflexible zeal — the intense devotion — the exclusive faith, infallible as light — the lofty self-denial — the austere morality — the all-comprehending love — the noble confession of the one God, and the one immortal life — the well-established claim of miraculous powers, — in a word, the unity, purity, fidelity, and all-conquering force of the great Christian republic, originally bound together, as Gibbon himself confesses, only by the ties of a common faith, are facts which do

* Hist. of the Decline and Fall of the Rom. Empire, ii. 264.

not explain themselves, but need to be explained by reference to some adequate cause. In matters like these, true philosophy goes beneath the surface, and sees, in energies and results so stupendous, the might of a supernatural life. It is the presence of the Deity among men; in other words, the presence of infinite love and pity in the hearts of primitive believers. " The love of Christ," says Paul, " constraineth us to live, not unto ourselves, but unto him who died and rose again." Hence, they " lived to Christ; " hence, also, they " died to Christ." Immortal, they rejoiced in shame, agony, and death. The death of the martyrs was the life of the church. Their superiority to all things outward, especially their superiority to suffering, struck the heathen. This it was which convinced the philosophers Justinus, Pantænus, Clemens, and Origen. This it was which conquered the Roman world. Their motto was, " Nothing for self, every thing for God." Do we need proof of this? Let the heathen themselves inform us. All their writers, who refer to this subject, speak of what they are pleased to call their " obstinate contempt of death." Pliny bears noble testimony to the purity of their lives. " They affirmed," says he, in his letter to the emperor, " that the whole of their guilt or error was, that they met on a stated day, before it was light, and addressed themselves in a form of prayer to Christ, as to some god, binding themselves by a solemn oath, not for the purpose of any wicked design, but never to commit any fraud, theft, or adultery; never to falsify their word, nor to deny a trust when they should be called upon to deliver it up; after which it was their custom to separate, and then reassemble to eat in common a harmless meal." After receiving this account, he adds, that he put two of their number, who were accustomed to serve in their religious functions, to the torture, in order to discover something more; but he could find nothing reprehensible, except their inflexible attachment to what he is pleased to designate their absurd superstition. "We declare and openly profess," says Justin Martyr, "in the midst of all your tortures, even while torn and bleeding, we proclaim that we worship God through Jesus Christ." "Torment, rack, condemn, crush us," says Tertullian, "the most exquisite cruelty you can devise avails you nothing, but rather induces the more to become Christians. As often as we are cut down by persecutions, we spring up the more abundantly. *The blood of Christians is the seed of the church.*" Hence the author of the Epistle to Diognetus, one of the earliest and most touching fragments of primitive Christian literature, unquestionably belonging to the early part of the second century, could say, as if the love of Christ were throbbing at his heart, and dictating his language, "They live in the flesh, but not after the flesh; they dwell on the earth, but have their mansion in heaven; they obey the existing laws, but in their lives are superior to all law; loving all men, they are persecuted by all; living unknown, they are condemned to death; they are slain, and behold they live; though poor, they make many rich; in want of every thing, they have abundance; in dishonor, they are but honored the more; when defamed, they are vindicated; when reviled, they bless; for insolence, they return respect; for well doing, they are punished as evil doers; and yet rejoice in their punishments, as being made alive. Rejected by the Jews, as aliens, they are persecuted by the Greeks; and, though hated by all men, none can show cause of enmity against them."

He then proceeds to show how God sent his Son to redeem the world from sin, and that, on this ground, vast but delightful responsibilities are laid upon Christians, and adds, "See you not that those who are delivered up to wild beasts, because they will not deny their God, are not overcome, but only increase the more, the more they are persecuted? This is the work not of man, but of God, and an evident token of his coming." *

* *Epistola ad Diognetum.* V. Hefele's *Patres Apostolici*, p. 228. For a translation of the whole of the *Epistola*, see Appendix F.

Some may be inclined to diminish the force of this testimony, by referring it to the partiality of sectarian preference. It is corroborated, however, by the heathen themselves, who, while accusing the Christians of atheism, in rejecting the false gods of the populace, are compelled, at least indirectly, to acknowledge the superiority of the Christian character. Thus Lucian, the satirist, in giving the history of an impostor, by the name of Proteus or Peregrinus, who deceived the Christians, by pretending to wonderful sanctity and wisdom, incidentally gives the following account of their views and habits.

"About this time," says he, "it was that he [Peregrinus] learned the wonderful wisdom of the Christians, being intimately acquainted with their priests and scribes. In a very short time he convinced them that they were all boys in comparison with himself, and became their leader, prophet, and grand president, in short, all in all to them. He explained and interpreted many of their books, and wrote some himself; insomuch that they looked upon him as their legislator and high priest; nay, almost worshipped him as a god. Their leader, whom they yet adore, was crucified in Palestine, for introducing this new sect; and this very circumstance was the foundation of all the consequence and reputation which he afterwards gained, and of that glory, of which he had always been so ambitious. For when he was in bonds, the Christians, considering it as a calamity affecting the common cause, did all in their power to release him, which, finding impracticable, they paid him all deference and honor. Old women, widows, and orphans were continually crowding to him; some of the principal of them even remained with him in prison, having, for the sake of doing so, bribed the keepers; suppers were brought in to them; they read together their sacred books, and the noble Peregrinus — for such he was then called — was dignified with the title of the new Socrates. Some of the Christian deputies came from the cities of Asia to assist in pleading for and comforting him. It is incredible with what alacrity these people support and defend the public cause; they spare nothing, indeed, to promote it. Peregrinus being made a prisoner on their account, they collected money for him, and he made a pretty respectable revenue from it. These poor people, it seems, had persuaded themselves that they should be immortal and live forever." The reader will notice especially what follows. "They despised death, therefore, and offered up their lives a voluntary sacrifice, being taught by their lawgiver that they were all brethren, and that, abandoning our Grecian gods, they must worship their own sage (sophist or rather philosopher,) who was crucified, and live in obedience to his laws, in compliance with which they looked with contempt on all worldly treasures, and held every thing in common — a maxim which they had adopted without just reason. If any cunning impostor, therefore, who knew how to manage matters, came amongst them, he soon acquired wealth, by imposing on the credulity of these weak and ignorant men."

But we shall best illustrate the spirit of the primitive church by giving one or two specimens, among many that might be cited, of early Christian heroism.

In the time of Marcus Aurelius, himself a philosopher, and upon the whole a good emperor, though permitting, and in some instances sanctioning, great enormities, Christians were often persecuted in an irregular way. Among these Justin, surnamed the Martyr, was brought, on some pretence, before the præfect, by Crescens, a Cynic philosopher, whose unblushing vices had been exposed by Justin, while defending Christianity against the attacks of his enemy. The name of the præfect was Rusticus, supposed by many to have been the teacher of the emperor in the Stoic philosophy. On this occasion, the following conversation occurred: —

Rusticus. First of all, offer sacrifice to the gods, and do homage to the emperor.

Justin. He who obeys Christ is guilty of no crime. (Meaning that he ought to be discharged.)

Rusticus. Of what sect [of philosophers] do you profess yourself? *

Justin. I tried all, and finally embraced that of Christ; though that is not agreeable to those who profess what is erroneous.

Rusticus. Do you profess that doctrine, unhappy man?

Justin. Yes; for it seems to me to be true.

Rusticus. What is the doctrine?

Justin. That we should worship the God of the Christians, whom we believe to have been from the beginning One; the Creator and Maker of all things, — of all things seen and unseen, — and the Lord Jesus Christ, the Son of God, who was predicted by the prophets, as the future Savior of mankind, their preacher and instructor in excellent doctrine — though I, being man, cannot speak adequately of his infinite divinity, that being only to be known by prophetic power. For the prophets spoke long before of him whom I spoke of as the Son of God, and of his presence on earth among men.

* Justin, after his conversion, continued to wear the philosopher's cloak. He was known, therefore, as a Christian philosopher.

Rusticus. Where do you assemble?

Justin. Wherever any one chooses.* Do you suppose we all meet in one place? Far from it. As the God of the Christians is without limitation, and invisibly fills the heavens and the earth, his faithful servants render him praise and worship every where.

Rusticus. Tell me where you assemble, and in what place your disciples are collected.

Justin. I live just above a certain man by the name of Martinus. And up to this time I know of no place of meeting but that. If any one chooses to come to me, I communicate to him the doctrine of truth.

Rusticus. Are you not then, after all, a Christian?

Justin. Assuredly I am a Christian.

[Here other Christians present, companions of Justin, — being addressed by Rusticus, avow themselves on the same side. After which he again addresses Justin as follows: —]

Listen to me, wise man, you who think you know the doctrine of truth. If you are scourged from head to foot, do you suppose you shall then ascend into the heavens?

Justin. I hope to enjoy the promise, if I suffer these things; for I know that all who so live

* The reply was made to escape the law against Hetæriæ.

will partake of the divine gift till the consummation of all things.

Rusticus. Do you imagine, when you ascend into heaven, that some recompense will be awarded to you?

Justin. I do not imagine, I believe; nay, I am certain of it.

Rusticus. Let us return, however, to the business before us. Come, then, all of you, and offer incense to the gods with one accord.

Justin. No right-minded man falls from piety into impiety —

Justin is here cut short by the præfect, who says, "If you do not obey, I shall punish you without mercy." To which Justin replies, —

"We give thanks to our Lord Jesus Christ that we, through suffering, shall be saved; for this will bring us freedom and salvation before the dread tribunal of our Lord and Savior."

In which the other martyrs concur, saying, —

Do what you will with us — we are Christians, and will not offer incense to idols.

Whereupon the præfect pronounces the following sentence: —

Those who will not offer incense to the gods, nor obey the decree of the emperor, having been scourged, shall be led away and punished capitally, according to the tenor of the law.

Such were the terrible tests to which the faith

of the primitive Christians was subjected, and such their mild but triumphant firmness.

" Swear," said the persecutors who had seized the venerable bishop, or pastor, of the church in Smyrna, " Swear by the genius of Cæsar; retract, and say, Away with the godless!" The old man gazed in sorrow at the frantic multitude, and, with his eyes lifted up to heaven, said, " Away with the godless!" " Swear, and I release thee," urged the heathen magistrate; " blaspheme Christ!" " Eighty and six years have I served Christ, and he has never done me an injury; how can I blaspheme my King and my Savior?" was the touching response. The proconsul again commanded him to swear by the genius of Cæsar. Polycarp replied, that he was a Christian, and requested a day to be appointed on which he might explain, before the proconsul, the blameless tenets of Christianity. " Persuade the people to consent," replied the ruler, overawed by the calm dignity of his prisoner. " We owe respect to authority," said Polycarp; " to thee I will explain the reasons of my conduct, to the populace I will make no explanation." The good man well knew that it was useless to reason with the passions of a ferocious multitude. The proconsul then threatened to expose him to the wild beasts. " 'Tis well for me to be released from this life of misery," was the only reply. He threatened to burn him alive. "I fear not the fire that burns for a moment; thou knowest not that which burns forever and ever!" His countenance was full of peace and joy, even when the executioner advanced into the midst of the assembly and thrice proclaimed, "Polycarp has professed himself a Christian." The multitude, composed of Jews and heathen, replied with an overpowering shout. They demanded that he should be cast to the wild beasts. The Asiarch excused himself, by saying that the games were over. Then a general cry arose that Polycarp should be burned alive. A hasty but capacious funeral pile was gathered of the fuel of the baths and other combustibles. He was speedily disrobed; he requested not to be nailed to the stake; he was only bound to it. In a dignified and simple manner, he then offered the following prayer: "O Lord God Almighty, the Father of the well-beloved and ever-blessed Son Jesus Christ, by whom we have received the knowledge of thee, the God of angels, powers, and of every creature, and of the whole race of the righteous who live before thee, I thank thee that thou hast graciously thought me worthy of this day and this hour, that I may receive a portion in the number of thy martyrs, and drink of Christ's cup, for the resurrection to eternal life, both of the body and the soul, in the incorruptibleness of the Holy Spirit; among whom may I be admitted as a rich and acceptable sacrifice, as thou, O true and faithful God, hast prepared, and foreshown, and accomplished. Wherefore I praise thee for all thy mercies; I bless thee; I glorify thee, with the eternal and heavenly Jesus Christ, thy beloved Son, to whom, with thee and the Holy Spirit, be glory now and forever."

The fire was kindled in vain, probably from some natural cause, though the early Christians deemed it supernatural.* Though the fire was kindled again, an executioner was sent to despatch the victim, and the blood which flowed from his side served to extinguish the flame. His body was subsequently reduced to ashes.

"Such was the death of the blessed Polycarp," says the Letter of the Church of Smyrna, "who, though he was the twelfth of those in Smyrna who, together with those from Philadelphia, suffered martyrdom, is yet chiefly celebrated by all men; insomuch that he is spoken of by the very Gentiles themselves, in every place, as having been not only an eminent teacher, but also a glorious martyr; whose death all desire to imitate, as having been every way conformable to the gospel of Christ." †

* *Patres Apos.*, (ed. Hefele,) p. 216.
† Ibid. p. 219.

The martyrdom of Polycarp took place in the early part of the second century, when Christianity was yet in the freshness and purity of its first love.

At the close of the second century, Christianity, by the simple force of its inherent virtue, was spreading far and wide in every direction. It was felt as a power, not only in Rome, the capital of the empire, but in Africa on the one hand, and Gaul on the other. It had made its way beyond the confines of Arabia and Syria, as far as Hither India; nay, more, it had penetrated, with more or less success, among the barbarians of the British Isles. We do not indeed mean to affirm, that in these countries polytheism was not the recognized and predominant faith; but we do mean to say, that Christianity was gradually taking its place, undermining its strength, and preparing its overthrow. The night of superstition was still deep and portentous, but the sunlight was piercing its depths, and glancing upwards and afar amid its broken shadows.

This was the age of conversion and proselytism, of struggle and self-sacrifice; consequently of simplicity, purity, and love. The might of the gospel was felt in the hearts of men; Jesus Christ was recognized as "Head over all to the church;" pastors and people, united by fraternal ties, had one Lord, one faith, one baptism; in a word, freedom and brotherhood united the whole, and made them one in Christ.*

* In the Appendix, note G, will be found some interesting testimonies from Bunsen, Guizot, Ranke, Gibbon, and others, touching the organization and government of the primitive church.

CHAPTER XV.

SAME SUBJECT CONTINUED.

The third century, in the history of Christianity, was one of struggle and transition, of partial corruption and splendid triumph. Embodied among men, it partook somewhat of their imperfections, and of the imperfections of the age. The times were evil, changing, and tumultuous. Corruptions the most horrible invaded the heart of Roman society. The old civic virtue was entirely lost. Scepticism and cruelty, luxury and lust, reigned among the patricians; discontent and greed, selfishness and disloyalty, among the people. Rome grew weaker and weaker at the centre, more feverish and disturbed at the extremities. Now and then a good and able emperor ruled well for a few years, but the good he accomplished was obliterated by some weak or wicked successor. The army ruled the state, controlled the emperor, made and unmade the laws. Occasionally the Christians were tolerated, but oftener persecuted. Indeed, this was preëminently the age of persecution. Blood flowed in torrents. Thousands were thrown to the wild beasts, or murdered by the frantic populace.

Christianity, however, made rapid progress. It numbered nobles and philosophers among its followers. It was preached among the Goths, and, in some degree, softened their ferocity. In Gaul and in Germany, far and near, churches were multiplied. Tours, Arles, Treves, Paris, Mentz, and other places, became the strongholds of its power. It occasionally invaded the palace of the Roman emperors, and exerted some influence even upon its most furious persecutors. When the monster Galerius was dying, he abated his persecution of the Christians, and asked their prayers on his behalf.

Christianity, however, in the hands of many, had lost something of its simplicity. Superstitions were ingrafted on its simple usages. Power was concentrated in the hands of metropolitan bishops. Vain speculations were indulged by some Christian philosophers. Philosophy, indeed, with all its treasures, was rapidly flowing into the bosom of the church. Plato and Philo were incorporated into the Alexandrian school, and much error was mingled with sublimest truth. In Clement and Origen, the highest speculative thought was combined with the profoundest piety; but in the end, while philosophy was exalted, piety suffered. All this, however, was inevitable, in the process of human thought. Offences must come, heresies and divisions, vain jangling, and foolish speculation. The converts to Christianity were from all nations, of all sorts of education and temperament. Many of them were men of vigorous intellects and rooted prejudices, who, though converted to Christ, retained many of their errors and defects. Hence, in their views of the Deity, and of religion, they followed their first, or their most popular instructors. Now they were of one school of philosophy, then of another. Few, if any, had just views either of secular or of ecclesiastical government. All were accustomed to centralization and despotism. They misconceived the free, expansive genius of Christianity. Hence, as Beausobre has remarked, "An Epicurean who embraced the faith was disposed to clothe the Divinity in a human form, and to define it, like Epicurus, to be *an immortal and happy animal.* A Platonist, on the contrary, according to his master's views, maintained God to be *incorporeal.** A Pythagorean, a follower of Empedocles, or of Heracleitus, considered the Deity as an intelligent fire or light," &c.

We may add that some of them were pantheists, and so represented the creation of all things as an emanation, and thus confounded matter

* And yet Plato himself represented "the manifested God," or the God of the outward universe, as "an animal;" — not an animal in the inferior sense, sometimes attached to the term, — but a living being, with a body as well as a soul.

and mind. Temperament also combined with these influences to deepen and extend the peculiarities of the Christian converts. Hence the materialism of Hermas and Tertullian, who believed in the regenerative power of water; the spiritualism of Justin Martyr, Clement, (of Alexandria,) and Origen, with their Platonic notions and symbolic interpretations; as, also, the various errors of the Gnostics and the Manichees, who mingled the truths of Christianity with their theosophic dreams, their pleromas and æons.

The age, too, was credulous and superstitious. Freedom and independence in matters of government and discipline were almost unknown. Thousands of converts, among them many teachers and preachers, were ignorant and superstitious. Hence the multiplication of forms and ceremonies, and the vast importance attached to external acts, to chrisms and genuflections, amulets and charms.

Nevertheless, the revolution in the views and manners of the converted heathen was immense. Idol worship was abandoned, and the one true and eternal Jehovah was loved and adored. The heart was cleansed of its idolatry and lust, the life of its folly and crime. It is well known, that among the heathen, a virtuous woman was a great rarity; among the Christian females, continence was the rule, vice the exception. Charity and chastity were the noble graces of the primitive church.

The contrast between the manners of the Christians and those of the heathen was obvious to all. The following description, in a letter of Cyprian, is by no means exaggerated. Writing to his friend Donatus, he says, "Imagine yourself raised above the earth, and looking down upon it, so as to perceive what is going on there. Behold the roads obstructed by bands of robbers; the sea beset with pirates; war every where! The very earth is wet with blood, and what is called murder, when committed by a private individual, is virtue when it is done by many; impunity being secured, not by the smallness, but by the greatness of the offence. If you turn your eyes to the cities, then you will find their very magnitude more offensive than the most wretched solitude. There gladiatorial shows are exhibited to gratify the lust of blood. Man is slaughtered for the pleasure of man; he who best knows how to kill is the most skilful; it is a trade, an art. The crime is not only perpetrated, but it is taught. What can be more inhuman? They combat with beasts, not as criminals, but from brute fury: sons behold their father, the sister sees the brother, in the amphitheatre.

"Turn your eyes to spectacles of another kind, not less repulsive and corrupting. In the theatre, the most vicious representations, parricide and incest reproduced in all their horror. Look at the comic actor, the very schoolmaster of vice. Adultery is learned by seeing it acted! The theatre panders to vice, and breaks down the modesty of women. What an incitement to vice in the gestures of the actors, who undertake to represent the whole course of sensual indulgence! If, from this, you could look into the retirement of the closed chamber, and see what is there transacted! But your eyes would be defiled by beholding it."

Cyprian then proceeds, in deepening colors, to depict still more horrible crimes, public and private, in the forum, the baths, the theatres, the places of public concourse, to some of which we have no parallel in modern times, crimes which it is impossible for us to repeat, difficult for us to conceive. Indeed, he describes that state of society, to which St. Paul, in his Epistle to the Romans, refers, as the most degraded and bestial.

All this, however, the early Christians renounced. Theatres, gladiatorial shows, popular amusements, the lust of the flesh, the lust of the eye, and the pride of life they abandoned in their baptism. They deserted the temples of the gods, and gave themselves to the cultivation of piety and virtue. Tested by the most powerful temptations, sometimes by appalling deaths, some yielded, but yielded reluctantly and with horror. This is freely admitted by the Christian fathers and church historians. But it is precisely what might have been expected. But many repented, while the great body of believers nobly stood the test. They preferred death to dishonor. Their purity, their fidelity, their triumphant faith astonished even the heathen. They gloried in the cross. Christ was in their souls, as strength and peace eternal, and willingly, nay, cheerfully, they passed through fire and blood, agony and disolution, to the glory of martyrdom. "Your cruelty," says Tertullian, addressing the heathen ruler, "will be our glory. Thousands of both sexes, and of every rank, will eagerly crowd to martyrdom, exhaust your fires, and weary your swords. Carthage must be decimated; the principal persons in the city, even perhaps your own most intimate friends and kindred, must be sacrificed. Vainly will you war against God. Magistrates are but men, and will suffer the common lot of mortality; but Christianity will endure as long as the Roman empire, and the duration of the empire will be coeval with that of the world." Look, for example, at the sublime serenity and triumph of that youthful company, Revocatus and Felicitas, Saturninus and

Secundulus, catechumens, and Viva Perpetua, a woman of good family and liberal education, and honorably married, who turned away from all human bribes, and gave themselves to the fury of the wild beasts. Entreated by the prayers and tears of an aged father to abandon her faith, Perpetua clung to the cross, amid shame, agony, and death. In prison and among the wild beasts, with her young child in her arms, she maintained her dignity and composure, as if she were an angel rather that a feeble woman. "When taken out to execution, they declined, and were permitted to decline, the profane dress in which they were to be clad; the men that of the priests of Saturn, the women that of the priestesses of Ceres. They came forward in their simple attire, Perpetua singing psalms. The men were exposed to leopards and bears; the women were hung up naked in nets, to be gored by a furious cow. But even the excited populace shrunk with horror at the spectacle of two young and delicate women, one recently recovered from child birth, in this state. They were recalled by acclamation, and in mercy brought forward again clad in loose robes. Perpetua was tossed, her garment was rent; but more conscious of her wounded modesty than of pain, she drew the robe over the part of her person that was exposed. She then calmly clasped up her hair, because it did not become a martyr to suffer with dishevelled locks, the sign of sorrow. She then raised up the fainting and mortally-wounded Felicitas, and the cruelty of the populace being for a time appeased, they were permitted to retire. Perpetua seemed rapt in ecstasy, and, as if awaking from sleep, inquired when she was to be exposed to the beast. She could scarcely be made to believe what had taken place; her last words tenderly admonished her brother to be steadfast in the faith. All were speedily released from their sufferings. Perpetua guided with her own hand the merciful sword of the gladiator which relieved her from her agony."

Similar to this, in features of moral beauty and heroism, was the martyrdom of Blandina at Vienne, in Gaul.*

The charity of the Christians of this age is beautifully illustrated, in contrast with the profound selfishness of the heathen, on the occasion of the devastating plague which broke out at Alexandria, as a consequence of the carnage which followed the insurrection in that city. The heathen fled, the Christians remained, and were unwearied in their attendance upon the sick and dying. Many of these perished in the

* See Milman's Hist. of Christianity, pp. 245, 246. See also p. 237 of the same work.

performance of their duty. "In this way," says the good Bishop Dionysius, with affecting simplicity, "the best of the brethren departed this life; some ministers and some deacons." They thus triumphantly disproved the slander of their enemies, who were wont to call them atheists and man haters.

A devotion similar to this was shown at Carthage, when the plague reached that city. "All fled in horror from the contagion, abandoning their relations and friends, as if they thought that by avoiding the plague any one might also exclude death altogether. Meanwhile the city was strewed with the dead bodies, or rather carcasses of the dead, which seemed to call for pity on the passers by, who might themselves so soon share the same fate; but no one cared for any thing but miserable pelf; no one trembled at the consideration of what might so soon befall him in his turn; no one did for another what he would have wished others to do for him. The bishop hereupon called together his flock, and *setting before them the example and teaching of their Lord*, called on them to act up to it. He said if they took care only of their own people, they did but what the commonest feeling would dictate — the servant of Christ must do more: he must love his enemies and pray for his persecutors; for God made his sun to rise, and his rain to fall on all alike, and he who would be the child of God must imitate his Father." To this appeal the people cheerfully responded; they formed themselves into classes; the rich gave of their abundance, the poor of their poverty, and no one quitted his post but with his life.

In the matter of government and discipline, the church of the third century was gradually yielding to a despotic, all-controlling unity. The Bishops of Carthage, Antioch, and Rome, especially the latter, exercised extensive influence and dominion over the neighboring churches. Gradually a hierarchy of presbyters and bishops was formed. Those who possessed talent and power, or who had done and suffered much in the cause of Christ, claimed a higher consideration. Episcopal authority was enhanced; and much bigotry and intolerance were developed. Heretics and apostates were denounced; the slightest deviations from dominant usage was punished with proscription and excommunication. Speculative notions also, as already intimated, began to prevail, and formal creeds were imposed upon the people. The Roman emperors occasionally flattered the bishops and leading members of the church, and a spirit of pride and intolerance was beginning to invade its purity. This, indeed, was often checked, if not altogether extinguished, by the terrible persecution through which they all passed; and upon the whole, the third century was one of remarkable spiritual progress. Piety of the noblest and most self-sacrificing kind adorned the character both of the pastors and their people. The gold was somewhat tarnished; nay, more, here and there it was mingled with dross; but it was gold still. Christ was enthroned in the church, and his peaceful reign extended among the heathen.

In two Christians especially, the one a bishop, the other a philosopher, is the spirit of Christianity at this era, both in its excellences and defects, strikingly developed; and to them, therefore, we will devote the remainder of this chapter. We refer to Cyprian of Carthage, and Origen of Alexandria, both of them great and good, yet erring and defective men.

Thascius Cyprianus was born at Carthage, of wealthy and influential heathen parents. He was educated with great care, and gave evidence of extraordinary talents. He paid much attention especially to oratorical studies, and was distinguished for his bold and fervid eloquence. His temper was warm and imperious, his passions quick and powerful. Yielding to the vices of heathenism, and despising Christianity, it seemed impossible that he should ever become a Christian; and indeed, he continued attached to the pagan faith till twelve years before his death. When his attention was called to the truth, he felt that in his case the transformation demanded was impossible. "Receive," says he in a letter to his friend Donatus,* "what must be experienced before it can be understood, not by external aids, or mere knowledge, but by the transforming grace of God. When I lay in darkness and blindness, tossed hither and thither, in the dismal night, amid the billows, wandering about with an uncertain and fluctuating course, according to my habits at that time, I considered it was something difficult and hard that any one could be born again, lay aside what he was before, and although his corporeal nature remained the same, become in soul and temper a new man."

"How could a man," said he, "already at mature age, undergo such a transformation, change his whole life and habits, which through constitution or the force of custom had become a second nature; learn economy and temperance when accustomed to luxury and dissipation; exchange gold and purple for a poor or simple dress? . . . Thus I have often said to myself. For as I was entangled in many errors of my former life, and did not believe that I could be emancipated from their control, I yielded to

* *Epistola Prima ad Don.*

the vice which clave to me, and despairing of reform, submitted to my evil passions, as if they belonged to my nature."

After a long struggle with himself, and aided by the pious counsels of Cecilius, a Christian presbyter whose name he adopted at his baptism, and whose wife and children he took into his own charge, after the death of Cecilius, Cyprian at length yielded to the overpowering evidence of Christianity, and became a new man in Christ Jesus. "Then," says he, "things formerly doubtful were confirmed in a remarkable manner; what before was closed became open, and dark things were illuminated; power was given to perform what before seemed difficult — the impossible was rendered possible; my former life, carnal in its origin and spent in sin, was an earthly life; my new life, animated and controlled by the Spirit, is a life in God."

Cyprian was reluctantly called, by the voice of the people, in a time of trouble and distraction, to the bishopric of Carthage. He nobly justified their choice. Though urging the loftiest claims to episcopal and church authority, and occasionally betraying what may justly be termed a vehement and intolerant spirit, he gave himself to the work of God with singular energy and zeal. His piety and benevolence, his charity and patience, were celebrated throughout Africa, wherever the Christian name was known. Persecution assailed the church. He nobly breasted the storm when necessary for the defence of his flock, but retired before its vehemence whenever by doing so he could best accomplish the ends of his pastorate. He thus escaped death during the persecution under Decius, and returned to Carthage when the edicts against the Christians were suspended by Valerian. He was soon, however, called to bear testimony to the faith, at the hazard of his life. All the bishops and teachers of the Christian church were condemned to death. It was a time of peculiar trial, and Cyprian felt that he must put himself at the head of his flock, and stand in the breach. He exhorted all to patience and endurance. When his sentence was about to be pronounced, he quietly awaited what might befall him, at his country residence near Carthage, which, in the fervor of his first love, he had sold, in order to assist the poor with the money, but which the attachment of his church had restored to him. In the former persecution he had yielded to the dictates of prudence; but now, no entreaties from friends, and even from men of note among the heathen, who proffered him an asylum, could induce him to decline that public confession which he believed the Lord had called him to make. But when he heard that he was to be taken to Utica, where the proconsul was then staying, that he might be executed there, he resolved to yield for a season to the advice of his friends, "since," as he said, "it was fitting that the bishop should confess the Lord before the church over which the Lord hath placed him, in order, by his confession, to do honor to the whole church; for what the bishop utters at such a time, by the inspiration of God, he utters as the voice of all."

All at once Cyprian was seized by a guard, and taken to the proconsul; but as long as the proconsul remained in the country for relaxation, Cyprian was not examined. Crowds of his brethren, friends, and church members gathered around him, and watched his prison during the night, so that no evil might befall him. The next morning, accompanied by a great multitude of Christians and heathen, he was led to judgment. The place was at some distance, and, as the proconsul had not yet arrived, he was permitted to retire to a solitary spot, where, exhausted, he lay down upon a bench that he found there. A soldier, who had apostatized from Christianity, offered him, — from love and reverence, and from a desire to secure his clothes as relics, (for the passion for relics then began to be entertained; a passion natural, but easily perverted,) — dry clothes instead of his own, which were dripping with sweat. But Cyprian answered him, "Shall I be anxious to be free from discomfort, when, perhaps, to-morrow I shall feel nothing at all?"

When at last brought before the proconsul, the latter thus addressed him:—

Are you Thascius Cyprianus?

Cyp. I am.

Pro. You have suffered yourself to be made a chief of these men holding sacrilegious opinions.

Cyp. I have.

Pro. The majesty of the emperor requires thee to perform the ceremonies of our state religion.

Cyp. That I cannot do.

Pro. Think of your own safety.

Cyp. Do what is commanded you. There is no room for deliberation in so clear a matter.

To the same deputy, a year before, he had replied, when commanded to perform idolatrous ceremonies, "I am a Christian and a bishop. I know no other deity than the one true God, who made heaven and earth, the sea, and all that therein is. This God we Christians serve; to him we pray day and night for ourselves and all other men, as well as for the safety of those very emperors."

Thus he had no further explanations to make, as the proconsul knew well the tenets of his faith, and that there was only one alternative. Hence

Cyprian's simple reply — "*Do what is commanded you.*"

The proconsul, after consulting with his council, pronounced the following sentence: "You have lived a long time in impiety, and have conspired to pervert other men — constituting yourself the enemy of the Roman gods — so that the pious and most sacred emperors have been unable to recall you to the observance of the holy ceremonies. Therefore, as you are the author and leader of these flagrant crimes, you shall be made a warning to those whom you have conjoined with you in your wickedness."

Cyp. God be praised.

He was followed by a crowd of believers, who wished to die with him; but the orders of the proconsul, it would seem, extended only to the principal men. His friends and disciples, therefore, were permitted to attend him to the place of execution, where, with a serene courage, springing from his confidence in God, after having presented the executioner with twenty pieces of gold, he sealed his testimony with his blood.

We now turn to Origen, whose genius and virtue were as illustrious as his piety and devotion to the cause of Christ. In him the philosophical spirit developed itself in connection with the faith of Christ, giving rise to some errors, and yet enriching the body of truth and the great stream of civilization with elements of beauty and power.

Origen was born in Alexandria, the magnificent capital of Grecian Egypt, in the year 185, and was instructed by his parents in the truths of the Christian religion. He received the best education that Alexandria afforded, and in early life gave indications of genius and strength of character. The old Grecian philosophy, extinguished by scepticism in its native haunts, revived in Alexandria with augmented splendor. As this prosperous city was the emporium of trade and luxury, thither flocked all sorts of persons, representatives of the different nations around it, merchants, artisans, politicians, and scholars. Learning and the arts were somewhat fostered by the government, and many distinguished thinkers were encouraged to open schools of philosophy. Plato revived in Philo. The theosophy of the east and the speculations of the west were mingled in Ammonius Saccas. In a word, Alexandria was equally eclectic in population, religion, and philosophy. Christianity came in as a new and all-comprehending power, first making its way among the common people, and then among scholars and philosophers. Pantænus and Clement were Christian instructors, and felt the necessity of adapting their teachings to the condition of the community.

Well read in Grecian learning, as well as in the writings of prophets and apostles, they discovered points of harmony where others had seen only discord and opposition. The grand ideas of the Platonic school especially found a response in their enlightened minds, and were easily blended with the revelations of Christ. Indeed, they saw in the fundamental principles of Christianity a manifestation of the true God and the everlasting life — a higher philosophy, in whose comprehensive unity all other truth might find its place. These were the teachers of Origen, in philosophy and religion. These inspired in their susceptible pupil the love not only of Christ, but of the beautiful and true in nature and in man. In his earliest years he evinced a certain grandeur of thought and feeling. Leonidas, his father, while he admired, had frequent occasion to check the inquisitive and aspiring spirit of his son. Yet he regarded him with a sort of reverence. It is related, that, when leaning over his sleeping boy, the father would reverently kiss that bosom as the chosen temple of the Holy Ghost. When his father was cast into prison, on account of his religion, during the persecution under Severus, Origen exhorted him rather to suffer martyrdom than renounce his religion.

This persecution was a severe one. It raged not only in Alexandria, but in the Thebais, and throughout Egypt. Multitudes suffered martyrdom. Origen himself burned to win a crown similar to the one that now hung over the head of his father. He could suffer as well as study for Christ! His mother besought him with tears not to expose himself to the fury of the persecutors. When this proved unavailing, she resorted to the expedient of secreting his clothes, and thus forced him to remain at home. It was then that he wrote to his father not to permit any considerations of his family to shake his fidelity to Christ. The good old man was led forth to death, and sealed his testimony with his blood. His property was confiscated; and the youthful Origen supported his mother and six brothers by teaching the Greek language and literature.

Shortly afterwards, the persecution was renewed with increased violence. The teachers of the Catechetical school sought refuge in flight. Origen was asked by Demetrius, the bishop, to supply their place. He did so, and nobly breasted the fury of the storm. He stood by the side of the martyrs during their trial, exhorting them to fidelity, comforted them in their prisons, and accompanied them to execution. His own life was frequently in danger, but he contrived to escape, as if aided by some miraculous power. Six of his pupils, according to Eusebius, suffered martyrdom; but he continued his instructions with a constant accession of students and hearers. His labors night and day were immense. He read and prayed alternately, fasted much, and gave alms of all that he had. Every delicacy, including wine, and even shoes, and sometimes sleep itself, were abjured. Undaunted and self-sacrificing, he became all things for Christ.

This feeling of ascetic severity, noble in its principle and impulse, was exaggerated; and Origen was led to mutilate himself, according to what he deemed the command of Christ, and for the sake of avoiding scandal amid the crowd of male and female pupils with whom he mingled — a sad mistake, yet indicating the iron energy and lofty self-denial of the man. Well might he be called by his contemporaries Adamantius; and well might Eusebius say that "he taught as he lived, and lived as he taught."

After the death of Severus, Origen went to Rome, where he gained many friends and admirers. After his return, he continued, at the desire of the Bishop Demetrius, his catechetical instructions. A popular tumult compelled him to flee to Palestine, where he was held in such esteem by the bishops, that they encouraged him to preach in the assemblies. His profound thought and persuasive eloquence won all hearts. Moved with jealousy, as it is supposed, his own bishop recalled him. Subsequently he was sent to Achaia, to heal some divisions there. On his way to Cæsarea, in Palestine, he was ordained a presbyter, which laid the foundation of difficulties and controversies with the Bishop Demetrius, who haughtily claimed entire jurisdiction over the movements of Origen, and finally degraded him from the ministry. But Origen had a great mission to perform, and he meekly continued to discharge his duties. He was encouraged and sustained by the churches in Achaia, Phœnicia, and Arabia. Denying the errors laid to his charge, he went to live at Cæsarea, where he taught the truths of Christianity with great success. In the year 231 his persecutor died, and Origen now enjoyed in tranquillity his well-deserved reputation. The celebrated Gregory Thaumaturgus and his brother Athenodorus employed him as their instructor, looking up to him with affectionate respect.

When peace was restored to the church, after the persecution under Maximin, during which Origen had lain in concealment, he took occasion to travel to Athens. Thence he went to Arabia, to which he was invited by the bishops of that province, to refute Bishop Beryllus, who denied the existence of our Savior's divine nature, previous to his incarnation. Origen spoke with such candor and eloquence, that Beryllus renounced his errors, and thanked him for his instructions. He was equally successful with other heretics — a circumstance which must be ascribed to the wonderful modesty, gentleness, and ability of the man.

In the new persecution under Decius, Origen played a conspicuous part. He was regarded as a pillar of the church, and thrown into prison, where he was subjected to the cruelest sufferings, which he bore with a spirit of calm heroism and Christian resignation. Exhausted by his sufferings, he died at Tyre, in the year 254.

Origen was a voluminous writer, but the most of his productions are lost. The others are somewhat mutilated, and, in all probability, interpolated. It is difficult, therefore, to form a just estimate of his philosophical or theological opinions. He spent years on the study of the sacred writings in the original tongues. He did much to preserve the integrity of the Greek and Hebrew text. His commentaries are often fanciful, and yet profound and pious. He uses the allegorical mode of interpretation, after the manner of Philo, and finds meanings under the literal import, sometimes extravagant, sometimes rare and beautiful. In this respect, however, he departed from the simplicity of Christ. In his great work, *Contra Celsum*, he vindicates Christianity, as a divine, infallible religion. His own soul rejoiced in Jesus Christ, as the "brightness of the Father's glory, and the express image of his person." Liberal and comprehensive, he cherished large and generous views, and cultivated a spirit of true Christian charity. Many of his speculations are simply suggestions and inquiries after the manner of Plato; he never pressed them as infallible dogmas. Not thoroughly appreciating the limits of human inquiry, and attaching too much importance to the methods of philosophy, at that time ill defined and variant, he allowed his thoughts to wander into the untried regions of speculative conjecture. Enamoured especially of Plato, he revelled amid the dreams of a profound, yet imaginative theosophy. Passing from the outward, and despising the body, he sought the essential and eternal archetypes of things in the bosom of God — saw there the unchangeable essence, and finite procession of the soul, and thus taught a dogma akin to the Platonic transmigration. Like Plato, he saw the spirit, once winged and holy, fallen into materialism and sin, from which, struggling upward, it must leave the body, and rejoin the immortals. From the same view he deduced the freedom of the human soul, and the final restoration of all to purity and God. To him all nature, as in the Platonic theory, was vital and conscious — the stars were the abodes, perhaps the bodies, of living souls, whose brightness or dimness corresponds precisely with the moral character of the spirits which occupy them. An endless succession of worlds preceded our own, and an endless succession will follow. The bad, revolving, so to speak, through various cycles and transformations, will yet, through the agency of their free will, and the love of Christ, reach new heavens and a new earth, prepared for their eternal abode.

Origen, while holding the humanity of Christ as an outer expression of his separate spiritual existence, maintained his supreme divinity. He saw in him the word or manifestation of the one eternal Father. In his Contra Celsum, replying to the objection of his opponent, founded on the worship paid to Christ, who, in the view of the heathen philosopher, was a mere man, he says, "We worship, therefore, as we have now shown, one God, Father and Son, and our argument remains as impregnable as before. We do not regard with an excessive veneration one who has but lately appeared among men, as though he had no existence before. We believe his own word, when he tells us, 'Before Abraham was I am,' as also when he says, 'I am the truth.' We are none of us so stupid as to think that the Essence of Truth had no existence before the time of Christ's appearance."* Hence, in his 8th Homily on Jeremiah, he says, "If the soul have not God the Father, if it have not the Son, saying, 'I and my Father will come to him, and will make our abode with him,' if it have not the Holy Spirit, it is desolate."

Thus Cyprian and Origen come together in their love and reverence for Christ, as the Way, the Truth, and the Life. This is the living stream which mingles with the philosophy, the literature, the politics, and the art of the modern world. We shall find it in all the centuries, coursing its way towards the grand consummation of truth, freedom, and righteousness, yet to come.

* *Contra Cel.* lib. viii. 12.

CHAPTER XVI.

CHRIST IN THE MIDDLE AGES.

We have seen how Christianity, thrown into the crude mass of humanity, vitiated and enfeebled by idolatry and lust, won amazing triumphs. It partook, however, in its actual embodiment and application, of the spirit and tendency of the age. At heart, the Roman empire was corrupt, and destined to destruction, and not even Christianity could finally save it. Indeed, its dismemberment was a matter not only of political, but of moral necessity. The revolution and reconstruction of nations is one of God's methods of elevating and purifying society. Old forms pass away. New energies are brought into free and generous play. Indeed, society, in its best form, is an amalgam; and it required the Roman and the Teutonic elements, moulded by Christianity, to give rise to the new and vigorous organization of modern society.

Taken, however, into the embrace of the state, first by Constantine, and subsequently by Charlemagne and Pepin, as an organized belief, with its hierarchy of forms and ministers, Christianity necessarily lost much of its original purity and power. Still, no amount of corruption could divest it of its inherent, life-giving energy.* It yet spread, after the disruption of the Roman empire, in lines of renovation and blessing. The idols of heathen worship were abolished, and the worship of the true God was established in many barbarous climes. Idolatry and slavery, polygamy and gladiatorial shows, with the more unnatural forms of lust, so common among the heathen, disappeared from the civilized world.

The church, however, having become national and hierarchical, was used as an engine of political power. Whole nations were brought into it by mere baptism or conquest, without the slightest reference to their spiritual state. The conversion of a warrior, king, or chief, insured the conversion of his people. All must come under the yoke of Christ, whether they understand the gospel or not. Some of the northern barbarians, who overran the Roman empire, were nominal Christians; others were pagans; but all eventually submitted to the church; some from superstition, others from choice, and many from policy and force. The consequences can

* It is of the greatest moment, in estimating the claims of Christianity, to distinguish between the mere human form, in which it is embodied, and Christianity itself, which never changes. The Christianity of Christ, or of the Bible, is often a very different thing from the Christianity of man, or of society.

easily be foreseen. Paganism was mingled with Christianity. The virgin mother was adored as "the queen of heaven," temples were turned into churches, and churches into temples, adorned with images of the saints, and smoking with incense. The supper of our Lord was made a sacrifice, having a greater affinity with superstition than with enlightened religion. The Catholic church, as it termed itself, with some grand redeeming elements, became a mere external organization, to which vast additions were constantly made, partly by persuasion, and partly by violence. Abjuring the first element of our Savior's kingdom, which is spiritual and divine, and thence to be advanced only by the regeneration of true hearts, in a free, spontaneous manner, the Papal organization formed itself into a hierarchy of material forms and despotic forces, and insisted upon the submission of the world. The Christian people were excluded from all share in the government of the church; and freedom, even on the part of the inferior clergy, was utterly excluded. The sword and the keys were conjoined, and what could not be effected by persuasion was effected by force. Racks and gibbets, imprisonment and death, as well as the preaching of the gospel, were the means employed to secure this result. Undoubtedly, both within and without the church Catholic, a constant protest was uttered against all this; and here and there, during the middle ages, we find multitudes of good Catholics, as well as Protestants or heretics, abjuring these anti-Christian principles, and cultivating, as best they could, the spirit of a pure Christianity. Rome, with all her unity, has ever been a unity of compromises; and, as she still possessed the word of God and the general theory of the gospel, as a system of reconciliation and reform, she retained, notwithstanding her corruptions, some regenerative power, some conservative social influence.

Hence, it has been well remarked, that "we ought to distinguish between Catholicism and Papacy." The Catholic church, in itself considered, may be regarded as a different institution from the Papal hierarchy. The latter is unquestionably anti-Christian; the former, imperfect and even corrupt, may yet embody, and undoubtedly does embody, much true piety. Immense, however, were the abuses of the Papacy, and through that of the whole Catholic body, at the time of which we are speaking. They had grown to such enormity in the days of Petrarch and Dante, that these two poets, Catholics both, denounced the Roman hierarchy, popes, cardinals, and monks, with unmeasured severity. Dante does not hesitate to put some of the popes in his Inferno, and boldly designates Rome as the Babylon of the Apocalypse, exclaiming,—

"Ah Constantine! to how much ill gave birth,
Not thy conversion, but that plenteous dower
Which the first wealthy father gave to thee." *

Petrarch, who had seen, especially at Avignon, the horrible corruptions of the Papal court, pours upon it a torrent of invective.†

* See *Inferno*, cxix. *Purgatorio*, xxxii.

† The following verses will give an idea of the energy with which Petrarch — ordinarily so gentle in the style of his composition — attacks the Roman see: —

" The fire of wrathful Heaven alight
And all thy harlot tresses smite,
Base city! Thou from humble fare —
Thy acorns and thy water — rose
To greatness, rich with others' woes,
Rejoicing in the ruin thou didst bear.

"Foul nest of treason! is there aught
Wherewith the spacious world is fraught
Of bad or vile, 'tis hatched in thee,
Who revellest in thy costly meats,
Thy precious wines, and curious seats,
And all the pride of luxury.

" The while, within thy secret halls,
Old men in seemly festivals
With buxom girls in dance are going;
And in thy midst old Beelzebub
Eyes, through his glass, the motley club,
The fire with sturdy bellows blowing."

Quoted from *Le Rime del Petrarcha*, (ed. Lod. Castelvetro,) tom. i. p. 325; in Dr. McCries' Hist. of the Refor. in Italy, p. 27.

The wonder indeed is, that Christianity could live in such a system at all, embarrassed by superstition, checked by bigotry, enfeebled by lust. But it certainly did, and this we regard as one of the proofs of its divine origin, its inherent, indestructible energy.* Roman Catholicism, while embodying pagan elements, was ever superior to paganism, and in a barbarous age exerted over society some conservative and reformatory influence. Even Merle D'Aubigné says that "important services were rendered by Catholicism to the existing European nations, in the age of their first formation." † All nationalities had been dissolved in the destruction of the Roman empire, and chaos brooded over society. Christianity formed a centre to the whole, and the old Teutonic nations crystallized around it. Thence order sprung from confusion, and all the vital elements of modern society were developed.

If the church, in consequence of her power, became corrupt, and oppressed her subjects, she did so to save them from the gulf of barbarism, into which, inevitably, they must have plunged. She was a severe and bigoted mother, but she preserved her children from fatal anarchy and absolute political destruction.

* This is what Bunsen (in Hippolytus) justly styles "*the miracle of the last fifteen hundred years.*" See Appendix, note H.

† Hist. of the Reformation, vol. i, p. 8.

Hence Ranke justly and strikingly remarks, "However defective the civilization we have delineated," (the combination of the spiritual and temporal elements, first in the Frankish empire, under Charlemagne, and then in the Germanic nations, Christianized and united under the Papal sway, both of which were thus preserved from destruction,) "it was necessary to the complete naturalization of Christianity in the West. It was no light thing to subdue the haughty spirits of the north, the nations under the dominion of ancestral superstitions, to the ideas of Christianity. It was necessary that the religious element should predominate for a time, in order that it might gain fast hold on the German mind. By this, at the same time, was effected the intimate blending of the Roman and Germanic elements. There is a community among the nations of modern times, which has always been regarded as the main basis of the general civilization, a community in church and state, in manners, customs, and literature. In order to produce this, it was necessary that the western nations should, for a time, form, as it were, a single state, temporal and spiritual." *

By this means the institutions of the church were preserved from destruction amid the general transition and change, while the church lent

* History of the Popes, vol. i. p. 40.

its aid to the formation of national character and virtue. The period indeed was abnormal, and preparatory to something higher and better, now partially developed by the reformations and revolutions of modern times; but it was necessary, under God, to the production of that form of Christian civilization yet to triumph in all lands.

It is for this reason that Macaulay speaks of the conversion of the Anglo-Saxons to Christianity, as "the first of a long series of salutary revolutions," and adds, "It is true that the church had been deeply corrupted both by that superstition and that philosophy against which she had long contended, and over which she had at last triumphed. She had given a too easy admission to doctrines borrowed from the ancient schools, and to rites borrowed from the ancient temples. Roman policy and Gothic ignorance, Grecian ingenuity and Syrian asceticism, had contributed to deprave her. *Yet she retained enough of the sublime theology and benevolent morality of her earlier days to elevate many intellects and to purify many hearts.* Some things, also, which, at a later period, were justly regarded as among her chief blemishes, were in the seventh century, and long afterwards, among her chief merits. That the sacerdotal order should encroach on the duty of the chief magistrate, would, in our time, be a great evil. *But that which in an age of good government is an evil, may in an age of grossly bad government be a blessing.* It is better that mankind should be governed by wise laws well administered, and by an enlightened public piety, than by priestcraft, than by brute violence, by such a prelate as Dunstan than by such a warrior as Penda. A society sunk in ignorance, and ruled by mere physical force, has great reason to rejoice, when a class, of which the influence is intellectual and moral, rises to ascendency. Such a class will doubtless abuse its power; but mental power, even when abused, is still a nobler and better power than that which consists merely in corporeal strength. We read in the Anglo-Saxon chronicles of tyrants, who, when at the height of greatness, were smitten with remorse, who abhorred the pleasures and dignities which they had purchased by guilt, who abdicated their crowns, and who sought to atone for their offences by cruel penances and incessant prayers. Those stories have drawn forth bitter expressions of contempt from some writers, who, while they boasted of liberality, were in truth as narrow minded as any monk of the dark ages, and whose habit was to apply to all events in the history of the world the standard received in the Parisian society of the eighteenth century. Yet surely a system which, however deformed by superstition, introduced strong moral restraints into communities previously governed only by vigor of muscle and audacity of spirit — a system which taught the fiercest and mightiest ruler that he was, like his meanest bondman, a responsible being, might have seemed to deserve a more respectable mention from philosophers and philanthropists." . . .

"Even the spiritual supremacy arrogated by the pope was, in the dark ages, productive of far more good than evil. Its effect was to unite the nations of Western Europe in one great commonwealth. What the Olympian chariot course and the Pythian oracle were to all the Greek cities, from Trebizond to Marseilles, Rome and her bishop were to all Christians of the Latin communion from Calabria to the Hebrides. Thus grew up sentiments of enlarged benevolence. Races separated from each other by seas and mountains acknowledged a fraternal tie and a common code of public law. Even in war the cruelty of the conqueror was not seldom mitigated by the recollection that he and his vanquished enemies were all members of one great federation." *

If, in the view of some, this statement require some slight modification, it must be admitted

* History of England, vol. i. pp. 6–8.

that the institution of Christianity, in its fundamental principles, was the means not only of individual regeneration, but of social and political progress, and that it possessed this character in spite of Papal assumption and superstition, especially in the earlier periods of its history. It was under the Pontificate of the second Gregory, (A. D. 590,) who, with all his ambition, was an honest, earnest man, that we see Christianity grasping the dissolving elements of society, and constructing them into those permanent forms from which Christendom has derived its civilization. It was then, too, that the Bishop of Rome acquired that dominion, which, beneficial in its first exercise, at last all but extinguished pure religion, as well as political freedom. Such was the desolation around him, that Gregory felt that society had come to its termination, and that the judgment was about to ensue. "Every where," he says, "we behold sorrow; on every side we hear groans. Cities are destroyed, fortresses are pulled down, the fields are laid waste, the land is become desolate. The villages are empty, and scarcely an inhabitant is left in the cities; and even this small remnant of the human race is daily and incessantly massacred. The scourge of divine justice does not rest, because no amendment has followed under it. We see how some are dragged to prison, some are mutilated, others are put to death."*

In these circumstances Gregory had not only to preach the gospel, and administer its consolations, but, as a vassal of the Greek empire, to take measures for the defence of the country, "placed between the Longobards, thirsting for conquest, the governors of the Greek empire, often forgetful of their duties, and a court full of intrigues." He was equal to the emergency. His influence grew apace. Italy was saved, and the northern barbarians were brought under the yoke of Christ.

That Gregory II., and many others devoted to the building up of the Roman church, and the aggrandizement of the Papacy, such as Boniface the apostle of the Germans, who caused his followers to swear allegiance to St. Peter and the see of Rome, were disinterested Christian men, cannot be doubted. Their influence, in one aspect of the case, may seem to be bad, as they sanctioned grievous errors and corruptions in the church of Christ; but in another, and that the most important, it was good, and only good. It gave Christianity and civilization to the Germanic nations.†

* Neander's Memorials, &c., p. 387.

† Upon this subject consult the works of Guizot, Hallam, Maitland, and Sismondi.

But it is in secret, and especially in the hearts of individual men, that God accomplishes his purposes of grace. It is the hidden leaven, which, in the long run, regenerates society. In the case of the church of the "dark ages," this work was perpetuated, even by means of imperfect institutions. And this is doubtless the reason why the providence of God permitted the Papal organization to exist, during this chaotic and transitional era. The thorns which grew up around the delicate flower of true religion, while they diminished its beauty and stifled its perfume, yet protected it from ruthless invasion. The church, in the period of her deepest degradation, was not all bad. Hence we find in her bosom noble spirits, devout and learned men, self-denying, and laborious missionaries. What beautiful details, for example, are given by Neander, in his Memorials of the Christian Life, Light in Dark Places, and the Life of St. Bernard, as well as in his Church History, of such men as Patrick and Columban, of Fulgentius and Severinus, Germanus and Lupus, Cæsarius of Arles, and Eligius, Bishop of Noyon, the venerable Bede, Gallus the apostle of Switzerland, the Abbot Sturm of Fulda, Martin of Tours, Anschar the apostle of the north, (who in his dreams heard a voice urging him to preach the gospel in Scandinavia, and saying, "Go, and return to me crowned with martyrdom,") Otto Bishop of Bamberg, and that strange, martyr spirit, mystic, philosopher, and missionary, Raimund Lulli! During the centuries designated by historians as preëminently "dark ages," some faithful Christian men and devoted missionaries were at work, in various countries, sowing the seed of life "beside all waters." All around them lay the thick shadows of ignorance and superstition; but by the blessing of Heaven, they kept the lamp of truth bright and clear, until the day dawned, and the day-star arose upon the nations.

Even monasteries, in early times the natural resort of persecuted Christianity, liable as they were to the grossest corruption, were frequently the refuge of piety and worth. Thence issued many of those self-denying men, who by their toils and prayers made the wilderness to blossom as the rose. Here, too, were preserved, for the benefit of succeeding generations, not only the word of God and the works of the Christian fathers, but all the extant literature of the times. "The church," says Macaulay, with reference to this fact, "has many times been compared by divines to that ark of which we read in the Book of Genesis; but never was the resemblance more perfect than during that evil time when she alone rode, amid darkness and tempest, on the deluge, beneath which all the great works of ancient power and wisdom lay intombed, bearing within her that feeble germ from which a second and more glorious civilization was to spring."

All must acknowledge that a certain moral as well as political grandeur attaches to the half-civilized Charlemagne and his Frankish kingdom, and the generous but unsuccessful efforts which he made to give unity and civilization to his empire. It paved the way for the Germanic confederation, and the civilization of France and Germany. The monk Alcuin and the schools which he founded, the mediæval philosophy, parent of modern speculative thought, and the transition from the Greek and Alexandrine schools to that of our more recent philosophy, were the fruit of Christianity. Some, who know little of it, affect to despise the scholastic philosophy; but, with all its faults, it marvellously disciplined the human intellect, and prepared the way for the high mental achievements of the present age. Full of defects, and even absurdities, like the age from which it sprang, after all, as Leibnitz suggests, there was *aurum in illo cœno.* One of its grandest features was its recognition of the absolute Jehovah, not simply in nature, where he seems an impersonal Power, but in Christ, where he reveals himself as "the Father of us all." This gave scope and strength to its speculations upon the true, the good, the holy, which all the efforts of Grecian genius could not reach. It assisted in laying the foundation of a vast structure, not only of speculative thought, but of Christian morality.

The mediæval church, as we call it, by which is usually meant the church of the twelfth century, — a strange gothic structure of truth and error, of barbarism and refinement, based upon the highest truths and the most extravagant assumptions, — was thus not without some aspects of beauty and worth. Beneath the magnificent abbey or cathedral, which symbolized its spirit, lay deep dungeons, and sometimes inquisitorial halls, where the groans of the poor persecuted heretic were heard at the dead of night; but the cathedral itself was a thing of beauty, and echoed a grand, and sometimes a heartfelt worship. As in Dante's great poem, which has been called the flowering of the middle ages, so here we find puerile superstitions and atrocious bigotries, mingled with lofty sentiments and graceful forms. Besides, a power was yet at work in the souls of men, and in the heart of society, which all the folly of the times could not extinguish. Truth struggled for supremacy, and kept its hold of the secret conscience. God had his chosen ones, both within and without the pale of the Papal church. The world was not deserted by the Son of God. His spirit of love yet throbbed in many penitent, believing hearts. Here and there, in mountains and in valleys, and even in the depths of cities, might be found clusters of holy confessors, and faithful Christians, bound to God and to one another by eternal ties. In the solitude of cloisters, with all their evils, Christian scholars meditated upon divine things, and sent forth into the world the light of eternal truth.

Such thinkers as Anselm and Aquinas, the one in England, the other in Italy, ranged through the loftiest realms of thought, combining the claims of reason and religion, and blending, not only in their works, but in their lives, the highest philosophy with the deepest piety.* The night indeed, so far as our common Christianity was concerned, seemed dark and portentous, but ever and anon the stars appeared in the peaceful heavens. The love of God, revealed in Christ as a secret power, brooded over the troubled elements. Angels of mercy visited the earth, in the persons of self-denying men; of devout, disinterested women. The river of life was hidden amid gloomy woods and precipices, but it kept its silent course,

* In Anselm, who may be called the Plato of the middle ages, the philosophy of that day culminated. His *Cur Deus Homo* gives, in its germ, the great fact or principle yet destined to solve the practical difficulties of "the higher philosophy." For some account of Anselm and Aquinas, see Appendix, Note I.

and in due time reappeared in the smiling landscape. There were reformers before the Reformation, martyrs for truth and freedom in the darkest days of bigotry and lust.*

Much fine character and many generous impulses were nourished by Christianity among the Germanic tribes. Superstitious and somewhat savage, but masculine and generous, the old German heart loved the truth, and, we may add, loved God. This gave them nationality and force of character. This nourished among them many lofty, self-sacrificing souls. They suffered indeed, a long night of despotism and bigotry, but at last the fire of freedom and Christianity began to burn. "The friends of God" (*Gottesfreunde*, as they called themselves) appeared. These were partly laymen, partly priests or monks, among whom were the mystics Eckart, Suso, Tauler, and the anonymous author of "The German Theology," all longing for purity and freedom, loving God and the truth. These uttered the first living word for evangelical Christianity, and exemplified it in their lives.†

* See the works of Bonnechose and Ullmann on Reformers before the Reformation.

† To the same class belong John Ruysbroek, Thomas à Kempis, and John Charlier Gerson. At least they were animated by the same, spirit and exerted the same influence. Luther refers to John Tauler, called *Doctor Sublimis et Illuminatus*, in terms of affectionate veneration. Writing to Spalatine he says, "Si te delectat puram, solidam antiquæ simillimam theologiam legere, in Germanica lingua effu-

A similar spirit animated many French divines and Christians. The Huguenots date far back for the first origin of their faith.* Peter Waldo and the poor men of Lyons were not alone in their attachment to the truth. It is well known that an immense influence was exerted in later times by Gerson, of Paris, the *Doctor Christianissimus* of the schools, a true Christian philosopher, who laid his vast learning at the cross of Christ, and deemed all science as nothing in comparison with the practical knowledge and love of God. He wrote a profound treatise on spiritual theology, called *Mystica Theologia.* In his old age he abandoned his literary and even ecclesiastical honors, and devoted himself to the education of little children, for whose benefit he wrote a remarkable treatise, De Parvulis ad Deum ducendis, *Of the art of leading little children to God.* Though he never left the Catholic church, and in

sam, sermones Johannis Tauleri, prædicatoriæ professionis tibi compare potes." The anonymous Little Book on German Theology (*Buchlein der Deutschen Theologie*) was first published A. D. 1516, by Luther, with a recommendatory preface, in which he says, "Next to the Bible and St. Augustine, I do not know of any book from which I have learnt better what God, Christ, man, and all things are." The true name of Thomas à Kempis was Thomas Hamerken of Kempen. He was sub-prior of the Augustinian monks on St. Agnes Mount near Zwoll, and died A. D., 1471. His Imitation of Christ, however, has been ascribed by some (Cousin, for example) to Abbot Gersen, or John Gerson. John Charlier Gerson, Chancellor of Paris, died A. D. 1429.

* See De Felice's History of the Reformed Church in France.

his earlier years defended some of its corruptions, he was a Protestant at heart, as his writings testify. His views were more conservative than those of Wicliff, nay, in some respects, opposed to his, yet, in the end, they exerted a similar influence. If Wicliff was "the morning star" of the Reformation in England, Gerson was such in France and Germany. The latter country, in which his writings advocating reform in the church were extensively read, received from Gerson a powerful impulse in favor of evangelical religion.

How many followers had Arnoldo of Brescia, and Savonarola of Florence, and what noble sentiments of civil and religious freedom did they promulgate, at the hazard of their lives. Blackened as their characters have been by the emissaries of the Papal church, both were men of singular piety and heroic virtue. Born out of due time, they sought for a freedom which they could not realize, and so died for the truth. One of his enemies, Tritemio, makes Arnoldo address the following words to the pope and cardinals: "I call heaven and earth to witness that I have announced to you these things which the Lord has commanded. But you despise both me and your Creator. Nor is it wonderful that you are about to put me, a simple man, to death, for preaching to you the truth, since, if even St. Peter were to arise from the dead this day, and were to reprove your many vices, ye would by no means spare him." *

In England, as early as the thirteenth century, we find Grostête (Greathead) Bishop of Lincoln protesting against the abuses of the Papacy, and vindicating his allegiance to Christ. He died rejoicing in the truth, having maintained his integrity to the end, in opposition to the power of Rome, and was recognized in that day, by the voice of the community, "as a searcher of the Scriptures, an adversary of the pope, and the despiser of the Romans." Sewal Archbishop of York professed similar sentiments; for "the more the pope cursed him, the more the people blessed him." Thomas Bradwardine, in the fourteenth century, chaplain of Edward III. and subsequently Archbishop of Canterbury, one of the most amiable and learned men of his day, and a humble follower of Christ, bore ample testimony to the fundamental doctrines of the gospel.†.

The Scriptures, or portions of them, must have been translated into Italian at a very early period, and hence, under the very shadow of the Roman see, the grace of God was found working in the

* Ego testem invoco cœlum, etc. Quoted from the North British Review from Tritemius.

† Some interesting details with reference to similar characters in England previous to the Reformation, may be found in the fifth volume of Merle D'Aubigné's History of the Reformation.

hearts of humble and inquiring souls. Fragments of such translations appeared in the fourteenth century. In 1471 a version of the Scriptures, by Nicolo Malermi, or Malerbi, was published at Venice, and is said to have gone through nine editions in that century, and twelve in the succeeding. A better one appeared in the beginning of the sixteenth century, by Antonio Brucioli. His edition of the New Testament was published at Venice for the first time in 1530, and the whole Bible two years later. Other versions rapidly followed. The revival of learning introduced not only the Greek classics, but editions of the Greek Testament and of the Septuagint, which fell into the hands of thoughtful scholars. The works of Augustine and other Christian fathers were also more or less studied. Giovanni Pico, one of the greatest scholars of his day, who had mastered twenty-two languages before he was twenty-five, and died in 1494, in the thirty-second year of his age, was a true Christian. His spirit, breathed through his writings, is remarkably evangelical. Indeed he narrowly escaped being burned as a heretic. Many valuable commentaries on the sacred Scriptures were written by learned and pious men, at a very early period, both in Italy and elsewhere. The relation of Nicholas Lyra to Luther was made the subject of a lively pun in the days of the latter: Si Lyra non lyrasset, Lutherus non saltasset. *If Lyra had not sung, Luther had not danced.*

In the days of Tasso and Queen Renée, a noble and pious woman, how many Italians were found in Ferrara and other parts of Italy, animated by the deepest piety, just at the breaking forth of the Reformation! It is true, the works of the Reformers had reached Italy, but they found in these Italian hearts a congenial soil. Some of these were members of the Papal church, and others were Protestants. Vittoria Colonna, the far-famed Marchioness of Pescara, the friend of Michael Angelo and Olympia Morata, was at heart a Protestant. After the death of her husband, she devoted herself to study and works of piety. Her poems and letters, some of them of great beauty, are imbued with a profoundly religious spirit. Her correspondence with Olympia Morata and others shows that her heart was given to Christ. How touchingly does she console a friend for the loss of her brother, "whose serene spirit had entered into eternal peace!" Thence she adds, that "she ought not to lament, since she could now converse with him; his absences, once so frequent could no longer hinder him being understood by her." Nor was her piety of a monastic order; for Aretino thus writes of her, "that it was certainly not her opinion that the muteness of the tongue, or the casting down of the eyes, or the coarse garment, availed any thing, but the pure soul."

Even under the shadow of the court of the polished but profligate Leo X. a few distinguished men of Rome had established the "Oratory of Divine Love" for their common edification. "In the church of S. Sylvestro and S. Dorotea, in the Trastevere, not far from the spot where St. Peter was thought to have lived and to have presided over the first meeting of Christians, they assembled for divine worship, preaching and spiritual exercises. They met to the number of fifty or sixty. Contarini, Sadoleto, Giberto, Caraffa, all of whom afterwards became cardinals, Gaetano de Thiene, who was canonized, Lippomano, a theological writer of great reputation and influence, and some other celebrated men, were amongst them. Giuliano Bathi, the priest of that church, served as a centre of the circle."

Quite an interesting group of pious souls, some of them men of considerable eminence, might be found, about the same time, in Venice. There the celebrated Benedictine monk Bernardino Ochino, one of the greatest preachers of the age, vindicated the doctrine of justification by faith, giving force, by the purity and elevation of his life, to the impassioned appeals of his eloquence. He was heard with delight by Bembo, Caraffa, and Vittoria Colonna. Afterwards persecuted as a Protestant, he delighted, by his sincerity and fervor, multitudes, who were subsequently horrified by his open Protestantism. "I opened my heart to him," says Bembo, "as to Christ himself. It seemed to me I had never beheld a holier man."

At the house of Pietro Bembo, subsequently cardinal, which was open to all who chose to attend, the conversation, though chiefly literary and often frivolous, sometimes turned upon more important matters. It assumed a deeper and more pious tone at that of the learned Gregorio Cortese, the Abbot of San Giorgo Maggiore at Venice. Marco of Padua was a man of the deepest piety. It was from him that Pole professed to derive spiritual nutriment. But the most eminent of all was Caspar Contarini, of whom Pole said that he was ignorant of nothing that the human mind could discover by its own research, and that he crowned his knowledge with virtue. Contarini wrote a treatise on the doctrine of justification, of which Cardinal Pole speaks in terms of the highest praise. "You have brought to light," says he, "the jewel which the church kept half concealed." Would to God that Pole himself had carried out his earlier and better views, for he speaks of this doctrine as "holy, indispensable, fruitful truth." "The gospel," says Contarini, in one of his letters, "is no other than the blessed tidings, that the only-begotten Son of God, clad in our flesh, hath made satisfaction for us to the justice of his eternal Father. He who believes this enters into the kingdom of God; he enjoys the universal pardon; from a carnal he becomes a spiritual creature; from a child of wrath a child of grace; he lives in a sweet peace of conscience."

In voluptuous Naples, then under Spanish rule, the same great truth was taught by Valdez, a Spaniard, secretary to the viceroy; but unfortunately his writings are lost. In 1540 a book was published entitled "Of the Benefits of Christ's Death," breathing the soul of evangelical religion, which, as a decree of the Inquisition expressed it, "treated in an insinuating manner of justification, deprecated works and meritorious acts, ascribed all merit to faith alone: as this was the very point which was at that time a stumbling block to many prelates and monks, it obtained extraordinary circulation." This book was written, as the decree of the Inquisition expresses it, by a monk of San Severino, a pupil of Valdez.* It spread every where, especially in

* It has been ascribed to Aonio Paleario, another celebrated Italian Protestant.

Italy, and produced an immense sensation. Revised by Flaminio, it prepared the hearts of many for the Reformation. Valdez, however, founded no sect. His book was the fruit of liberal study and Christian piety. He enjoyed the quiet retreats of nature in the vicinity of Naples, in profitable conversation with his friends. "A portion of his soul sufficed," says one who knew him, "to animate his frail, attenuated body; the larger part of his clear, untroubled intellect was ever raised aloft in the contemplation of truth." One of his friends was Vittoria Colonna, already mentioned, who, after the death of her husband, occupied a beautiful retreat on one of the islands in the vicinity of Naples, and spent much of her time in literary and pious conversation with such persons as Valdez. The Duke of Palliano, and his wife Giulia Gonzago, reputed to be the most beautiful woman in Italy, adopted the same sentiments, and took part in these conversations.

Indeed, many bishops and distinguished laymen favored the doctrines which subsequently entered the Reformation, and formed its animating spirit. Those, indeed, who became open Protestants in Italy were cruelly persecuted by the Papal hierarchy. The prisons of Ferrara, of Venice, and of Rome heard the groans of the martyrs. Some, as the noble Carnessechi, were beheaded or burned at the stake. Calabria was deluged with Protestant blood. But the inference is a legitimate one, that multitudes, in preceding ages, must have loved the Savior, who had neither the strength nor the opportunity, perhaps not even the desire, to leave the Papal church.* The churches of the Waldenses have lived through a period of at least eight hundred years. They date beyond the days of Peter Waldo, and derive their name rather from their mountain home, than from any human teacher. Stigmatized and persecuted by the dominant church, like the Paulicians of the East, or the Albigenses of the West, they clung to the word of God amid all changes and trials. Numbering even now thirty thousand, they have endured the most appalling persecutions. They have passed through thirty wars, twelve of which were intended to be wars of extermination.†

The Catholic church in Germany, corrupt as it was in the days of Tetsel, preserved some spirit

* For details respecting Protestantism in Italy, see McCries' Annals of the Reformation in Italy. See also Ranke's History of the Popes, i. pp. 96, 101, and Baird's Protestantism in Italy.

† For information on the Waldenses, see Dr. Baird's Protestantism in Italy, Allix's Churches of Piedmont, Leger's Histoire des Eglises Evangeliques, the Ancient Valenses and Albigenses, by G. S. Faber, Morland's Hist. of the Evangelical Churches, &c., Henderson's "Vaudois," and Gilly's Waldensian Researches.

36 *

of freedom and of piety. Staupitz, the friend and spiritual teacher of Luther, never left the order of the Augustinians. It was from him, as well as from the Bible, which Luther first saw chained in the convent at Erfurth, that he received the doctrine of justification by faith. He carefully studied the writings of Augustine, as well as those of Occam and Gerson. It was an old monk who enlightened him respecting the doctrine of the forgiveness of sin, and by God's blessing brought it home to his heart, in a season of deep depression.* On another occasion we find him referring with affectionate respect to one of his old friends, John Braum, "holy and venerable priest of Christ and of Mary." Ursula, the wife of Conrad Cotta, both good Catholics, and others of his old acquaintances, were truly pious. Speaking of the former, he says, "There is nothing sweeter than the heart of a pious woman." Undoubtedly many such women might have been found in the old German church, even in the times of ignorance and superstition. Claudius of Turin, Peter de Bruys, Gabriel Biel, John de Wickliff, John Huss, Jerome of Prague, John Knox, and Thomas Cranmer, all received their training in the dominant church.†

* D'Aubigné's History of the Reformation, vol. i. p. 154.

† No thanks, however, to the Papal hierarchy, the whole endeavor of which has been to crush and extinguish such men. Could the

In a word, there is abundant evidence to show that Christ was in the church of the middle ages, as a regenerative power, and that from this source sprang the Reformation of the sixteenth century.

Catholic, and even the Roman, or Italian church, only throw off this Papal incubus, and return to primitive simplicity, it might yet bless the world.

CHAPTER XVII.

CHRIST IN THE REFORMATION.

THAT a system, divine in its origin, and supernatural in its resources, should, in consequence of its embodiment among men, be corrupted and abused, is not only quite conceivable, but altogether probable. It cannot, however, in its essence, either be tarnished or extinguished. It lives, it struggles to be free, it eventually casts off the tyranny and superstition of ages. Thus one thing, and one alone, produced the Reformation of the sixteenth century, though many things concurred to aid its development. It was a natural, it was also a supernatural movement; for the Spirit of God, transforming the hearts of good men, and controlling the actions of bad ones, is visible through the whole. As usual, however, in mighty revolutions, which change the current of human affairs, and affect the welfare of states and empires, all things were prepared beforehand. In this respect, as of old, it was "the fulness of time." Thence it was not an insulated event, but rather the result of many previous events, and many invisible forces, working long and silently under the surface of things. It has been said that the germ of the reformation lay in the heart of Wickliff and Waldo. So also it lay in the heart of Augustine, of St. Paul, of Jesus Christ. Luther was its principal agent in Germany; but it was not, as some have designated it, Luther's Reformation. Nor was Lutheranism its proper result. That was a mere incident in its history. Its result is even now revealed only in part. By and by the ages will discover it. A free Bible — a free church — a free Christianity — love, purity, joy, activity, hope in God and for God, in the world and for the world — that is its result. Its latent or ultimate cause is the presence of Christ among men. The more obvious and immediate causes, or what we call such, were various movements and changes in the hearts of individuals, and in the state of society which preceded the sixteenth century. It is interesting, however, to see the streams of history converge, to see the waters, from various quarters, commingle and flow in one resistless tide.

The civilized world began to awake from the slumber of ages. The authority of the schoolmen was doubted or rejected. The superstitions of the twelfth century were losing their hold of reflective minds. Learning and science revived together. A spirit of inquiry, blind, impulsive, irregular, but hopeful, diffused itself over Europe. Kings and emperors were becoming impatient of the Papal sway. They were casting off, or curtailing, one by one, its despotic interference with their governments. They did not abandon the church, but they were quite willing to abandon the pope, whenever, at least, it suited their ambitious views. The popes themselves seemed struck with fatal blindness and imbecility. Even Pope Leo X., "the Magnificent," as he has been termed, failed utterly to check the Reformation, or give security to the Papacy. He was at the height of human prosperity. His troops had entered Milan, and victory had perched upon his standard. He was filled with exultation; but in that moment he died. "Pray for me," said he to his attendants; "I still make you all happy." He loved life, he loved the world, but his hour was come. He had not time to secure the viaticum or extreme unction. "So suddenly, so early, so full of high hope, he died as the poppy fadeth."

The historian adds, "The Roman people could not forgive him for dying without the sacrament, for spending so much money, and for leaving debts. They accompanied his body to the grave, with words of reproach and indignity. "You glided in like a fox," said they, "you've ruled like a lion, you have died like a dog."*

* Ranke's History of the Popes, p. 70.

Leo, indeed, had some generous qualities; his, too, was a great epoch in the advancement of the race, to which, perhaps, he contributed something, though vastly less than is generally supposed. For, as Carlyle justly suggests, he was but a splendid pagan. Passionately fond of music, sculpture, and painting, he encouraged these beautiful and humanizing arts. Ariosto, neglected by him in old age, was one of the companions of his youth. Machiavelli wrote several of his productions at his suggestion. Bembo revolved around him as one of the brightest literary stars of his court; Raphael filled his chambers, halls, and galleries with immortal beauty; and Michael Angelo, to whom he was frequently unjust, erected for him the dome of St. Peter's. His admirers speak of him as learned and bountiful, and some of them (devotees of the Papal court) go so far as to call him amiable and religious! But Leo was a lover of pleasure more than a lover of God. He indulged in feasting and sports, in luxury and sensual delights. "He spent the autumn in rural pleasures; he took the diversion of hawking at Viterbo, of stag hunting at Corneto, and of fishing on the Lake of Bolsena, after which he passed some time at his favorite seat at Malliano, where he was accompanied by men of those light and supple talents which enliven every passing hour.

In the winter he returned to the city, which was in the highest state of [material] prosperity.* Never was the court more lively, more agreeable, more intellectual; no expenditure was too great to be lavished on religious and secular festivals, or amusements and theatres, on presents and marks of favor. It was heard with pleasure that Giuliano Medici, with his young wife, thought of making Rome his residence. "Praised be God," Cardinal Bibbiena writes to him, "the only thing we want is a court with ladies!" The historian might have added, that several of the cardinals had sons and nephews to provide for; and the character of Leo himself was not free from the taint of impurity.†

* Ranke.

† We append the testimony of Prescott, the historian, and Mariotti, a distinguished Italian writer, with reference to the character of Leo. After showing the impropriety of calling him the Mæcenas of literature, and proving that he had less to do with the advancement of the arts than is generally supposed, Prescott adds, "Ariosto, his ancient friend, he coldly neglected, while he pensioned the infamous Aretin. He surrounded his table with buffoon literati, and parasitical poets, who amused him with feats of improvisation, gluttony, and intemperance, some of whom, after expending on them his convivial wit, he turned over to public derision, and most of whom, debauched in morals and constitution, were abandoned, under his austere successor, to infamy and death. He magnificently recompensed his musical retainers, making one an archbishop, another an archdeacon; but what did he do for his countryman, Machiavelli, the philosopher of his age? He hunted, and hawked, and caroused; every thing was a jest, and while the nations of Europe stood aghast at the growing heresy of Luther, the merry pon-

The schools of philosophy, fostered by the predominant taste, were infidel in their tendency. The most distinguished philosopher of that day, Pietro Pomponazzo, denied the immortality of the soul. Erasmus expresses his astonishment at the blasphemies he heard in Rome. An attempt was made to prove to him, a foreigner, from the works of Pliny, that there was no real difference between the souls of men and of beasts. The lower orders were degraded and superstitious, the higher sceptical and Epicurean. A few longed for better things; but even Bembo, the elegant, the half religious poet and cardinal, never forsook the beautiful Morosina; and yet so nice was he in his notions, that he was wont to speak of the Holy Spirit as "the sacred or divine zephyr"! How amazed was the youthful Luther, when he visited the Eternal City, (in the time of Pope Julius,) to witness the impieties of the people and clergy! He informs us that, at the very moment

tiff and his ministers found strange matter of mirth in witnessing the representation of comedies that exposed the impudent mummeries of priestcraft." — *Miscellanies*, p. 522.

"The memory of Leo," says Mariotti, "as an Italian prince, is disgraced by a system of irresolute, improvident, unprincipled policy; as a Roman pontiff, by a lavish, venal, simoniacal abuse of his sacred ministry; as a private man, by a free indulgence in a wanton and sometimes even vulgar epicurism. . . . The epoch of the greatest triumph of letters . . . the age of Leo and Clement was also that of the utmost depravation of morals." — *Italy*, &c., vol. i. p. 352.

the offering of the mass was finished, they uttered words of levity and blasphemy which denied its efficacy. Machiavelli, in his Dissertation on the First Decade of Livy, says, "that the greatest symptom of the approaching destruction of Christianity (the Papal religion) is, that the nearer we approach the capital of Christendom, the less we find of the Christian spirit in the people." . . . "The Italians," he adds, "are principally indebted to the church for having become impious and profligate." It was the tone of good society at Rome to question the evidences of Christianity. "No one passed," says P. Ant. Bandino, "for an accomplished man, who did not entertain heretical opinions about Christianity; at the court the ordinances of the Catholic church, and passages of holy writ, were spoken of only in a jesting manner; the mysteries of the faith were despised."

The atrocities of Pope Alexander VI. and of his son Cæsar Borgia are well known, and need not be detailed here.

Indeed, Rome was beginning to be recognized by multitudes throughout Christendom as the Babylon of the Apocalypse. It was worse than in the days of Petrarch, who describes it as "impious Babylon," "avaricious Babylon," "the school of error," "the temple of heresy," "the foul nest of treason," "the forge of fraud," "the hell of the living."* Whatever it might have been in the early centuries, and whatever benefits it might have conferred on society, it was now "the visible Antichrist," sitting in the temple of God, and calling itself divine, yet "drunk with the blood of saints," and tyrannizing over the bodies and the souls of men. This, therefore, prepared the way for the great change that ensued. Thousands, in England, Scotland, Germany, and France, were longing for the rise of a better faith and a purer morality.

Yet with all its vice, the pretensions of Rome to supreme authority and infallibility were never more lofty and clamorous. Poor Germany, honest at heart, but superstitious, was priest-ridden, and fleeced to supply not only the extravagance of her own clergy, but the rapacity of Rome. Peter-pence and indulgence brought immense sums into the Papal treasury; and if any sincere soul, hungering for the bread of life, or disgusted with the vices of the clergy, dared to utter a voice of protest, he was branded as a heretic, and dragged to imprisonment or execution. The ignorance, superstition, and bigotry of the monks, Dominican and Franciscan, were open to the day, and excited the disgust of all pure and thoughtful men. Reuchlin and Erasmus, after Wickliff and Huss, poured upon them unmeasured scorn.

* *Petrarchi Opera*, tom. iii. p. 149.

Most decisive upon some of these points is the testimony of Duke George of Saxony, a member of the Papal church, and one of Luther's most determined enemies, as given at the Diet of Worms. Opposed to the Reformers, yet favorable to the removal of abuses within the Church itself, he made the following reply to the Papal nuncio, who wished Luther and the Reformation to be involved in the same sentence of condemnation. "The Diet," said he, "must not lose sight of the grievances of which it has to claim redress from the court of Rome. How numerous are the abuses that have crept into our dominions. The annats, which the emperor granted of his free will for the good of religion, now exacted as a due; the Roman courtiers daily inventing new regulations to favor the monopoly, the sale, the leasing out of ecclesiastical benefices; a multitude of offences connived at; a scandalous toleration granted to rich offenders, while those who have not wherewithal to pay to purchase impunity are severely punished; the pope's continually bestowing reversions and rent charges on the officers of their palace, to the prejudice of those to whom the benefices rightly belong; the abbeys and convents of Rome, given *in commendam* to cardinals, bishops, and prelates, who apply the revenues to their own use, so that in many convents, where there ought to be twenty or thirty monks, there is not one to be found; stations multiplied to excess; shops for indulgences opened in every street and square of our cities; shops of St. Anthony, of the Holy Ghost, of St. Hubert, of St. Vincent, and I know not how many more; societies contracting to Rome for the privilege of setting up this trade, then purchasing from their bishop the right of exposing their merchandise to sale; and finally, to meet all this outlay of money, squeezing and draining the last coin out of the poor man's purse; indulgences, which ought to be granted only with a view to the salvation of souls, and procured only by prayer, and fasting, and works of charity, sold for a price; the officials of the bishops oppressing men of low degree with penances for blasphemy, or adultery, or drunkenness, or profanation of this and that festival, but never addressing so much as a rebuke to ecclesiastics who are guilty of the same crimes; penances so devised as to betray the penitent into the repetition of his offence, in order that more money may be extracted from him, — these are but a few of the abuses which cry out on Rome for redress. All shame is laid aside, and one object alone incessantly pursued — money! evermore money! So that the very men whose duty is to disseminate the truth, are engaged in nothing but the propagation of falsehood; and yet they are not merely tolerated, but rewarded;

because the more they lie, the larger are their gains. This is the foul source from which so many corrupted streams flow out on every side. Profligacy and avarice go hand in hand. The officials summon women to their houses on various pretences, and endeavor, either by threats or by presents, to seduce them, and if the attempt fails, they ruin their reputation. O, it is the scandal occasioned by the clergy that plunges so many poor souls into everlasting perdition. A thorough reform must be effected. To accomplish that reform, a general council must be assembled. Therefore, most excellent princes and lords, I respectfully beseech you to give this matter your attention." *

The word of God had been sought out of dirty corners, and studied in the original tongue. It was translated also to some extent, and made its way into some homes and hearts. Copies here and there, in Latin or in the vulgar tongue, fell into the hands of thinkers, and opened their eyes to the beauty of primitive Christianity, in contrast with the errors of Rome. In Germany, the writings of St. Augustine, Gerson, Thomas a Kempis, and others were read and studied by pious monks; for happily amid the prevalent corruption there were some sincere souls. When these failed to convert them, they yet discovered

* Preserved in the archives of Weimar.

the mournful condition of Christendom, and prepared the way for a better order of things.

Some attempts, too, had been made, but without success, within the bosom of the church itself, to reform its abuses. This was the professed object of the Council of Constance. Princes and electors, dukes and ambassadors from all nations, with learned church dignitaries, doctors of theology, and representatives from the universities, gave dignity and importance to the occasion. But alas! instead of reforming the church, they gave Huss to the flames. A commission, however, was appointed, of deputies from different nations, to propose a fundamental reform. The Emperor Sigismund, who violated his safe conduct to Huss, supported the proposition with all the weight of his influence. The council concurred unanimously. The cardinals bound themselves by a solemn oath, that he among them who should be elected pope, — for this duty, among others, had to be performed by the council, which, in furtherance of its objects, had deposed three popes, — would not dissolve the assembly, or leave Constance, without accomplishing the desired reformation. The election fell upon Colonna, under the name of Martin V. With intense interest the members of the assembly awaited the result. "The council is at an end!" cried Martin V., with startling Papal consistency, the moment he had placed the tiara on his head. A cry of grief and indignation arose from Sigismund and the clergy; but it was no more heeded than the idle wind which fanned the flames of John Huss. " On the 16th of May, 1418," says the historian, "the pope, arrayed in the pontifical robes, mounted a mule richly caparisoned; the emperor was on his right hand, the Elector of Brandenburg on his left, each holding the reins of his palfrey; four counts supported over the pope's head a magnificent canopy; several princes surrounded him, bearing the trappings; and a mounted train of forty thousand persons, composed of nobles, knights, and clergy of all ranks, joined in solemn procession outside the walls of Constance." Thus did Rome laugh at reform, and fasten the fetters of her tyrannous dominion.

" There are three things," says Vadiscus, a traveller introduced into the tract which Ulrich Von Hütten published, after his return from Rome, "which we commonly bring away with us from Rome: — a bad conscience, a vitiated stomach, and an empty purse. There are three things which Rome does not believe in: the immortality of the soul, the resurrection of the dead, and hell. There are three things which Rome trades in: the grace of Christ, the dignity of the church, and women."

These grievous moral and political wrongs

stirred the hearts even of worldly men, and awakened sometimes, in the breasts of kings and rulers, educated under Papal influence, a longing for redress and reform. "I will destroy the name of Babylon," (*Perdam nomen Babylonis,*) were the words stamped upon a medal issued by the impetuous Louis XII. Maximilian of Austria, grieved at the treachery of Leo X., exclaimed, "This pope, like the rest, is, in my judgment, a scoundrel. Henceforth, I can say, that, in all my life, no pope has kept his faith or word with me. I hope, if God be willing, that this one will be the last of them." Similar sentiments were occasionally expressed by poets and historians, among others by Machiavelli, who charges upon them all the political difficulties of Italy, the wars of the Guelphs and Ghibellines, and the destruction of Italian liberty and nationality.* This acted, of course, to some extent, upon the people, many of whom were weary of the Papal sway.

But not all these causes combined could produce the Reformation. That was effected by the

* In the first book of his History of Florence, after stating how these difficulties had lasted from the days of Theodosius, he adds, "So that all the wars which foreigners afterwards made upon Italy were chiefly owing to the popes; and most of the several inundations of barbarians that poured themselves into it, were, in a great measure, occasioned by their incitement and instigation; which practices, being continued even to this time, have so long kept, and still keep, Italy weak and divided."

reproduction, among those who read and believed the word of God, of the spirit of primitive Christianity. Once more the Son of God took possession of selected agents, great, generous, courageous hearts, "born from above," who, fired with the love of truth, went forth to oppose error, and proclaim "glad tidings of great joy to all people." The first great impulse in continental Europe issued from Wittemberg, and thence spread itself in successive waves to the remotest parts of the Christian world.

The Reformation was not a speculation or a theory, springing from some profound or original intellect; neither was it a preconcerted plan of wise, far-seeing men; above all, it was not a mere social or political change. Those chiefly concerned in it, at first, thought nothing of the stupendous result to which they were irresistibly conducted. Luther himself was as clay in the hand of the potter. Long years intervened, after he opposed indulgences, before he dreamed of opposing the Papacy, or abandoning the Roman church. It was the love of Christ, of truth, and of the souls of men, which impelled him to the sublime issue. Over and over again, Luther declares, that not "of choice, but of necessity," — a necessity which he could not resist if he would, and would not resist if he could, — he was carried forward in his perilous career. "God," he says, on one occasion, "does not conduct, but drives me, and carries me forward. I am not master of my own actions. I would gladly live in peace, but I am cast into the midst of tumult and changes."

Gladly he would have retired from the combat, if Rome would only permit him and other "poor sinners" to live in peace and follow Christ. Nay, he would never have entered into it, unless compelled for his soul's sake, and the truth of God. To oppose the church of his fathers, and, above all, to leave her, was agony and crucifixion, only compensated by the thought that God was with him, and that the gospel would stand forever. "I began this affair," is his own testimony, wrung from the depths of his heart, "with great fear and trembling. What was I at that time; a poor, wretched, contemptible friar, more like a corpse than a man? Who was I, to oppose the pope's majesty, before which not only the kings of the earth, and the whole world, trembled, but also, if I may so speak, heaven and hell were constrained to obey the slightest intimation of his will? No one can know what I suffered those two first years, and in what dejection, I might say despair, I was often plunged. Those proud spirits, who afterwards attacked the pope with such boldness, can form no idea of my sufferings; though, with all their skill, they could have done him no injury, if Christ had not inflicted upon him, through me, his weak and unworthy instrument, a wound from which he will never recover. But whilst they were satisfied to look on, and leave me to face the danger alone, I was not so happy, so calm, or so sure of success; for I did not then know many things, which now, thanks be to God, I do know. There were, it is true, many pious Christians, who were much pleased with my propositions, and thought highly of them. But I was not able to recognize these, or look upon them as inspired by the Holy Ghost; I only looked to the pope, the cardinals, the bishops, the theologians, the jurisconsults, the monks, the priests. It was from thence that I expected the Spirit to breathe. However, after having triumphed, by means of the Scriptures, over all opposing arguments, I at last overcame, by the grace of Christ, with much anguish, labor, and great difficulty, the only argument that still stopped me, namely, that I must hear the church; for from my heart I honored the church of the pope, as the true church, and I did so with more sincerity and veneration than those disgraceful and infamous corrupters of the church, who, to oppose me, now so much extol it. If I had despised the pope, as those persons do in their hearts who praise him so much with their lips,

I should have feared that the earth would open at that instant, and swallow me up alive."

No, it was Christianity itself, rising from the grave of superstition in which it was intombed, taking possession of the hearts of Luther, Myconius, Melancthon, and others, and going forth, as of old, to regenerate the world. This was the real secret, the true power of the Reformation. No other religions have ever reformed or reproduced themselves, with fresh and living energy. Divested of their original power by formalism and corruption, they have ever remained so, or passed away. Separate from Christianity, Judaism has no power of reproduction and revival. Indeed, all other religions, even in their best state, are local or national, and remain stationary or die out altogether. But Christianity renews itself, rises above the corruption with which it is invested, and exhibits the same vital, regenerative power as in the days of Christ and his apostles.

The agents by which this was accomplished, in the Reformation of the sixteenth century, were in themselves human and insignificant. They derived their success, as they frequently and frankly testify, from an unseen power, controlling events, and working mightily in them and others. What had the son of the poor miner of Mansfeld, born at Eisleben, as

Christ was born at Bethlehem, to do with reformations and revolutions? Nay, what had the poor monk of Erfurt, groaning over his sins, and despairing of the grace of God, to do with such things? What even had the humble Wittemberg professor, a submissive doctor of the Papal church, lecturing on Paul's Epistles to the Galatians, to do with them? He wanted only to live, to serve God, to confide in Christ, and teach any pious souls, who might desire it, the way of life, and this in connection with the church of his fathers, of whose infallibility even then, he had no doubt. In vain had learning and genius, in vain had diplomacy and theology attempted to reform the Papacy. It had wealth, talent, numbers, organization, influence, all at its command. It had burned John Huss, and it could easily burn Luther. The Emperor Charles V., was just as likely to yield to the power of Rome, as Sigismund was when he delivered up the Bohemian reformer. But Christ was in the movement, as a spirit of wisdom and power, transcending all calculations, overcoming all obstacles, and bringing thousands of willing hearts to the foot of the cross. It was through Christ, and Christ alone, endowing him with a matchless energy on behalf of the truth and the souls of men, that the poor feeble monk became the reformer of Christendom.

All say, even the Papists say, that Luther had power. "I cannot bear," said one of his opponents, "those deep-set eyes." "He is possessed of the devil," said others, "and nothing stands before him." What was that power? Was it sincerity, simplicity, vigor of intellect, learning, courage, rough eloquence, resolution, perseverance? These, doubtless, are elements of power and means of success, within certain limits. But John Wickliff, John Huss, Jerome of Prague, Peter Waldo, Arnold of Brescia, all had these elements of character; but they failed as reformers. Nay, some of the opponents of Luther, though wrong, utterly wrong, had these qualities, in more or less measure. Luther, however, had a power beyond them all. What was it? We unhesitatingly reply, *The power of God, through Jesus Christ, in large and abundant measure.* God, indeed, uses fit vehicles. He puts great grace into great souls. Thus it was with Luther. Christ was in him as a fit vehicle of his divine might.

Hence Luther had no special theological dogmas or quiddities to plead. If some of these were embodied in the creed of the Reformation, they were never used by Luther, in his grand contest with the Papacy, or in preaching the word for the comfort and guidance of "weary souls." He believed, and he taught, with a depth of conviction, and a force of eloquence, unequalled since the days of Paul, the doctrine of justification by faith; for this was the doctrine of grace, the doctrine of life, the only hope of the sinner, the only hope of the world. No, no; he who had rejected the doctrine of indulgences, and consequently of all commerce and barter in religion, could not introduce it into Christ's free gospel. Not by purchase, not by works, but by grace, free and boundless as the nature of the God from whom it springs, can the sinner be emancipated. He must believe, he must trust, he must love, in order to obey. He is not a slave; he is a child, an erring child indeed, but a child to be forgiven, to be taken to the bosom of God, and thus to be redeemed and disinthralled forever. "Justified freely by his grace, through the redemption that is in Christ Jesus."

Faith in Christ, after terrible struggles, had emancipated his own spirit, and filled him with the life of God, and Luther wanted the whole world to enjoy the mighty blessing. But special dogmas of predestination, election, general and particular atonement, &c., did not trouble him. In themselves, too, he cared little for external forms and usages. He observed them as decorous, but would neither abolish nor indorse them. He might have remained a Catholic for all this. Some one wanted a cassock to preach in, to which more scrupulous persons objected. "Let him have three cassocks, if he wishes them!" cried Luther. Perhaps he was not sufficiently enlightened about some things. Indeed, he left many evils unreformed. He had some false ideas and superstitions of his own. He was not a perfect man. But he loved Christ. He loved the truth. He loved the souls of men. In a word, Christ was in him, as a great, strong, loving, self-sacrificing, Christian heart. Hence he was willing to die for Christ, to suffer for the truth, to yield his life for the church. "I do not refuse to die," said he over and over again, "if it be God's will." "Take my life," said he to the pope, "but I must stand by the truth." "What is about to happen," said he in a time of danger, "I know not, nor do I care to know, assured as I am that He who sits on the throne of heaven, has from all eternity foreseen the beginning, the progress, and the end of this affair. Let the blow fall where it may, I am without fear. Not so much as a leaf falls without the will of our Father. How much rather will he care for us! It is a light thing to die for the Word, since the Word, which was made flesh, hath himself died. If we die with him, we shall live with him; and passing through that which he hath passed through before us, we shall be where he is, and dwell with him forever."

The Reformation had transpired in Luther himself, before it transpired in Germany. A superstitious Catholic, bending beneath the burden of a false and degrading faith, fearing "Christ himself as a tyrant," ignorant of God's method of justification, macerating his body by penances, and his soul by sorrows, he was led, insensibly, to the word of God, and thence to the cross of Christ. Gradually he discovered the "riches of grace," and found peace in believing. Still he clung to the Papacy, to masses and pilgrimages, purgatories and penances. From all these, however, he was gradually emancipated by the word, the providence, and the Spirit of God. Then he exulted in the God of his salvation, and not all the powers of pope or devil could move him from his integrity. He became a Protestant; say rather a Christian, simple, sincere, devout, noble-hearted, and self-sacrificing. Then "to live was Christ, and to die gain." "Though as a monk," says he, "I was holy and irreproachable, my conscience was still filled with trouble and torment. I could not endure the expression — the righteous justice of God. I did not love that just and holy Being who punishes sinners. I felt a secret anger against him; I hated him, because, not satisfied with terrifying by his law, and by the miseries of life, poor creatures already ruined by original sin, he aggravated our sufferings by the gospel. But when by the Spirit of God I understood these words — when I learned how the justification of the sinner proceeds from God's mere mercy by the way of faith — then I felt myself born again, as a new man, and I entered by an open door into the very paradise of God. From that hour I saw the precious and Holy Scriptures with new eyes. I went through the whole Bible. I collected a multitude of passages which taught me what the work of God was. And as I had before heartily hated that expression, 'the righteousness of God,' I began, from that time, to value and love it, as the sweetest and most consolatory truth. Truly this text of St. Paul was to me as the very 'gate of heaven.'"

Hence he taught this great truth, in all his preaching and writings; and because he was forbidden to teach it, on pain of Papal condemnation, he opposed the Papacy by teaching and preaching it the more. This was his great weapon against all the errors and corruptions of Rome. "I see," said he, at a critical moment, "that the devil, by means of his teachers and doctors, is incessantly attacking this fundamental article, and that he cannot rest or cease from this object. Well then, I, Doctor Martin Luther, an unworthy evangelist of our Lord Jesus Christ, do confess this article, that faith alone, without works, justifies in the sight of God; and I declare, that in spite of the Emperor of the Turks, the Emperor of the Tartars, the Emperor of the Persians, the Pope, all the cardinals, bishops, priests, monks, nuns, kings, princes, nobles, all the world, and all the devils, it shall stand unshaken forever! that if they will persist in opposing this truth, they will draw upon their heads the flames of hell. This is the true and holy gospel, and the declaration of me, Doctor Luther, according to the light given to me by the Holy Spirit. . . . There is no one who has died for our sins but Jesus Christ, the Son of God. I repeat it once more: let all the evil spirits of earth and hell foam and rage as they will, this is nevertheless true. And if Christ alone takes away sin, we cannot do so by all our works. But good works follow redemption, as surely as fruit appears upon a living tree. This is our doctrine; this the Holy Spirit teacheth, together with all holy Christian people. We hold it in God's name. Amen!"

And thus he proclaimed it to the world, proclaimed it to his dying day; and the reformation in Luther's heart reproduced itself, by the power of Christ, in Germany, Switzerland, Holland, England, and Scotland. The word of God had free course — it ran and was glorified.

Some, unfriendly to the Reformation, have denied the presence of Christ in the spirit and work of Luther, because of his roughness and violence. Doubtless he was an imperfect, nay, sinful man, and he himself was the first to confess it; but this is not to be charged to Christ or the Reformation. God commits the treasure of his grace to earthen vessels. Our adorable Redeemer condescends to dwell in sinful hearts. Doubtless Luther, though at heart a gentle, loving man, was often violent and impetuous; but such also is the lightning's flash, which cleaves the atmosphere, and goes crashing through the resounding heavens. A Luther, or a John Baptist, or a John Knox, is no puling sentimentalist. At times the word of God is as fire shut up in his bones. He is indignant at oppression and wrong. He longs to strike the hoary lust from its throne. His words, rough, vehement, jagged, tumultuous, are "half battles." They go burning and crashing amid the idols of superstition. He must be honest, he must be true, and sometimes he must be vehement, fearfully vehement. And as he is only a man, sometimes he may be imprudent, and both say and do things which subsequently he regrets. But in the main he is honest, terribly, gloriously honest. Let him then speak out, let him lay stunning blows on the head of despotic error and fiendish lust. Let him trample in the dust the mean arguments and meaner wiles of his opponents. Are they not the enemies of God and man; and has not the

Almighty made him the battle axe to grind them to powder? Men stood aghast when Luther burned the pope's bull; but to us it is a magnificent sight. With what generous and beautiful disdain he tears it to atoms, and commits it to the flames as a weak and worthless thing, which it behoves all honest men to despise! "Too much imprudence displeases men," replies Luther to Spalatin, who had counselled him to sobriety, "but too much *prudence* is displeasing to God. It is impossible to make a stand for the gospel without creating some disturbance and offence. The word of God is a sword, waging war, overthrowing and destroying; it is a casting down, a disturbance, and comes, as the prophet Amos says, as a bear in the way, as a lion in the forest. I want nothing from them. I ask nothing. There is One above who seeks and requires. Whether his requirements be disregarded or obeyed affects not me." "No," he continues, "I dare not withdraw from the contest. I commit every thing to God, and give up my bark to winds and waves. The battle is the Lord's. Why will you fancy that it is by *peace* that Christ will advance his cause? Has not he himself, have not all the martyrs, poured forth their blood in the conflict?"

Yet Luther clearly distinguishes between what is his own and what is the Lord's. The former he was ever willing to yield, the latter never.

He readily acknowledges his faults; he acknowledges this very imprudence and impetuosity. In his letter to Pope Leo X., and in his address before the Diet of Worms, he is willing to retract all this, any thing, in fact, which is his own; only he takes his stand on the word of God, and contends for the truth. Reform the church, preach the gospel, or let the gospel be preached, and he is satisfied. "I have attacked," says he, addressing the pope, "it is true, some anti-Christian doctrines, and I have inflicted some deep wounds on my adversaries on account of their impiety. I cannot regret this, for I have in this Christ for an example. Of what use is salt, if it hath lost its savor, or the sword blade, if it doth not cut? Cursed is he who doth the Lord's work coldly. O most excellent Leo, far from conceiving any evil design against you, I wish you the most precious blessings for all eternity. One thing only have I done. *I have defended the word of truth. I am ready to give way to every one in every thing;* but as it regards that word, I will not, I cannot abandon it."

The facts and principles to which we have referred, as lying at the basis of this great revolution, are strikingly illustrated in Luther's appearance before the Diet of Worms, at which point the Reformation seemed to culminate. It is one of the sublimest passages in history, and deserves the study of all who would understand the spirit of Luther and the Reformation.

Every one familiar with history knows the nature and object of that august assembly or Diet, which, under Charles V., of Germany, was held at Worms, and before which Luther was cited to appear and retract his heresies. He had received a safe conduct from the emperor, but his friends feared that it would not protect him, and that his life would be endangered. Already condemned by the pope, it was only necessary for the secular authorities to execute the sentence. Every where his books were burned by order of the Papal court, and although his friends were numerous and powerful, his enemies were yet more numerous and powerful. He was sick and feeble, but he felt that he must appear at Worms, and testify to the truth. His brethren earnestly dissuaded him; but he must go. A few friends accompanied him on his journey. At Weimar he heard of the condemnation and burning of his books. The herald asked him if he would proceed. "Yes," replied Luther, "though I should be put under interdict in every town, I will go on. I rely on the emperor's safe conduct."

In some of the towns on the way, particularly at Erfurt, he was welcomed with joy. Here he preached, with vigor and comfort, on the great doctrine of salvation through Christ. He never once alluded to the object of his journey; his whole mind and heart were engaged on the glorious theme. At Eisenach he was taken suddenly ill. They bled him, and administered cordials, and on the following morning he resumed his journey.

Crowds of the common people followed him, in all the towns through which he passed. "Ah," said some, "there are plenty of cardinals and bishops at Worms. You will be burned alive, and your body reduced to ashes, as they did with John Huss." Luther replied deliberately, "Though they should kindle a fire whose flame should reach from Worms to Wittemberg, and rise up to heaven, I would go through it in the name of the Lord, and stand before them. I would enter the jaws of Behemoth, break his teeth, and confess the Lord Jesus Christ."

One day, as he was entering an inn, one of the crowd, who pressed around him, made his way to him and said, "Are you the man who has taken in hand to reform the Papacy? How can you expect to succeed?" "Yes," answered Luther, "I am the man. I place my dependence upon Almighty God, whose word and commandment is before me." The officer, deeply affected, gazed on him affectionately, and said, "Dear friend, there is much in what you say; I am a servant of Charles, but your Master is greater than mine. He will keep and protect you."

On Sunday, the 14th of April, Luther arrived in Frankfort. The pope's emissaries were amazed and alarmed. They had no idea that he would obey the summons. They expected to condemn him unheard. It was their intent, therefore, to stop his progress; and they did every thing to effect their purpose. His own friends were undecided. But the reformer never once hesitated. He was going in the strength of God, and, whatever might be the issue, he must honor Christ before kings and emperors. It was intimated to him that the emperor's confessor, Glapio, who had come on purpose to prevent, or, at least, to retard his arrival, wished to see him. "I shall go on," said he, "and if the emperor's confessor has any thing to say to me, he will find me at Worms."

Spalatin, his friend and counsellor, and the elector's chaplain, on whom Luther much depended for protection and aid, in case of difficulty, was himself filled with apprehension. The elector was yet undecided, and might abandon Luther to his enemies. He heard from all quarters that the safe conduct would be violated. Alarmed, he despatched a servant to meet Luther a little way beyond the city, with this message: "Abstain from entering Worms." Luther fixed his eyes sternly on the messenger: "*Go tell your master*," said he, "*that though there should be as many devils at Worms as there are tiles on its roofs, I would enter it.*" Thus rose the high spirit of Luther, as he drew near the scene of danger and trial. He felt himself "strong in the Lord, and in the power of his might." The messenger delivered the astounding message. "I was then intrepid," said Luther, a few days before his death; "I feared nothing. God can give this boldness to man. I know not whether now I should have as much liberty and joy."

Some young noblemen and others rode out of the city to meet Luther, and escorted him within the walls. The place was filled with excitement. Nothing was thought of, nothing talked of, but the arrival of the intrepid monk. At a late hour, he rested in his hotel, the gates were shut, and all was still. Whether he should ever go beyond these guarded walls, God only knew. Luther himself enjoyed perfect peace. He was filled with a holy enthusiasm. It seemed as if Christ was standing by him all the time. He calmly awaited his citation before the Diet on the following day. In the morning, however, his strength suddenly failed him. His mind was agitated by a profound and fearful struggle. He seemed to drink of the cup of Christ. He threw himself with his face upon the earth, and uttered, in broken cries and sobs, expressions which God alone can appreciate, expressions never to be interpreted literally, and which the deep and terrible anguish of the spirit alone can justify. In these, however, we discover the complete sincerity and self-abnegation of the man, and the simple, childlike faith he was wont to exercise in God. They are the cry of a wounded spirit, dreading to be severed from God in the hour of its deepest trial. "O God, Almighty God everlasting! how dreadful is the world! behold how its mouth opens to swallow me up, and how small is my faith in thee! O, the weakness of the flesh, and the power of Satan! If I am to depend upon any strength of this world, all is over. . . . The knell is struck . . . Sentence is gone forth. . . . O God! O God! O thou my God! help me against all the wisdom of this world. Do this, I beseech thee; thou shouldst do this, . . . by thine own mighty power. . . . The work is not mine, but thine. I have no business here. . . . I have nothing to contend for with these great men of the world! I would gladly pass my days in happiness and peace. But the cause is thine, . . . and it is righteous and everlasting! O Lord, help me! O faithful and unchangeable God! I lean not upon man. It were vain! Whatever is of man is tottering, whatever proceeds from him must fail. My God! my God! dost thou not hear? My God! art thou no longer living? Nay, thou canst not die! Thou dost but hide thyself. Thou hast chosen me for this work. I know it! Therefore, O God, accomplish thine own will! Forsake me not, for the sake of thy well-beloved Son Jesus Christ, my defence, my buckler, and my stronghold."

After a moment of silent struggle, he continues: "Lord, where art thou? My God, where art thou? Come, I beseech thee, I am ready. . . . Behold me prepared to lay down my life for the truth, . . . suffering like a lamb. For thy cause is holy. It is thine own! . . . I will not let thee go! no, nor yet for all eternity! And though the world should be thronged with devils, and this body, which is the work of thy hands, should be cast forth, trodden under foot, cut in pieces, . . . consumed to ashes, . . . my soul is thine! Yes, I have thine own word to assure me of it. *My soul belongs to thee, and will abide with thee forever!* Amen! O God, send help! . . . Amen!"

Here is revealed the secret of Luther's power, and here the secret of the Reformation. If Christ was not in it, Christ was never in the garden, or on the cross.

Four o'clock arrived. All things were ready. Luther set out, God had heard his prayer.

Through a dense crowd he reached the town hall; a passage was cleared by the soldiers. The place was crowded; above, below, windows, staircases, all were filled. As he drew near the door which was to admit him into the presence of his judges, George Freundsberg, a valiant knight, seeing Luther pass, touched him on the shoulder, and shaking his head, grown gray amid the din of battle, said kindly, "My poor monk, my poor monk, thou hast a march and a struggle to go through such as neither I nor many other captains have seen the like in our most bloody battles. But if thy cause be just, and thou art sure of it, go forward in God's name, and fear nothing! He will not forsake thee."

And now Luther stood in the presence of Charles V., "whose kingdom extended across two hemispheres, associated with electors, dukes, margraves, archbishops, bishops, and prelates, ambassadors from various countries, including France and England, deputies of free cities, and a great multitude of counts and barons, the pope's nuncio, and other dignitaries.

His very appearance there, so dreaded by the Papal court, was a victory. Some princes were near him, one of whom, affected by his dignified appearance, whispered, "Fear not them who are able to kill the body, but cannot destroy the soul." Another said, "When you are brought before kings, it shall be given you by the Spirit of your Father what you shall say."

Luther was addressed, at the command of the emperor, by the imperial counsellor Eck, who said that he had been called before the imperial Diet to answer these two questions: "First, whether you acknowledge these books (a large pile of which lay on the table) to be yours, or not; secondly, whether you will retract them or not, or whether you will adhere to them still."

Before Luther replied, Schurf, his counsellor, said, "Let the titles of the books be read." Then the official read over the titles, among which were Exposition of certain Psalms, Treatise on Good Works, Explanation of the Lord's Prayer, and others, mostly of a practical character.

Luther acknowledged that the books were his. But "touching the next point," he added, with noble simplicity and prudence, "whether I will maintain these or retract them, seeing it is a question of faith, and of one's salvation, and of the word of God, which is the greatest treasure in heaven and earth, and deserving at all times our highest reverence, it would be rash and perilous for me to speak inconsiderately, and affirm, without reflection, either more or less than is consistent with truth; for in either case I should fall under the sentence of Christ, 'He that denieth me before men, him will I deny before my Father which is in heaven.' Therefore I beg of your imperial majesty time for reflection, that I may be able to reply to the question proposed without prejudice to the word of God or to my own salvation."

Though it was intimated that he did not deserve the clemency, it was granted by the emperor.

The gravity of the question at issue, and this solemn suspense, only heightened the interest of the occasion.

What were Luther's feelings at this time we learn from one of his letters. After informing his friend what had transpired, and that he had asked time for deliberation, he adds, " This is all the time I asked, and all that they would give. But, Christ being gracious to me, I will not retract one iota."

His friends crowded around him with words of cheer; and he received from the warrior-poet and reformer, Ulric von Hutten, the following inspiring letter, addressed to his " holy friend, the invincible theologian and evangelist:" " Fight courageously for Christ, and yield not to wrong, but go forth confidently to meet it. Endure as a good soldier of Jesus, and suffer that the gift which is in you may be called out, and be assured that He on whom you have believed can preserve what you have committed to him till that day.

I also will take strong hold of the work; but there is this difference in our undertakings, that mine is human, while you, far more perfect, cleave wholly to divine things." Von Hutten had at other times proffered Luther the aid of "carnal weapons," but Luther uniformly declined all such help. His reliance was on the arm of God.

On the succeeding day, in the afternoon, Luther was again summoned to the Diet, when, after waiting some time, the lamps being lighted, and the immense crowd eager and expectant, the official called upon him to answer to the question previously laid before him. Luther replied with modesty and calmness, but with the utmost clearness and decision. He classified his books, saying that in some he had treated of works of faith and piety with such Christian plainness and simplicity, that even his enemies did not deny their harmlessness, utility, and worth. To retract these would be to condemn the truth confessed by all. The second class of his works were directed against the Papacy and the Papists, as corrupting and injuring all Christendom with their teaching and example. He urged that by the laws and teachings of the Papacy, souls are enslaved and injured, and that goods and possessions, especially in Germany, are devoured by their incredible tyranny. They themselves have ordained by their own decrees, that the laws and doctrines of the pope, which are contrary to the gospel and the teachings of the fathers, be regarded as erroneous. Were *he* to revoke this class of books, he would but increase the strength of tyranny, and leave open not merely a window, but a door and a gate, to wickedness, wider than ever. The third class of his books were personal, and written against those who had opposed reform, and vindicated the tyranny of Rome. Against these, he had, he acknowledged, been more violent than was becoming. But even these books he could not retract, because by this means he would give his influence to Roman tyranny, which would crush the people's rights more mercilessly than ever.

But as he was a man, and not God, he would not do for his books otherwise than Christ had done for his doctrines, who, when questioned respecting them by Annas, and smitten on the cheek by the servant, said, "If I have spoken wrong, then show it to be wrong." On which ground he respectfully urged them to cause plain proof to be brought against them from the words of Christ and his holy apostles, and he would be the first to cast them into the fire.

When his address was ended, though exhausted by the effort and the extreme heat, he was requested to repeat it in Latin, for the benefit of those who did not understand German. After a slight hesitation, he complied with the request, in a calm, clear, deliberate voice.

He was accused by the imperial orator of evading the question, and urged to give a plain, categorical answer, whether he would retract or not. He replied, "Since your imperial majesty and lordships desire a direct answer, I will give one which has neither horns nor teeth; and it is this: Unless I shall be convinced by the testimony of Scripture, or by clear and plain argument, (for I do not believe either in the pope or in the councils alone, because it is plain and evident they have often erred and contradicted each other,) I am held by those passages which I have cited, and am bound by my conscience and the word of God, and therefore I may not, I cannot retract, inasmuch as it is neither safe nor right to violate my conscience. *Here I stand, I cannot do otherwise, so help me God. Amen!*"

Thus nobly and courageously Luther clung to the word of God. If that failed, he failed — if that stood, he stood. "Hier stehe ich — Ich kan nicht anders! Gott helfe mir. Amen!"

After much discussion, Luther was finally condemned by the emperor; but as he had a safe conduct, which even Charles V. did not dare to violate, he was permitted to go unmolested. Hundreds were ready to defend him; but he needed no defence, but the consciousness of right and the protection of the Almighty. Much effort had been made, before the final sentence, to induce him to retract. But he stood firm as a rock; "he had given his answer, he could not retract." He was willing even to forego his safe conduct, and "resign his person and life to the emperor's disposal; but as to the word of God — never!"

In leaving Worms, Luther's heart was filled with unutterable peace and joy. "Satan himself," said he, "kept the pope's citadel; but Christ has made a wide breach in it, and the devil has been compelled to confess that Christ is mightier than he."

The Diet of Worms decided the fate of the Reformation. Thenceforward the Elector of Saxony, and many others, gave themselves to it, heart and soul. The echo of that occasion resounded far and near, in Germany, France, and Switzerland, and even as far as England and Scotland. The word of God was more precious than ever. Thousands, in the spirit of Luther, exclaimed, "Here we stand — we cannot do otherwise. God help us. Amen!"

On his arrival at Frankfort, Luther, rejoicing in God, wrote the following familiar, energetic letter to his dear friend Lucas Cranach, the painter, of Wittemberg — "My service to you, dear Master Lucas. I expected his majesty would assemble fifty learned doctors to convict the monk outright. But not at all. Are these books of your writing? Yes. Will you retract them? No! Well, begone! There 's the whole history. Deluded Germans, how childishly we act!—how we are duped and defrauded by Rome! Let the Jews sing their yo! yo! yo! But a passover is coming for us also, and then we will sing Hallelujah! We must keep silence, and endure for a short time. 'A little while and ye shall not see me, and again a little while and ye shall see me,' said Jesus Christ. I trust I may say the same. Farewell. I commend you all to the Eternal. May he preserve in Christ your understanding and your faith from the attacks of the wolves and the dragons of Rome. Amen."

Luther was shut up in the Castle of Wartburg, in the depths of the old Thuringian forest, and many thought him dead; but the word of God was not bound. Christ crucified, the hope of the soul, was every where proclaimed and believed. The movement spread on all the wings of the wind. Great numbers deserted the Papacy, and turned to the Lord. Luther reappeared, as faithful as ever, and maintained the long struggle. He suffered much, and was willing to die. Indeed, he was weary of the world, so full of contention, oppression, and sin. But his trust was in God his Redeemer. He departed in peace at Eisleben, the place of his birth. Three times quickly he repeated the words, "Father, into thy hands I commend my spirit; thou hast redeemed me, thou faithful God." Then he was quiet. The attendants shook him, rubbed him, and spoke to him; but he closed his eyes, and made no reply. Jonas and Cœlius then spoke to him very loud, and said, "Venerable father, do you die trusting in Christ, and in the doctrine which you have preached?" and he answered distinctly, "Yes," and turning upon his right side, slept a short period, when, with folded hands, with one gentle breath and sigh, he passed away.*

There were many obstacles to the progress of the Reformation; some confusion, some disorders were the result; but God raised up many great and good men, in various places, to preach the gospel of Christ, and the work of renovation advanced. Christ was in it as a power of hope

* We have dwelt upon the Reformation chiefly as it developed itself in the centre of continental Europe. We might trace, were it necessary, the action of the same principles in England and Scotland. In these countries the Reformation had an independent origin, though vastly aided by the movement in Germany. For information upon the history of the Reformation in England and Scotland, see Burnet's History of the Reformation, Blunt's History of the English Reformation, D'Aubigné's fifth volume of his History of the Reformation, Neale's History of the Puritans, McCries's Life of John Knox, Hetherington's History of the Church of Scotland. For an admirable exposition of the spirt and aim of Knox, see the Westminster Review for July, 1853.

and transformation to many souls and many lands. It was as if the frosts of a long winter had dissolved, and quickening spring was breathing through the forests of Germany, and the mountains of Switzerland, and far off amid the plains of England, and the hills of Scotland. The waters of life, long pent up among frozen rocks, let loose by the breath of God, were rolling and flashing under the deepening radiance. The wilderness and the solitary place were glad, the desert rejoiced and blossomed as the rose.

In all violent transitions, however, much evil is developed along with the good. Human passions and interests ever mingle with divine institutions. Individuals, as well as churches and communities, are only partially "sanctified." Some are grievously defective, others are selfish and tumultuous. Besides, action and reaction ever correspond to each other; if the pendulum is held far in one direction, it will swing the farther in the other. Some tumult and irregularity mingle in the grandest revolutions.

All this we see in the Reformation of the sixteenth century; yet it was the revival of primitive Christianity. It was a power of life and blessing to the nations, and to myriads of individual souls, who "justified by faith," had, in life and in death, "peace with God through Jesus Christ our Lord." The word of God was emancipated. Noble reformed churches were established. Thence sprang freedom and justice, activity and advancement. Thence came Bacon, Newton, and Howard, John Milton and Thomas Chalmers, with that high, progressive civilization, yet destined to cover the earth.*

* It might be interesting here to show how the Reformation reacted powerfully on the Papal church, and, consequently, on all Roman Catholic countries. Its spirit is diffused beyond Protestant bounds. It is at work among all civilized nations. It is the leaven which must leaven the whole mass. But the facts are obvious; and we leave the matter to the reflection of intelligent men.

CHAPTER XVIII.

CHRIST IN MODERN SOCIETY.

In all ages, among the modern as well as among the ancient nations, we find the influence of two great elements, or factors — the finite and the infinite, the human and the divine. In the finite and human is the tendency to imperfection, consequently to division, disorder, and death. In the infinite is the tendency to perfection, consequently to unity, order, and life. And as the finite and the infinite, in their action, are blended in the constitution and course of things, we find the manifestations of the latter, in the moral sphere, greatly modified by circumstances. Hence the striking variations and contrasts in history, the singular ebb and flow of society, its convulsions and revulsions, its retrogression and progression. In some ages, and among some nations, we meet an apparent predominance of evil, yet ever with a struggle and tendency to good. God does not leave himself without a witness, either in nature or in society. Every where he works after the counsel of his own will. The process is invisible and mysterious, and often to our view, sadly checked and disarranged. Still it advances, and, in due time, discovers its resistless force. Individuals arise who recognize "the divine," and endeavor to advance society in the direction of God and perfection. Organs of the infinite, certain institutions, and certain races, are found better adapted than others for the reception and communication of the truth. Opposition and difficulty exist among all, because imperfection and sin exist in all. But the divine element struggles onward and upward. Its tendency is ever to unity and perfection. In its higher development, as in Christianity, which is only the infinite organized and embodied in human forms, we see this great fact strikingly revealed. Order and perfection are its law, but opposing influences come into collision with it; and hence it is sometimes the cause, or rather occasion, of disturbance and disorder. But its movement is always in the right direction. Like the pillar of cloud by day, and of fire by night, before the Jewish army, it leads society in the wilderness. Obstacles vanish, or fall into its train, while the race is moved onward to its goal.

Ages, however, are needed for the mighty evolution. The infinite is slow, but sure. It moves through time, as if time were eternity. Indeed, time is as nothing to the infinite. "One day is with the Lord as a thousand years, and a thousand years as one day." But that which endures conquers at last. Therefore the kingdom will come, and the whole earth be subdued to God. "The movements of Providence," says Guizot, looking at the successive developments of human civilization, "are not restricted to narrow bounds; it is not anxious to deduce to-day the consequence of the premises it laid down yesterday. It may defer this for ages, till the fulness of the time shall come. Its logic will not be less conclusive for reasoning slowly. Providence moves through time, as the gods of Homer through space; it makes a step, and ages have rolled away! How long a time, how many circumstances, intervened before the regeneration of the moral powers of man, by Christianity, exercised its great, its legitimate influence upon his social condition! Yet who can doubt or mistake its power?"* Thus the Reformation of the sixteenth century has come and gone; and now all things are preparing for a second and grander reformation. Obstacles oppose it; yet who doubts that it will come? Who doubts that the whole world shall yet see the glory of God?

We are not to be surprised, then, if in Christianity, and in the Christian form of civilization,

* History of Civilization, vol. i. p. 28.

we find the constant, and even violent struggle of opposing powers. But Christianity, like the infinite factor, is never defeated, above all, never extinguished. Cast down, and, to all appearance, fit only for the grave, it rises again, renews its energies, augments its resources, and goes forth among men conquering and to conquer. It thus vindicates its title to the character of a supernatural power. It works together with God; its tendency is to universal dominion.

Hence Christianity will generally be found associated with the strongest races; rather, perhaps, it will assist in forming the strongest races. How rapidly it allied itself with the Romans, the strongest race on the globe! but finding Rome, with all its resources, debauched by vice, and consequently imbecile at heart, it left it for the Germanic and Anglo-Saxon tribes. It seized upon those rude, muscular races, and brought them into unity and order. It gave them laws and civilization. At first, it seemed to oppress them, but it finally lifted them up, giving them freedom and power. And now they are the central races, the strongest and most influential of all.

The process, to our view, has been difficult and slow, with many interruptions and convulsive throes; but its movement has now become more clear and decisive. The Reformation was one step in advance, much impeded we grant, and even now only partially developed. The result however is grand and beautiful, and so obvious, that he who runs may read it. That result is nothing less than the possession by Christianity, as a central or supernatural power, of the most valuable portions of the globe, and the leading forces of modern civilization. In some of the nations professedly Christian, Christianity is developed with greater purity and vigor than in others; but in all she occupies a position of influence and command. Individuals, nay, whole masses, may reject her claims, while others misapprehend and misapply her principles; but she keeps her place notwithstanding, and by invisible influences guides and controls even her enemies. Often checked and abused, she only bides her time to bring all into unity and submission. Those who oppose her sometimes blindly fulfil her designs. Yet Christianity is the very reverse both of scepticism and despotism. She will yet convert the one, and extinguish the other. With this view, and as by a natural instinct, she allies herself to science and art, to literature and commerce. She works even through revolutions. They prepare the way of the Lord; they make straight in the desert (of despotism) a highway for our God. All improvements in mechanics, and the means of locomotion through the world, aid her progress. She goes forth over all seas and lands, on tours of exploration, takes possession of favorable positions all along the lines of business and travel, plants her colonies and schools here, there, every where, and thus prepares herself, one of these days, to occupy the whole.

Thus, after the fall of the Roman empire, and the destruction of the ancient civilization, Christianity took possession of Germany, France, and Scandinavia, then of England and Scotland, then of the United States of America, with Canada and Australia. And now, especially through Great Britain and the United States, she commands an approach to all quarters of the globe. Comparatively feeble in Russia and France, she yet holds these two nations in her grasp; here, as in England and Germany, she may yet reform the church and the people. These nations can never become pagan or Mohammedan. If they advance in civilization, Christianity will advance also, or rather Christianity will advance in them as a power of civilization; unless indeed, like Rome of old, through the force of despotism and vice, they should break to pieces, and give to Christianity, released from the thraldom of tyranny, a wider and more glorious field. Among all the Anglo-Saxon races, Christianity is strong, free, and progressive. Should these races advance as they have done,

Christianity will advance with them to universal conquest. Much of this is the direct result of the Reformation of the sixteenth century, as the Reformation itself was the direct result of primitive Christianity. By the singular changes associated with that event, or resulting from it, we find the purest and freest form of religion, at this moment, occupying the most commanding positions in both hemispheres, and wielding the forces of the most vital, the most enterprising extant civilizations. From England, the United States, and portions of continental Europe, she is planting her institutions in all pagan countries, and acting powerfully upon the less advanced nations around her.

She has thus, for the first time in the history of the world, become closely and permanently identified with the progressive races, and with all those powers in society upon which their advancement depends — freedom, activity, commerce, science, and education; and as these, by a necessary law, tend to unity and universality, so Christianity tends to unity and universality.

But to make this clear, let us go back a little, and view the actual state of the world. It has obviously come into new positions and relations, as Christianity has come into new positions and relations.

Three forms of religion, or of civilization,

divide the globe — the pagan, the Mohammedan, and the Christian. The pagan and the Mohammedan civilizations are confined chiefly to the Oriental world. They are found also in Africa, but in a comparatively feeble, abnormal condition. It is in the ancient and hoary East we find the seat of their power. Here all things are either stationary or decaying. Except in the places invaded by the influences of Christian civilization, all India, on this side and on that side the Ganges, is old and decrepit. None of the pagan nations advance. They make no discoveries, plant no colonies, secure no conquests. They do not increase, but rather diminish, in numbers. When spreading among other nations, they seem to lose themselves like streams in the sandy desert. Their resources, physical and social, are gradually becoming exhausted. They fall before the stronger and advancing races. The religions of the heathen nations are antiquated and puerile, stricken with a fatal imbecility, and ready to vanish away. Budhism and Brahmanism, which divide the whole of India beyond the the Ganges, already totter to their fall. Hindostan is in the hands of England, and China is convulsed with revolution, which, in that land, may extinguish idolatry.

The Mohammedan form of civilization, once so wide and powerful, has been gradually restricted and weakened. At one time ready to swallow and extinguish the whole Christian civilization, both of Asia and Europe, it is now in its turn ready to be absorbed or extinguished by the advancing forces of European civilization. It is true that it gives some signs of reviving life, but it is only galvanic life. The influence which has excited, perhaps inspired it a little, is European and Christian. The nations under its sway do not advance. Their religion has lost its ancient fire. It is feeble and effete. Turkey can scarcely be called a power in the world, except by the support or sufferance of others. She has numbers, to be sure, and through the force of Christian ideas, exhibits a commendable liberality in some things; but she has no vital unity, no coherent power. Her religion cannot reform itself — cannot, therefore, reform the people. It must gradually yield to the superior forces around it. These forces constantly press upon it, nay, more, penetrate, as an element of dissolution, into its very heart. She has made advances, politicians affirm. She is even said to promote European tactics, railroads, and electric telegraphs. In other words, she is putting new wine into old bottles. Her venerable sages shake their heads; her sacred muftis declare that her glory is departed. Turkey has no living faith, no intensity of feeling, no capacity of real and permanent advance.

The rest of the world, containing the richest and most powerful nations, are more or less under the influence of Christianity and the Christian form of civilization. Moreover, the most of these are advancing, and that, too, with amazing rapidity. Christianity, simply as a social or civil power, may be said to control the physical resources of the world. She exerts a strange influence, even in pagan and Mohammedan lands. Hers are the ships, the roads, the steam engines, the electric telegraphs, the languages, the science and the literature of the nations. She can use them all, and does use them all, for the accomplishment of her designs.

But Christian countries, as they are called, themselves differ much. Some are far in advance of the others. Two or three are feeble, almost as feeble as Mohammedan countries. If not reformed and elevated, they will grow feebler and feebler, every day, and may finally become extinct, like the empires of antiquity, which perished in their sins. "That nation that serveth not me," saith God, "shall perish." Such are dashed to pieces like a potter's vessel. Their power and their glory pass away forever. Hence all the revolutions and convulsions in the past history of the world. Hence the volcanic condition of some European, as well as Asiatic states. "I will overturn, overturn, overturn," is the declaration of the Almighty, by his prophet, "till he come, whose right it is, and I will give it [the dominion] to him."

But what is peculiarly striking in the present condition of the Christian nations, with all their imperfection, is, that Christianity is strongest in the strongest of these. Leaving France, Spain, and some other Papal countries out of the account, which are growing weaker and weaker by the force of despotism, or internal revolution, saying nothing also of Russia, with its peculiar position, and semi-barbarous races, Christianity has taken up her abode more especially in Great Britain and North America, and through them reaches with a controlling influence both the eastern and the western hemispheres. To speak, however, with more precision, England and the United States, it is well known, have now nearly the one fourth part of the globe under their control. England sways her sceptre over a hundred and fifty millions of the human race; the United States govern about twenty-five millions, so that these two command for Christianity, and Christian uses, one sixth of the population of the human race. Both, too, are increasing in numbers and resources beyond all former precedent. England is increasing rapidly, especially in her colonies, which are penetrating both Asia and Africa, while the United States indulge in no extravagant expectation, when they hope, at the close of the nineteenth century, to have a population, within their borders, of a hundred millions.

These two are the great commercial nations. Every where they diffuse themselves, and plant extensive colonies. Two thirds of all the roads and railways, and nearly the whole of the oceanic steam navigation of the world, at this moment, are in their hands. Their language, their influence, their usages, their ideas, are becoming all but cosmopolitan. With the single exception of France, and even in her case to a very limited extent, Papal nations are planting no colonies, and exerting little influence beyond their own sphere, while all the Protestant nations, especially England and the United States, are taking possession, we trust for Christ, of some of the most interesting and influential portions of the globe.

The manner in which, by a long course of preparation, Christianity has taken possession of the German or Teutonic race, including the Anglo-Saxon, which we maintain to be the *leading* or central race, in modern times, is one of the most singular and striking events in history. The only other race that can compete with this is the Slavonic, including the Bohemians, Hungarians, Russians, and some others; but this race is partly Protestant, and in the case of the Greek church, not without hope of improvement and reformation. Still, every one must allow, that the Slavonic race, as a mass, is far inferior to the Anglo-Saxon in freedom and education, in science, art, and commerce. What is called the Keltic or Celtic race is, in the judgment of some of the most acute and learned historians, Niebuhr, Thierry, Arnold, and others, entirely lost.* The Latin races, as for convenience they are designated, sometimes spoken of as Celtic, are a mixed people, partly Teutonic, yet differing somewhat from what we call the German or Saxon stock, and deriving something of their character and tendencies from the admixture of the old Roman or Italian elements. In these we include the Italians, Spaniards, and to some

* "In the fourth century before the Christian era, the Kelts or Gauls broke through the thin screen which had hitherto concealed them from sight, and began for the first time to take their part in the great drama of the nations. For nearly two hundred years they continued to fill Europe and Asia with the terror of their name; but it was a passing tempest, and if useful at all, it was useful only to destroy. The Gauls could communicate no essential points of human character in which others might be deficient; they could neither improve the intellectual state of mankind, nor its social and political relations. When, therefore, they had done their appointed work of havoc, they were doomed to be themselves extirpated, or to be lost amidst nations of greater creative and constructive power; nor is there any race which has left fewer traces of itself in the character and institutions of modern civilization." — Arnold's *History of Rome*, vol. i. p. 499.

extent, the French, all belonging to the Latin or Papal church. The south of Germany is partially occupied by people of similar affinities, and may be spoken of in the same category. By the German or Saxon race, we mean the Germans proper, who came from beyond the Rhine, who were never subdued by the Roman empire, and who in all ages, whether pagan or Christian, have exhibited singular energy and independence of character.* To this class belong the Saxons, Anglo-Saxons, and even Normans, the inhabitants of Denmark, Norway, Sweden, the north of Germany, the English, and the Scotch. All have a common origin, and common characteristics. Even in a mixed state, they betray their peculiar affinities and tendencies. Gazing beyond the Rhine, the ancient frontier of the Roman empire, and the limit therefore of two distinct worlds, and modes of existence, Roman and Teutonic, Dr. Arnold says, "Far beyond us lay the land of our Saxon and Teutonic forefathers — the land uncorrupted by Roman or any other mixture; the birthplace of the most moral races of men that the world has yet seen — of the soundest laws, the least violent passions, and the fairest domestic and

* *Ger-man* means *fighting man*. His is that old, tough, independent, indomitable race, admired by Tacitus, which subdued the Roman world.

civil virtues. I thought of that memorable defeat of Varus and his three legions, which forever confined the Romans to the western side of the Rhine, and preserved the Teutonic nation, the *regenerating element* in modern Europe, safe and free." *

"Our English race," says the same acute and philosophical thinker, in his Lectures on Modern History, developing the great fact to which we have referred, "is the German race. And that this element is an important one, cannot be doubted for an instant. Our English race is the German race; for though our Norman fathers had learned to speak a stranger's language, yet in blood, as we know, they were the Saxons' brethren; both alike belong to the Teutonic or German stock. Now, the importance of this stock is plain from this, that its intermixture with the Keltic and Roman races at the fall of the Western empire, has changed the whole face of Europe. It is doubly remarkable, because the other elements of modern history are derived from the ancient world. If we consider the Roman empire in the fourth century of the Christian era, we shall find in it Christianity, we shall find in it all the intellectual treasures of Greece, all the social and political wisdom of Rome. What was

* Life and Correspondence, App. No. iii. 1. Quoted in his Lectures, p. 59.

not there, was simply the German race, and the peculiar qualities which characterize it. This one addition was of such power that it changed the character of the whole mass; the peculiar stamp of the middle ages is undoubtedly German; the change manifested in the last three centuries has been owing to the revival of the older elements with greater power, so that the German element has been less manifestly predominant. But the element still preserves its force, for good or for evil, in almost every country of the civilized world."

This German or Saxon element is becoming more and more prominent and decisive in its influence upon society. It has embodied itself in books, laws, and institutions. It is increasingly active, aggressive, and diffusive. It animates especially the free enterprising portions of Christendom. In a word, it has been enthroned by Christianity, as a central and pervading power. Emancipated by the Reformation, it has founded institutions and empires. It has given to mankind freedom and hope. From its favorite centres between the great oceans and continents of the east and west, it is spreading civilization, commerce, and Christianity, over the world.

We shall here, however, be asked, whether the race in Germany, especially in the north of Germany, has not forsaken Christianity for infidelity.

We reply most decisively, No! A confused, transitional state has occurred there, and some vague, speculative infidelity has been evolved; but it is temporary. The heart of Germany is sound, and will yet be given to Christ, with the full fervor of its strength. The learned men of Germany, the theologians and the philosophers, are coming rapidly to the acknowledgment of the supernatural character and claims of Christianity, as the religion of God. Strauss is already effete. The essence of faith is all but universally acknowledged, and the rest, we doubt not, will come in due time. "I say with Meier," says Bunsen, "and with almost all German writers of note, that the doctrine of the Father, Son, and Holy Ghost is the fundamental doctrine of Christianity, and that without it, Christianity, as a theological and philosophical system, cannot rank much above Rabbinism and Mohammedanism." * Spiritual religion, too, is advancing among students and thinkers. The common people are joyfully receiving the gospel from the lips of Oncken and others. A new reformation, like that of Luther, seems on the eve of being inaugurated among the whole German people.

But it is in England and North America we see the Anglo-Saxon race in its glory and strength, rejoicing in the truth, and giving the gospel to

* Hippolytus, vol. i. p. 303.

mankind. Unconquerable, (for the old Teutonic or German stock, neither in its native haunts beyond the Rhine, nor in any other part of the globe, into which it has emigrated, has *ever been subdued by a foreign power*,) persevering, self-reliant; self-sacrificing, if need be; loving freedom, and contending for it as the heritage of all; enlightened and enterprising, covering all lands and all seas with its science and commerce; venerating the Bible, which it has translated into more than a hundred and twenty languages, or nearly all that are spoken on the earth; clinging to Christianity, as the support of the soul, and the hope of the world; and disposed, by means of her missionary army, to preach it to every creature under heaven, — we may well recognize the Saxon race as the central and chosen people, through whom Christ shall win the empire of mankind.

We will not, however, confine ourselves to any narrow or local view of this great subject. God has his chosen ones in all places, centres of influence and means of blessing, in all lands, and among all races. Christ is every where. His footsteps are seen in Burmah and China, as well as in Germany and England. He is walking among the churches of the Armenians and the Nestorians, of the Sandwich and Polynesian Isles. Far away in the depths of Africa, and on the bleak shores of Greenland, on the plains of Australia, and amid the golden fields of the Pacific slope, his benign presence is felt and seen.

It has been intimated that, in the present day, and especially in Christendom, the tendency of all things is to unity and universality, and that it is by their tendency we can predict their issue. We are encouraged to do this, especially when we find the various forces actually moving and converging to a common result. Now, every one will allow that such is the direction of Christianity. It is a universal religion, being adapted to man as man, and therefore its resistless aim is to spread over the world, and bring the whole into spiritual unity. In the same line, and apparently under the same influence, like scattered streams flowing into one vale, and so forming one river, we see the other forces of society converging to a common issue. Thus commerce is overleaping all its ancient barriers, spreading over all seas and lands, and bringing the nations into commercial brotherhood. They are finding out, in spite of themselves, that the interest of one is the interest of all. Thus, while commerce diffuses and distributes its energies, it also unites them in a common system. While it spreads to the circumference, it attracts to the centre. It links land to land, and sea to sea; it gathers community to community, and tribe to tribe; it calls to the remotest races, and invites them to unity of interest and aim. It diminishes the fierceness and frequency of war, gives facilities for the spread of common blessings, Christianity among the rest, and thus makes it the interest of one and all to live in harmony and peace.

The same tendency may be seen in science. All the particular branches of science have a common tie, and are found to belong to one great system. They have a tendency, therefore, among all who cultivate them, though far separated from each other by land or ocean, to produce common ideas. They unite rival nations by the ties of thought and interchange of discoveries. In this way the science of one, in process of time, becomes the science of all. Bigotries and superstitions give way under the gracious influence of extending knowledge, while an open field is cleared for the conquests of the cross.

Such is the tendency also of modern speculative philosophy. It seeks unity and order, and consequent universality. It recognizes, sometimes produces, a common type of thought, and not only this, but a common type of humanity. Moreover its singular vacillations and contradictions find their centre in Christ, as the manifestation of the true God and eternal life. Thus, in the present day, philosophy is eminently eclectic and free. It belongs to no class permanently, and in its higher spiritual relations aims to recognize a common Christianity, producing thereby a common life and destiny. It has not reached this as yet, but such is its tendency.

The tendency even of *politics*, in all the enlightened nations, flows in the same direction. Gervinus, in his Introduction to the History of Modern Europe, has, by a laborious analysis, demonstrated this great fact. Through many changes and struggles, an advance towards equal, and consequently universal rights is visible. How strikingly and beautifully is this developed on the North American continents! The longing and the struggle for these rights is visible enough in other lands. The end is universal liberty, a recognition of the rights of God and the rights of man — what the socialists dream after, but for the want of solid Christian principle, and the sure light of eternal truth, they cannot realize, equality, freedom, fraternity, that is, order, unity, universality, under Christ and Christianity.

Thus, too, language, the great civilizer, with all the elements of social life, is tending to unity and universality. How the Saxon tongue and Saxon literature, for example, are spreading over the whole western hemisphere, and bringing different peoples into unity and repose! See, too, how in the other hemispheres it penetrates vari-

42

ous lands, pagan and Mohammedan. Such, also, is the tendency of the French and the German tongues, and with them, of course, their knowledge and power. All seek unity and universality. The German especially is beginning to assert its rights; it is spreading fast and far. A new reformation in the fatherland will send it, by the mouth of missionaries and preachers, to the ends of the earth.

But it is the Bible and Christianity which are exerting the greatest influence, through various languages, in producing the sublime result of which we speak. Distant and dissimilar communities are thus calling to each other — China to Europe and Europe to China; Burmah to America and America to Burmah, in the common speech of Christianity. The prodigious influence of this peculiar force can scarcely be realized. Much of it is so delicate, and so far removed from the domain of the senses, that it will only be recognized, when it has produced some stupendous result.

We are not, indeed, blind to adverse influences even in the bosom of Christendom. But we are not speaking now so much of Christendom, defective, and far behind its ideal, as of Christianity itself, a force amid the forces of society, all of which are rapidly converging to unity, and consequent universality.

Christianity, in its present form of embodiment in the world, is only partially developed. It is still checked and hindered by many obstacles. But its real resources are boundless, and will yet be discovered on a scale of grandeur which will astonish the world. Like Christ, Christianity is immutable and immortal, and must prevail. Changes may come, dynasties may rise and fall, revolution, as of old, may follow revolution ; but the gospel will survive as a supernatural, self-existent mystery. Opinions, too, may fluctuate, and many conflicting theories be propounded among men, but Christ, as a Life, divine and indestructible, will remain the same. In all ages his empire of love is one. It can no more be destroyed than God himself can be destroyed ; for it is the embodied Divinity. The true church, then, or that which forms the essence of the true church, is but his heart of love beating among men. It already counts its subjects by millions, millions who would die for their Lord and King. It is secretly spreading among the nations. It is "gathering" men of all times and of all lands to the cross. And, as good must finally overcome evil, Christianity, like an atmosphere of light, radiant and peaceful, shall envelop the globe.

APPENDIX.

APPENDIX.

ADDITIONAL NOTES AND ILLUSTRATIONS.

Note A.—PAGAN RELIGION.

The following estimate, though partial and one sided, of the moral value of the religions of the ancient heathen world, coming from one of the profoundest scholars of the age, de serves consideration. "All the moral theories of [pagan] antiquity were utterly disjoined from religion. The supposition that the ancient pagan systems of religion were introductory to some scheme of morals, is an anachronism. It is the anachronism of unconsciously reflecting back upon the ancient religions of darkness, and as if essential to all religions, features that never were suspected as possible, until they had been revealed by Christianity, [including Judaism.] Religion, in the eye of a pagan, had no more relation to morals than it had to ship building or trigonometry. But, then, why was religion honored among pagans? How did it ever arise? What was its object? Object! it had no object, if by this you mean ulterior object. Pagan religion arose in no motive, but in an impulse. Pagan religion aimed at no distant prize ahead; it fled from a danger immediately behind. The gods of the pagans were wicked natures; but they were natures to be feared and to be propitiated; for they were fierce, and they were moody, and (as regarded men, who had no wings) they were powerful. Once accredited as facts, the pagan gods could not be regarded as otherwise than terrific facts; and thus it was, that in terror, blind terror, as against power in the hands of divine wickedness, arose the ancient religions of paganism. Because the gods were wicked, man was religious; because Olympus was cruel, earth trembled; because the divine beings were the most lawless of Thugs, the human being became the most abject of sycophants.

"Had the religions of paganism arisen teleologically; that is, with a view to certain purposes, to certain final causes ahead; had they grown out of *forward* looking views, contemplating, for example, the furthering of civilization, or contemplating some interest, in a world beyond the present, there would probably have arisen, concurrently, a section on all such religions devoted to positive instruction. There would have been a *doctrinal* part. There might have been interwoven with the ritual of worship, a system of economies or a code of civil prudence, or a code of health, or even a secret revelation of mysterious relations between man and the Deity; all which existed in Judaism. But as the case stood, this was impossible. The gods were mere odious facts, like scorpions or rattlesnakes, having no moral aspects whatever; public nuisances; and bearing no relation to man but that of capricious tyrants. First arriving upon a basis of terror, these gods never subsequently enlarged that basis; nor sought to enlarge it. All antiquity contains not a hint of the possibility that *love* could arise, as by any ray mingling with the sentiments in a human creature towards a divine one. Not even sycophants pretended to *love* the gods.

"Under this original peculiarity of paganism, there arose two consequences, which I will mark by the Greek letters α and β. The latter I will notice in its order, first calling the reader's attention to the consequence marked α, which is this: In the full and profoundest sense of the word *believe*, the pagans could not be said to believe in *any* gods; but in the ordinary sense, they did, and do, and must believe in *all* gods. As this proposition will startle some readers, and is yet closely involved in the main truth which I am now pressing, viz., the meaning and effect of a simple *cultus*, as distinguished from a high doctrinal religion, let us seek an illustration from our Indian empire. The Christian missionaries from home, when first opening their views to Hindoos, describe themselves as laboring to prove that Christianity is a true religion, and as either asserting, or leaving it to be inferred, that, on that assumption, the Indian religion is a false one. But the poor Hindoo never dreamed of doubting that the Christian was a true religion; nor will he at all infer, from your religion being true, that his own must be false. Both are true, he thinks: all religions are true; and all gods are true gods; and all are equally true. Neither can he understand what you mean by a false religion, or how a religion could be false; and he is perfectly right. Wherever religions consist only of a worship, as the Hindoo religion does, there can be no competition amongst them as to truth. That would be an absurdity, not less nor other than for a Prussian to denounce the Austrian emperor, or an Austrian to denounce the Prussian king, as a false sovereign. False? How false? In what sense false? Surely not as non-existing. But at least, (the reader will reply,) if the religions contradict each other, one of them must be false. Yes, but that is impossible. Two religions cannot contradict each other, where both contain only a *cultus;* they could come into collision only by means of a doctrinal or directly affirmative part, like those of Christianity and Mohammedanism. But this part is what no idolatrous religion ever had, or will have. The reader must not understand me to mean that, merely as a compromise of courtesy, two professors of different idolatries would agree to recognize each other. Not at all. The truth of one does not imply the falsehood of the other. Both are true as *facts:*

neither can be false, in any higher sense, because neither makes any pretence to truth doctrinal.

"This distinction between a religion having merely a worship, and a religion having also a body of doctrinal truth, is familiar to the Mohammedans; and they convey the distinction by a very appropriate expression. Those majestic religions, (as they esteem them,) which rise above the mere pomps and tympanies of ceremonial worship, they demonstrate '*religions of the book.*' There are of such religions three, viz., Judaism, Christianity, and Islamism. The first builds upon the Law and the Prophets, or perhaps sufficiently upon the Pentateuch; the second upon the Gospel; the last upon the Koran. No other religion can be said to rest upon a book, or even to admit of a book. For we must not be duped by the case where a lawgiver attempts to connect his own human institutes with the venerable sanctions of a national religion, or the case where a learned antiquary unfolds historically the record of a vast mythology. Heaps of such cases (both law and mythological records) survive in the Sanscrit, and in the pagan languages. But these are books which build upon the religion, not books upon which the religion is built. If a religion consists only of a ceremonial worship, in that case there can be no opening for a book; because the forms and details publish themselves daily, in the celebration of the worship, and are preserved, from age to age, without dependence on a book. But, if a religion has a doctrine, this implies a revelation or message from Heaven, which cannot, in any other way, secure the transmission of the message to future generations, than by causing it to be registered in a book. A book, therefore, will be convertible with a doctrinal religion: no book, no doctrine; and again, no doctrine, no book.

"Upon these principles we may understand the second consequence, (marked β,) which has perplexed many men, viz., why it is, that the Hindoos, in our own times, but equally, why it is that the Greek and Roman idolaters of antiquity, never proselytized; no, nor could have viewed such an attempt as rational. Naturally, if a religion is doctrinal, any truth which it possesses, as a secret deposit consigned to its keeping by a revelation, must be equally valid for one man as for another, without regard to race or nation. For a doctrinal religion therefore to proselytize, is no more than a duty of consistent humanity. You, the professors of that religion, possess the medicinal fountains. You will not diminish your own share by imparting it to others. What churlishness, if you should grudge to others a health which does not interfere with your own! Christians, therefore, Mohammedans, and Jews originally, in proportion as they were sincere and conscientious, have always invited or even forced, the unbelieving to their own faith: nothing but accidents of situations, local or political, have disturbed this effort. But on the other hand, for a mere 'cultus' to attempt conversions, is nonsense. An ancient Roman could have had no motive for bringing you over to the worship of Jupiter Capitolinus; nor you any motive for going. 'Surely, poor man,' he would have said, 'you have some god of your own, who will be quite as good for your countrymen as Jupiter for mine. But if you have *not*, really I am sorry for your case; and a very odd *case* it is; but I don't see how it could be improved by talking nonsense. You cannot beneficially, you cannot rationally, worship a tutelary Roman deity, unless in the character of a Roman; and a Roman you may become, legally and politically. Being *such*, you will participate in all advantages, if any there *are*, of our national religion; and without needing a process of conversion, either in substance or in form. *Ipso facto*, and without any separate choice of your own, or becoming a Roman citizen, you become a party to the Roman worship.' For an idolatrous religion to proselytize, would be not only useless, but unintelligible.' — *De Quincey.*

There is much of truth in all this; although De Quincey has not made sufficient allowance for the universal prevalence in man of the religious element, which, in favorable circumstances, infuses even into false religions a certain amount of moral and political influence. This, and not *fear* alone, is their true origin. Indeed fear is the natural exaggeration of the religious element, in circumstances of profound or general ignorance. The religious instinct must satisfy itself somehow, even if it originate gods "whom guilt makes welcome." It is true, however, that the ancient pagan nations, even the most enlightened and polished, for example the Greeks and the Romans, might be described as "without God and without hope in the world." Notwithstanding the traditional fragments of a better faith, and the lofty imaginings of their philosophers, their public *cultus* was a gross, often an immoral nature worship. It was sustained by no body of living truth, and exerted upon the community at large no transforming moral influence. Indeed, those who were virtuous were often virtuous in spite of their religion. The chaste Lucretia, as Rousseau remarks, adored the unchaste Venus. The popular Jupiter was a licentious bandit, who, in modern times, would have deserved a place in the jail or penitentiary. And yet who can fail to see, through the whole, the strugglings of the great human heart, made for God, for duty and immortality, the dim sense of the infinite, the consciousness of guilt, and the longing for redemption? The ancient religions, especially the elder, are not absolute untruths; they are only perversions and corruptions of that which is highest in man.

NOTE B. — ORIGINAL SIN UNIVERSALLY ACKNOWLEDGED.

SPEAKING of "original sin," which Coleridge designates "self-originating sin," that distinguished thinker remarks, "that it is no tenet first introduced or imposed by Christianity, and which, should a man see fit to disclaim the authority of the gospel, would no longer have any claim on his attention. It is no perplexity that a man may get rid of, by ceasing to be a Christian, and which has no existence for a philosophic Deist. It is a fact, affirmed indeed in the Christian Scriptures alone, with the force and frequency proportioned to its consummate importance; but a fact acknowledged in every religion that retains the least glimmering of the patriarchal faith in a God infinite, and yet personal; a fact assumed or implied as the basis of every religion of which any relics remain of earlier date than the last and total apostasy of the pagan world, when the faith of the great I AM, the Creator, was extinguished in the sensual Polytheism, which is inevitably the final result of Pantheism, or the worship of nature; and the only form under which the Pantheistic scheme — that according to which the world is God, and the material universe itself the only Absolute Being — can exist for a people, or become the popular creed. Thus, in the most ancient books of the Brahmins, the deep sense of this fact, and the doctrine grounded upon obscure traditions of the promised remedy, are seen struggling, and now gleaming, now flashing, through the mist of Pantheism, and producing the incongruities and gross contradictions of the Brahmin mythology; while, in the rival sect — in that most strange *phenomenon*, the religious atheism of the Buddhists, with whom God is only universal matter, considered abstractedly from all particular forms — the fact is placed among the delusions natural to man, which, with other superstitions, grounded on a supposed essential difference between right and wrong, the sage is to decompose or precipitate from the *menstruum* of his more refined apprehensions! Thus, in denying the fact, they virtually acknowledge it.

"From the remote East, turn to the mythology of the Lesser Asia, to the descendants of Javan, who dwelt in the tents of Shem, and possessed the isles. Here again, and in the usual form of an historic solution, we find the same fact, and as characteristic of the human race, stated in that earliest and most venerable *mythus* or symbolic parable of Prometheus — that truly wonderful fable, in which the characters of the rebellious spirit, and of the divine Friend of mankind, (Θεὸς φιλάνθρωπος,) are united in the same person; thus, in the most striking manner, noting the forced amalgamation of the patriarchal tradition with the incongruous scheme of Pantheism. This and the connected tale of Io, which is but the sequel of the Prometheus, stand alone in the Greek mythology, in which elsewhere both gods and men are mere powers and products of nature. And most noticeable it is, that soon after the promulgation and spread of the gospel had awakened the moral sense, and had opened the eyes even of its wiser enemies to the necessity of providing some solution of this great problem of the moral world, the beautiful parable of Cupid and Psyche, was brought forward as a rival of the fall of man; and the fact of a moral corruption connatural with the human race was again recognized. In the assertion of original sin, the Greek mythology rose and set.

"But not only was the fact acknowledged of a law in the nature of man resisting the law of God, (and whatever is placed in active and direct oppugnancy to the good is, *ipso facto*, positive evil,) it was likewise an acknowledged mystery, and one which, by the nature of the subject, must ever remain such — a problem of which any other solution than the statement of the fact itself was demonstrably impossible. That it is so, the least reflection will suffice to convince every man, who has previously satisfied himself that he is a responsible being. It follows, necessarily, from the postulate of a responsible will." — *Aids to Reflection.*

NOTE C. — INFLUENCE OF JUDAISM.

THE following passage, from A. Coquerel's *Christianisme*, will throw light on the relations of the Jews to the neighboring nations, and especially their influence upon the Oriental Magi.

"There are innumerable texts in the sacred writings of both covenants, which express the idea of the mission or privilege of the Jews, and of their title of people of God. This mission may be summed up in four distinct, but closely united points: the knowledge of the true God; the promise of the Savior; the drawing up and preservation of the Old Testament; and lastly, the accomplishment of the redemption in the very bosom of their nation.

"'Abraham was called.' Gen. xii. 1. 'By faith Abraham, when he was called to go out into a place which he should after receive for an inheritance, obeyed; and he went out, not knowing whither he went.' Heb. xi. 8. On all the great occasions of his life, it was said of him. 'In thee shall all the families of the earth be blessed.' Gen. xii. 3; xviii. 18; xxii. 18; xxvi. 4. 'And he [Abraham] believed in the Lord, and it was accounted to him for righteousness;' that is, Abraham, with confidence, accepted his great destiny, and devoted himself to his holy task, (xv. 6;) thus he became the father of all them that believed, (Rom. iv. 11;) that is, the first head of particularism, the first head or guardian of religious truth. 'For I know him, [said the Lord,] that he will command his children and his household after him, and they shall keep the way of the Lord, to do justice and judgment; that the Lord may bring upon Abraham that which he hath spoken of him.' Gen. xviii. 19. 'Now, therefore,' it is said to the contemporaries of Moses, 'if ye will obey my voice indeed, and keep my covenant, then shall ye be a peculiar treasure unto me above all people.' Exod. xix. 5. . . .

'That thou mayst be a holy people unto the Lord thy God, as he hath spoken.' Deut. xxvi. 19. 'For the Lord will not forsake his people for his great name's sake; because it hath pleased the Lord to make you his people.' 1 Sam. xii. 22. 'He hath not dealt so with any nation; and as for his judgments, they have not known them.' Ps. cxlvii.

"'Unto you first,' said St. Peter to the Jews, 'God having raised up his Son Jesus, sent him.' Acts xii. 26. 'Who are Israelites, to whom pertaineth the adoption, and the glory, (Ex. xi. 34, 35; 1 Sam. iv. 22; 2 Chron. vii. 1, 2,) and the covenants, and the giving of the law, and the service of God, and the promises; whose are the fathers, and of whom, as concerning the flesh, Christ came.' Rom. ix. 4, 5. 'Now I say that Jesus Christ was a minister of the circumcision for the truth of God, to confirm the promises made unto the fathers.' xv. 8.

"This divine commission, given to Israel, constituted particularism, and made the Jewish religion a national religion.

"Yet Providence prepared afar off the return to universalism; not only at the moment of the captivity, and by the dispersion of the Jews over Asia, at a period when Greece and Italy were comparatively barbarous; but we may see the light of universalism faintly dawning in some degree, even in the age when Solomon erected the temple of a unique and local worship, in the prayer of dedication, this prince says: 'Moreover, concerning a stranger that is not of thy people Israel, but cometh out of a far country for thy name's sake; . . . when he shall come and pray toward [in] this house, hear thou in heaven thy dwelling-place, and do according to all that the stranger calleth to thee for, that all the people of the earth may know thy name, to fear thee.' 1 Kings viii. 41–43; 2 Chron. vi. 32. Isaiah proclaims their rights, and reassures the proselytes, and even eunuchs, (who, in whatever manner they had become so, were not considered as Jewish citizens.) Deut. xxiii. 1. 'Neither let the son of the stranger, that hath joined himself to the Lord, speak, saying, The Lord hath utterly separated me from his people; neither let the eunuch say, Behold, I am a dry tree, (I shall be cut off as a barren tree.) For thus saith the Lord: Those that choose the things that please me, and take hold of my covenant, even unto them will I give, in mine house, and within my walls, a place.' Isaiah lvi. 3, 4, 5. Ezekiel, when he promises to the Jews a new division of the Holy Land, meaning by this image to give them assurance of a restoration after the captivity, does not forget the strangers or proselytes who were soon to be more numerous than ever. 'And it shall come to pass that ye shall divide it [the country] by lot for an inheritance unto you, and to the strangers that sojourn among you, which shall beget children among you; and they shall be unto you as born in the country among the children of Israel; they shall have inheritance with you among the tribes of Israel. And it shall come to pass, that in what tribe the stranger sojourneth, there shall ye give him his inheritance, saith the Lord God.' Ezek. xlvii. 22, 23.

"A curious passage in Isaiah, the complete explanation of which would require a separate dissertation, opened to the Mosiac system a vast perspective of extension. 'In that day,' says the prophet, 'shall five cities [five several, the definite for the indefinite number] in the land of Egypt speak the language of Canaan, [a figurative expression — the language of the worship of the true God,] and swear to [by] the Lord of hosts. . . . And the Lord shall be known to Egypt. . . . In that day shall there be a highway out of Egypt to Assyria, [there shall be frequent and intimate communication,] . . . and the Egyptians shall serve the Lord with the Assyrians. In that day shall Israel be the third with Egypt and Assyria.' Isaiah xix. 18-24. This whole passage, extremely poetic in style, is a prophecy of the progress which should be made by the Jewish religior under the Ptolemies, during which period there were a million of Jews established in Egypt, whose teaching and example must have greatly diffused the knowledge of the true God and of revelation, and from whom even the nations of the interior of Asia derived benefit. It was impossible more effectually to undermine particularism than by placing Israel as *the third* with two strange nations in the service of the true God.

"The intention of Providence of gradually preparing universalism by diffusing among strange nations some hopes of the advent of a Messiah, and the wisdom of the means employed to this end, find a striking confirmation in the narrative of the arrival of the Magi at Jerusalem. Of these Magi, tradition has made kings; the first interpreters of Scripture opened the way to these errors, by interpreting literally some expressions of the prophets and of the Psalms, and resting upon the ideas of the Jews, who expected a temporal Messiah, the King of kings, before whom all men should bow: the Psalmist, in describing the glory of Solomon, says, 'The kings of Tarshish and of the isles shall bring presents; the kings of Sheba and Seba shall offer gifts.' Ps. lxxii. 10. Isaiah, in one of his Messianic prophecies, has said, in a more explicit manner, kings shall see and arise, princes also shall worship. Isaiah xlix. 7. These passages probably contain the origin of those legends of tradition which has also endeavored to fix the number of kings, viz., three, solely because three kinds of presents, 'gold, and frankincense, and myrrh,' are mentioned in the gospel. These fables have not the slightest historical foundation, and deserve no attention, notwithstanding the endeavors which have been made to consecrate them, by erecting to these imaginary kings in a cathedral (Cologne) a cenotaph loaded with jewels. The word *Magus* is of Persian origin, and very ancient; it signified priests, wise men, philosophers; it appears that, from the earliest historical times in Asia, these

Magi formed sorts of colleges or institutions, which corresponded with one another, obeyed a supreme head, and were principally occupied with drawing up calendars, consequently, therefore, with astronomy, astrology, medicine, and physics, and preserved the old traditions. Since the time of Alexander, their credit, science, and numbers had been greatly diminished; the current of philosophy had flowed back towards Europe, in consequence of the Greek and Roman ascendency; and the foundation of Alexandria had greatly favored this change. It is, however, certain from the testimony of contemporary writers, or nearly so, with the gospel, that men addicted to these studies, and known by this name, were still dispersed in Asia, and especially in Persia and Arabia. In the interval between the overthrow of the Jews under Nebuchadnezzar, and their restoration under Cyrus, Daniel, the author of the prophecy of the seventy weeks of years which were to elapse between Cyrus and the gospel, had been the head of these Magi. The recollection of this remarkable prophecy would naturally be preserved among them, and would be strongly awakened at the moment, when, according to the impartial testimony of three Roman historians, a rumor was every where diffused that a master of the world was about to show himself in the East. The appearance of a meteor, perhaps of a comet, struck these Magi, who were always occupied with astrology. They believed that this phenomenon, coinciding with the date of Daniel's prophecy, announced its accomplishment; the personage whose advent was predicted by Daniel, must, according to their ideas, be a king; some of them, therefore, following the universal custom of the ancients, that of undertaking journeys for the purpose of verifying facts of science, went into Judea, not to a village like Bethlehem, but to the capital, and inquired, 'Where is he that is born King of the Jews for we have seen his star in the East,' Matt. ii. 2; that is, according to the erroneous ideas of astrology, the star announcing his birth. This circumstance of the nativity, when thus explained, far from presenting any difficulty, is a confirmation, both of the fact that the expectation of the Messiah was general, and of the meaning of the prophecy of weeks. The presents offered by the Magi afford an example of the ancient and universal usage of the Eastern nations, followed even in the present day, never to approach princes or great personages without bringing gifts, among which are always some pieces of gold; and it must be remarked that in the whole conduct of the Magi there is nothing religious."

Note D. — THE ESSENES.

The following is Philo's account, in his book called "*Quod Omnis Probus Liber*." It is obviously exaggerated and rhetorical. In other parts of his works he makes different and modified statements. "There is no lack, in Palestine and Syria, of practical virtuous men. Some of them are called Essenes, on account of their holiness. Their number is about four thousand. They are truly pious; they do not bring sacrifices, but are striving after purity of heart. They do not live in cities, but in the rural districts. They avoid the former, that they may not be polluted by their vices. Their daily occupations are agriculture and mechanics; but they neither deal in nor make instruments which are used in war. They serve and aid each other. They do not lay up money, nor care for riches; these have no attractions for them, and, therefore, they do not strive to secure them. When they have sufficient to maintain themselves with frugal meals, they are satisfied. Frugality is their only treasure. They do not trade, and, therefore, they are not tempted by avarice. They are free men, and serve each other gratuitously. They reject all employments in the service of rulers, considering such service as inhuman and unjust, because it is opposed to the common law of nature and of man. They say that nature has not created us to be nominal, but real brothers; and that it is only avarice that weakens the brotherly tie, changes unity and harmony into discord and strife, and disunites friends. They are engaged in the study of philosophy, to aid in the promotion of virtue, but avoid all kinds of sophistry and display. From natural philosophy they have selected only those departments which treat of creation and the Creator; they cherish, however, the idea that nature is above our comprehension. Morals are with them a daily study, in accordance with the laws of their fathers, which laws, they hold, cannot be interpreted without the aid of inspiration. They employ, for that purpose, more especially the seventh day, which they keep holy, doing no common business in it. When they are in the temple, or in the synagogue, the young men sit next to the old, and listen to their teachings. They give instruction, not only in the fundamental virtues, purity of manners, holiness and integrity of life, but also in the art of performing public and domestic duties. Their morals are based upon a threefold foundation — the love of God, of virtue, and of our neighbors. This is the test of their actions. Chastity, in their view, is the first of the virtues, which they vow to observe for life. They never tell a falsehood, swear, or take an oath. They are not nominal saints; this is proved by their renouncing all earthly goods, which the human heart desires, as riches, honor, and pleasure. Upon all these things they look with contempt. They lead a life of toil, but are temperate and free from cares. They make no show; they are humane, modest, and never deviate from their regulations, but exhibit a firm character. Their benevolence is the best proof of their philanthropy. Their equality and community are admirable. Their dwellings are open to any stranger of their order. None of them has a dwelling which he may call his own; but all live and eat in common.

What any one earns daily he puts into the treasury for common use. The sick are maintained from their common contributions. The youth cherish for the aged filial reverence and submission, and support the grayheaded, when not able to support themselves. Philosophy raises such heroes in virtue. This philosophy, indeed, does not boast of Grecian high-sounding phrases, but proves its excellence by inducements to sublime acts, through which eternal freedom is obtained.

THERAPEUTÆ, OR THERAPEUTES.

In the *De Vita Contemplativa,* Philo thus describes the Therapeutæ, who, if not precisely the same as the Essenes, were closely allied to them. Doubtless they had a common origin. They were the monks — perhaps we might say the mystics of Judaism. "The institution or the philosophic school of the Therapeutes is sufficiently explained by its name. They call themselves Therapeutes, and Therapeutrides, that is, physicians; but in a higher sense of the word, because they are chiefly engaged in curing the maladies of the soul, which men contract through their evil desires; and also because they have learned from nature and the Holy Scriptures how to worship the only God. These Therapeutæ will rise higher and higher in their contemplation of that which is divine, when all visible things shall have passed away. Their institute is founded neither on tradition nor on proselyting; but in the principle inherent in man, to yearn after the supernatural; or a kind of inspiration which impels them to the vision of God, for which they hope. From the moment one enters their institute, he is, so to speak, dead to the world, and alive only to heaven and immortality. They give their possessions to their children, friends, or relatives. They leave father and mother, brothers, sisters, and children, kindred, friends, and country; they free themselves from all those worldly ties, which, to them, are of no value. They leave the towns and retire into the country, where they live in solitude, not from misanthropy, but that their manners of life may be free from the corrupting influence of the conversation of those not initiated. This order of men may be found in many parts of the country above alluded to, and are tolerated and owned by Greeks and barbarians. They exist also in many parts of Egypt, and live chiefly in the neighborhood of Alexandria. From their dwelling-places they send the ablest of their men as emissaries, to choose the most convenient place for settlement. They chiefly select the country around the Lake 'Mœris,' on account of its temperate climate and safe situation, as it is surrounded by villas, country seats, and villages. These settlements are uncommonly productive, being exposed to neither great heat noı cold. Their houses are neither too near nor too remote from each other, in order that they may enjoy some kind of conversation in their solitude, and have immediate assistance in the case of necessity. Every one of them has his own closet for prayer and devotion, which they call "σεμνεῖον," and "μοναστηϱίον." For use in these closets they have the laws and the oracles of the prophets, hymns and ascetic writings, as also scientific works. God is the only object of their worship, to whose honor they perform their duties. Their dreams, therefore, are always of an elevated character, full of divine images. There are many instances of their dreams explaining the most difficult problems of philosophy. They pray twice a day, morning and evening. In the morning they pray for protection and blessing during the following day, and for the illumination through the heavenly light; and in the evening they pray for divine assistance in their meditations in the law, and ascertaining the truth in the Sanhedrim. Before their prayers they endeavor to expel every sensual thought. The remainder of the day they are engaged in meditation and contemplation. As soon as the book of the sacred writers is opened, it is expounded through the assistance of the traditional philosophy, allegorically; as they hold that in the literal sense is concealed a mysterious one. They possess also many commentaries from the authors of their society, whom they strictly follow. They write also hymns and songs for religious worship in various metres." Compare Josephus, Antiquities xv. 10, 4. Jewish Wars, lii. c. 8, § 8 & 9.

It would appear, from all this, highly probable that Philo was himself one of the Therapeutæ, at least in theory. His opinions correspond with theirs. He reveres the sacred writings, but interprets them allegorically. His system is partly philosophical, and his philosophy is partly traditional. He is devoted, like them, to mystical contemplation; he claims a kind of inspiration. It is quite evident that he rejects the ordinary view of sacrifices, if not their use, and spiritualizes the whole Mosaic ritual. He believes in "the vision of God," pours contempt upon government and policy, and longs for the suprasensible and supernatural. His great aim in all his books is to "expound the ancient lessons of holy wisdom," and in fact his works are mainly "allegorical commentaries" on the "law and oracles of the prophets." If he admired the Platonic and Oriental philosophers, he ascribes their origin to the legislation and writings of Moses. His classification of mankind corresponds to the notions of the Therapeutæ — 1. The earthly, who are devoted to pleasure; 2. The heavenly, who are occupied with human sciences; and 3. The divine priests and prophets, who are the true "citizens of the world of ideas." In a word, he exhorts all men to withdraw from external engagements, and lose themselves in the universal reason.

We must acknowledge, however, that Philo vacillates somewhat in the practical application of his views, and in one of his tracts (*De Decalogo*, § 22) he attempts a conciliation between the theoretical and the practical. In the *De Migra. Abra.* he informs us that his own experience had taught him that he could not rid himself of himself, and attain to the vision of God, by going into the wilderness and abandoning society; that it is not "change of place which brings evil or good," but that "all depends upon that God who steers the ship of the soul in the direction he pleases." Perhaps a more intimate acquaintance with himself and others abated his lofty estimate of the Therapeutæ; hence we find him, in the *De Profugis*, castigating those who pretended to great interior sanctity, yet indulged in secret vice. He exhorts men first to exercise themselves in the duties of common life, before rushing into Therapeutic solitude. He maintains (*De Profugis*, § 6) "that *human virtue* should go first, the *divine* follow after."

For information on the subject of Philo and the Philonic philosophy, see Ritter's Anc. Hist. iv. p. 407, *et seq.* Neander's Church Hist. i. 52, 60. Dahne's Hist. of the Jewish Alexandrian Religious Philosophy, Halle, 1834. See art. on Philo, by the same author, in the Theol. Studien u. Kritiken, p. 984, *et seq.*, 1833.

Note E. — SACRIFICES.

"The idea of *sacrifice* is so much the natural and necessary foundation of every religious worship, that it appears as such, not only in the dispensation of God's revelations by the Scripture, but in all pagan religions, from the Hindoo and Greek down to the negro and the inhabitant of California. The horrors and abominations which the desire of effecting the sacrifice produced, for instance in the service of Moloch, prove only how deeply the same is founded in human nature. When man feels his indestructible connection with the Divinity, in consequence of that voice of conscience which St. Paul mentions when speaking of the pagans, this connection appears to him either as that of a dependence upon an almighty and benevolent power, or as that of a separation from a more intimate connection, a real union broken by acts which provoked the divine wrath. The first feeling will prompt him to thank, the second to attempt to *propitiate*. As his prayers will be those of thanksgiving or those of penitence, so the acts by which he feels the want to show and manifest his feelings, will be attempts either to thank God or soothe his wrath. All such acts fall under the denomination of sacrifices, which implies that what is offered to God as a gift is considered on the one side as our property, and part of ourselves, and on the other as belonging to him.

. . . .

"Now, it is a mere corollary from the first truth revealed to us in Scripture on the fall of mankind, that man by himself could neither effect such a real atonement for his sins as might appease divine justice, nor that act of thanksgiving which would answer eternal love. For in order to offer this latter sacrifice, his mind ought first to be entirely relieved and delivered from the consciousness of sin and the divine wrath, that is to say, a perfect, everlasting, and all-relieving atonement ought first to have been found; and again there being and remaining the fear and consciousness of the divine wrath in the mind of the natural man when approaching the Deity, every attempt to find and effect such an atonement, by offering even the dearest thing or person, or by excruciating himself, must only increase the despair of being reconciled to God, or confirm men in external rights and ceremonies.

"Only one way remained, therefore, for a divine revelation which for ages would prepare what was once to be accomplished, and this is the system of the Levitical worship and sacrifice, as a type, and such a consoling promise and hope of what was reserved to the people of God, and through the same to all the nations of the earth.

"The sacrifices of the Old Testament are typical, and

according to their peculiar character, all are sacrifices of thanksgiving, with the exception of that great and awful sacrifice of propitiation or atonement, which in its typical character is so clearly described and explained in the Epistle to the Hebrews. Christ was the real victim of propitiation, his death the only all-satisfactory sacrifice of atonement."—*Bunsen's Hippolytus*, ii. 200–202.

Note F.—THE EPISTLE TO DIOGNETUS.

This fragment of Christian literature is published sometimes in the works of Justin Martyr, and sometimes in those of the apostolical fathers. Some ascribe it to Justin Martyr, and others to an unknown author, who lived about the same time with Justin, (the middle of the second century,) or perhaps earlier. This is the opinion of Neander, who says "that the Christian simplicity which reigns in the letter bespeaks its high antiquity, which is further supported by this circumstance, that the author classes Judaism and heathenism together, and does not appear to deduce the Jewish *cultus* from a divine origin; and yet there is nothing properly Gnostic in the treatise — a phenomenon which could only exist in a very early age." Semisch, who has written learnedly on the life and times of Justin Martyr, concurs in this opinion. So also does Hefele, who has published the letter in his edition of the Patres Apostolici. Tzschirner (Fall des Heidenthums) says, "that, in all probability, it was written in the days of Justin, as it has been ascribed to him, and does not contain any thing which can with propriety be referred to a later age. Its tone of elevated piety, and the picture which it gives of the Christians, as a persecuted yet widely-spread community, justify us in assuming that it belonged to an age when the new faith had begun to raise its voice with greater boldness, and to make a more marked progress."

THE EPISTLE TO DIOGNETUS.

I observe, excellent Diognetus, that you earnestly desire to be informed respecting the religion of the Christians, and are particularly careful to ascertain what God they trust, and what may be their form of worship; for while they contemn the world and despise death, they deny the gods of the Greek, and disregard the religion of the Jew, and manifest a tender affection for each other. What, then, is this new sect or institution; and why has it made its appearance now, and not before? To these questions, highly commendable on your part, it shall be my happiness to inquire; beseeching God, who bestows the faculties of speech and understanding, to grant that my reply may be a benefit to you, and that you may never have occasion to reject the instructions received.

Come, then, after having freed your mind from prepossessions, and the force of delusive habit, and becoming, as it were, an entirely new man about to listen, by your own confession, to a new doctrine, discern the true character of your acknowledged gods. Is not one of them, like the stone, trodden under foot; another of brass, fit only to be wrought into vessels for common use; another of wood, ready to decay; another of silver, which one must guard lest it be stolen; and another of clay, not superior to that used for the vilest purposes? Are they not all of perishable materials, and are they not forged by means of iron and fire? Is not one of them the work of the stonecutter, another of the brazier, another of the silversmith, another of the potter? By such artificial skill they were moulded into their present shape, previous to which they might be exchanged for each other; and even now may they not be thus exchanged? Nay, could not those very gods be changed into vessels? Are they not all deaf, and dumb, and blind? Are they not lifeless, insensible, and immovable? Are they not all liable to decay? May they not all be destroyed? Yet such you call gods, adoring and serving them, and so becoming altogether like them. For this reason you hate Christians, because they refuse to worship such gods. After all, do you not, even while you maintain their divinity, treat them with yet greater contempt? Do you not contemn and wrong them more? Those of stone and earth you leave unguarded; while those of gold and silver you watch by day, and shut up by night, lest they should be stolen. You rather punish than honor them by your services, if you suppose them endowed with sense; if not, you convict them of it, by worshipping them with blood, and the smoke of burning fat. Who of you would allow this to be done to himself? Indeed, no rational man would voluntarily endure the infliction. But a stone allows it, because it is without sense. Thus you yourselves convict your gods of their senselessness. From all such bondage Christians are free, of which I might speak at greater length; but it is unnecessary to enlarge.

I presume you wish to know the difference between the worship of Christians and that of the Jews. Although the latter may be free from the idolatry of which I have spoken, and worship only one God, regarding him as the sole Ruler of the universe, yet they greatly err when they pay their worship even to him with heathenish conceptions. The Greek shows his folly by offering sacrifices to dumb idols; but the Jew may well deem it equally irrational and impious to present his sacrifices to the Deity, as if he needed them. For the Creator of heaven and earth and all they contain, and from whom we derive all our blessings, cannot need from any of his creatures what he has himself given to those who imagine they give to him. Those who offer to him sacrifices, blood offerings, fat offerings, and burnt offerings, supposing that by such means they do him honor, vainly bestowing gifts upon him who needs them not, differ little, in my opinion, from those who exhibit the same devotion to senseless idols, unconscious of the homage paid them.

I need not inform you of the scrupulousness of the Jews respecting meats, their observance of fasts, new moons, and Sabbaths, or their boasted practice of circumcision. These things are too ridiculous to be worthy of notice. For can it be right to accept as good some of the things created by the Deity for the use of man, and reject others as bad or superfluous? Is it not wicked falsely to accuse God of having forbidden the doing of good on the Sabbath day? Is it not despicable to boast of the mutilation of the flesh, as a mark of the special favor and choice of the Almighty? Who does not regard watching the stars, and the changes of the seasons, and the appropriation of some to festivity and others to mourning, with the superstitious observance of months and days, as a stronger proof of folly than of piety?

Doubtless you have sufficiently learned that Christians abstain from the common vanity, boasting, and pretension of the Jews. But the secret (μυστήριον) of their peculiar religion you cannot hope to be taught by any man. For Christians are not distinguished from other men by their place of residence, their language, or their manners, for they do not dwell in separate cities, use any peculiar kind of speech, or follow any unusual mode of life. They propose no mysterious system devised by man, nor any human dogma whatever. They live in Greek or foreign cities, each where his lot is cast, and in matters of food, clothing, and the like, comply with the customs of the place. And yet they exhibit a life and conversation of wonderful paradoxes. They inhabit their native land, but only as sojourners. They take a part in all things as citizens, but endure all things as foreigners; every foreign country is to them a native land, and every native country a foreign land. They marry like others, and rear children, but never expose their offspring. They have all things in common, but rigidly observe their marriage vows. They live in the flesh, but not after the flesh. They pass their time on earth, but their citizenship is in heaven. They obey the existing laws, but in their lives transcend all laws. They love all, and are persecuted by all. They live unknown, and are condemned to death. They are slain, and behold they live; though poor, they make many rich; in want of every thing, they have abundance; in dishonor, they are crowned with glory; when defamed, they are vindicated; when cursed, they bless; for injury, they return kindness; for well doing, they are punished as evil doers; persecuted to death, they rejoice as being made alive. They are treated by the Jews as barbarians and foes, and by the Greeks are persecuted; but their bitterest enemies can assign no reason for hating them. In a word, what the soul is to the body, that Christians are in the world. As the soul is diffused through the whole body, so are these Christians scattered through all the cities of the world. The soul, indeed, occupies the body as its dwelling, but is not of the body; so Christians dwell in the world, but they are not of the world. The soul lodges unseen in the body; so Christians are known as existing in the world, but their devotion to God is unseen, unknown. The flesh hates and contends against the soul, though the soul injures not the flesh, but simply hinders it from indulging its pleasures. So the world hates Christians, because they oppose the pleasures of the world. The soul loves the body even when it opposes it; so Christians love those by whom they are hated. The soul sustains the body in which it is detained; so Christians preserve the world in which they are imprisoned. The soul, itself immortal, occupies this perishable tabernacle. So Christians inhabit these dying bodies, looking forward to the everlasting felicity of heaven. The soul, checked and impaired by sense, only triumphs the more; so the Christians, refined and disciplined by persecution, only increase the more in numbers and in elevation of character. God has appointed them to this important post, which they dare not and cannot forsake.

For, as I have already stated, it is no earth-born invention which has been committed to them. It is no mortal wisdom which they so sedulously guard; no human mysteries which have been intrusted to their keeping. The almighty and invisible God himself imparts from heaven, and establishes in men's hearts the truth and the holy and incomprehensible Word. His messenger to men is not, as some might imagine, any servant of his, angel or potentate, intrusted with divine or earthly power. But he has sent the Creator and Governor of all things, who framed the heavens, and set bounds to the sea that it cannot pass; to whom all things are subject, the heavens and all that are therein, the earth, the sea, and all that in them is, fire, air, and the intermediate spaces of immensity. This Being he sent to man. And was this done, as some might imagine, to strike them with fear, or oppress them by tyranny? So far from this being the case, he sent him in mercy and love, like a king sending his son — himself a king. He sent him to man as their Savior, whose lips should speak words of gentleness, and not threats of violence, for violence is not in God. In mercy, he has sent him to fulfil the kind offices of invitation and of grace, not to sit in judgment; though he will yet commission him to go forth in judgment, and who shall then be able to abide his coming! Do you not see that those who are exposed to wild beasts are not overcome, but only increase the more, the more they are persecuted? This is not the work of man, but of God, and an evident token of his coming.

How miserable the condition of men before the advent of Christ! How could men form any just conception of God before his coming? Or do you confide in the vain and frivolous speculations of the philosophers, some of whom declare that fire is God, (calling that God which they are themselves rapidly approaching;) and others water, and others again some of the other elements created by God? Even supposing any one of these opinions admissible, God might, with equal truth, be predicated of every created thing. But they are all the lying wonders and impostures of jugglers. None of these ever saw God, or had any knowledge of him. But he has revealed himself to faith, by which alone God is seen. For the supreme Creator and Governor of all things ever was, and is, and will be merciful and gracious, true, faithful, and long suffering. He alone is good. He formed a great and unutterable purpose, known only to his Son. Wrapped in secrecy, he seemed to neglect us. But when, through his beloved Son, he began to reveal the things he had from the beginning prepared for us, he unfolded to us the whole, giving us all things freely to know and enjoy.

In time past God suffered us to be carried away by our own passions; not that he delighted in our sins, but because he bore with them; not approving of our unrighteousness, but thereby convincing us of guilt, and preparing us for the reception of his grace. By discovering our guilt and inability, he would thus fit us joyfully to enter the kingdom and become partakers of his grace. But when the measure of our sins was filled, and nothing but punishment and death awaited us as our recompense, when the time came for the disclosure of the divine mercy, and power, and exceeding love for mankind, then he hated us not, nor cast us off, nor remembered against us our iniquities; but he was slow to anger, and took upon himself our sins. He gave his Son a ransom for us, the Holy One for the unholy, the sinless for the sinful, the just for the unjust, the incorruptible for the corruptible, the immortal for the mortal. What but his righteousness can cover (*hide*) our sins? And by whom, in our guilt, can we be justified, but by the Son of God? O the unsearchable grace! O the unexpected blessing! that the sins of many should be cancelled by one act of sacrifice, that many should be justified by the righteousness of one! Having shown us the impossibility of obtaining salvation ourselves, and then having revealed an all-sufficient Savior, he now calls for our faith and confidence in him as our supporter, teacher, physician, and counsellor, as our light, glory, strength, and salvation, that we should be careful for nothing pertaining to the present life.

Were you, Diognetus, only to receive this faith, then you should know God as a Father. For God has loved us men, for whose benefit he created the world, upon whom he bestowed reason and intelligence, permitting us alone to aspire to him. He formed us in his own image, and sent us his only-begotten Son, and has promised, to those that love him, a heavenly kingdom When you have known this, with what delight will you be filled! How will you love him who first loved you! And loving him, you will become an imitator of his goodness. Wonder not that man can become like unto God. By the grace of God, this is attainable. To acquire authority over others, to gratify ambition and oppress the poor, that is not happiness. One cannot thus imitate God; such things are abhorrent to his majesty. But he who loves, who bears his neighbor's burden, who helps those beneath him, and imparts his goods to the poor, becomes, so to speak, a god to those he benefits. Such a one is an imitator of God. Then, while yet on earth, you will behold Him that reigns in heaven. Then shall you begin to declare the mysteries of God. Then shall you admire and love those who are persecuted for righteousness' sake. Then shall you rebuke the folly of the world, while you have yourself entered into the enjoyment of the true heavenly life. You will despise the horrors of death itself, while you fear that eternal death, reserved for those who are condemned to final and irrevocable destruction.

I am not here treating of matters unknown to me, or inconsistent with reason; but having been a disciple of the apostles, I am become a teacher of the Gentiles. The things delivered unto me I minister to those who are sincere disciples of the truth. For who, that is rightly instructed in divine knowledge, does not desire to learn thoroughly what was communicated clearly by the Word (Λογος) to the disciples whom the Word enlightened, conversing freely with them; not comprehended by unbelievers, but explained to the disciples? Those accounted faithful have known the mysteries of the Father. For this cause, he sent the Word, that he might be manifested in the world. He sent the Word, who, despised by his own people, was preached by apostles, and was believed by the Gentiles; who was from the beginning, yet appeared and was found a new being on the earth, and for the same reason is ever new born in the hearts of believers. By him the church is enriched; through him grace abounds in the saints, conferring understanding, unfolding mysteries, discovering the future, conferring joy upon the faithful, and even bestowing it upon them that seek to be obedient to the rules of faith and heavenly wisdom. Then is celebrated the dignity of the law, the inspiration of the prophets is acknowledged, the faith of the gospel is confirmed, the teaching of the epistles is defended, and the grace and joy of the church made to abound. If you do not grieve this grace, you shall know the communication of the Word, when and by whom he wills. For whatever we are commanded by the will of the controlling Word to utter, that we are impelled to utter, and share with you the things revealed, in labor and in love.

When you have read and studied these with diligence, you will find what God bestows upon those who sincerely love him, who become a delightful paradise, within each of which springs up a beautiful and luxuriant tree, adorned with various fruits; for here are planted the tree of knowledge and the tree of life. It is not knowledge, but disobedience that destroys. So that it is not without significance, that the Scriptures declare that God, in the beginning, planted the tree of life in the midst of paradise, revealing life through knowledge; which our first parents not using lawfully, were despoiled of their heritage through the wiles of the serpent. With this view were the trees planted near each other, because without knowledge there is no life, and no real knowledge without true life. The apostle, perceiving this, and wishing to condemn the knowledge which exists without obedience unto life, declares that knowledge puffeth up, but love buildeth up. Whoever thinks it possible to attain true knowledge without obedience and life, is deceived by the serpent. But whoever, with love and reverence, has knowledge, and seeks life, plants a life-giving fruit. May you have the knowledge of the heart. May your life be the true word of God inwardly received. From the tree of knowledge growing up within you, you will always gather such fruits as are desired in the presence of God, which the serpent never troubles. Then Eve is not corrupted, but a virgin soul believes; salvation is displayed, the apostles are made wise; the feast of the Lord proceeds; the praising multitudes gather together, in beautiful order, praising the Lord; and the Word, instructing saints, rejoices, through whom God the Father is glorified. To him be glory forever. Amen.

Note G. — TESTIMONIES RESPECTING THE ORGANIZATION AND GOVERNMENT OF THE PRIMITIVE CHURCH.

"The constitution of the Christian church, like the political constitution of the Germanic races, rested upon the idea of a community freely submitting to a divine order of society which calls mankind to freedom, and makes man free. Christianity was a free, and in some sense a secret, association. At a time when Egypt was suffering under the most iron despotism, and when the Aramaic races of Asia were in a state of the most revolting religious and moral debasement, he formed a free people, and a people of God, by organizing it at first as a secret religious community.

It was by this agency he threw off the bondage of an empire, mighty both in Africa and Asia, and united the tribes of Israel, who were dissevered and trodden under foot, into a nation of universal historical importance. Jesus and his disciples formed a secret society first out of the children of that nation, at the last turning-point of its history, when subjected to the most cruel despotism of republican emperors, and amid the despair of a highly-civilized but dissolute world. This society was based upon the freedom of its members from the Levitical law, on their equality as children of God, on their brotherhood as men. It was this society, established upon this freedom, this equality, and this fraternity, which dissolved the greatest empire in the world, and led to the forming of a vast association, embracing the whole human family throughout the world-wide dominions of Rome. . . .

"Every town congregation of ancient Christianity, the constitution of which we have to delineate, was a church. The constitution of that church was a congregational constitution. In St. Paul's Epistles, in the writings of Clemens Romanus, of Ignatius and of Polycarp, the congregation is the highest organ of the spirit as well as power of the church. It is the body of Christ, the embodiment of the person of Jesus of Nazareth, in the society which was founded by him and through faith in him. This congregation was governed and directed by a council of elders, which congregational council, at a later period, was presided over, in most churches, by a governing overseer, the bishop. But the ultimate decision, in important emergencies, rested with the whole congregation. The bishop and elders were its superintending members; its guides, but not its masters.

"In most of the customs and ordinances transmitted to us, we find this active interference on the part of the congregation considerably weakened. Already a hierarchy has been established. Nevertheless the congregation elects its bishop, and invites the bishops of the neighboring localities to institute him into his office with prayer and the imposition of hands. If the congregation is still to be formed, the bishop names the elders, three at least, and inducts them with prayer and a benediction. They form with him the congregational council. The bishop elects at least one deacon, as his assistant, and appoints widows and young women to take care, both spiritually and bodily, of the orphans, the sick, and the poor. If the bishopric of a congregation, already formed, become vacant, the form of episcopal election remains the same: the clergy elect with the people, &c. . . .

"The hypothesis, therefore, of the Presbyterian divines of the sixteenth and seventeenth centuries, that the bishop, as the first of his peers, (*primus inter pares*,) sprang from the elders of the congregation, falls to the ground as unhistorical. But their idea of elders, as both an officiating and ruling body, is quite correct. The ancient church knows no more of a single presbyter than of clerical government and election. It was only in very small places, manors, (*villæ*,) that the collegiate form was not adopted. There, a single clergyman, who, according to the use of the word *bishop* in the Epistles of St. Peter and St. Paul, was called a country bishop, (chorepiscopus, i. e., country curate,) managed the small community in its ordinary emergencies.

"The Lutheran view, again, especially that of the German Lutherans, according to which the clergy formed the order of teachers in the ancient church, is entirely erroneous. The church was a government, and the bishops and elders were magistrates; they directed the congregation, but without legislative power. Teaching and praying were open to every one in the church of the apostles; every man acting as a priest, and anointed of the Lord. . . .

"The nature of things, however, led, as early as the second century, to collective congregations. The small village communities in the vicinity of the town, already, to a certain extent, formed such an association with those of the city. This, however, was only the first, and an imperfect arrangement; because the integral parts, with the exception of the town, had no complete organization. The principal towns in the then existing provinces of the empire (and all the apostolic Epistles are addressed to these) formed central points for the province or island, as mother towns or metropolises. The bishops assembled then in synod. Believers had the liberty of attending the sittings, and hearing their discussions. The first bishop, in age or importance, presided.

"As to Rome, Alexandria, and Antioch, however, the bishops had, in early times incorporated with them a more considerable portion of the province. . . .

"The churches, which grouped themselves around a great church, stood in an organized, but strictly hierarchical connection with it. It was natural that common interests should be treated of in common, and decided upon under the presidency of the bishop of the metropolis. The other bishops were joint elders in this council. They formed, with the parish clergy of the capital, the presbytery of the chief bishop. This is the origin of the college of cardinals.

"This second stage in the development of the church's constitution is, therefore, already infected with the decay of the times. There were no longer then any free nations, but only municipal unions. The ancient world did not know a free nation beyond the municipal limits, and therefore had no representative government. Christianity prepared this by clerical senates and synods; it could not create nations. The congregation was free, and her life the only living and free life of the age. But this free element in the Christian community remains within the narrow limits of the municipal constitution; all beyond that is unfree, as regards the congregation. Independent and autonomic in their parochial concerns, the congregations are excluded from the general church affairs. . . .

"A century after Hippolytus, Christianity became, under Constantine, from a persecuted sect, a recognized religion, and, with the passing exception of Julian, the religion of the rulers and of the imperial army by which they were governed.

"Even before the end of the fourth century, it was the dominant religion, and the Catholic church enjoyed exclusive privileges. From the time of Theodosius downwards, the emperors carried out a system of persecution, and the bishops rivalled them in an almost apocalyptic manner. Christianity was from the very beginning admitted into the empire as an episcopal and catholic corporation, which centred more and more round the great imperial cities of Rome, (and New Rome,) Alexandria, and Antioch. The protector considered the bishops partly in the light of helpmeets, and partly in the light of subjects; and this is the point of a convivial joke of the Emperor Constantine, which has been immortalized by Eusebius, comparing himself with the bishops as an episcopus (overseer) of the external affairs of the state. His system was despotic monarchy; so was theirs. It is just as rational to build upon this a right of supremacy, as it is to establish the theory of passive obedience, and the right divine of absolute princes, by referring to Christian government the words of the gospel and apostles, meant for Nero and Neronian prefects. Constantine was the first, but already a complete Byzantine despot, and would have remained so, had he survived his baptism. The first result of the protectorate of the Christian emperors, was that in their codes they converted church ordinances (that about baptism, for instance) into statute laws. . . . Evangelical and religious freedom then received its death blow from the same police crutch which was given it for its support." — *Bunsen's Hippolytus.*

"At first the church was governed according to republican forms; but these disappeared in proportion as the new faith attained the mastery. Gradually the clergy separated themselves altogether from the laity.

"It appears to me that this was the result of a certain internal necessity. The rise of Christianity involved the liberation of religion from all political elements. From this followed the growth of a distinct ecclesiastical class, with a peculiar constitution. In this separation of the church from the state consists, perhaps, the greatest, the most pervading and influential peculiarity of all Christian times. The spiritual and secular powers may come into near contact, may even stand in the closest community, but they can be thoroughly incorporated only at rare conjunctures, and for a short period. Their mutual relation, their position with regard to each other, form, from this time forward, one of the most important considerations in all history.

"The constitution of the ecclesiastical body was necessarily formed upon the model of that of the empire. The hierarchy of bishops, metropolitan patriarchs, arose, corresponding to the graduated ranks of the civil administration. Ere long, the Roman bishops assumed preëminency above all others. The pretence that primates, whose supremacy was acknowledged by east and west, existed in the first centuries of the church, is, indeed, utterly groundless; but it is unquestionable that they soon acquired a consideration which raised them above all ecclesiastical authorities. Many things contributed to secure this to them.

"If the importance of every provincial capital conferred on its bishop a peculiar weight and dignity, how much more must this have been the case in the ancient capital of that vast empire, to which it had given its name! Rome was one of the most eminent apostolical seats; here the greatest number of martyrs had perished; during the persecution, the bishops of Rome had displayed extraordinary firmness and courage; their succession had often been rather to martyrdom and death, than to office. But now, independent of these considerations, the emperor found it expedient to favor the rise of a great patriarchal authority. In a law which became decisive for the supremacy of Christianity, Theodosius the Great ordains that all nations who were subjects to his grace should receive the faith which had been delivered by St. Peter to the Romans. Valentinian III. forbade the bishops, both in Gaul and in the other provinces, to depart from ancient usages without the approbation of the venerable man, the pope of the holy city. From this time the power of the Roman bishops grew up under the protection of the emperor himself." — *Leopold Ranke, History of the Popes.*

"In its primitive state, in its childhood, Christian society presents itself before us as a simple association of men possessing the same faith, the same sentiments and opinions. The first Christians met to enjoy together their common emotions, their common religious convictions. At this time we find no settled form of doctrine, no settled rules of discipline, no body of magistrates.

"Still it is perfectly obvious that no society, however young, however feebly held together, can exist without some moral power, which animates and guides it; and thus, in the various Christian congregations, there were men who preached, who taught, who *morally governed the congregation.* Still there was no settled magistrate, no discipline; a simple association of believers in a common faith, with common sentiments and feelings, was the first condition of Christian society.

"But the moment this society began to advance, and almost at its birth, (for we find traces of them in the earliest documents,) there gradually began to be moulded a form of doctrine, rules of discipline, a body of magistrates, of magistrates called *πρεσβύτεροι*, or elders, who afterwards became riests; *επίσκοποι*, inspectors or overseers, who became bishops; and of *διάκονοι*, or deacons, whose office was the care of the poor, and the distribution of alms.

"It is almost impossible to determine the precise functions of these magistrates; the line of demarcation was probably very vague and wavering; yet here was the embryo of institutions. Still, however, there was one prevailing character in this sacred epoch; it was, that the power, the authority, the preponderating influence still remained in the hands of the general body of believers. It was they who decided in the election of magistrates, as well as in the adoption of rules of discipline and doctrine. No separation had as yet taken place between the Christian government and the Christian believers, who exercised the principal influence in the society.

"In the third period, all this was entirely changed. The clergy were separated from the people, and now formed a distinct body, with its own wealth, its own jurisdiction, its own constitution; in a word, it had its own government, and formed a complete society of itself — a society, too, provided with all the means of existence, independently of the society to which it applied itself, and over which it extended its influence. This was the third state of the Christian church, and in this state it existed at the opening of the fifth century. The government was not yet completely separated from the people; for no such government as yet existed, and less so in religious matters than in any other; but as respects the relation between the clergy and Christians in general, it was the clergy who governed, and governed almost without control." — *Guizot, History of Civilization.*

"The societies which were instituted in the cities of the Roman empire were connected only by the ties of faith and charity. Independence and equality formed the basis of their internal constitution." — *Gibbon, Decline and Fall, &c.* ch. xv.

To these testimonies from distinguished laymen we might add the testimonies of nearly all, and especially the more eminent, ecclesiastical historians and writers upon church history. See, for example, Mosheim, *De Rebus Christianorum*, Sæc. i. Sect. 48. In his ecclesiastical history he uses similar language: "Through the greater part of this century [the second] the churches were as yet self-governed; nor were they united in any alliance or confederation. Each society was a sort of little state, governing by its own laws — laws either introduced or approved by the people." — Century ii. p. 2.

See also Augusti, Hist. Eccles. Epit., § 21. "The form of the Christian republic, as we detect it in the first and second centuries, may be called, in a sense, *democratic*, because with the entire assembly of the people lay the right and power of choosing the presiding officers, teachers and ministers. To the assembly, (*εκκλησία*, church,) in the stricter sense, belonged only the *believers*, (*πιστοί*,) those Christians who partook of the sacraments," &c.

Compare Dr. George Campbell's Lectures on Church History, 4th, 5th, 6th, 7th, 8th, and 9th Lectures. Gieseler's Ch. Hist., vol. i. § 30 and § 50. Neander's Planting and Training of the Church, as also his Church History, (Torrey's Trans.,) vol. i. p. 179, *et seq.* Whately's Essays on the Kingdom of Christ, p. 138, *et seq.*, 3d ed. Barrow on the Pope's Supremacy, Works, vol. vii. p. 302. To these correspond the views of Guericke, Bretschneider, Hase, M. J. Matter, and others of equal eminence as theologians and church historians.

Note H. — THE MIRACLE OF THE LAST FIFTEEN HUNDRED YEARS.

"Taking this high ground, that Christianity is based upon that which is eternally God's own, (reason and conscience,) and, therefore, as indestructible and as invincible as he is himself, I am truly thankful to find that there is visible and traceable, in the history of Christianity, the overruling power of the divine Spirit. This Spirit I believe to be infused into the universality of the human conscience, which is identical with the God-fearing and God-loving reason, and which answers, in those sublime regions, to what, in things connected with the visible world, is called common sense. This divine power of reason and conscience, I find to have been so great, that it has overruled all the imperfections and errors, both of ancient communities and formularies. Any Protestant Christian, who, taking a Protestant view of the world's history, and leading a Christian life, goes naturally and conscientiously through the history of Christianity, can feel himself in perfect communion with the churches of the east and west, and see the working of the Spirit in the Scholastic, and even in Tridentine definitions, if he will only interpret the Scriptures honestly, and according to the general rules of interpretation; if he will only take the writings of the fathers, according to the spirit, as a limited part of the development of Christianity, and judge their speculations, not as aggressive dogmatism, but as philosophical explanations, given in self-defence; and, finally, if he consider the decrees and formularies of these churches, not in the light of his own system, but as they were understood by the members of those churches." — *Hippolytus*, i. 175, 176.

"If there is any manifest proof of a divine ordinance [government?] of human destinies, it is the history of the church. There were certainly many circumstances which wonderfully facilitated the spreading and the maintenance of Christianity. The ancient nationalities were worn out. Judaism had merged into Rabbinism; and the destruction of Jerusalem had extinguished the sanctuary, with which, since Ezra, the Jews had been identified. Heathenism had also lost its natural basis and local faith; the unbelief of the Romans was grosser than that of the Greeks; so was their remaining superstition. The human mind was yearning after some high and restoring union and fusion of the different nationalities; and the idea of a common truth, born out of Christianity, was the fulfilment of the world's deepest longings. But, then, look at the difficulties. First, then, was the decaying civilization of an effete world; and, on the other side, the barbarism of a fresh and noble, but wholly undeveloped, conquering race. There was no nation, no national life, the only sound supporters of a pure and hallowing religion: there was a general decay in literature, in learning, in philosophy; there was a universal despair as to the destinies of mankind. The world seemed to be actually governed, not by God, but by the devil. Then look to the inward difficulties. There was a very imperfect representation of the Christian church in all the councils, to begin with that of Nice — a system excluding any action of the laity, which means the Christian people, and representing only a part even of the clergy. Then there were all the intrigues of Byzantine emperors and empresses, imperial aid-de-camps, and palace eunuchs. There were the passions and ambitions of an uncontrolled clergy. There was the *odium theologicum* of the doctors. Finally, there was the rage of the ruling powers of the age for realizing Christianity, not in social institutions, not in the duties and works of love, but almost exclusively in hierarchical discipline, and for making the sole test of communion with Christ and God, consist in certain speculative formularies, which necessarily brought their antagonistic principles, and, therefore, schism and persecution, along with them. This rage was intimately connected with the despair of the human mind, and with the death of all nations, and of all national life. Debarred from such an existence, the end for which man was created, (because the only means of realizing God's purpose with the world,) having no fatherland to cling to, no national institutions to defend, all the leading Christian minds were seized with the appalling idea that this world was drawing to its end, and shared, so far, the despairing feelings of the rest of mankind. They looked to another world with faith; but they did not feel a vocation to make this world itself, with its social and national institutions, the object of their Christian thoughts and efforts. Now, the great miracle of the history of the last fifteen hundred years is that the world was renewed, notwithstanding all this, and that the fundamental records and ideas of Christianity have been saved, and although very imperfectly developed, and preserved for future development, in the whole of Christendom, as it exists at present in the east and west." — i. 177, 178.

Note I. — ANSELM AND AQUINAS.

"The true metaphysician of this period is St. Anselm, born at Aosta, in Piedmont, Prior of Abbe and Bec, in Normandy, and at his death Archbishop of Canterbury. [Born 1034, died 1109.] To him was given the appellation of the second Augustine. Among his numerous works are two, the titles of which I will at least mention, for the titles indicate their spirit, and reveal, moreover, a remarkable progress. One is a monologue, wherein St. Anselm supposes an ignorant man who is seeking truth by force of his reason only — a very bold fiction for the eleventh century, and the antecedent to the Meditations: [Cousin here refers to the 'Meditations' of Des Cartes, the father of mental philosophy in modern times] it is entitled *Monologium, seu Exemplum meditandi de Ratione Fidei;* Monologue, or example of the manner in which one may account for his faith. The second work is called *Proslogium, seu Fides quærens intellectum;* Allocution, or the faith which tries to demonstrate itself. In the first work, St. Anselm does not suppose himself in possession of the truth; he is seeking it: in the second, he supposes himself in possession of the truth, and he tries to demonstrate it. The name of St. Anselm is attached to the argument, which draws from the idea of an absolute maximum of greatness, of beauty, of goodness, the demonstration of the existence of its object, which can be only God. Without citing St. Anselm, whom he did not probably know, Des Cartes has produced the same argument, &c. . . . Leibnitz, in taking up the Cartesian argument, refers it to St. Anselm; but he was able to go farther back; he had found it in the genius of Christian idealism, and it was worthy of St. Anselm, of Des Cartes, and of Leibnitz, to draw it from that source, and diffuse it through modern philosophy." — *Cousin, Hist. of Mod. Philosophy*, Wight's trans., vol. ii. p. 21.

"St. Thomas Aquinas was born rich, and of an illustrious family, [at Aquino, near Naples, in 1225,] who naturally wished to give him a good position in the world. He refused it, and entered quite early into the Order of the Dominicans, in order that he might give himself wholly to philosophy. He carried into his order the same disinterestedness; he constantly refused all dignities, and would consent to be only a professor, and was called *Doctor Angelicus*, the Angel of the School. He understood the importance of the Arabic and Greek philosophers. He greatly encouraged the translation of their works, and Europe is infinitely indebted for all the translations he caused to be made. If Albert [Albert the Great, called Albert of Böllstadt] was more learned, and, above all, better acquainted with the natural sciences, St. Thomas was a better metaphysician, and especially a better moralist. He did not fall into asceticism as did his compatriot, John of Fidanza, otherwise called St. Bonaventura, who nearly brought theology to mysticism, thereby obtaining the name of *Doctor Seraphicus*, the Seraphic Doctor. St. Thomas Aquinas remained faithful to the philosophic spirit. If he submitted reason to the rule of faith, he never misconceived the extent and legitimate authority of our faculties. The masterwork of St. Thomas is the famous summation, *Summa Theologiæ*, which is one of the greatest monuments of the human mind, in the middle age, and comprehends, with profound metaphysics, an entire system of morality, and even of politics, and that kind of politics, too, which is not at all servile. Among other things, you find in it a defence of the Jews, who were then persecuted, and were so serviceable not only to commerce, but to science. He could not dream of the civil equality of our days; but as a Christian, he recommended humanity in regard to them, even as a matter of policy. St. Thomas is particularly a great moralist." —*Idem*, p. 26.

www.ingramcontent.com/pod-product-compliance
Lightning Source LLC
LaVergne TN
LVHW021258110826
845150LV00003B/419

* 9 7 8 1 4 2 5 5 6 0 3 9 3 *